DATE DUE

OC 21 '04			

DEMCO 38-296

THE WHITE WOMAN'S
OTHER BURDEN

R

THE WHITE WOMAN'S OTHER BURDEN
Western Women and South Asia During British Colonial Rule

Kumari Jayawardena

Routledge — New York & London

Published in 1995 by
Routledge
29 West 35th Street
New York, NY 10001

Published in Great Britain in 1995 by
Routledge
11 New Fetter Lane
London EC4P 4EE

Library of Congress Cataloging-in-Publication Data

Jayawardena, Kumari.
The white woman's other burden: Western women and South Asia during
British colonial rule / Kumari Jayawardena
     p. cm.
     Includes bibliographical references and index.
     ISBN 0-415-91104-4 (cloth) — ISBN 0-415-91105-2 (pbk.)
1. White women – Great Britain – Colonies – History. 2. Women social reformers – Great
Britain – Colonies – History. 3. Women – South Asia – Social conditions. 4. Great Britain –
Colonies – Asia – History. I. Title.

HQ1593.5.J39   1995   94-28881
303.48'4'0954—dc20   CIP

British Library Cataloguing-in-Publication Data also available

To the memory of Serena Tennekoon (1957–1989), anthropologist and feminist, and Dr. Rajani Thiranagama (1954–1989), fighter for minority and women's rights.

For my aunt Eva Ostergaard.

And for Anil de Silva-Vigier, Vivienne Goonewardena, Jeanne Moonesinghe, Dr. Manorani Saravanamuttu, and Hedi Stadlen.

CONTENTS

Preface   *ix*

Introduction: The Noble and the Ignoble
         White Women as Goddesses and Devils   *1*

PART I
   SAVING THE SISTERS FROM THE SACRED COWS
   Christianity and "Civilization"

1   The Imagined Sisterhood of Women   *21*

2   Christianity and the "Westernized Oriental Gentlewoman"   *33*

3   Going for the Jugular of Hindu Patriarchy
    American Women Fund-Raisers for Ramabai   *53*

PART II
   MOTHERING INDIA
   Women Social Reformers from the West

4   Radical and Secular Reformers   *65*

5   The Medicine Women
    The Struggles of Western and South Asian Women Doctors   *75*

6   "Children of Children"
    The Child Marriage Controversies and India   *91*

PART III
   "CONSOLATION IN AN ALIEN SOCIETY"
   Women Theosophists and Orientalists

7   "The Light of Asia" or "Hooey from the Orient"?   *107*

8   "Sandals in India and Shoes in the West"
    Annie Besant's "Passage to India"   *123*

9   From London's West End to Jaffna
    Florence Farr as George Bernard Shaw's "New Woman"   *135*

10 "Blazing the Trail for Indian Women's Freedom"
    Margaret Cousins in India   *147*

11 "O Free Indeed! O Gloriously Free"
    Women Orientalists, Writers and Funders   *157*

PART IV

WHITE WOMEN IN SEARCH OF BLACK GODS

12 Western Holy Mothers as Soul Mates of Indian Gurus   *175*

13 Irish Rebellion and "Muscular Hinduism"
    Margaret Noble as Vivekananda's "Lioness"   *183*

14 From Admiral's House to Gandhi's Ashram
    Madeleine Slade in India   *195*

15 The "Jewish Mother" of Pondicherry
    Mirra Alfassa Joins Aurobindo   *207*

PART V

COMRADES IN ARMS
Western Socialist Women Fight Imperialism

16 Women and Revolution   *221*

17 Comrade or Evil Temptress?
    American Socialist Women and Indian Left Leaders   *229*

18 Red Flags in the Emerald Isle
    European Socialist Women Intervene in Sri Lanka   *245*

Conclusion: An Asian Feminist Gaze   *261*

Notes   *269*

Bibliography   *293*

Index   *303*

PREFACE

Take up the White Man's burden —
Send forth the best ye breed —
Go, bind your sons in exile
To serve your captive's need;
To wait in heavy harness
On fluttered folk and wild -
Your new-caught, sullen peoples,
Half-devil and half-child.

—From Rudyard Kipling, "The White Man's Burden" 1899

WESTERN WOMEN IN THE COLONIES WERE EXPECTED TO PLAY SUBORDINATE roles and help the white man with his very "masculine" burden of ruling the Empire. But not all foreign women in South Asia were "Women of the Raj" who thought of India as the "jewel in the Crown" or Asians as "half-devil, half-child." In collecting material for an earlier book on feminism and nationalism in Asia and the Middle East, I came across numerous examples of dynamic foreign women who were not *memsahibs* but were linked to nationalist, Socialist, reformist, missionary and medical projects in South Asia.

In colonial society, Western women may have often been of the same race and class as the rulers, but many of them had a consciousness of gender difference that often developed into a feminist consciousness. Many "daughters in exile" spoke with other voices, and shouldered other burdens. They crossed boundaries of accepted race, gender and class positions, proclaiming "sisterhood," and taking political stands against colonial rule, thereby problematizing many issues of feminism and nationalism. To the colonial rulers, these women were a strange array of holy rollers, spinsters, busybodies, eccentrics, divine mothers, fanatics, whores, agitators, anarchists and Communists, some more troublesome than others, with the potential to embarrass, shame and threaten the white man in his business of ruling the "sullen peoples." To Asian women and men, however, these same Western women appeared in a different light—some as goddesses, others as devils, depending on their attitudes to local nationalism, women's equality and social change.

Writing in the 1990s, I attempt with hindsight to cast an Asian "feminist gaze" on the activities, in India and Sri Lanka during British colonialism, of women missionaries, reformers, doctors, theosophists, disciples of gurus and Marxists, to highlight their contribution to the cause of women's liberation and, in the case of some, to national liberation. I question both the British Liberal view and the standard nationalist interpretation of the role of these foreign women in the colonies, who have often been erased from memory and history in both Asia and the West.

I began this research while at the Bunting Institute (Radcliffe College) as an affiliate fellow. I obtained material from archival and other sources in India and Sri Lanka, from the British Library in London, from the New York Public Library, the Widener Library, the Divinity School Library and the Schlesinger Library of American Women's History in Cambridge, Massachusetts.

I particularly express my thanks for interviews and correspondence to Doreen Wickremasinghe, Hedi Stadlen, Jeanne Moonesinghe and Alys Faiz who figure in the book. For advice and comments my warm thanks are due to Jasodara Bagchi, Maeve Bhavan, Kamla Bhasin, copyeditor John Bohannon, Valentine Daniel, Malathi de Alwis, Mangalika de Silva, Howard Fast, Yolanda Foster, Elizabeth Harris, Michael Holroyd, Pradeep Jeganathan, Ram Manikkalingam, Chitra Maunaguru, Sucheta Mazumdar, Ritu Menon, Valentine Moghadam, V. Murugesu, Anita Nesiah, Vasuki Nesiah, Karen Offen, Arjuna Parakrama, Paru Parathalingam, Judith Waters Pasqualge, Pradeepa Perera, Ros Petchesky, V.K. Ramachandran, Sibnarayan Ray, Jennifer Robertson, David Scott, Neelan Tiruchelvam, Nira Yuval-Davis, and Suriya Wickremasinghe. Any errors in the book are, of course, mine. For help in research, locating documents and editing my thanks go to Rasika Chandrasekera, M. Jacob, Colvin Karunaratne, Karen Lambert, A.Mukhopadhyay, B.P.K.L. Pushpakumari and Kapila Silva.

I am deeply grateful to Marlie Wasserman of Routledge for the interest she has taken in the book, and to Mary Carol De Zutter, Adam Bohannon, and Kimberly Herald of Routledge for their invaluable help.

Kumari Jayawardena
Colombo, Sri Lanka.

INTRODUCTION

THE NOBLE AND THE IGNOBLE
White Women as Goddesses and Devils

The difference is that Margaret Noble works from within outwards, while [Katherine] Mayo tries to work from without inwards.... Sister Nivedita's outlook is noble like her birthname; but Miss Mayo's method is ignoble, warped and seeks to dress up abuse as argument.

—K.R. Shastri, *The Bombshell of Today* (1931:19)

THE PUBLICATION IN 1927 OF *Mother India*, A SENSATIONALIST BOOK BY AN American, Katherine Mayo, caused a storm of outrage and protest. The book's condemnation of Indian family life and child marriage was traumatic for Indians at that time; it went into forty-two printings in ten years and continues to be denounced even today. Mayo was reviled as a white American racist, as an agent of British imperialism, and as an old, childless spinster with a prurient interest in the sex life of Indians. Almost every famous Indian reacted with sharp criticism; Gandhi dismissed it as a drain inspector's report. Particularly insulting was Mayo's declaration that Indians were not fit for self-government because of their terrible oppression of women. Some Indian males replied in anger, defending Indian womanhood and denouncing the sexual mores of the "decadent West." For reformers who basically agreed with Mayo's social critique, there were questions of voice, location and politics; it was not *what* was said, but *who* was saying it, and from what vantage point, that was important. Complicity with or resistance to imperialism became the crucial test.

Reading *Mother India*'s critics sixty years later, the most revealing reaction was that of the Indian judge Shastri; he contrasted Katherine Mayo with Swami Vivekananda's Irish disciple Margaret Noble (Sister Nivedita) who had celebrated Hindu family life, spoken of the empowering aspects of Kali worship and linked this with the political awakening of India. These two women, Shastri said, were polar opposites. The Indian male's perception of foreign women, dividing them into categories of noble/good and ignoble/bad, made me realize that Western women in South Asia during the colonial period problematize important issues of gender and race, of feminism and nationalism. It became clear that for some South Asian males the "bad" Western woman was the critic, "muck-raker," social reformer or missionary, attacking local customs and religions from the standpoint of values said to be derived from outside South Asian civilization, and also acting in support of other sinister agendas such as those of Christianity and British imperialism. The "good" Western woman, in contrast, was the theosophist, Holy Mother, Orientalist or devotee of a guru who found Hinduism or Buddhism liberating, found traditional South Asian society more attractive and acceptable than her own, and, most important, sympathized with and supported local nationalist aspirations. To many, the "good" woman also included foreign women who independently, or as a wife or partner of a local political leader, fought against colonialism and entered into active politics for national liberation, Socialism and women's rights. Thus, along with white "female devils" from the West, South Asians have also had white "goddesses" whose centenaries are remembered, who have city suburbs, streets and schools named after them, and whose memory has been kept alive long after independence from foreign rule.

In retrieving the histories of numerous foreign women who had lived and worked in South Asia in the colonial period, I found myself compelled to reconsider the issue of colonialism in terms of race, gender and feminism. I began to think about the multiple roles of white women in a colonial situation and felt the need to re-examine the role of some Western women who, despite colonialism, were speaking with a "different voice," especially on issues of local women's status and political change. I was also concerned to put forward a critique of nationalist attitudes which was not a defense of imperialism, and to see if the "West-East discourse" could be liberated from what Romila Thapar calls "the polemics of the colonial age" (1989:23).

The subjection of Africa and Asia entailed war, conquest, and genocide, and the domination and humiliation of colonial peoples by the "master-race." But colonialism was also multi-faceted; the colonizers themselves were fragmented and there were many ways of seeing the colonized. Colonialism was also gendered, and this book highlights (among other issues) the feminist content of the work of Western women under British colonialism in South Asia. Colonialism was also the domination by European males of colonized women, a point that has not been adequately emphasized. The colonized woman was the "Other" to the European in several senses, as a woman and as a member of a subject *race* and *class*. One contrast was between the "noble savage" woman, portrayed as sensuous and living close to nature, and the Western wife, safe at home, chaste and subordinate. As Tiffany and Adams noted, "the white, civilized lady of temperate climates opposes that dark primitive woman of the torrid zones," adding that Joseph Conrad in *Heart of Darkness* describes Kurtz's African mistress as "savage and superb, wild-eyed and magnificent" in contrast to his polite, English fianceé (1985:30–31). The "savage" woman was also predatory, giving rise to myths of Amazons, matriarchs, man-eaters, untamed and sexually uninhibited women who had to be dominated by Man-the-Hunter.

The metaphor of "woman" was even appropriated to describe the colonized regions themselves and colonial literature is full of such sexually-charged references. As a British naturalist in 1825 said, "Guiana still whispered in my ear and seemed to invite me once more to wander through her distant forests" (ibid:17). These notions shaded off into the fantasy of the "Oriental woman," as reflected in writings such as Baudelaire's poem "A Une Dame Créole," Hugo's "Farewell to the Arab Hostess," and Conrad's numerous "half-caste" women. At the level of popular culture too, Oriental clichés proliferated; harems, geishas, dancing girls and princesses, along with Madame Butterfly and Mata Hari figured in a background of the erotic and exotic. This was the fantasy; the reality was that colonized women were also an economically exploited group—an important source of cheap labor in plantations and factories.

If in Europe "us" and "them" had meant the upper class and the working people, the colonial context required a differentiation based on race, for the rulers were very concerned to show that "us" meant *all* whites, rich and poor, including *all* white women. It was one of the unwritten rules of colonialism that there should be no breach in the ranks; hence, the alacrity with which white male and female agitators and communists, as well as gamblers and prostitutes, were expelled from the colonies as "undesirable Europeans." In 1920, for example, the British authorities deported a Russian woman who was a "disgrace to the European community in Ceylon…constantly seen in the company of sailors…wandering about the public streets drunk and indecently dressed" (Bracegirdle Commission 1938:421). While European men had liaisons with local women, by the early 20th century these were strongly discouraged and in the case of civil servants, actually prohibited in 1909 by circulars from the Colonial Office (Strobel 1991:4). White women were considered the guardians of the purity of the race, and those who did not conform to this image were therefore a threat to colonial rule. Those who had local friends were accused of "going jungli" and their socializing with local men was seen as racial betrayal. As Strobel notes, the marriage of the Maharaja of Patalia to Miss Florry Bryan in 1893 "unsettled" the Viceroy of India, for "his social status and her lower class background confused…the racial, sexual and class hierarchies of Empire" (ibid:4). In 1902 a British official deplored the recent "craze of white women for running after black men," adding that "it pervades all classes of society" from peeresses to working-class women (Ballhatchet 1980:119–20). White women who married Indians were denounced as deviant, "unless she is sexually perverted," wrote an Englishman in the early 1900s "she has violated her own nature in marrying a man of coloured race" (MacMillan 1988:216).

If therefore some gender analysis is called for in taking another look at colonialism, we must start by differentiating between various groups of white women in colonial situations. This book is not about the *memsahibs* (master's women)—the wives of European men who served as bureaucrats, merchants, planters or in the armed forces. These were the famous "Women of the Raj" who have been written about extensively and are depicted in literature, films and television serials as brave, long-suffering and strong, or as racist, stupid and neurotic. There was even a popular male view that it was the white woman who not only caused the Indian rebellion of 1857, but also eventually "lost the British their empire, alienating the friendly native with her petty snobberies and sexual jealousies" (Haggis 1990:105). What has not emerged, however, was the reality of the colonial wife, living in a sort of doubly refined bondage—isolated in the home as a *woman* and alienated in the colony as a *foreigner.* This book does not deal with them.

It does deal, however, with other categories of women who had different perceptions of the East. To the missionaries and social reformers there was nothing noble or exotic about "savagery" and they saw their task as "saving" their Asian sisters from devilish beliefs, moral degradation and from sexual and social oppression. However, this deliverance was to be achieved within the framework of colonialism, which was seen as the agent of modernization and social development. They may have conflicted with the British rulers on some issues, but generally their objectives ran parallel with those of the colonial rulers. In striking contrast to those who wanted to Christianize and "civilize" the colonized were other foreign women—theosophists, Orientalists and Holy Mothers who also rejected the savagery hypothesis and wanted to Orientalize and "civilize" the colonizers of the West. They perceived Asia as the model of an alternative society that was also the site of their ideal of womanhood. Asia had, in their eyes, achieved a degree of wisdom and spirituality far superior to the materialist development of the West; as far as womanhood was concerned, they were particularly attracted by concepts of woman's power (shakti) in Hinduism, by androgynous deities, female goddesses such as Kali, and by the claims of high status of women in ancient Hindu and Buddhist societies. These perceptions placed them in a position of direct antagonism to colonialism, which they saw as a destructive force. But there was also a group of foreign Socialist women who rejected Christianity and reformism as well as shakti, Kali, and local gurus, and who wanted their Asian "sisters" to free themselves politically from foreign rule, and socially from oppressive structures and traditional religious and cultural practice.

All these groups of white women had their origins in the reality of the "new woman" who was asserting herself on all fronts. Women all over the world had made one of the most remarkable "leaps" in history in the late 19th and early 20th centuries. Spurred on by the principles of the French revolution and the *Declaration of the Rights of Man*, women took up the challenge and proclaimed "the Rights of Women." While groups of "blue stockings" or learned women of the privileged classes had existed in all cultures of the world, in the 19th century, women's education in the West and East advanced to include higher education and expanded to bring within its scope other social strata. There were campaigns not only for women's legal and political rights, but also for sexual freedom and birth control. Many women were able to make their mark as writers, artists, travelers, and actresses, leading independent lives and often breaking away from the accepted family roles for women and from patriarchal domination. Others, who were radicals, joined movements for social change and were active in political and trade union struggles. Defiance of social convention and dissidence in politics and religion became the attributes of the independent woman of the period. In the colonies, the British rulers were clearly rattled at the boldness of those Western women who were undermining white supremacy by consorting with the colonized.

The search for other less oppressive religions, philosophies and cultures, and other less exploitative ways of life attracted the "new women"; this search also had a sympathetic basis in the currents of thought that questioned accepted religious and social orthodoxies. It was argued that no religion or culture was better than another and that white people had no "imperial destiny" to colonize and impose their ideologies on others. It was even suggested that Western society needed to learn from other cultures. Thus, Hindu and Buddhist beliefs and cultures interested certain liberal intellectuals, especially those linked to spiritualist and theosophist movements. Asian nationalist males who were themselves attacking the imperial state and church were attracted by these new allies—independent, educated, rebellious Western women who were in revolt against oppression and subordination. The ruling class, unwilling to grant rights to either women or colonial peoples, could do little to prevent some bonding and networks between the "advanced" women of the West and the Asians fighting for national liberation, two groups with common enemies.

While feminism at home and nationalism in the colonies were anathema to the British "establishment," those South Asian male students, intellectuals and religious and political activists who visited Britain were delighted to link up with the "enemy within"—namely the "new women" who were battling the authorities at all levels. Swami Vivekananda wrote to Margaret Noble, his Irish friend, in 1895 urging her to come to India, and arguing that India needed not a man, "but a woman; a real lioness, to work for the Indians, women especially" (Chatterjee 1968:207). His requirements were clear; he needed someone who had "education, sincerity, purity, immense love, determination and above all Celtic blood." The Celtic blood was the added bonus, as colonial peoples had a special sympathy for Ireland's struggle for "Home Rule." Vivekananda was preceded by many others. Sixty years earlier Rammohan Roy had a circle of English women admirers, most of them Unitarian radicals like Mary Carpenter, Harriet Martineau and Lucy Aikin, who in 1831 noted Roy's amazement at "the mental accomplishments of English ladies" (Carpenter 1850:106). Keshab Chandra Sen, the Bengali reformer also had many close friends among women social reformers in Britain, and the Indian leader Aurobindo's second name was Ackroyd, after Annette Ackroyd, who had started a secular girls school in Calcutta in 1872. Many of the Indian nationalists of later years were also influenced by Western feminists, a notable example being Gandhi, who in his early career was inspired by meetings with famous women of the time including Annie Besant and Olive Schreiner.

This brings me back to the question of Western women living and working in South Asia during the period of colonial rule, and of course the reason for the differentiation made between white devils and goddesses. Women theosophists, devotees, wives and companions were all accepted in their own right. And in the heyday of imperialism, some of the most renowned leaders (Vivekananda, Aurobindo, Krishnamurti), leaders of national liberation movements (Gandhi, Nehru, Krishna Menon, Subhas Chandra Bose) and Communist pioneers of the region (M. N.Roy, V.Chattopadyaya, S.A.Wickremasinghe, Pieter Keuneman)—along with numerous other prominent Indian and Sri Lankan figures in public life—had Western women as their advisors, soul-mates, companions or wives. Many of these foreign women were not in the shadow of the "great man" but had their own identities and like many other independent Western women, spoke out for political freedom and women's rights in South Asia. Problems arose only when foreign women who had not openly allied themselves with Indian and Sri Lankan nationalism dared to take a critical look at local religions, cultures, family practices and the condition of women. Here they touched a raw nerve, for criticism is acceptable when made by a member of that society or someone sympathetic to its aspirations, but not when made by anyone guilty of ambivalence or—worst of all—of complicity with foreign rule.

In a colonial context, however, there were other reasons for hostility to foreign critics. For one, the nationalist discourse was also an exercise in identity and national pride, the assertion of a superior culture, an ancient past, and a mythic golden age of freedom, prosperity and self-sufficiency; in contrast, the evils of poverty, sickness, degradation, violence, drunkenness and other social evils were blamed on colonialism. In this context, criticism of local religions and cultures was an attack on the "nation." Legislative interventions by the colonial state to improve women's status, while welcomed by a few local reformers, were an unwarranted alien intrusion into local gender relations. The confining of women to the home became the crux of the issue; for as Partha Chatterjee has pointed out, there was a clear demarcation by Indians between the world (bahir) and the home (ghar), an "identification of social roles by gender to correspond with the separation of social space." The Indian venturing into the outside world and exposed to a dominant material culture could be westernized and acquire the latest in science, technology, economic organization and political strategy; this was permissible only as long as the private space—the home—was preserved as the center not only of a superior spiritual culture, but also of "true" identity. This was the sphere of women and family where man was sovereign, a status he had lost in the outside world dominated by foreign rulers. "In the world, imitation of and adaption to Western norms was a necessity; at home they were tantamount to annihilation of one's very own identity" (Chatterjee 1989:239).

One can add to this argument by suggesting that the home (and women) were not merely a representation of the spiritual, and the locus of ideological domination and power, but also an area of material interest to males in terms of unpaid labor and services. Any suggestion by missionaries, reformers or the colonial government that some aspects of Indian home life were unacceptable and needed change through legislative decree was thus doubly abhorrent. Indian men would decide how much social reform and education for women was necessary and how much tradition had to be preserved (or invented) in terms of women's dress and behavior. It was bad enough when British bureaucrats and busybodies interfered in the privacy of Indian home life, but the thought of the white man's woman daring to interfere was even more offensive.

In situations of conflict and confrontation, women of the enemy are often the target of violence and invective, and during colonial rule, European women were frequently demonized. It is a part of nationalist discourse at its more populist and demagogic level that "whites" as individuals are attacked and criticized for their inferiority in terms of religion, culture, morality, behavior and cleanliness; the stereotype of the white woman was that she was not much better than a prostitute—immodest in dress and indulging in drinking, smoking, dancing and promiscuous behavior. Who were these low creatures, barmaids and landladies' daughters from a decadent civilization, who dared lecture and criticize Asians on their treatment of women? Why didn't missionaries preach to their own poverty-stricken working class, blacks and oppressed groups in Europe and America? Why didn't social reformers deal with problems at home, and what had Katherine Mayo to say about crime, vice, racism and the Ku Klux Klan in the United States? And what is more, sixty years after Mayo wrote her book, are Western feminists—coming from societies rampant with drugs, crime, and violence—daring to continue probing into South Asian family life with the help of their local agents, in the form of Indian, Pakistani, Bangladeshi and Sri Lankan feminists? And therefore is it surprising that Mary Daly should urge "Feminist Seekers/Spinsters" not to have "fears of criticizing "'another culture'" and should "search out and claim such sisters as Katherine Mayo"? (1978:129).

In this book I discuss the various types of Western women with a "cause" who were linked to South Asia in the colonial period. I make a distinction on the one hand between those Western women who were bringing Christianity, Western education and values, social reform, women's rights, and some modernizing processes to the women of Asia within a framework of the acceptance of British rule, and, on the other hand, Western women who were rejecting Christianity, negating Western values and rediscovering Oriental religions and cultures in a context of Home Rule and nationalism, or even Socialism. But whether spiritual or secular, many of these Western women were inspired by a movement which led them to abandon their home countries to live, and in most cases die, in South Asia. Hence the sense of the "white woman's other burden"—which was an attempt to liberate women, in terms of a Western or Eastern ideal, and in terms of a vision of a better society. But did this vision have a feminist content? How did it relate to local nationalism? And which was more important, to take the pledge of feminism or of nationalism? This is what I have set out to examine. For example, did the "women's work for women" approach of the missionaries have a feminist agenda as well as a vision of global sisterhood? Were the women doctors, social reformers and fund-raisers inspired by bold new ideas about women's rights in Europe and the United States? Were the strong, independent, often single women who became important missionaries, theosophists, Orientalists and Holy Mothers feminists in their own way? Did feminism inspire women scholars, travelers and writers to become interested in South Asia, and what part did feminism play among Western Socialist women involved in anti-imperialist struggles and movements for social change?

The word feminist as Sheila Rowbotham remarks, has been given "a range of shifting meanings," but its origins are however still uncertain (1992:3). In France the suffragist Hubertine Auclert used the term in the 1880s and in later years in France, Britain, and the United States, it was used to denote the campaign for women's emancipation (Offen 1988:126). Various types of feminisms emerged—liberal, Socialist and conservative—and women ranging from Christians to Socialists in all parts of the world were involved in projects to gain political rights and equality for women. This was also the era of the "new woman" who broke from traditional family ties and conventional beliefs and behavior to assert her independence from patriarchal restraints. Feminism can be defined as a consciousness of injustices based on gender hierarchy, and a commitment to change. Such injustices arise from the exploitation and oppression of women in male dominated societies, and the changes envisaged range from the achievement of "equal rights" to "liberation." All such definitions, of course, lead to further queries and differences of opinon, to the insistance that there is no one feminism and to the denial of "grand theories." For the purpose of this book, however, the basic definition is adequate because the study deals with a wide range of women; some of them were more feminist, others less feminist, and in their own way consciously or otherwise, were involved in projects to change the lives of women. But what is it to be "more" or "less" feminist? There was the "independent" woman, unmarried, mobile and sometimes conservative and conformist in social attitudes (like missionaries), distinguishable from the "new woman" who defied tradition and social conventions and considered herself to be *avant garde* in politics and culture and liberated in terms of her sexuality. The feminists, however, had all these traits and more; their concern was not merely personal liberation from patriarchal shackles, but public and organized resistance to structures of oppression that denied women their rights.

Feminism in the 19th century could mean not only a critique of patriarchal structures, including church and state, but also a challenge to colonialism and the subordination and exploitation of women in the colonies. Whether they accepted the title feminist or not, many Western women who worked in South Asia, were involved in such critiques and concerned with women's status in the family and society; this book therefore highlights the various aspects of such concern. Missionaries, nuns and social reformers felt they had a moral duty to uplift, sanitize and modernize traditional societies (and especially family life) through the Christianizing and "civilizing" mission; in doing so they often had to fight their own male hierarchies of church and state. Quakers and Shakers were no doubt the "Mothers of Feminism" (Bacon 1986 and Desroches 1971) but what about women missionaries and reformers in the "Age of Empire"? Barbara Ramusack described them as maternal imperialists "mothering India and Indians" (1992:133). Antoinette Burton called them imperial feminists "who collaborated in the ideological work of empire" (1992:151–2). While it is true that we cannot ignore the religious, racist, maternalist and imperialist connotations of their work, I argue that the feminist content in missionary and social reform activities has to be further reconsidered, analyzed and problematized.

What are the basic issues of feminism and nationalism in a context of foreign women in a colonial situation—with agendas of conversion, modernization, reform and revolution? Colonized people faced two key issues: one was to rid the country of foreign rule and achieve national liberation; the other was to promote democracy and social change, which would provide a better life for women and men free of exploitation and oppression. This of course raised a perennial problem—are there stages and priorities or is it a combined process? And does national liberation take precedence over all other issues including women's liberation? These are some of the questions that arise when discussing the "good" and "bad" foreign women who lived in South Asia in the colonial period. The irony often was that some of those who were "good" on nationalism, were lukewarm on women's rights for fear of offending locals; and those who were all for the sun never setting on the British Empire, were often "advanced" on the issue of women's oppression and did not care too much about offending South Asian males or their own patriarchs. But if for many men in the region, the only foreign women worth honoring were those who sympathized with or joined the struggle for independence—how did local women see the question of "global sisterhood" under colonialism? Here the tricky question often arises—can outsiders in any circumstances speak out and criticize, or is the formula the old one—that this would be unwarranted interference in internal matters? Can there be then, a "universalist discourse" on the rights of women, irrespective of race, ethnicity, class, cultural differences and political agendas? Or do we have to highlight the importance of difference and multi-culturalism and avoid the risk of homogenizing on the basis of gender and class?

In this book I advocate a perspective that combines universalist discourse with the recognition of difference, which Nira Yuval-Davis has called "universality in diversity" (1994:422). This approach does not lose sight of the universal condition of subordination that women are subject to, and claims the right of every woman to speak out against women's oppression and exploitation everywhere. But it also recognizes the distortion that can arise from a universalism that only takes gender into account, as well as the pitfalls of focusing exclusively on ethnic or racial collectivities, disregarding internal class and gender divisions.

In a post-colonial era, one should look back with a new focus at the foreign women who participated in what they considered universal causes and historic movements. The missionaries may have been insensitive about local culture and religion, but they were ahead of the state and local reformers on women's issues and in their efforts to highlight social evils. The theosophists and Holy Mothers may have romanticized local religions and tradition, but they were sharp in their critique of Christianity and "cultural colonialism." Yet it was the foreign women Socialists, in their quest for liberation and social change, who were perhaps way ahead in their synthesis of the missionary and social reformist outrage at social evils, with a sense of history and the recognition of "difference" of the theosophists, Holy Mothers and Orientalists. Echoes of these debates still prevail and are of continuing concern to feminists. The attitudes of antipathy to Western social reformers that I have analyzed through the dichotomy of "good" and "bad" is evident even today in attacks on feminism construed as a Western import, marshalled generally in terms of universalist values and/or cultural difference. The bogey of "white imperialist feminism" hardly applies in a South Asian context; for as Lata Mani has pointed out, there is no direct white presence or "the boot of imperialism upon one's neck" in the region. The immediate resistance is to local issues— the "nation state, dominant social and political institutions, and religious "fundamentalisms" of various kinds" (1990:29). For women of South Asia, the main enemy is within.

In the euphoria and enthusiasm of the women's movement of the 1970s and early 1980s, the essentialist universal concept of women, without differentiation, united under the slogan of global sisterhood was attractive and inspiring; many feminists established links of "sisterhood" internationally and regionally, and met at historic "universal" gatherings in Mexico, Copenhagen, Nairobi and now Beijing. During this period, however, the criticism was made that apart from gender oppression, women were victims of class and race oppression, and that women also had other important identities based on ethnicity, race, religion and class. Even gender oppression operated differently as it was influenced by factors of class, ethnicity, age, and even region. African-American women alleged that white feminists were ignoring minority cultures and were generalizing on the basis of white society (hooks 1981, Mohanty 1988). Similarly, "white feminism" was seen as very middle-class, not taking up issues that were of concern to working-class women. Women of Africa, Asia and Latin America also began to claim that concepts like "sisterhood" were misleading unless contextualized. Western women are critiqued by Marnia Lasreg for not recognizing heterogeneity and "discoursing about others" of the "Third World" by merely universalizing "First World" experience (1988:99); and Gloria Anzaldua accuses white feminists of wanting to "minimize racial differences by taking comfort in the fact that we are all women" (1990:xxi).

The shift to a notion of difference and multiple identities, taking into account such factors as race, religion and ethnicity, was important in that it not only stressed crucial areas of difference between societies, but also made theorizing on women purely on the basis of middle-class, white society no longer acceptable (Anthias & Yuval-Davis 1983). But rejecting universalism also had its dangers; it enabled some to make excuses for the oppression of women in their societies, arguing that its particular manifestations were part of their specific culture or religion. But there are many Third World feminists who do not fall into this trap; they denounce the xenophobia and chauvinism of their own societies and oppose the currents of fundamentalism and anti-Western populism that are supportive of gender oppression. Valentine Moghadam, for example has warned against such "insular thinking" and the "nativist mentality" of some Third World intellectuals who denounce "any concept, practice or institution that originates in the "West" as Orientalism or neocolonialism." What is privileged is "authenticity"; what is sought for is "identity" she adds, noting that this often leads to a rejection of democracy, socialism, secularism and feminism as "alien and culturally inappropriate" (1989:88).

These debates have added another dimension to the struggles of Third World feminists, who, in their advocacy of democracy and social change, are already in a battle on the home front against nativism and populist nationalism. They also raise many other questions. In attempts to challenge class, caste and gender inequalities in our societies, how do we react when foreign women say we are backward and need "experts" from the West to teach us how to improve? Such attitudes tend to make us culturally defensive, finding arguments to justify the oppressive features of our own societies—from caste and religious fundamentalism to women's exploitation and subordination, and sometimes even sati (widow immolation on the husband's funeral pyre). On the other hand, how do we react when foreign women who have a romance with the Orient, appropriate the "Other" and not only denounce feminism as irrelevant and foreign, but also tell us that our societies are the "alternative" model, that we should not change by industrializing or modernizing, but should reactivate and preserve traditional societies, and honor our self-sacrificing Third World women?

There are many dilemmas for feminists in a Third World context, where anti-feminist attitudes and policies are shared by many males spread across the political and social spectrum. The left often agrees with right wing fundamentalists in their denunciation of feminism. Muslims, Hindus and Sikhs in India, and Sinhalese, Tamils and Muslims in Sri Lanka, while in conflict on ethnic or religious issues, would be in agreement on the question of feminism, giving the impression of a homogeneity of opinion that transcends class, caste, political, religious and other boundaries. Local feminists, they say, are bourgeois women inspired by foreign ideology and Western patterns of behavior, and are bribed with foreign money to promote chaos in the family, divisions in political movements and cultural degeneracy. In addition, all religious and ethnic groups concerned with their "identity" have also begun to argue falsely that women had already been liberated by Hinduism, Islam or Buddhism as the case may be, and that women in the "golden age" of all these cultures had an equality and freedom unheard of in the West. If women's status had declined it was due to colonialism, and the remedy was to return to a precolonial type of society, based on the myths of a self-sufficient peasant economy, where social harmony, equality and traditional values prevailed—and, of course, where women were free.

In recent years, I too have been involved in defending South Asian feminists from charges of being Western and bourgeois, and raising the questions: "What is Western?" "What is bourgeois?" In a confrontation with a Pakistani leftist who alleged that the book *Women in Pakistan* (by Shaheed and Mumtaz) was about "a handful of elitist, Westernized bourgeois women," I questioned his use of such emotive words and asked whether "Westernized" meant "modern" as opposed to "traditional." Did it indicate life-style, use of the English language, of computers, cars, television sets? Did it mean "degenerate behavior?" Or did it include secularism, Socialism and feminism? And was the word "bourgeois" used not to define a class, but pejoratively to suggest conspicuous consumption, individualism or ill-gotten wealth? My conclusion was that these were red herrings—crude attempts to denounce the women's struggle, resorting to language and arguments that colonialists used to vilify movements of national liberation and are used today by right-wing and authoritarian regimes to deny women their rights (Jayawardena:1988).

Part I of this book deals with two basic themes. First, the efforts by women missionaries, while spreading the gospel, to improve education and health for women, and their "civilizing mission" to challenge old structures like the caste and family systems and ameliorate the condition of Asian women. Missionaries have been looked upon generally with hostility by the non-Christian intelligentsia of South Asia, even though many of them benefitted from the services offered by these foreigners. These missionaries have been stereotyped as racist "agents of imperialism" at worst, and well-meaning but ludicrous proselytizers at best, who along with Christianity were offering some tempting products of Western society. Nuns fell into the category of rosary-clutching, simple women, misguided in their blind faith, but with attractive offers of making "ladies" out of "backward" local girls. Missionaries and nuns were treated as if they were all the same; differences of Christian belief and tactics in reaching out to the local population were often ignored by those to whom all aspects of Christianity were "bad news." This book presents some of the approaches to local women adopted by these Western women in South Asia, their own difficulties with the male hierarchies of Church and State and their attitudes to imperialism. Second it also discusses the influences of missionaries on local women, and the way in which Christian education produced not only "good wives and mothers," but also the early women professionals, feminists and some women Prime Ministers of South Asia. These themes are discussed through some case studies of old-style American Methodist missionaries of the 1820s and their narrow fundamentalism; the Church of England's infusion of the Protestant ethic of work, achievement and modern education in a girls' high school in Sri Lanka and the network of girls' schools in India started by the Irish Catholic Loreto nuns that provided a modern Western education and unwittingly produced the Indian "new woman." The links and contradictions between funders and funded is seen in the study of fund-raising by Christian women in the United States for homes for Indian child-widows started by Pandita Ramabai.

Part II of this book deals with those Western women whom Ramusack calls "secular missionaries" (1992:133) who took up issues of medical reform, changes in legislation and the eradication of social evils. They often had to fight on two fronts: against the colonial government that paid lip-service to reform but was reluctant to disturb local opinion, and against those Indians who thought that legislation by the British, and denunciations by outsiders of social evils, like child marriage and prohibitions on widow re-marriage or sati, were an intolerable interference in the sacred area of family life. But to the reformers, these questions could not be left to the whims of men—whether British bureaucrats or the local bourgeoisie. Some of the urgent tasks that the "new women" of the West also felt they had to undertake included the establishment of women's hospitals and medical education for women in India. This book focuses on the lives of two pioneers, Dr. Edith Pechey and Dr. Mary Scharlieb; the campaigns for female education and other reforms by Mary Carpenter; the secular girls' school started by Annette Ackroyd and the highlighting of the evil of child marriage by numerous women ranging from the controversial missionary Amy Carmichael, to the liberal member of parliament Eleanor Rathbone and the "muck-raker" Katherine Mayo.

Indians were also wary of social reformers like Annette Ackroyd who claimed to put gender before race when she opposed the attempt by British liberals to appoint Indian magistrates with powers over European residents; her opposition, she said, was not because the magistrate was Indian, but because he was an Indian *man* who was presumed to be unenlightened on the question of women, and she, a *woman*, did not want to be judged by him. Many Western women reformers like Eleanor Rathbone also faced criticism in spite of their support for Indian women's issues, because of their reluctance to put Indian independence on their agenda. And Katherine Mayo was the ultimate abomination, since her pro-British political stand against Indian nationalism was extreme in its reactionary and racist content. In this, South Asian women agreed with their men—that there was not much point in foreign women devoting their lives to good causes unless they also supported the most important of good causes—namely liberation from foreign rule. But whatever their enthusiasm and commitment to education, health and social reform, these Western women, as well as the missionaries, could not enter the pantheon of white goddesses as long as they worked either within the ideological framework of Christianity and Christian culture, or with a belief in the benevolence of British rule. Opposition to political agitation was a distinguishing feature of missionary schools, which not only delighted in proclaiming loyalty to the throne, but also often banned "seditious" literature or "disloyal" talk in their schools. Ultimately, as the locals knew, the missionaries and reformers would support imperialism. Hence, while benefitting from the various services provided, they were not prepared to elevate any foreign woman missionary or reformer—and less so any local woman Christian like Pandita Ramabai—to the status of "national hero."

Part III of this book deals with the revolt against Christianity in the West, the rise of numerous alternative beliefs, and the link-up between such tendencies in the West with religious revival and emerging nationalism in the colonies. For the Hindus, Muslims and Buddhists of South Asia, Christianity had been a malediction that had hit their societies, denouncing their beliefs and practices and linking social evils to their religions. Their antagonism to Christianity found expression in movements of cultural and religious revival infused with a nationalist content. Apart from the hostility to Christianity as the "outsiders" religion, there was also the fact that opposition to Christianity could be expressed as a "religious" question without fear of charges of sedition and treason against the ruling power. Patriotic issues in 19th century India and Sri Lanka were formulated in cultural and religious terms before political expressions of nationalist views were possible (Jayawardena 1972). Religion thus became a useful method of mobilizing the masses, using the argument that their holy religion and their traditional beliefs and practices were threatened by the religion and culture of their foreign masters. These revivalist-cum-nationalist currents were influenced by Darwinism, Free-thought and by anti-

Christian trends in Europe. While some women had come to theosophy from occult and spiritualist cults, others had been in social reform, Socialist movements and women's suffrage struggles. Many women intellectuals, scholars and writers were associated with the theosophists. What then was the attraction of theosophy, Vedanta and Kali worship to women intellectuals and radicals who were rejecting Christianity as superstition and were critical of Victorian patriarchy and the Church and State? How could, what H.L. Mencken called, "the Hooey from the Orient" find a response among intelligent women, especially when theosophy and occult phenomena had been exposed to sharp criticism and ridicule by intellectuals both in Europe and South Asia?

This book discusses these questions through the lives and experiences of some unorthodox Western women in South Asia who went against the stereotype; these included the woman Orientalist (Caroline Rhys Davids and I. B.Horner), traveler (Alexandra David-Néel); funder of Buddhist causes (Mary Foster) and art critic (Ethel Coomaraswamy) who wrote about the need to preserve traditional arts and crafts from industrial capitalism. Women theosophists included the co-founder of the Theosophical Society, Helena Blavatsky; Annie Besant, atheist, Socialist, feminist and supporter of birth control of the 1870s and 1880s, who made India her home in the 1890s, championing Home Rule and Krishnamurti—the new Messiah; Margaret Cousins, a militant Irish feminist and participant in the suffragist struggles of the early 20th century; and actress Florence Farr, member of the Golden Dawn occult group, friend of Bernard Shaw, W.B.Yeats, Ezra Pound and P.Ramanathan, who ended her life in Sri Lanka as the "lady principal" of the first Hindu girls' school.

Part IV of this book concerns the foreign women disciples of Indian gurus, who were more than simple Holy Mothers following a saint. They were committed not merely to the leader personally, but also to political struggles—both national and international—of their time, and they defied all the accepted gender and race roles of white women in a colonial situation. The earliest was the dynamic Sister Nivedita (Margaret Noble) who made her home in Calcutta in the 1890s as the "daughter" of Swami Vivekananda. Her solidarity with militant nationalist agitation was the key to her popularity in India. Another extraordinary Holy Mother was Mirra Richard, of Egyptian Jewish origin from France, a liberated feminist who moved in impressionist artistic circles and dabbled in spiritualism; she joined forces with the Indian philosopher Aurobindo, became the famous "Mother" of Pondicherry, and was involved in creative education and in setting up an international community in Auroville, South India. Equally famous was Madeleine Slade, from an upper-class British family who became Gandhi's devoted follower, assuming the name Mira Behn. It was highly embarrassing for the British rulers to have a woman of their class and race, (who should normally have been a memsahib) cooking and washing for Gandhi and acting as his secretary and adviser. While the British ridiculed her and dismissed her as eccentric, the Indians (however surprised they were by the strange sight of a six-foot English woman in flowing khadi robes) respected her for the choice she had made to identify with Gandhi, the arch enemy of the British Empire.

But other women who were not disciples chose to perform a secular, political role by allying with South Asian Communist leaders. Such women have received little attention or recognition and were often demonized as dangerous revolutionaries, abhorred by both the imperial rulers and local bourgeoisie. The British rulers had from the early 20th century been on the lookout for persons described as terrorists, anarchists, Socialists and Communists. While locals could be jailed, the authorities were faced with a problem of "foreign agitators," and had to have special legislation to deport such undesirable foreigners who threatened the British by their presence. After the 1917 Russian Revolution, a strict watch was kept on Western Communists visiting or living in South Asia. Many were deported, including several women who resided in, or tried to visit India and Sri Lanka. But some married local Communists and lived in the region, while others worked for the local nationalist and left movements from abroad.

Those considered in Part V of this book include Agnes Smedley, the American Socialist and feminist who lived with Virendranath Chattopadyaya in Berlin in the early 1920s organizing Indian revolutionaries in Europe, and the other important but forgotten figure, Evelyn Trent, (wife of India's pioneer Communist M.N. Roy), who worked between 1917 and 1925 with Indian revolutionary groups in the United States, Mexico, Soviet Union, Germany and France. And there were many others like her—German, Austrian, British and American women who married Indian and Sri Lankan nationalists and leftists. Some of their stories are lost to history because both sides were embarrassed by their existence; but there were other left leaders whose wives came to live in the region and work for political causes and became nationally known public figures. One such person was a British woman, Doreen Young, from a family of Socialists, who married Dr. S.A. Wickremasinghe, for many years the Chairman of the Communist Party of Sri Lanka. She was one of the pioneers of Left politics, the anti-imperialist campaign, modern education, and the women's movement in Sri Lanka and became the first foreign woman to be elected to the Sri Lankan parliament. Another Sri Lankan Communist leader, Pieter Keuneman, married Hedi Simon, a Viennese of Jewish origin who had left Austria to study in Cambridge, England in the 1930s; her militant actions in the strikes and political struggles in Sri Lanka during the years 1940 to 1945 are a part of left folk history of the island.

This book takes a feminist perspective in examining the lives of some of these forgotten women. In their time they became famous while pioneering movements, stirring controversy, confronting the patriarchs and creating scandal. When the history of the period was written, however, these women were often ignored or marginalized and soon became a distant memory. I have deliberately reversed the usual trend, foregrounding the women and relegating the "important" male performers—bishops and priests, reformers, gurus, nationalist politicians and left leaders, to the background.

The women I have discussed are the controversial ones about whom there could be two types of perception, ranging from "devils"—reviled, condemned, jailed and deported, to "goddesses"—worshipped, honored and celebrated. But there was no agreement on who were goddesses and who were devils, and those who were goddesses to some were devils to others. And there was much sexism in the use of both these categories; those who praised South Asian social practices were deemed noble and those who dared to speak out on women's subordination and oppression were ignoble. The British rulers and local men and women also had differing views; among the foreign women themselves, there was occasional bonding, but there were "multiple hatreds" and differences—missionaries despising secularists, theosophists, Holy Mothers and Socialists—who in turn were critical of them all and did not care for any messiah whether Christ or Krishnamurti. Foreign women in a colonial context are thus a useful category for focusing and exploring many angles of race and gender and for problematizing issues of feminism and nationalism; they serve to highlight the ways in which feminism is seen as divisive and disruptive of race and identity, while nationalism is faulted for subsuming issues of gender. This book takes a new look at these women whose lives, while being of historical interest, help us understand some of the critical problems in current feminist East/West dialogue and diatribe, and the need for "universality in diversity."

I

SAVING THE SISTERS FROM THE SACRED COWS
Christianity and "Civilization"

I

THE IMAGINED SISTERHOOD OF WOMEN

See that heathen mother stand
Where the sacred current flows
With her own maternal hands
'Mid the waves her babe she throws

Send, Oh send the Bible there,
Let its precepts reach the heart,
She may then her children spare
Act the tender mother's part.

—From "Songs for the Little Ones at Home," mid-19th century hymn
(Burke 1958:131)

"The holy church—now alas steering its malignant way through the Indian Ocean."

—W.B. Yeats (around 1905), letter to Florence Farr (Bax 1946:55–56)

The nineteenth century has been called "Woman's Century" and the "Century of Missions"; the dawn of one brought light to the other.

—Mrs. F.A. Butler, *History of the Woman's Foreign Missionary Society* (Butler 1904:23)

UNDER BRITISH RULE, WOMEN MISSIONARIES FOUND SPACE IN THE PUBLIC domain and opportunities for achievement denied them at home. While they spearheaded movements for Christianizing and modernizing Asian societies through the education of women, many questions were raised about their motives and the kind of education provided. Was it patriarchal, puritan, riddled with middle-class values and supportive of imperialism, or was it liberating, freeing local women from feudal constraints and traditional social practices oppressive to women? Were Christians keeping women subordinate by creating "good wives and mothers" or were they championing women's rights to education and promoting ideas of equality? Were they self-less "angels" helping to alleviate social evils in South Asia or "devils" subverting local religion and culture and opposing movements for national liberation?

This chapter gives some background for discussing the complex and diverse roles of Christian women during British colonial rule. It deals with these women's dilemmas and their confrontations with Christian patriarchs and local nationalists.

Some Christians were in India from the 4th century A.D., long before parts of Europe had been Christianized, but with the advent of European colonial powers in South Asia, missionaries followed the flag and began the task of proselytizing the "heathens." The Portuguese and the Dutch in the 16th to 18th centuries introduced their brands of Christianity to the regions they ruled in South Asia, but it was with the subsequent British conquest in the 18th and 19th centuries that a new wave of missionary activity began, which was to have important consequences for local women. The Christian impact on South Asia in the late 18th century was linked to the imposition of a system of production and exchange relations designed to serve imperial interests. In this context, Christianity had a dual role—conversion and modernization. In the first role, missionaries claimed that they were bringing salvation and the light of true faith to people steeped in the darkness of the devil. In the second role, missionaries contributed to the breakdown of traditional beliefs and social structures, imposing Western systems and values on local societies.

From the earliest years of mission activity, it was understood that Christianity and Western values formed a superior and joint product to be imposed on heathens whose "barbaric" and "savage" way of life was a result of false beliefs.[1] Christianizing the natives meant attacking their religious and social practices and presenting alternatives at both ideological and institutional levels. As the first Baptist missionary in India, William Carey wrote in 1800:

> It is not to be thought that the moral character of a people should be better than that of their Gods. Men make themselves idols *after their own hearts*, and therefore to look for good morals among idolaters is the height of folly…the Hindoos…are literally sunk into the dregs of vice. (Potts 1967:6)

The Evangelicals advocated confrontation not only to Christianize "heathens," but also to introduce them to concepts of the rights of man, to a better material life, and to Western education. A similar view (without religious content) was also held by the British Utilitarians of the time. As Pathak notes, "Adam Smith in economics, Jeremy Bentham in ethics and law, and James Mill in logic and philosophy advocated Utilitarian remedies for India" (1967:13). Mill in 1817 was particularly insistent in his advocacy of legal reform, taxation, and good government for the Indians, along with reason and Western knowledge. Political despotism and priestcraft had made Hindus "in mind and body…the most enslaved portion of the human race," he said, describing

Hinduism as "the most enormous and tormenting superstition that ever harassed or degraded any portion of mankind" (ibid:14). For most missionaries, the first ideological task was to revile local religions, cultural practices and social customs, equating them with ignorance, superstition, immorality and dirt. The description of non-Christian religions in some missionary writing of the 19th century was intended to inspire horror and loathing mixed with a sense of pity, and the missionary task was seen as educative and purifying.[7]

The missionaries also realized quite early that the massive task before them was not purely religious. Rev. Miron Winslow, an American Methodist noted this problem:

> As the whole fabric of idolatry rests on that same foundation with the most absurd systems of geography and astronomy, and the most stupid fictions in natural science, (they believe that the earth is flat) which could be overthrown at once by the demonstration and experiment, it was seen that to extend true science would be to undermine this fortress of Satan. (1840: 284–85, emphasis added)

Winslow therefore wrote of the need for translators and writers "who should be able to transfer some of the treasures of European literature and science into the native languages" (ibid). Similarly, in 1835, Alexander Duff, a leading missionary in India from the Free Church of Scotland, believed that "every branch of Western knowledge would destroy some corresponding part of the Hindu system, and so one stone after another would be thrown from the huge and hideous fabric of Hinduism" (Pathak 1967:57). Acting on these assumptions, many missionaries began to learn local languages, compile dictionaries and start schools for the general education of boys and girls. Through education they succeeded not only in winning some converts, but also in "Christianizing" a far larger number. This was done through the inculcation among non-Christians of a set of values, which led to the questioning of traditional beliefs and social practices.

Foreign missionaries, while involved in their primary task of conversion and taking the "Good News" of the Bible to "Greenland's icy mountains," and India's "coral strand," also claimed to bring other "good news," which was economic, political and social. In their work of conversion, missionaries, while defending imperial policies and championing laissez-faire capitalism, emphasized the rights of individuals to freedoms based on "self-evident truths" such as the right to life and liberty. The interest displayed by the Baptists, Methodists, Unitarians and other non-conformists in social reform and women's rights in the colonies was based on a particular vision of a civilizing and modernizing mission; they hoped that the state would actively intervene to redress injustices in the name of Western progress and enlightenment. Some even spoke of a "social Christianity" that had roots in many radical movements.

The imperialist rationale was that foreign rule was bringing civilization to (Kipling's) "lesser breeds without the law." The mood of the epoch of "civilizing missions" was captured by Bishop Reginald Heber's verses in a famous hymn composed in 1811 for the Society for the Propagation of the Gospel:

> What though the spicy breezes
> Blow soft o'er Ceylon's isle
> Though every prospect pleases
> And only man is vile!
>
> Can we whose souls are lighted
> With wisdom from on high
> Can we to men benighted
> The lamp of life deny?

If the men were vile and benighted, then the women were even more degraded and in need of salvation. As a result, from the early years of British rule in India and Sri Lanka, Christianity began to assume an additional role in challenging prevalent social customs and family structures that affected the status of women. While Christian mission activity has often been presented as a single-purpose proselytizing movement in league with the colonial powers, there were various denominations of Christian opinion. In a colonial context, the established church was the Church of England (Anglican) and the others were tolerated, with some reservation, such as the Roman Catholics who had the largest local following and the non-conformist "low church" Methodists and Baptists who could irritate the British rulers by their emphasis on social reform. There were also shifts in attitudes and policies among the missionaries over the years—essentially reflections of the critiques of Christianity and missionary activity, emphasising the need for more tolerant attitudes to local religions and customs.

South Asians have regarded missionaries as agents of imperialism, as purveyors of false beliefs and Victorian puritanism, as ignorant catechists preaching "Bible and Beer," trying to win over the "heathen" through material inducements ranging from trinkets and food, to education and health facilities. (Jayawardena 1972:61) Recent feminist research however has shown that women's foreign missions and fund-raising organizations were important women's movements of the 19th century (Rendall 1985 and Hill 1985). During this period, in the United States and Europe, a network of Christian women emerged proclaiming "global sisterhood" and venturing out of their homes into the male world of work, travel and adventure in the name of the "noble cause" to serve God and improve the condition of women. The main concern of the women missionaries was the amelioration of the lives of colonized women. But in the "Age of Empire," Christianity was linked with imperialist conquest and capitalist expansion, and the main current of missionary activity became identified with colonial rule.

There were, however, radical dissenting strands of Christianity which promoted equal rights between the sexes, the concept of a female messiah, the abolition of private property, refusal to accept Church and State orthodoxy and a vision of the millennium(Desroches 1971:57). Heresy and women's rights were closely linked and the earlier tradition of women's active participation in Christian movements never died out.[3] The Society of Friends, popularly known as the Quakers, a group originating in 17th century radical Puritanism shared many of these beliefs.[4]

> Concepts of political democracy, of common ownership of land, of the levelling of class differences and even a primitive form of communism all thrived during this yeasty period.... The authority of both church and state was questioned as men and women took seriously the consequences of their newly acquired freedom to read the Bible for themselves and to reason with their peers about its message. (Bacon 1986:5–6)

Quaker women have been called the "mothers of feminism" because they were the first to have separate women's meetings. The movement also produced many of the women social reformers, including leaders of the anti-slavery agitation and women's rights movement of the 19th century (ibid). Even more interesting from a feminist point of view were the Shakers whose female messiah was Mother Ann Lee, a former English cotton-mill worker. Several startling feminist and socialist principles characterized the Shaker community, including the abolition of private property and the rejection of marriage and child bearing. As Mother Ann claimed, "Marriage of the flesh is a covenant with Death and an agreement with Hell (Desroches 1971:139).[5]

Even if the Quaker/Shaker type of radicalism remained peripheral, it served to make feminist issues known among fellow Christians. This leads to the question of whether there was feminist consciousness in the missionary project. It was true that missionaries and nuns approached local women with narrow objectives of Christianizing them and producing good Christian wives and mothers. But missionary women were also part of the feminization of Christianity, the increase of female educational opportunities and the challenges to male hierarchies in all spheres of life. This made missionaries and nuns very conscious of the status of local women, and their work for women in health and education reflected awareness about women's problems. In addition, they were daring travelers and courageous pioneers, willing to under-take hazardous ventures in hostile territory, which was evidence of the new-found independence and mobility of women. Women not only assumed leadership roles in missions and convents, but also formed maternal associations and kept in contact with the larger Christian networks abroad. Their tussles and conflicts with their own male church hierarchies were continuous, and their struggles for equal recognition, equal remuneration, the rights of single women and for the autonomy of Christian women's organizations were important manifestations of resistance to patriarchal control. But their lasting contribution was the unintentional creation of a "feminist" consciousness in local women through modern schools, which imparted a liberal education. They gave equal educational facilities at all levels to girls and introduced a curriculum that promoted higher education including university education for women. It is not surprising that many South Asian feminists were products of mission schools and convents.

WOMEN AS MISSIONARIES

Women played a crucial role in almost all areas of Protestant and Catholic missionary endeavor. In the home country, they were fund-raisers and recruiters for mission work abroad; they were also missionaries' wives who continued in the traditional roles of home builders for male missionaries. But most important were the single, independent women missionaries and nuns who from the early 19th century onward, began traveling to Asia and Africa.[6] This latter group formed a vanguard that started women's groups, girls' schools, orphanages, and convents, and were able to enter the homes of married or secluded women to teach languages and other skills and, it was hoped, to spread the gospel. In the years before medical missions, untrained women missionaries also tried to introduce new methods of tackling health problems, and in later years missionary women doctors pioneered female medical education. Thus a large part of the work in the two crucial areas of education and health were undertaken by foreign women. In funding, recruiting and servicing mission activities, women played key roles and gained importance in areas outside the home; and as missionaries and nuns in foreign countries, they had perhaps more influence and power than were accorded at that time to women in Europe and the United States. Women missionaries and nuns also had their own networks of female support, locally and internationally. Through church work at home and missionary activity abroad, single and married middle-class women were able to take part in socially acceptable work in the public sphere; women, as Harriet Martineau remarked in the mid-19th century "pursued religion as an occupation" (Rendall 1985:78).

The establishment of separate women's mission organizations was a bold-er innovation. In Britain, the "Ladies Association for the Promotion of Female Education among the Heathen" was formed in 1866 with its own funding, staff and magazine; the objectives were to recruit women as teachers who could help in the education of girls and to support girls' schools. (Forbes 1986:WS3). The secretary from 1866 to 1895 was Louisa Bullock, who was the "pulse of the organization guarding it from male domination…and from any possible charge that its goals, values and personnel were not ladylike" (ibid).[7] In the United States, Methodist women started the Women's Foreign Missionary Society in Boston in 1869 with branch societies in other states. It was considered a "heroic" move, being the first occasion when a women's church group in the United States was able to both collect and disburse funds (Butler 1904:27). As Mrs. F.A. Butler, who edited the *Women's Missionary Advocate* (1880), writing in later years commented, "At that time a new venture was rarely proposed that did not suggest the daring scheme of some smuggler of new opinions who was trying to introduce "woman's suffrage" (ibid:29).

During the years of intense campaigning on the abolition of "dreadful practices" in India, British Baptists made pioneering efforts to involve women in the work of the missions and to start schools for girls.[8] The first independent woman to come out for missionary work was Miss Chaffin, a nurse, who arrived in Bengal in 1813.[9] At the time there was a belief that literate girls would be early widows; respectable people would not send their daughters to schools run by missionaries, not only because the teachers were men, but also because they might meet the "corrupt and vicious of their own sex." This meant that, at first, only the "very poorest and lowest castes" would enroll in the school (Potts 1967: 122–23). However, a group of Anglo-Indian (Eurasian) women educated by the Baptists formed a society for the education of Indian women, and by 1822, they had six schools with 160 pupils (Fuller 1899:255).

From the 1820s onward, missionary girls' schools and convents were organized in almost every major town in India and Sri Lanka, giving primary and in some cases secondary education. These schools were class-based; some provided education only in the local languages to poorer sections of the population, while others gave an education in English to daughters of upper and middle-class families. Toward the end of the 19th century, these schools— mainly run by the new generation of Western women graduates—were geared to foreign examinations and trained girls for graduate studies, locally and abroad. They thereby created a group of Westernized women, qualified in English, who were not merely Christian wives and mothers (as originally intended) but who became the first women professionals in the region.

Apart from religious conversion through day schools and boarding schools, women missionaries had a clear advantage in the establishment of other categories of "women's work for women," such as zenana education for women at home and the setting up of orphanages for girls. The system of sending missionary women into zenanas (women's quarters of the house) where women were secluded or denied access to education became acceptable to some wealthy men who were interested in having educated wives. During the mid-19th century, the movement for home education in the zenanas developed fairly rapidly. In 1854, Rev. John Fordyce of the Free Church Mission convinced some rich Hindu Bengalis to pay for the instruction of their women at home by "his ablest teacher, a European governess who knew Bengali perfectly." Fordyce also printed a hand-out that had a wide circulation in India, calling upon Hindus to educate their daughters at home and, as Fuller writes, "one by one, and afterwards at an increasing ratio, *Zenana* doors flew open" (ibid:260). In London, the Indian Normal School and Instruction Society was started in 1862 for sending out missionaries for zenana education. The same year, Miss Britain, of the undenominational Women's Missionary Union in the United States, came to Calcutta for similar work. By 1872, she claimed that 800 Indian women were being taught by her organization and 1700 others by women of additional missionary societies (ibid:260).

Zenana education could only have very limited success in terms of conversion; Hindu, Muslim and Parsi males (from upper and middle-class families) were anxious to have wives with some education in English and a knowledge of European manners; but they wanted privatized female education at home, without the Christianity, whereas the missionaries' main interest was to reach out through education and Christianize the upper layers of society. The limited success they had in zenana education led to a reconsideration of this policy in favor of more generalized female education of all classes, over individualized education of the privileged; moreover, experience showed that it was easier to "civilize" Indian girls in school "since education in the zenanas allowed old habits to linger" (Forbes 1986:WS7). Nevertheless, missionary access to the homes of Indians provided educated Western women, who came from societies where the issue of female education was being fought out, a unique opportunity to observe the daily lives of Indian women and to try to educate and influence them and their families.

MISSIONARY ACTIVITY AND WOMEN'S EMANCIPATION

Women's missionary activity was not purely a question of converting "heathens," doling out charity, or providing basic amenities in health and education for women. It also had a strong ideological component; the strength of missionary zeal derived from the belief that something had to be done for the women of India and Sri Lanka, in terms not only of saving their souls but also eradicating social evils and introducing other patterns of living. In Britain, Priscilla Chapman wrote a book, *Hindoo Female Education* (1839), alerting her readers to "the poor idolatrous females in bondage" and wrote of "the necessity of an avowed Christian direction to the efforts which may effect the elevation of the Hindoo females from their present degradation to their proper level" (1839: 74, 175). And in 1878, Isabel Hart (of the Baltimore Women's Foreign Missionary Society) described heathen women as "degraded, secluded and helpless" and reminded American women of their "responsibility and duty" to support missionary work, adding that "in the needs and opportunities of this work for women by women, you have heard the voice of the Master calling for you" (Butler 1904:66).

But with women missionaries there was the added influence of the movement for democratic rights, including some women's rights. In the case of women missionaries and nuns, women's rights included the right to travel abroad, to head schools, convents and missions, and above all to be accepted and respected as independent single women; in many cases, they had also to constantly combat the authoritarian attitudes and male chauvinism of the church hierarchies as well as face ridicule in outside society. Women in activities away from the home were figures of fun. Charles Dickens in *Bleak House,* (1853) immortalized a comic character, Mrs. Jellyby, who neglected her own children, but devoted herself

> to an extensive variety of public subjects at various times and is at present (until something else attracts her) devoted to the subject of Africa, with a view to the general cultivation of the coffee berry—and the 'natives'…of Borrioboola Gha—on the left bank of the Niger. (Dickens, 1980:49, 53)

But missionaries were not all naïve evangelists; many were reformers concerned about local women and anxious to make changes in society. Some were more liberal and sophisticated in their views; others were bigoted and conservative. But all were full of enthusiasm about their mission to rescue their "sisters," looking upon Christianity as a liberating factor for women in both the West and East.[10] Thus in the 19th century, sections of British and American women became aware of a mission to bring "light" to their own households and also to the outside world. The housewife was urged to introduce "her special qualities into the public arena through school-teaching or church work" on the ground that "a woman's nurture and refinement carried the miraculous potential to conquer and redeem the entire world" (Hunter 1984:xiii). Even Catherine Beecher's famous book for housewives, written in 1842, claimed that:

> To American women, more than to any other on earth, is committed the exalted privilege of extending over the world those blessed influences, which are to

renovate degraded man, and "to clothe all climes with beauty." (ibid:xiii)

Women in the "Age of Imperialism" also had a world vision, a concept of global duties and obligations toward women of other countries. They believed, according to Hunter, that "Christianity was responsible for the elevated status of Western women" and that "in preaching the gospel they were only sharing what they had received in such bounty." This meant that American women missionaries were moved to action by both "the heinousness of heathen womanhood and gratitude for their own Christian womanhood" (ibid: xv). Many have noted that such attitudes were a kind of "Imperial feminism," (Burton 1992:151), but it is also possible, as Jane Rendall claims, that early 19th century evangelicalism was one of the sources of feminist "sisterhood." According to her "women increasingly found within their church a means of associating with other women." Moreover, their newly found moral strength "gave them an acceptable way of asserting their own standards in the creation of the home as a refuge from the harshness of the market economy, or against a specifically male morality—the double standard of sexual behaviour, the culture of the pub or club." Women were not only morally superior, but also "more emotional and affectionate than men," and therefore "potentially closer to God" (1985: 74–75). In addition, evangelical missions gave women a crusade, enabling them to leave home and, also as pious women, to urge men to conform to a higher standard of sexual morality (Hill 1985:23–25).

In both America and Britain, there was a whole cult of missionary work, highlighting the "romance of missions." Women who were "doers" could fight oppressive conditions at home and boldly venture abroad to expose the "wrongs of women." Magazines, popular novels and poetry on women's work among "heathen" women abounded; there were journals like "The Heathen Women's Friend," "Women's Work for Women" and "Helping Hand," and books such as *Life and Light for Heathen Women* were published by the Women's Board of Missions. Popular novelists also latched on to the theme of missionary adventure, introducing a new genre of daring missionary heroines in exotic settings fraught with dangers of various kinds, as well as the rebel missionary in revolt against discrimination at home. Emma Southworth (in *Fair Play,* 1868) created a character, Britomarte Conyers, whose main desire is to leave America and save other women. "Oh my sisters! my sisters!" she exclaims, "as Christ died to save the whole human race, so I would die to free you."

> The Board of Foreign Missions are in want of teachers to join a company of missionaries…to India. I shall offer my services to go with them. It is better to labor for nothing in the vineyard of the Lord among the heathen, than to

slave here where your cruel laws and customs in regard to women dishonour Christianity. (ibid:10–11)

In another best-seller, *Rebecca of Sunnybrook Farm* (1903) by Kate Douglas Wiggins, the heroine is deeply influenced by her meeting with missionaries who visited her village; "Rebecca sat entranced, having been given the key of another world; she saw blue skies and burning stars, white turbans and gay colors" (ibid:16). Even by the 1920's in Ellen Glasgow's *Barren Ground* (1925), one character who admires missionaries has a recurring dream "about India's coral strand and Africa's sunny fountains…and palm trees and ancient rivers and naked black babies thrown to crocodiles" (ibid:20).

But there were other Christians who challenged the "babies thrown to crocodiles" approach. There had been a few earlier missionary pioneers of "dialogue" and the study of other religions, but the significant shift in missionary attitudes to local religions and societies occurred in the latter quarter of the 19th century. There was even talk of Christian Socialism by the American, Isabella Thoburn of the Women's Foreign Mission Society, the first independent woman representative of her organization; she opened a girls school in Lucknow in 1870 which became an important social center where Christian and non Christian could meet.[11] Thoburn had very bold objectives; "*our social Christianity or Christian socialism is largely in the hands of women,*" she stated, adding that "we have a part in bringing together into one all these diverse Indian tongues and peoples" (Baker 1898:186, emphasis added).

Serious attempts were made to recruit a more intellectual type of missionary with a better understanding of other religions and cultures. Comparative religion was introduced to theological seminaries in the 1890s; qualified graduates were sent as missionaries and emphasis was placed on starting Christian colleges for higher education for both men and women in India; these included the Isabella Thoburn College for Women in Lucknow (1895), Kinnaird College, Lahore (1913) and the Women's Christian College in Madras (1915) from which many students went to its sister college Mount Holyoke, in Massachusetts (Jeffery 1938:173). By the early 20th century, Christianity was also being linked with the prevalent discussions on democracy. Some missionaries claimed that the women's movement in all countries had a common source—namely Christianity. Helen Montgomery writing of *Western Women in Eastern Lands* (1910), discussed the "common consciousness" of Christian principles, which included the importance of the individual, and the obligation of unselfish service laid on all irrespective of sex. Christianity was "the most tremendous engine of democracy ever forged" and was destined "to break in pieces all castes, privileges, and oppression" (1910:206).

But missionaries had to also face the realities of rising nationalism in India and Sri Lanka. Especially after the 1920s, some Christian missions became more flexible and tried to adjust to demands for self rule. But the tradition of the white man's and white woman's Christian burden continued the belief, among many, that "premature independence for India would be...an abdication of the ordained exercise of Christian rule" (Studdert-Kennedy 1990:22–26). A conservative member of parliament who opposed political reforms for India, which were being discussed in the early 1930s, wrote:

> ...the whole ideal of British laws, justice and administration...exactly interpret the Ten Commandments...our idea of government is the nearest approach to Christianity, and to exchange it for government which may lean towards...the worship of Shiva or Kali is...a "spiritual abdication." (ibid:26)

But whether "radical" or "reactionary," the Christian imperialist discourse was linked, as Studdert-Kennedy notes, to a view of history, a belief in the "rational process of historical evolution under providential sanctions."

> It was the tradition of Christian belief and Christian values of social service and self-discipline, cherished in the great middle-class foundations and institutionalized in the machinery of imperial trusteeship, that was leading decayed civilizations away from their aberrant paths. (ibid:21)

The scope for a study of missionary activity among women is thus very wide. The following sections, however, attempt to narrow the focus and deal more specifically with social reform and "women's work for women" in India and Sri Lanka by missionaries and nuns; it deals with their attempts to Christianize and modernize the women of the region and the problems they faced not only because of local resistance to their reforming efforts, but also their struggles as women against church hierarchies. The following studies from India and Sri Lanka on Methodist, Catholic and Anglican proselytizing and educational activity and the fund raising in the United States for Pandita Ramabai, illustrate Christian concern about the status of women. They also reveal the weak link of the missionary project, namely the failure among many missionaries to come to terms with national liberation movements and the unrealistic vision that persisted of a permanent British presence in South Asia.

2

CHRISTIANITY AND THE
"WESTERNIZED ORIENTAL GENTLEWOMAN"

Until the females are raised by education as to hold their proper rank in society, and until their hearts are brought under the influence of Christianity, there is little hope that the people of India will rise from idolatry and sin to the dignity and happiness of a Christian people.

—American Mission Report, Jaffna (1839:9–10)

From the first days of the mass conversions [in India] the fathers were very much concerned about the education of the girls. "Sisters! we need Sisters!" …Without the help of the nuns, they felt that an essential wheel was missing in the machine.

—Mother Mary Colmcille, *First the Blade, History of the IBVM (Loreto) in India* (1968:168)

They learnt to live with girls of different nationalities and ages, being taught to care for their own clothes and health, and were not subordinated to the activities of their families or the whims of their ayahs.

—Mabel Simon, *A History of CMS Ladies' College* (1957:21)

MUCH HAS BEEN WRITTEN OF THE DETRIMENTAL EFFECTS OF MISSIONARY education, but the question raised in this chapter concerns the feminist and reformist content of such education. The focus is on three case studies of missionary girls' schools and convents in India and Sri Lanka started by Methodists, Catholics and Anglicans. The examples chosen highlight controversial issues including sexism, caste prejudice and nationalism during different historic epochs. One study is on the Uduvil Girls School started in the 1820's by simple, pious wives of American Methodists in the north of Sri Lanka to convert and educate Tamil girls; they met with resistance at many levels, especially on caste issues. The second deals with the network of convent schools run by the Loreto order of Irish Catholic nuns in India over the 19th and early 20th centuries and their conflicts with church hierarchies. The third study is of Ladies' College, Colombo, founded at the onset of the 20th century by British women to provide a modern high school education for the daughters of the urban bourgeoisie on the lines of similar schools in Britain, but which had to deal with issues of rising nationalism.

The missionaries themselves were more sophisticated, university graduates by the turn of the century compared to their naive religiosity of the early years. Moreover, in the early phase of British rule all such schools had a narrow aim of conversion and of merely producing good Christian wives for male converts. With capitalist development and the emergence of a non-Christian bourgeoisie, there was a demand for girls' high schools providing a modern Western education, which not only almost equalled that of parallel boys' schools, but also gave women access to higher education, the professions and other employment.

METHODISTS AND THEIR METHODS

Methodism was an evangelical movement founded by John Wesley in Britain in the 18th century. It was linked to early heretical Christian sects that preached primitive communism and female equality, and, by the 19th century, it endorsed Liberal politics and the working-class movement in Britain. Dynamic Methodist women joined missions to Asia, continuing Methodism's tradition of female activism and female preaching. The American Methodist Mission to Ceylon (now Sri Lanka) in 1816 is an early example of missionary women's participation in religious and educational work for women abroad. An early pioneer was Harriet Winslow (1796–1833), who spent thirteen years as a missionary from 1820 to her death. She was born Harriet Wadsworth Lathrop in Connecticut and married Rev. Myron Winslow in 1818, sailing (with other missionaries) soon after to Sri Lanka for missionary work, with a "colored woman" Amy as servant (Winslow 1840:302). Harriet Winslow devoted her main endeavors to girls' education in Jaffna, and articulated the need for a strong female presence in mission work. The constraints of traditional society in terms of female education, caste hierarchies and customs had to be faced head-on by these American missionaries, in their attempt to produce the "new" Tamil wife and mother who was Christian and educated. In this endeavor, the idea that foreign women should work for improving the status of local women was never far from their minds.

Harriet Winslow visited the Methodist schools in Colombo and commented critically that women would be better teachers than men; "when I see missionaries, habituated to the use of words beyond the comprehension of the ignorant, attempting to instruct children, I am more and more convinced that *females* also should be employed among the heathen" (ibid:185). No judicious person could deny that "females are needed in all missionary establishments," she wrote in 1821, adding significantly that a female "need not...imagine that all her talents must be wasted on petty things." She did not deviate from the prevalent view of wifely duties, admitting that a husband "is to find all his society" in his wife, and be encouraged by her prayers, advice and by "her considerate attention to all the family"; but Winslow nevertheless claimed that in spite of this "multiplicity of cares, *there is time to do much for the female sex, which...must be done almost exclusively by females*" (ibid:274, emphasis added).

Winslow's activities included the creation in Jaffna of a separate Maternal Society for women missionaries based on and linked to a similar society in New England.[1] For Winslow, this coming together of women was a source of inspiration:

> Today all the sisters met...to enjoy a little season of Christian fellowship, and to make arrangements for forming a *maternal society*. I have not promised myself so much from anything since I came to India. It has been a day long to be remembered. (ibid:234)

In 1822 Winslow wrote, "I do not forget the circle of sisters who used to meet; we have had fellowship together—have lived and loved, and soon we shall meet, if we are children of God, where our happiness will be perfected" (ibid:259). Female education became the main area of Winslow's activity.[2] "In the degraded condition of our sex here, we see much to turn from with abhorrence" (ibid:238). While the concern of the missionaries was to propagate Christianity, this was also linked with an attempt to advance female education; "We consider every female child added to our number as a great acquisition," wrote Winslow, "on account of prejudice and custom against females being instructed" (ibid:239). The earliest activities of missionaries in South Asia had been in education and proselytization of boys, trained to become "native" preachers and teachers. But female conversion lagged behind because converted men faced the danger of lapsing back into "heathenism" if they married non-Christian women. It was argued that "pious and educated young men" should have similar companions, because "a heathen companion is a source of constant trial to her husband, and not unfrequently of ruin to the children" (American Mission Report 1839:10). By the 1820s a few girls were attached to each mission in Jaffna, but converting local women in the early years was not an easy task; missionary women seemed ludicrous because of their strange appearance and weird beliefs.

For the early missionaries, education had to be synonymous with conversion, but conversion was often an uphill task and met with resistance. In 1820, Winslow describes her encounter with thirteen women who came to her house "with burdens on their heads."

I went to speak to them of Christ…they told us they did not wish to know anything about the Saviour…and with a levity which deeply grieved us, went their
way. This is a fair specimen *of the manner in which we are received by most of our sex.* When
they sometimes appear attentive, we may unexpectedly find every opportunity
embraced to turn aside their heads and laugh. (1840:211, emphasis added)

Winslow had several such unsuccessful encounters with women and
despaired of the "ignorance, hardness and careless ease" of "these stupid, dead
heathen" which "constitutes our greatest missionary trial." She used to question women on god, sin, heaven and hell, but was exasperated by their evasive
answers or replies of "we don't know." Winslow tried unsuccessfully to "show
them…the insufficiency of all their sacrifices, bathing in the holy waters, and
rubbing ashes on their bodies, to cleanse them from sin," but was dismayed by
their attitudes. "How painful it is to see these poor creatures," she exclaimed
"on the borders of an awful eternity, disregarding our most solemn admonitions" (ibid:219). But Winslow persisted in her meetings with women and
attempted to get girls to attend school. In 1821 she records that she had "a pleasant time at one place with a number of women, until…a very boisterous
woman came up and almost drove me away" (ibid:241). However, the inducements of food and clothing offered to orphans and poor children brought
results. In 1824 the bold step was taken of starting a female boarding school in
Uduvil, Jaffna with Harriet Winslow and her husband in charge. Another such
school was established in Varany, Jaffna. The task of persuading parents to send
their daughters to school was difficult, for "reading and writing were not considered becoming in a female…those who finally gave up their daughters to
be instructed, were subjected to no small degree of reproach for this departure from national and immemorial usage" (American Mission Report 1839:3).
The Uduvil School started with twenty-nine girls aged between five and
eleven, the numbers rising to fifty in 1833 and to 100 by 1837. The girls were mainly from the highest caste (vellala) with three or four of the karaiyara caste and
around eight of other castes (ibid).

The policy of the missions was "to pay special attention to the children of
those of respectable standing in society," though mixing the castes at the
school, especially at mealtimes, was certainly an innovative act (ibid:5). The
girls were supported with donations of not less than $20 a year by benefactors
mainly from Massachusetts, Connecticut, Maine and Maryland whose names
they adopted; among the girls in the school in 1824, for example, were
Charlotte Burnell, Ann Louise Payson and Mary Sweetzer (Harrison 1925:11).
The girls went home only once in two months to keep them "as much as possible from heathen influence until old enough to form a steady Christian
character" (American Mission Report 1839:6). The subjects taught, apart from

a heavy dose of the Bible, were Tamil, English, geography, astronomy, arithmetic, plain sewing and singing; the teachers included American women missionaries and some local teachers (ibid:7).

The products of the school served as teachers in other mission schools or were married to "pious native assistants who were educated in Mission schools," the school itself serving as a marriage bureau. By 1833, twelve of the early pupils of the school were given dowries and married (Harrison 1925:16).[3] The missionaries noted that up to 1843, seventy-two girls "were thus married, and are mothers of more than 100 children, whom they train up in a Christian manner" (American Mission Report July 1843:6). The missionaries congratulated themselves that they had broken "one of the greatest obstacles to the progress of Christian truth; viz. *the inveterate prejudice of the community at large against female education*" (ibid:7, emphasis in original).

The mission schools also concentrated on challenging tradition and local social practice, discouraging "corrupt" habits in favour of "civilizing" American customs. The schools stressed neatness, cleanliness, obedience and modesty, while encouraging specific patterns of behavior such as eating together with males and with persons of other castes and races. Winslow observed that among the Tamils "husband and wife must never eat together, and a man cannot even touch a woman's hand in public without disgrace," reassuring herself that though "they sometimes remark upon our familiarity" they are "convinced that it is not improper for us" (1840:265). Some mission schools also experimented with changes in modes of eating; the Varany Girls' Boarding School reported in 1843 that "tables and spoons for eating have been introduced, with which girls seem pleased," but noted cautiously that this "must be regarded only as an experiment" (American Mission Report Oct. 1843:5–6).

Another break with tradition was in the age of marriage of girls from the Mission schools. The prevalent custom was early marriage or betrothal of girls as young as nine years, and one mission report claimed that in Jaffna "the people thought it strange, at first, that girls of fourteen or fifteen years of age should remain unmarried, and frequently spoke about it" (ibid:4). The missionaries also claimed that the girls who had been at their school were exemplary in "their cleanliness and modesty in dress, and the care they maintain in their domestic affairs as well as their anxiety to keep their children from the bad morals, and the corrupt conversation of the heathen" (American Mission Report 1839:8). The rules imposed on Tamil girls reflected the missionary culture of the period, which tried to promote Christian meekness in women, while discouraging local customs and habits such as wearing ear and toe rings and chewing tobacco and betel leaves (Harrison 1925:23–25).

A typical "successful" product of the Uduvil school from the missionaries' point of view was one who was intelligent, pious, courageous in breaking tradition, and with qualities of leadership. Such a student was Betsey C. Pomeroy, born in 1805, whose Tamil name was Chinnachi Vyravi. She came to the school as one of its first students in 1821, converted to Christianity and studied there until 1826.[4] Betsey had also pioneered the breaking of caste taboos by dining with Christians and was the first pupil who "took her food on the Mission premises when it was considered disgraceful" (American Mission Report 1843:5). At the age of twenty-one she married Samuel Davis, another Tamil convert, lived "through many trials," and by 1835 was a widow, working at the Varany boarding school for girls. Other students such as Harriet Newell Ambrose, became teachers in mission schools and in later years some of the Uduvil Tamil girls went abroad; among them Caroline Chester whose husband was sent to Penang as a catechist, and Anna Maria Spence who married a Tamil Christian and went to teach a Hindu princess in South India (Harrison 1925:25).

Harriet Winslow's short life was typical of the harsh lives of the early missionaries. While involved in gruelling work at the Mission, she also gave birth to nine children, five of whom died. She herself died in child-birth at thirty six in 1833, after thirteen years in Sri Lanka without returning home. After her death, the school was run by Rev. and Mrs. Spaulding, but the latter was "hampered by her duties to her children from taking a very active part in the School." As a result, the Mission in 1834 considered asking for an "unmarried female" to be sent from America, but abandoned the idea as being "too revolutionary a measure" (ibid:17). A few years later, the local mission was bold enough to make a request for "three unmarried females," and in 1839, Eliza Agnew (1809–1883) of Scotland, thirty-two, arrived in Jaffna; several Mission Boards had offered to send her abroad for missionary work on condition she married, but she had refused. "Please Sir, where is Mr. Agnew" asked a girl from Uduvil after Eliza Agnew's arrival. She also boldly insisted that her salary be equal to that of a single man. During her stay the school expanded to include new school rooms, dormitories and dining halls (ibid:50–54). Agnew specialized in teaching the Bible; she served forty-three years in Jaffna with only one break, and after her retirement, stayed on there until her death, being known as the "mother of a thousand daughters" (Leitch & Leitch 1890:118).

By the 1880s, Uduvil had started to change its emphasis; it hired graduate teachers and concentrated not only on Bible studies, but also on a knowledge of English and academic success. This was in response to the growing local middle and lower middle-class that serviced the colonial economy or had branched out into trade and independent professions. The need was not merely for a Christian wife, but for a westernized, English-speaking one, who would be an asset in colonial society. Missionary policies also changed and a more modern education for girls was introduced. In 1877 Uduvil school had introduced English as a special subject requiring a fee. The "new era" had a new principal, Susan Howland, (the daughter of two American missionaries who had worked in Jaffna). She spoke Tamil and, as a graduate of Mount Holyoke, Massachusetts, was "always receptive to new ideas," bringing back "from every furlough some modern method or theory to be tried out at Uduvil (Harrison 1925:141).

The curriculum was revised, new subjects introduced and more classes added. In 1885 Mary and Margaret Leitch, sisters from the United States, started a training school at Uduvil to produce teachers for other schools run by the Mission; they were called Queen's scholars and "tried hard to be worthy of their name" (ibid:78–80). The first local trained teachers, Sarah Daniel and Hester John, joined Uduvil school in 1887. The demand for full education in English for girls increased, and in 1897 a separate English school was opened, teaching all subjects in the English medium. The school also had an advanced class that prepared students for the examinations of the Calcutta University, helped by teachers such as Helen I. Root, a Cornell University graduate who had joined the staff in 1899. The English school began with forty-four pupils and by 1899 two students had qualified for the Calcutta University entrance, and the next year the entire class of four passed this examination; but many students left school to get married (ibid:94–95).

While things were going smoothly in the educational field, the Uduvil school was "shaken to its very depths" by the caste question. From 1824 the policy had been to take "girls of good caste and with some property," which meant that the majority of pupils were from the highest caste. When a girl from the nallavar caste was admitted in 1902, and allowed to dine with and use the same well as other students, some parents took away their daughters and started a policy of harassment, including burning the school hedges, and instigating the school laundrymen to boycott the school. The struggle lasted a year. The missionaries were surprised at the "depth and bitterness of the feeling," but were determined to stand by democratic principles. In 1903 the Christian girls were addressed by a visiting missionary and they promised to give up caste prejudice. The "low caste" girl was accepted by the students; many who left returned and the school continued to take some "low caste" girls (ibid:98–100).

By the turn of the century, diplomas for girls had caught on in Jaffna and became an important aspect of school life.[5] In 1916, 234 were enrolled in the English school, the numbers rising to 353 by 1923. By then, thirty-six percent of the English school students were from Hindu homes (ibid:110–11). The next decade produced the first batch of graduates from Uduvil, the first university

Harriet Winslow—Pioneer Methodist Missionary in Sri Lanka.
(From Rev. Miron Winslow (1840), *Memoir of Mrs. Harriet Winslow.*
In author's collection.)

graduate being Daisy Anketell (whose mother and grandmother had been at
Uduvil). She received a B.A. from Women's Christian College, Madras in 1923,
and went on to obtain a B.A. in Mathematics and Physics at Mount Holyoke
College, and an M.A. at Columbia University, New York (ibid:136–37). By the
time of the Uduvil girls school centenary in 1924, Tamil women had made the
first breakthrough into the professions and entered public life in a wide range
of activities. While women in Jaffna who had an early educational headstart
were forging ahead and breaking away from traditional society in the north
of Sri Lanka, in the capital city of Colombo, and other parts of the island,
Sinhala, Tamil, Muslim and Burgher women were also receiving a modern
secondary education in English in girls' high schools, with access to higher
education and employment.

GOOD CATHOLIC GIRLS
Another input into local girls' education was provided by Catholic convent
schools. Catholicism obtained a foothold in India and Sri Lanka in the 16th
century in the course of Portuguese invasions, and succeeded in making converts; however, with the demise of Portuguese political power, Catholics were

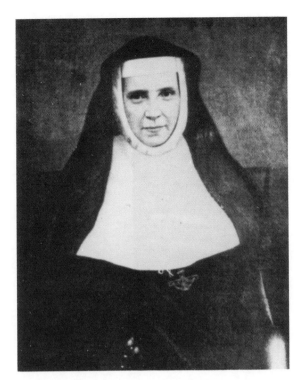

Mother Delphine Hart (1841). (From Mother Mary Colmcille (1968), *First the Blade: History of the I.B.V.M. (Loreto) in India.* Widener Library, Harvard.)

subject to legal discrimination and survived as an underground network. The situation changed with the repeal of discrimination in Britain against Catholics in 1829; this made possible the arrival in Calcutta in 1834 of English, Irish and French Jesuits who revived church activity and education. A boys school in Calcutta, St. Xavier's, was one of the first schools to be opened, inevitably leading to discussion of the need for good Catholic wives for the products of St. Xavier's. A committee was set up, composed of a cosmopolitan group of Irish, Portuguese and Anglo-Indian women of Calcutta who collected money to open up a girls' school. This desire for female education led to a flow of European Catholic nuns, from the orders of Loreto, Good Shepherd, Holy Family and Jesus & Mary among others, who started orphanages and convents all over South Asia. By 1911 there were 2.2 million Catholics in India and 3,615 nuns (Capucin Mission Unit, 1922, Tables I and VI).

The popular image of Catholic nuns in a colonial context was that of passive women in eternal prayer, concerned with conversion and charity, who perpetuated archaic feudal values, especially with regard to women. For example, when there was discussion in the early 1860s on the question of a Holy Family Convent in Sri Lanka, a famous local liberal, Charles Lorenz, protested that the project was retrograde in a country that was trying to promote "modern attitudes, a convent where young women are to be secluded from male society, where the head is to be shaved, and the rosary to be the test of continuous prayer—what do the people of Ceylon want with such an establishment?" he queried in the legislature (Blaze 1948:190). Nevertheless, the first batch of six nuns opened a convent school in Jaffna led by Sister Marie Xavier Marchand, described by the Bishop as "a woman full of experience and practical common sense endowed with piety and devotion."[6]

The Holy Family sisters began the Jaffna Female Seminary. It became one of Jaffna's leading girls schools, and its first principal was Sister Helen Winter. The subjects taught were English, arithmetic, sewing, painting and music. Other schools and orphanages were also begun by the sisters in the Jaffna peninsula and other parts of the island, including Kurunegala (1868), Anuradhapura (1877), Wennappuwa (1884) and Chilaw (1894). The most prestigious was the Holy Family Convent in Colombo (1903), teaching in English up to the levels of the Junior and Senior Cambridge examinations; its popularity grew, and by 1922 it had 500 students. The activities of the Holy Family sisters also extended to training local nuns, opening teacher training colleges and serving as nursing nuns in hospitals all over the country (Peiris 1980). However, being predominantly interested in female education, the energies of the Holy Family sisters were concentrated in schools that produced wives and mothers who were not merely good pious Catholics, but also had been inducted into "Western civilization."

While the stereotype of nuns as backward and reactionary prevailed, the reality was sometimes different, for the nuns involved in education were products of European patterns of education and training, and their aim in the colonies was to produce well-educated and accomplished Catholic women who had also imbued Western ways of living and thinking. Catholic education was thus a part of the modernizing process,[7] which inevitably was also a process of denationalization and therefore gave rise to fierce criticism from Buddhists and Hindus. The nuns themselves were also not uniformly subservient; many were in conflict with the patriarchal church hierarchy and resisted male authoritarianism. One may add that in the 1970s, the Holy Family nuns in Sri Lanka became key proponents of liberation theology and participants in campaigns for human rights, minority rights and women's emancipation. These were, of course, the exceptions, but nevertheless they broke the traditional image of nuns as purely religious beings with conservative attitudes. Catholic schools also had their quotas of professional women as well as the world's first woman Prime Minister Sirima Bandaranaike, her daughter

Chandrika Bandaranaike Kumaratunga, the President of Sri Lanka (products of St.Bridget's Convent, Colombo), and Benazir Bhutto (educated at the Jesus and Mary Convent in Lahore) the Prime Minsiter of Pakistan. A more detailed picture of 19th-century nuns, the problems they faced and the education they imparted, emerges in the following account of the famous Loreto nuns in India.

THE LORETO PHENOMENON

The first response to the search for nuns by the Calcutta Catholics came from the Loreto Abbey near Dublin, Ireland, an elite school for girls which belonged to the Institute of the Blessed Virgin Mary.[8] When the Bishop of Calcutta, on a visit to the Loreto Abbey, made a request for nuns for educational work in Calcutta, there were many eager volunteers. Leading the Loreto team to India was Mother Mary Delphine (1818–1889). The nuns were greeted in India by a huge crowd: "The whole of the Christian population had turned out in gala attire. There were many Hindus and Mahommedans in the crowd, anxious to have a sight of the 'Christian Priestesses'...black robed figures with the veils drawn down over their eyes...like purdahed ladies" (Colmcille 1968:19). Several convents were opened in Calcutta. The main Loreto convent had Mother Mary Delphine as its Superior. Mother Teresa Mons was put in charge of another Loreto school (for the poor) at Bon Bazaar in the heart of Calcutta and another was opened in Chandernagore. Loreto schools and orphanages spread all over India with the arrival of more nuns from Ireland. Although the Loreto nuns of this period were devoted to women's education, they themselves did not have the benefit of either higher education at universities or of theological scholarship at Catholic seminaries. They taught in parallel schools with Jesuits in India, but they did not have a similar training. The nuns were mainly the products of good Irish secondary girls' schools where the emphasis was on religion, English literature, French, music and the arts. When Irish girls joined the Loreto Abbey as novitiate nuns they were trained to be teachers who would impart a similar type of Victorian education to others.

Convent education in India thus successfully reproduced British upper class education in an atmosphere of strict discipline and catered to the needs of resident Europeans, wealthier Anglo-Indians and Indians who wanted their daughters to be refined, well-educated, accomplished ladies who would make suitable wives for upwardly-mobile bourgeois men. The Loreto convents fulfilled this task admirably. It was claimed that girls, who were languishing without much education, exposed to the risks of "coarse speech," the wrong accent and "heathen immorality," were given a good education as well as lessons on decorum, correct speech and chaste conduct as well as Western cultural accomplishments considered desirable in young women. The syllabus of Loreto House in Calcutta, for example, offered English, arithmetic, geography, history, French and needlework, with painting, music and dancing as extras. The nuns were able to provide more than a basic education in the three R's. Mother Delphine "could turn her hand to most subjects" which included "producing grand plays"—*Balthazar's Feast*, *Queen Esther* and *Le Medecin Malgre Lui* (in French), to the delight of ambitious parents. Describing the intellectual background of Mother Mary Gonzaga Joynt, Colmcille says she was typical of the "Catholic gentlewomen of her generation" who "fed their emotions on Longfellow, Mrs. Hemans and Tennyson, and their intellect on Goldsmith and Gray" (ibid:90).

There was, however, a clear intellectual difference among the nuns who ran the paying schools, and those in charge of the orphanages and schools for the poor. There was also a class division between nuns who were better educated and were from middle-class families, and those lay-sisters from the Irish poor who did menial tasks.[9] One such was Sister Gabriel Doyle, who came to Calcutta in 1841 and went to the Darjeeling Loreto convent in 1846 "not to leave it for a single day till she died there in 1905." She baked bread, cooked, fetched water, cut firewood, swept the grounds and did "all the rough outdoor work, and went out to find what the villagers could provide." Another of the many such "quiet lives" that Colmcille contrasts with the "more spectacular works of the teaching sisters," was that of Sister Alphonsus Geraghty who spent sixty-seven years in household tasks, forty of them as the portress of Loreto House (ibid:94–96).

CONFLICTS WITH THE MALE HIERARCHY

It is not often realized that in India, Loreto nuns had to fight many battles against domination by the Catholic male hierarchy. The nuns had many trials; on arrival in Calcutta Mother Delphine had to cope not only with the arduous taks of starting the school, teaching, and looking after the nuns, but also with "the calls on their charity, whether in slum schools or the epidemic hospitals" (ibid:90). But more difficult were the problems arising from the tension between the Loreto Order and the Jesuit Archbishop of Calcutta, Monseignor Carew, described as "domineering" with "absolute or authoritarian" tendencies. He believed that all nuns should be directly under his control (ibid:35).[10] Mother Delphine resisted many of his intrusions, refusing to move from Loreto House, and fighting back in many ways; "they held out, yielding in unessentials, unbending where the spirit of their vocation was concerned; and by their perseverence, ensured that the education of Catholic girls in Calcutta and Bengal was never interrupted" (ibid:40). But nevertheless, the atmosphere was oppressive, and Mother Delphine, feeling the pressure on her, gave up her post to Mother Joseph Hogan, staying on as her assistant. She came back to become Chief Superior of the Loreto convents in and around Calcutta from 1855 to 1881, visiting Ireland twice to recruit new nuns. After retirement she spent ten years in a convent she had started in 1874 in the health resort of Hazaribagh, where she died in 1889.

Mother Joseph Hogan,[11] who held the post of Superior for nearly three years continued the fight for the right of self-management of Loreto House. But interference in other matters continued; the Archbishop imposed nominees on the convent as novices, ordered others to leave and in 1845 demanded that the nuns undertake the running of the women's section of the Hospital for Indians, which was part of the Medical College. Loreto nuns had specialized in teaching, for which the demand increased as the schools multiplied, and Mother Hogan was reluctant to allow her nuns to be diverted to nursing, particularly because a contract for the nuns to serve in the hospital for two years had been signed without consultation.[12] When Mother Joseph decided to appeal to the Pope, the Archbishop backed down. But she paid the price for her stand and a new Superior, Mother Xaveria McDonnel was appointed to Loreto House. The tension with the Archbishop continued and after a year, the new Superior also asked to be transferred. In the meantime, in Ireland, Mother Teresa Ball had found the Archbishop "rather an impossible person to deal with, and had decided to send no more members to his vicariate." During this time "the removal of all the Loreto nuns from the Vicariate of Archbishop Carew" was discussed, but in the end, Mother Xaveria and the nuns stayed on to survive and expand their educational work to many other parts of the country (ibid:44–45).

EXPANSION OF LORETO CONVENTS

From the mid-19th century onward Loreto convents were opened in many parts of India, their success associated with the pioneering work of individual nuns. For example, in 1848, Mother Joseph Hogan became Superior of the convent at Darjeeling, which gained in importance as tea plantations were established and the town became a popular resort. By 1862 there were sixty boarders and an infant school for fifteen boys. In the 1860s and 1870s, the Darjeeling Loreto convent became known for its annual concert; it had "excellent standards in music and drama, performances on three or four pianos...classical plays, French conversation" and perhaps most important of all for cultivated ladies, "really good elocution, without a trace of che-che accent" (ibid:122–23). With the growth of industry, plantations and the road and rail networks, the demand for female convent education increased among all communities. In the earlier years Loreto education for girls was notable for its Anglo-Indian (Eurasian) input and produced several generations of Anglo-Indian lay teachers and nuns who in turn became teachers in the Loreto convents; the first Superior at the Entally Convent, Mother Christine Finch, was an Anglo-Indian as were many of her successors (ibid:98).

Changes in Loreto education took place in response to demand. From the 1880s onward, there was growing clamor for higher education for women. Some had already entered universities, and were doing medical and other studies locally and abroad. The pattern of education in Loreto convents was inadequate in the new situation; the correct convent accent and accomplishments were not enough and there was also a demand for higher academic attainment, such as the Cambridge School-leaving certificate, and for the teaching of science. The nuns had to adjust to these new trends and some of them began studying for higher degrees. The Loreto Teachers College for nuns and Indian girls, which began in 1912, was affiliated to a university and also provided intermediate courses in science and qualifying studies for Medical Colleges (ibid:162).

The Loreto venture had started as a religious mission to make converts of orphans and create good Catholic wives and mothers, full of the virtues of "godliness and cleanliness." As a Catholic priest reported, "You'd hardly believe the difference…between pagan households and those of our new Christians. What surprises you first is the cleanliness of their houses…which is often the only sign that we have arrived at a Christian home." As Colmcille wrote, "It was obvious to missionaries that, if Christian children were to develop a Christian mentality, they must be removed far from idolatrous villages" (ibid:170); as a report on a boarding school in Ranchi for tribal girls stated:

> they are good little girls, simple and sweet minded…. To see them in church, in class…you would say they behaved like the best girls in Catholic Schools in Europe; so grave, so modest, so good in every way…They will make excellent mothers of Catholic families. (ibid:171)

But apart from the "excellent" Catholic wives and mothers, the Loreto convents also produced wives for members of the emerging Indian bourgeoisie, who were anxious to "modernize" some aspects of their lives. In addition, the Loreto and other Christian schools succeeded in creating a new group of local women who overcame the narrow rigors of Catholic education. They profited from their good secondary education and were able to do further studies, including studies abroad, and also enter the professions. The Hindu and Muslim students of the convents also benefitted from being exposed to other religions, thereby developing tolerance and a broad eclectic attitude to different beliefs. They were also exposed to important activities—music, singing, dancing and art, as well as to social service in village and town and in orphanages run by Catholics. Ironically, the Irish, Catholic, conservative sisters of the convent were instrumental in advancing local women's emancipation—a concept they probably did not consciously believe in. In this sense, they differed from Western women theosophists who challenged the modernizing process and advocated a return to tradition, to the ideals of ancient Hindu and Buddhist society and to an even more orthodox concept of female education (see Chapter 8).

THE PROTESTANT ETHIC FOR "LADIES"

Similar to the movement in the West, the demand grew in South Asia for girls' schools where equal education and academic excellence were stressed, rather than merely the production of good wives with some basic education. These schools in India and Sri Lanka, staffed by teachers with higher education, were important centers of modernization, producing several generations of university graduates and professionals. An example from Sri Lanka of a conscious effort in this direction was the founding in 1900 of Ladies' College Colombo by the Church Missionary Society (CMS). Members of this Anglican body had arrived in Sri Lanka in 1818 and had started schools in the country for the poor and the lower middle-classes. By the 1890s, the promotion of upper-class female education had become missionary policy; there were also requests by "leading residents" of the island for the "establishment by Government of a superior school for girls on the model of Royal College," established in 1834 by the government as a secular boys' school for the sons of the local bourgeoisie. This school was run on the lines of a British public school and prepared boys for the Cambridge local examination and, in some cases, for studies in Indian and British universities. The government, though unwilling to start a parallel girls' high school, supported the CMS project for such a school (Muller 1957:10).

Funds were raised from church sources and from local patrons and benefactors. These were mainly the old rich landowning families and the new class of plantation owners, liquor merchants and traders, whose sons, in the second half of the 19th century, were qualifying for the professions in foreign universities. Some of the daughters of these families were educated privately at home, the richest having British governesses and tutors; but other sections of the bourgeoisie clamored for a high-class girls' school that would give their daughters an education comparable to that of the boys' schools.

The model for Ladies' College was the prestigious Cheltenham Ladies' College in Britain, which had been started in 1854 and was geared to high scholastic achievement for the "daughters of Noblemen and Gentlemen" (Clarke 1953:26). The subjects taught were scripture, English, Latin, French, geography, history, music and needlework, with German, Italian and dancing as "extras." Its most famous principal, appointed in 1858, was Dorothea Beale (1831–1906). In 1848, Beale was one of the first students of Queen's College, London, an institution for training young women to be teachers and governesses, linked to the University, giving a certificate, but not a degree. Under her influence, Cheltenham Ladies' College became the first girls' school to have annual examinations conducted by outside University lecturers. In 1865, Beale gave evidence before the Schools Enquiry Commission—along with other famous fighters for women's education, Frances Mary Buss and Emily Davis—emphasizing the need for girls' schools to have qualified teachers and "inspectional examinations" of schools (ibid:55). This extension of the Schools Enquiry Commission to include girls' schools was a landmark for women's rights. Soon after there was another victory when Cambridge Local Examinations were opened to girls on an equal footing.[13]

By 1897 the influence of the Cheltenham Ladies' College was widespread. Forty headmistresses of important schools in Britain and overseas were from Cheltenham; sixteen students of the school had become doctors, several famous scholars, like Jane Harrison, had been students there, and thirty former students were missionaries. Also a product of Cheltenham Ladies' College was Lilian Nixon, (1874–1945) the first principal of Ladies' College, Colombo. She came from a devout Protestant Irish family and had been inspired by Miss Beale. She may have also been influenced to do missionary work by the example of Pandita Ramabai, the Indian widow who started a school for child widows and who, in 1884, had taught Sanskrit at Cheltenham Ladies' College. On leaving school, Lilian Nixon went to the Royal University of Ireland, Dublin, obtaining an honors degree in modern literature. From there she followed a teachers' course at the Women's Training College, Cambridge (which had been started in 1885) and then moved on to a CMS missionary training school. Because of her success she was chosen at twenty-six to start the Ladies' College, in Colombo, a "first class educational institution" for girls. Elizabeth Whitney, a Canadian who had studied art in Montreal was there to help her. The school started in 1900 with two pupils, and had 225 students and sixteen teachers six years later. By 1905, of 200 pupils, 175 were Christians, the others Buddhists, Hindus and Muslims. The proportion of non-Christians rose in later years. For upper-class girls, the boarding school was also a new experience in self-reliance and inter-mixing (Simon 1957).

Nixon ran the school and taught scripture, English, French, German, Latin and mathematics in the higher classes while Whitney supervised the "housekeeping" (Wilson 1975:68–69). Their assignment was "educational work for the children of the upper classes, both Christian, and non-Christian, but particularly for the families that attend the Evangelical Churches in Colombo" (Simon 1957:17). The CMS Committee had to deal with the thorny question of how to reconcile the demand by the local bourgeoisie for superior female education with the desire of the missionaries to propagate Christianity. Some of the Committee felt that "so much teaching of secular subjects in English, which parents insisted on, was tending to overshadow the missionary aim"; one parent wanted his daughter to learn "French, English, Latin and mathematics" and had come to the school only "to get a *good* education" (ibid:18).

Lilian Nixon was innovative. She started a Kindergarten, a boys' preparatory school, a program for training teachers, and also introduced the teaching of science and mathematics as well as sports. The school had many non-missionary British teachers working for a few years at a time, such as Miss M. Hall, a graduate with a Cambridge Teachers Diploma who joined in 1905. The long-serving staff, however, consisted of the foreign missionary graduates. In the early years, they included Constance Browne, a B.Sc. of the University of Wales, who taught science in the school, and Anne Norseley, who had a classical tripos from Cambridge University, and joined the school in 1908 (ibid:30). Male teachers were also employed to fill the gaps in some subjects, but for the sake of propriety, "Miss Nixon used to sit at a side table in the same room correcting exercise books" (Hitchcock 1957:55).

From the earliest years, the Protestant ethic of hard work prevailed and the race was on at Ladies' College for academic achievement. Six girls of the school passed the Cambridge local examinations in 1902, and by 1904 there were nine successes, many winning government scholarships. Pressure was put on pupils to study hard, even Saturdays being used for extra teaching (Simon 1957:23–24). Other accomplishments such as music were encouraged as "there had been some fear that the girls would become blue-stockings"; but even in music the "exam craze" set in and by 1904, girls of the school had won four out of six music prizes offered by the Trinity College of Music, London (ibid:25). Even as early as 1906, Nixon, while claiming credit for the school's achievements, felt the need to correct "an impression...that we work for examinations alone." She also disclaimed any tendency to "cramming and mere memory work" (ibid:33).

In spite of these denials, the pressure for results was there, the school urging girls to "do your best." The inspiration for further studies came from the staff members who had been part of the movement for higher education for women, in which the "battle of the sexes" featured prominently—namely, competing with and excelling the men in higher education. Local girls caught the spirit of academic success. "Don't work later than ten o'clock at night," Nixon urged the girls, complaining that some of them studied until twelve, and got up early in the morning to work again (ibid:24). Results came quick and fast and some of the early women doctors were from Ladies' College. While in Cheltenham, Lilian Nixon had absorbed the idea that her school was "a place of sound learning…for a full, varied, natural life" and "a place for spiritual growth within the life of the Church" (Hitchcock 1957:107). In the case of the Colombo Ladies' College, although Christianity was the inspiration of the founders, the school became more concerned with acquiring fame for "sound learning" as well as excellence in sports and cultural activities. There was an emphasis on achievement and much satisfaction when the girls of the school beat the leading boys' schools in examinations, debates or other competitions. Succeeding generations of students were always reminded that the school produced the first woman Oxford graduate, as well as early women lawyers, doctors, diplomats, professors, and public figures.

But as the school grew in popularity, Lilian Nixon's problems increased. Faced with large debts, Church officials suggested that the school apply for a government grant that was conditional on government inspection and educational proficiency. Nixon rejected this prospect of government interference; because of this, and perhaps other areas of disagreement, (which remain unknown) she went on leave to Britain and resigned, or was made to resign, in 1914 "to the shocked surprise of her pupils and friends" (ibid:50). Nixon was succeeded as principal of Ladies' College by Gwen Opie (1887–1944), a graduate in science of Canterbury College, New Zealand. In her time as principal, from 1917 to 1945, the school facilities and activities expanded rapidly. New classrooms, boarders' quarters, sports fields, a chapel and library were built. The number of students and staff, the courses taught and the extra-curricular activities increased and pupils continued to succeed in entering the Ceylon University College, the Law and Medical faculties and universities abroad.

While such expansions were taking place, political changes in the country gave rise to serious qualms among missionaries. In response to a growth of national sentiment, the government ruled that grants were conditional on children also learning their mother tongue. As a result, from 1915, Sinhala and Tamil classes were begun, and in later years Christianity was made optional in mission schools. In the 1920s gradual constitutional reforms were introduced in Sri Lanka, and in 1931 universal suffrage was granted, ushering in an era of electoral politics. The 1930s form a period of growing nationalist sentiment as well as the rise of the first left political groupings.

With the growth of female education, and opportunities to participate in the political process, women increasingly took an interest in politics. Schools like Ladies' College, which had become pillars of the colonial establishment— and which (as the leading Anglican girls' school) was the favorite haunt of the Governors, colonial bureaucrats and Bishops on prize giving days—were faced with serious questions. How can you educate women up to university level, and yet isolate them from social and political currents of change in Sri Lanka, and from knowledge of massive protest movements against British rule in

India? How could Miss Gwen Opie, born in 1887 in the heyday of Empire, who had diehard views on King, Country, and the Christian missionary project, accept the new realities of anti-colonial sentiment, Buddhist and Hindu resurgence and political challenges to the church and colonial state?

Opie was also a puritan moralist; "In dress she would see that we were decent and did not attract unhealthy notice, and she never tolerated artificial beauty aids" wrote a former student. Others recalled her admonitions at the annual prize-givings. "I'd like every boy and girl to be able to say truthfully I'd rather die than tell a lie." And as the school historian notes, Opie's speeches included issues that aroused her "moral indignation"—ranging from the dowry system and "unjustifiable luxury" to "the dangers of nationalism" (ibid:82). In the early 1930s, when leftists and nationalists, including a British Socialist woman (see Chapter 18) started a movement to challenge the celebrations organized by the British on Armistice Day, Gwen Opie openly denounced this movement at school assembly and warned the students not to get involved in such displays of disloyalty.[14] Nevertheless, it was difficult to isolate the school from outside developments. Just as other schools and convents that intended to merely produce Christian wives, inevitably produced the first emancipated women, Ladies' College, which intended to create emancipated women, has also over the years produced its share of dissident women—nationalists, Socialists, feminists and human rights activists.

3

GOING FOR THE JUGULAR OF HINDU PATRIARCHY

American Women Fund-Raisers for Ramabai

> I beg of my Western sisters not to be satisfied with…the outside beauties of the grand philosophies…and the interested discourse of our educated men, but to open the trap doors of the great monuments of the ancient Hindu intellect, and enter into the dark cellars where they will see the real working of the philosophies they admire so much.
>
> —Ramabai (1896) quoted in Chakravarti (1989:75–76)

> The Christian ladies, trying to infiltrate our society under the cloak of women's education and their supporters—however learned—would be regarded by us as enemies of the people, of Hinduism and also of the cause of women's education.
>
> —B.G. Tilak (1892) in Pradhan and Bhagwat, *Lokmanya Tilak* (1959:58)

AN IMPORTANT AREA OF "WOMEN'S WORK FOR WOMEN" WAS FUND-RAISING by Western women for good causes abroad, including missionary work. One of the famous campaigns in America, carried out by women of various denominations, was in support of Pandita Ramabai's project for the education of child widows and orphans in India. I chose this particular case because it provides an early example of the dilemmas of "global sisterhood" and the predicaments caused by policy disagreements between Western fund-raisers and Eastern recipients. Important issues of feminist consciousness among Indian and American women arise in considering Ramabai's fierce challenge to Hindu patriarchy. But her feminism and Christianity came into conflict with emerging Hindu nationalism and led her into serious problems with both local nationalists and foreign funders. Feminism, nationalism and Christianity became then the key issues in the famous cause of Ramabai.

Pandita Ramabai (1858–1922), was the daughter of a Sanskrit scholar of
Maharashtra, of the exclusive caste of Chitpavan Brahmins who had deviated
from orthodoxy by teaching his wife and children to read Sanskrit, the classical language of India. By the age of twelve, Ramabai was highly proficient in
the Hindu texts. The family lived a nomadic life moving all over the country
visiting sacred sites.[1] One aspect of Ramabai's unorthodox upbringing was
that, contrary to tradition, she had not been married off in childhood. Instead,
Ramabai married Bipin Bihari Madhavi, a graduate of Calcutta University,
who also belonged to the reformist Brahmo Samaj. He was of a lower caste
than Ramabai, and the marriage was a civil ceremony, because both had liberal
views and rejected Hindu orthodoxy. The two had a daughter, but Madhavi
died suddenly of cholera, leaving Ramabai in the unfortunate position of
being a sonless widow in India. Rather than crushing her, this setback led to
the beginning of "her career as an Indian widow" (Dyer 1900:29). Ramabai
returned to Pune where she had relatives, and by 1883 she was active in the
reformist group, Prarthana Samaj, and began speaking out on women's education, condemning child marriage, and urging that women be instructed in
Sanskrit and their own local language. Several women from leading high-
caste Pune families joined her in forming a women's association, The Arya
Mahila Samaj. Because of her erudition, Ramabai was honored with the title
Pandita. Proceeds from her book *Stree Dharma Nithi* (Moral Law for Women)
enabled her to travel to England where she lived with the sisters of St. Mary's
Home, Wantage. She converted to Christianity in 1883 and taught Sanskrit at
the Cheltenham Ladies' College, a school that became a model for girls' high
schools in South Asia (see Chapter 2).

In India, Ramabai's conversion caused shock because she was appropriating
the religion of the imperial rulers during a revival of Hinduism. To Ramabai,
the situation in the 1880s seemed bleak for women. There was little evidence of
social reform, with Indians and British rulers reluctant to make radical
changes affecting women's positions in society. Moreover, the plight of
women seemed without hope as long as they were bound by the constraints of
Hindu tradition. A sharp break was needed and she made this by converting to
Christianity. After four years in England, Ramabai went to Philadelphia to
attend the graduation of a relative, Anandibai Joshi, who had completed her
medical studies at the Women's Medical College of Pennsylvania. The College
Dean, Rachel Bodley, was impressed by Ramabai and assisted her in the publication, in 1887, of *The High Caste Hindu Woman*.[2] The book discusses in detail
certain discriminatory aspects of Hinduism, especially child marriage and widow's status, and traces them back to Hindu theological texts, particularly the
Code of Manu. Ramabai referred to the need for self-reliance (rather than life-

long dependency on men) for education, and for Indian women teachers in a country where "caste and the seclusion of women are regarded as essential tenets." The goal would be to create a body of Indian women who would teach other women "by precept and example" (Ramabai 1887:130). Ramabai urged that a useful beginning could be made by concentrating on high-caste women, because these women had "quickness of perception and intelligence," and only needed education to become "competent teachers" (ibid:131).

Pandita Ramabai's feminism was way ahead of her time. Her challenge was not merely a demand for the abolition of a few social evils, but an attempt to expose and reject the patriarchal basis of religion and culture. In this she differed from the male social reformers who were highlighting the need for reforms through legislation and education, without themselves challenging the structures of oppression. Many of the reformers did not practice what they preached, some of them even taking child brides, or marrying off their children, while campaigning against the system.[3] As Kosambi has pointed out, Ramabai "was a solitary woman leader of the women's cause" who has long been "eclipsed by the storm over her conversion to Christianity and her consequent neglect by contemporary mainstream Hindu society, which was acutely vulnerable to assaults on its religious identity" (1988:W.S. 38).

THE FORMATION OF THE RAMABAI ASSOCIATION

Pandita Ramabai's book aroused interest among Christian circles in America. In a message to the readers Ramabai said, "Tell them to help me educate the high-caste child widows; for I solemnly believe that this hated and despised class of women, educated and enlightened, are, by God's grace, to redeem India!" (Ramabai 1887:xxiv). Ramabai's proposal was for homes for child widows, "where they can take shelter without the fear of losing their caste or being disturbed in their religious belief" and could become teachers, nurses and housekeepers. Ramabai appealed for funds from abroad since "the great majority of my country-people being most bitterly opposed to the education of women, there is little hope of my getting from them either good words or pecuniary aid" (ibid:139). She asked for help for a period of ten years, to prove that her project could succeed, and made an emotional appeal to Americans to free Indian child widows from "life-long slavery and infernal misery" and from their tormentors: "Let the cry of India's daughters reach your ears and stir your hearts" (ibid:142). In the introduction to Ramabai's book, Rachel Bodley referred to the English missionary, William Carey, who said, on his departure to India in 1793, "I will go down into the deep mine, but remember that you must hold the ropes." Bodley hoped, "that among the favoured women of this Christian land there might be found a sufficient number to hold the ropes for Ramabai," and added,

When in that great Hindu nation about to come to birth, the women are moved
to arise in their degradation, and cry "Help or we perish…a corresponding multitude of women must be found elsewhere, willing…to send this help." (ibid:xxii)

In 1887 at a large public meeting, the Ramabai Association was formed in
Boston and addressed by Ramabai under the auspices of the Unitarians,
because they were "free from sectarianism"; it was reported that the "audience was moved to tears and laughter by Ramabai's pathos and keen wit"
(Ramabai Association 1897:14). Membership of the Ramabai Association
entailed a pledge to give not less than one dollar a year for ten years. Provision
was also made for a scholarship of one hundred dollars annually for ten years,
and for donations to the building fund. From the outset there was strong liberal influence on the workings of the Ramabai Association, whose first
president was the leading Unitarian clergyman of Boston, the Rev. Edward E.
Hale, a doctor of divinity. He was known for his open-minded views on other
religions and was involved in social reform in Boston[4] (Ramabai Association
1893:24—25).

The women vice-presidents of the Ramabai Association, included Frances
E. Willard (1839—1898) who had been president of the Evanston College for
Ladies and in 1888, wrote, *Women in the Pulpit,* arguing the case for women's ordi-
nation (Hardesty 1980:109). She was active in temperance, women's rights and
socialist movements. The Ramabai Association also had a Board of Trustees
of ten persons "equally unsectarian" and composed of "some of the best business and professional men of Boston" (Ramabai Association 1897:14). The
"men" included three women, Phoebe Adam, Ellen Mason and Pauline
Agassiz Shaw (1841—1917).[5] The important work of the Ramabai Association was
carried out by the nine women of the Executive Committee. They were of all
denominations associated with a variety of church, humanitarian and philanthropic activities. Thus, while the main work of the Association was done
by activist women, many of them veterans of earlier struggles for the abolition of slavery, the necessary status and legitimacy for fund-raising was provided by men who were the "pillars" of ecclesiastical and secular Boston
society. The Ramabai Association also had two Indian Advisory Boards in
Pune and Bombay, consisting entirely of distinguished Indian reformers and
professionals.

In 1887 and 1888 Ramabai toured the United States, speaking, forming groups
and observing new methods of education. By December 1889, there were fifty-
seven Ramabai circles all over the United States and Canada with a
membership of 4,069, the largest contributors being those of Brooklyn,
Chicago, Cornell University, Indianapolis, New York, Smith College,
Philadelphia, Richmond (Virginia), the Pacific Coast and Toronto (Ramabai

Ramabai (left) with missionary friend. (From
Helen Dyer (1900), *Pandita Ramabai: The Story of her
Life*, Schlesinger Library, Radcliffe College.)

Association 1890:12). All these Ramabai Circles were affiliated with the main
Association in Boston. At the end of the second year of its activities the
Association reported that it was in a "strong position," having a balance of
$27,000 from an income of $36,000 (ibid:11). The Ramabai Association also published a bulletin, *Lend a Hand*, which gave details of the work of the Association,
and news about Ramabai.

RAMABAI'S RETURN TO INDIA
Ramabai returned to India via Hong Kong, where she received a rousing reception given from the Indian community.[6] In Bombay she started Sharada
Sadan, a school for high-caste widows. Helping her was Miss Dennison, a
young American who had traveled back with her. The opening ceremonies
were described as "rather novel" because Ramabai rejected advice to invite an
important British official or a local dignitary to preside and chose a woman
writer Kashibai Kanitkar. The school was specifically intended to be for child
widows of the three high castes, the restriction ensuring that women would

not refuse to come to the school on grounds of caste taboos about eating and living with those of low castes. The caste restriction, however, prevented Ramabai from applying to the government for a grant and land for school buildings. The school began with two pupils, increasing to twenty-two in three months. The number gradually grew over the years and by the end of ten years, 350 child widows and girls had attended the school, of whom fourteen were trained to be teachers, eight to be nurses, seven as missionary assistants, seven as matrons, two as house-keepers, and ten "of the once despised widows were happy wives in homes of their own" (American Ramabai Association 1903:15–16).

Sharada Sadan was shifted in 1891 to Pune; one of the innovations being the Kindergarten training class based on the Froebel system (Ramabai Association 1892:25). After the famine of the mid-1890s, the school was again shifted to Kedgaon. There, with help from her daughter Manorama, a new school, the Mukti Sadan, was started in 1896 for famine victims of the lower castes. But by this time, the ideology of the Ramabai project had narrowed. For ten years the Sharada Sadan had been run as a secular school, according to the wishes of the American funders, but "the Kedgaon establishment became openly Christian, with a church and regular missionary activity" (Kosambi 1988:w.s. 42). Up to her death in 1922, Ramabai remained in Kedgaon and was active in educational work, vocational training in teaching, nursing, weaving, printing and tailoring, as well as translating the Bible into Marathi. By this time, she and her daughter found solace in a revivalist type of Christianity. Nevertheless, the project had achieved world fame; missionaries had publicized her work, and every winter tourists were "daily at the gates" wanting to look around the school. There were, in 1907, six English, American and Swedish women residents. In other parts of Asia, women were also inspired by Ramabai; one notable case being Kartini, the Indonesian pioneer of female education.[7]

But in India, the reactions to Ramabai were mixed, especially in view of her hesitation to ally publicly with nationalist causes. For Christians in India and their supporters abroad, the crucial question of social reform was linked to British rule. It was not merely that "enlightenment" and progress was thought of as part of the blessings the British had conferred upon India, but also that the end of British rule was seen as reversion to conflict, ignorance and superstition. Ramabai, who had been attacked by B.G. Tilak and the political extremists, was particularly aware of this issue. As the agitation in India increased, especially the ferment in Bengal around 1905, Ramabai was faced with the dilemma: is benevolent foreign rule in any circumstance preferable to self-government? She had a clear answer. Christianity had to continue its noble work in India. And for this, British rule was necessary. In 1909 she described the "makers of this unrest in India" as "fine well-educated people, trying to do good to the country in their own way"; but she faulted them for failing to see that India was not a nation.[8] She added that because it took the British many centuries of "Christian training" to arrive at their "love of the right principle," it would take Indians some centuries to "come up to the mark" (American Ramabai Association 1909:16–21). What is ironic, however, is that by this date the American funders and the American public may have been more sympathetic to Indian nationalism than Ramabai. During the last decade of her life, Ramabai had moved toward a more fundamentalist Christianity, being also preoccupied with Bible translations and constant prayer sessions, while Ramabai's American funders were more interested in possible political changes in India (ibid:39). [9]

THE FUNDERS VERSUS THE FUNDED

Relations between funders and recipients of funds are inevitably complex and the case of the Ramabai Association and Ramabai was no exception. The officials of the Association were anxious initially to emphasize their advanced attitudes, the liberal content of their activities, and to disassociate themselves from the more fundamentalist and crude evangelical aspects of missionary activity abroad. Ramabai's strength had been that she was Indian and not the typical foreign missionary preaching Christianity to "natives."[10] Although anxious that Indians should create their own forms, the Ramabai funders occasionally felt impelled to intervene. Even by 1889, the Ramabai Association agreed that Ramabai could not cope alone with all the problems of running the school. It spoke of her "lack of experience in teaching, organizing, and in business matters" and of the need for "help and sympathy of a woman of experience, judgement and courage." The committee sent Sarah Hamlin, "a woman of cultivation and refinement, of experience in teaching, organizing and traveling" who had been Ramabai's "most loyal friend" on the Pacific Coast, to help her (Ramabai Association 1890:22).

The Ramabai Association was also clearly worried that "even the *appearance* of breaking faith" was to be avoided as "the Hindus have put such confidence in the word of Ramabai and of the American people that the school shall be strictly secular, countenancing no interference with Hindu beliefs and customs" (Ramabai Association 1890: 28). Sarah Hamlin took a close look at the school and made frequent reports on Ramabai to the committee in Boston. While praising Ramabai's work, Hamlin was also conscious of the possible dangers of the school becoming too closely associated with Christianity. The question arose because several pupils used to participate with Ramabai in morning prayers in her room.[11] But Ramabai defended her right to openly practice Christianity and to have prayer meetings in her room, and because the school was dominated by her charismatic personality, it was difficult to prevent pupils from being attracted to Ramabai's religious practices. The issue was an explosive one, and in 1892 and 1893, there was a crisis in India over the proselytization of child widows in Ramabai's school leading to the resignation of the Indian Advisory Board.[12] The controversy became public, and well-known reformers and the press were involved. The most damaging attack came from leading nationalists, like B.G. Tilak, who alleged that Ramabai's Sharada Sadan was merely a cover for proselytizing.

There were two considerations that affected the American funders' attitude to Ramabai's strong Christian views. One was the general liberal climate of interest in Asian religions and a reaction against dogmatic and fundamentalist Christianity. Second, the Unitarians, Methodists and other non-conformist Christians of the Association were disconcerted, if not disappointed, by Ramabai's dogmatism. They asked whether Ramabai had broken her pledge to the American funders that she would run the school in a nondenominational and non-sectarian manner, where students could worship as they pleased. As a result, significant changes occurred in the relationship between Ramabai and her American funders in 1898; ten years had elapsed since the formation of the Ramabai Association, and Pandita Ramabai went to the United States for the annual meeting in 1898. The Association dissolved itself and a new one, the American Ramabai Association, was formed, to which the property was transferred.[13] The next crisis for the funders occurred in 1902 when Ramabai, without the approval of the American Ramabai Association, took the Sharada Sadan from Pune to Kedgaon (because of the bubonic plague problems and "other plagues"). In Ramabai's words, "This action of mine has naturally displeased many of my friends in America, and consequently the subscriptions for the Sharada Sadan have fallen off (American Ramabai Association 1904:18). By 1902 the issue of Christian proselytization at Ramabai's school again became a matter of controversy.

But perhaps the most disturbing question for the funders was the way in which the Ramabai issue became a confrontational one with Hindus and theosophists at a time when liberal Christians were trying to promote a new approach to non-Christians. Ramabai's project was obviously unacceptable to orthodox Hindus from the outset. As a Brahmin widow, her conversion, denunciations of Hinduism, attack on caste taboos and the promotion of Christianity in her schools, were reasons to cause scandal. Ramabai was also strong in her advocacy of women's rights long before such ideas were generally acceptable in either the West or India, and she was ahead of her time in her challenge to patriarchy. By focusing mainly on the condition of child widows, Ramabai was choosing an area of action that hit out against Hinduism, Brahmin oppression and male domination. To her, the condition of Hindu widows was not merely a social evil to be reformed, it was a symptom of the disease that had to be eradicated. Her challenge was thus a basic one, questioning Hinduism; even Indians who might have agreed with Ramabai on the condition of Hindu women, could not agree with her appeal "to take the Real Remedy, the Gospel of Christ, to millions of India's women" (Fuller 1899: 13). Moreover, Ramabai's conversion and her denunciation of Hinduism as the root cause of women's oppression, occurred at a time when nationalism and Hindu revivalism were growing in strength. It was also a period during which the West was becoming acquainted at first hand with the views of leading Hindus, such as Swami Vivekananda.

The popularity of Ramabai in the United States caused a problem for Vivekananda, and when he criticized Ramabai's activities, there were "accusations and counter-accusations of mis-representation." This conflict between Americans was an interesting confrontation on gender lines—American women coming out in defense of Ramabai against the Indian "man of the hour"—Vivekananda—and his sponsor Dr. Lewis James of the Brooklyn Ethical Society. The problem began when, at this society's invitation, Vivekananda spoke in December 1894 on "Indian Religions." This led to a controversy in the pages of the *Brooklyn Eagle* between Dr. James and Mrs. McKeen of the Brooklyn Ramabai Association, alleging that Vivekananda in his public lecture had denied that Hindu widows were undergoing suffering. Vivekananda's intervention clearly caused some anguish among the Boston Ramabai Association, which in 1895 referred to "the grave misstatements made by some of the Hindus visiting this country, not only in regard to child wives and widows, but concerning Ramabai and her school" (Ramabai Association 1896:28). While foreign missionaries living in India were very supportive of Ramabai, it was to be expected that foreign women theosophists and women followers of Swami Vivekananda were highly ambivalent if not critical of her.

In turn, Ramabai regarded Westerners like Annie Besant and Sister Nivedita, who were championing the cause of Hinduism, with feelings bordering on contempt. There was no open confrontation between Annie Besant and Ramabai, but when Besant gave a lecture on Theosophy in Pune "Ramabai consented to depart from her usual custom of not appearing in public, and attended the lecture where she was cheered by the audience" (American Ramabai Association 1899:19–20). But she was critical of Besant and other Westerners who were attracted by Hinduism; writing to her American funders, Ramabai described the horrors of child widows and remarked that the world was going backwards since Mrs. Besant had the nerve to say that Hindu widows should never remarry. "Let us hope that better days are coming for the poor, despised Hindu widows," she wrote, "in spite of all the seeming obstacles in their way of progress" (American Ramabai Association 1904:21–22). Annie Besant on her part alleged that Ramabai's conversion to Christianity and her use of the widows' school for making converts had been a set-back to female education in India. On her first visit to India in 1893, Besant had wanted to concern herself "with the question of the education of girls," but had been discouraged by "thoughtful Indians" (see Chapter 8) because of Ramabai's Christianity and her attempts at converting child widows and orphans under the guise of education (Besant (1904) 1913:318).

How much did Ramabai's conversion harm the cause of women's education? It certainly provided an ideal excuse for traditionalists to warn against female education—linking it with dangers of exposure to Christian influences and westernized behavior and the rejection of Hindu religion and culture. It also, in the 1890s, made theosophists extremely cautious about moving ahead to start girls' schools (See Chapter 8). But although Ramabai's conversion was an excuse, it is also true that Ramabai, who started so fearlessly in her challenge to Hindu patriarchy, destroyed her chances of leading women's struggles by her narrow preoccupation with Bible translation and conversion. The women of India could hardly benefit by moving from the patriarchal domination of the Brahmins to the patriarchal ideology of Christian fundamentalism. Moreover, in seeing British rule as the protector of Christianity, Ramabai also lost the opportunity to emerge as a truly national woman leader who could also challenge colonialism. What her American funders could clearly see—namely, the need for secular institutions and a sympathy for Indian nationalism—bypassed Ramabai and proved to be a real set-back for women's rights in India. But Ramabai's pioneering work for women was not forgotten and the voice of Indian women in protest, which she articulated as early as the 1880s, was kept alive by succeeding generations of Indian women for whom her attacks to the "jugular" of Hindu patriarchy made her a true hero and a pioneer feminist. There was another group of Western social reformers who continued to raise issues that Ramabai had been concerned with but who were not, however, primarily motivated by the spread of Christianity. Their cases will be considered in the following chapters of this book.

II

MOTHERING INDIA
Women Social Reformers from the West

4

RADICAL AND SECULAR REFORMERS

From the first to the last day of a residence in India, the point which most painfully strikes the mind is the position of Hindoo women.... May many more English women arise, who shall devote themselves to the glorious and blessed work of raising their Eastern sisters to fill their place in society.

—Mary Carpenter (1867), *Six Months in India* (1868:74, 83)

His feeling for women in general, still more than the admiration he expressed for the mental accomplishments of English ladies, won our hearts.

—Lucy Aikin (1831) on the Indian social reformer Rammohan Roy, in Mary Carpenter, *The Last Days in England of Raja Rammohun Roy* (1850:106)

AN IMPORTANT DEVELOPMENT OF THE 19TH CENTURY WAS THE DE-LINKING in the West of Christianity and social reform. The missionaries' work for reform was so closely bound with their religious beliefs that it was often not possible to discuss the issues separately. But the appearance of radical women reformers was a crucial break, for it was linked with a positivist vision of the good society here on earth, without necessarily juxtaposing it with religious "truth." Those from backgrounds of "advanced" or dissident Christianity were able to make this break; two women reformers from Unitarian families, Mary Carpenter and Annette Ackroyd are cases in point.

Western women concerned with South Asia in the colonial period included reformers, social critics, fund-raisers and professional women who had strong beliefs in the "civilizing mission," but were not part of the Christian or missionary project. Their concern for the colonized in most cases was an extension of their interest in social reform movements in Britain and the United States. Even before the advance of female education and employment, women in the West were occupied in a wide range of charity and social service activities concerned with institutional reform, poverty alleviation, sanitation and moral elevation. Social work became an accepted area of outside activity for middle-class women who were appalled by some of the social consequences of industrial capitalism.[1] And many women who were wealthy in their own right became important funders and fund-raisers for women's projects in South Asia.

More specific agitation for the reforms of existing institutions, laws and social practices were also taken up. Elizabeth Fry (1780–1845) was concerned with prison reform, especially highlighting the appalling conditions in which women and children were kept in prison (Murray 1982:284). Josephine Butler (1828–1906) carried out a successful campaign against state-regulated prostitution and the double standards of the Contagious Diseases Acts of 1864, whereby women considered to be prostitutes could be forcibly examined, hospitalized and imprisoned. After their repeal in 1886, Butler lobbied for the repeal of similar legislation in India. The best-known reformer of the period, however, was Florence Nightingale (1820–1910), who pioneered professionalism in nursing and continued all her life to agitate for the amelioration of women's health in the colonies where the "Nightingale method" of nursing was introduced.

In earlier chapters, mention has been made of the impact of missionary literature that described the condition of Indian women and the way in which the issue of child widows was taken up by reformers in the United States and Britain. Social reform in India and fund-raising for Indian women became areas of activity where British women assumed a special responsibility for improving conditions in the colonies. Women's rights in India and women's status in the family and social evils like sati, female seclusion, polygamy, child marriage, and the ban on widow remarriage became widely discussed topics. And those expressing concern ranged from Queen Victoria to feminists, liberals and socialists. Action taken by women reformers was linked to social reform movements initiated by the Indians themselves.

Many Indians had been activated into taking up issues of social reform as a result of missionary criticism, as well as concern expressed by liberals and radicals in the West; but the key motivation was the belief that for a national awakening to take place in India, some reform and modernization of local society was necessary. Pioneering this movement was Rammohan Roy (1772–1833),[2] a learned Bengali who had been exposed to British liberalism and non-conformist liberal Christianity and was the friend of British women radicals such as Mary Carpenter and Harriet Martineau. The famous social reformer of a later period was Keshab Chandra Sen (1838–84), who visited Britain several times to mobilize support for social reform and was in close touch with Mary Carpenter and Annette Ackroyd. The most active movements of social reform were in West India, where from the mid-19th century, the cities of Bombay and Pune became centers of intellectual debate on religious and cultural issues. The movements for the reform of Hinduism and the eradication of social evils were led by Dr. Pandurang, Jotirao Phule, Gopal Deshmukh, and M.D. Ranade.[3] Parallel to these movements in India were the Western women reformers and fund-raisers who exposed Indian women's oppression and agitated for changes to eliminate social evils. The British government was not too keen to highlight social evils affecting the family life of local people and was in no hurry to legislate on social issues, because this was considered to be politically risky and a potential cause of unrest. But to British women reformers with a feminist awareness, the main justification for British rule was to cleanse local societies of social evils affecting women.

During the years of controversial debate in India about women's rights, many Western women educationalists, doctors, reformers and writers became involved in speaking out loud and clear about social evils in India. They visualized a righteous British Empire where social justice prevailed, and thought it their task to publicize and agitate on issues affecting women thereby often legitimizing "imperial authority" (Burton 1991:49). But some were more "imperialist" minded than others and there were many shades of political opinon and activities—ranging from pioneer work of women doctors to the secular work of reformers like Mary Carpenter and Annette Ackroyd, and the continued agitation and exposure on the issue of child marriage by Eleanor Rathbone and Katherine Mayo. The following sections deal with their work in the context of the campaign in Britain and India for women's rights.

MARY CARPENTER, THE UNITARIAN RADICAL

Of the radical Christian groups, one of the most influential was the Unitarians who were associated with many of the liberal causes of the 19th century in Britain and America. Unitarians rejected the Orthodox belief in the Trinity, holding that God rests in the Father alone. They championed "freedom, reason and tolerance" and were "especially responsive to the spirit of the age" in which they lived, many of them becoming "leaders and transmitters of current thought," varying from "liberal traditional to extreme modernist" (New Encyclopedia Britannica, 1986, Vol 26:264). Unitarians took an intellectual approach to religion and were receptive to the study of non-Christian religions. One of the outstanding Unitarians of the 19th century was Mary Carpenter (1807–1877), a renowned 19th-century social reformer with a keen interest in India. Born in Exeter, her father Rev. Lant Carpenter and mother

Anna were both teachers and Unitarians—a group linked to radical causes, political and social reform, philanthropy and liberal attitudes to religion and education. Rev. Carpenter became a famous minister in Bristol, a center of non-conformist and radical political thought, trade union agitation, and Christian socialism. "Concern for the poor became a habit...(and) was to give Mary a career and a claim to fame as impressive as any of the great company of outstanding women who were her contemporaries" (Saywell 1964:2).[4]

Mary Carpenter's father died in 1840, and until 1845, along with her mother and sister, she ran a school for girls. In 1846, funded by Unitarians, she started the Ragged School which was attended by twenty poor boys. According to Carpenter, her school was at the beginning "literally a Ragged School. None have shoes or stockings, some have no shirt and no home, sleeping on casks on the quay or on steps and living...by petty depredations." She also ran a night school for 160 pupils which attracted a lot of attention and praise from the school authorities (ibid:4). Carpenter taught at the school and wrote on educational methods. Her essay "Ragged Schools, their Principles and Modes of Operation" described her ideas on "religious and moral training, intellectual and industrial training, self respect and cleanliness" (ibid:5).[5]

In an article, "Reformatory Schools for the Children of the Perishing and Dangerous Classes" (1851), Carpenter wrote of the responsibility of parents for delinquent behavior in children, but also stressed the need for society to assume responsibility for the child (ibid:6). In 1852, she set up the "Kingswood Industrial School for Boys and Girls," with funding from Lady Byron, the widow of the poet. In 1854, the Youthful Offenders Act was passed, which provided for the establishment of voluntarily-managed reformatory schools under the Home Secretary, whereby young offenders would be imprisoned for two weeks and then sent to a reform school. The Kingswood School subsequently became the Boys' Reformatory, with Carpenter in charge; she also started a girls' reformatory school, relying on the efforts of enthusiastic women. Lady Byron again helped in the purchase of a house known as "Red Lodge," which became the first girls' reformatory school in England.[6] The aim of Carpenter's innovative work was to treat the children with kindness rather than use the traditional coercive methods, in order "to act on the child's inner nature." Her school became famous in Britain and attracted many visitors (ibid 1964:9—10).

Mary Carpenter's interest in India was influenced by the visit to Britain in 1831 of Raja Rammohan Roy, the noted Bengali reformer and scholar who had campaigned for the abolition of sati. Roy was heartily welcomed and extensively praised in reform circles in Britain; he met the Unitarians, liberals, political radicals and even the Utopian Socialist, Robert Owen.[7] Roy, like many other famous Indians after him, had a wide network of unusual British women

Mary Carpenter (From Ruby J. Saywell (1964), *Mary Carpenter of Bristol*, Widener Library, Harvard.)

friends, who were radicals and Unitarians holding "advanced" opinions and were keen to mix with Asians. One of these celebrated friends was Harriet Martineau (1802–76). She was from a Unitarian family and had been a "fanatical disciple" of Rev. Lant Carpenter before she became an agnostic. By the early 1830s, when she met Rammohan Roy she was earning a living writing stories and essays to popularize economic and political themes, which had a huge success. Her radical interests included the abolition of slavery in the United States and reform in India. In 1857, soon after the rebellion in India, she wrote "British Rule in India—An Historical sketch" and "Suggestions towards the Future Government of India" (1858). Another of Roy's close friends was Lucy Aikin who, writing about Roy to the leading American Unitarian, Dr Channing, stated:

> Just now my feelings are more cosmopolite than usual; I take a personal concern in a *third* quarter of the globe, since I have seen the excellent *RAMMOHUN ROY*.... He is indeed a glorious being—a true sage...with genuine humility...and more fervour, more sensibility, a more engaging tenderness of heart than any *class* of character can justly claim. (Carpenter 1850:105, emphasis in original)

Aikin also praised the way Roy exposed "the many cruelties and oppressions to which females in his country are subjected by the injustice and barbarity of the stronger sex," and remarked on the way in which he pleaded "for pity towards them with such powerful, heartfelt eloquence as no woman, I think, can peruse without tears and fervent invocations of blessing on his head" (ibid:107). Apart from being the guest of the Carpenters, Roy also stayed in the Bristol home of Catherine Castle—a young heiress and her aunt Ann Kiddell, who lived nearby at "Stapleton Grove" (ibid:117–18). Unexpectedly, the lionized guest died in Bristol in 1833, at sixty-one, and was buried at Stapleton Grove. This was an occasion of shock and sorrow for all his British friends, and many women wrote poems and hymns on his death.[8] In the early 1860s , Mary Carpenter's interest and sympathy with India and female education was rekindled by visiting Indians. She noted that God had given her:

> the unspeakable privilege before leaving this world, of going to distant India and there working with the spirits of my beloved father and the noble Raja for the elevation of women, and perhaps also for the planting of a pure Christianity. (Ramusack 1990:310)

From September 1866 to March 1867 she visited India and produced a book, *Six Months in India*, dedicated to Rammohan Roy, "who first excited in the author's mind a desire to benefit his country." She describes her visits to jails, asylums and girls' schools in Bombay, Ahmedabad, Madras, Calicut, Calcutta and Dhaka, deploring especially child marriage and female illiteracy. In her jail visits, she paid particular attention to the condition of women prisoners. About their plight in the Ahmedabad jail she wrote:

> I felt grieved and shocked that in any part of the British dominions, women who were rendered helpless by being deprived of liberty…should be so utterly uncared for, as to be left under the superintendence of male warders (Carpenter 1868, Vol. 1:51)

In India, she also gave many public lectures on female education, which were attended by large numbers of British residents and Indians; and in Calcutta in December 1866 she spoke at the inauguration of the Bengal Social Science Association at which many prominent Bengali reformers were present. She discussed a range of topics—female education, normal schools, juvenile offenders, reformatories, jail reform, sanitation, popular health and working-class housing. Before returning to England she also sent a memorandum to the Indian authorities on girls' schools, reformatories and jails, and in London she lobbied the Queen and the India Office on these issues

(*Dictionary of National Biography* 1968:1069). Her subsequent visits to India in the winter months of 1868 to 1869 and 1869 to 1870, convinced her that there was "more to be done by the influence she could exert at headquarters" in Britain than by "personal work in India itself." In 1870, a visit from Keshab Chandra Sen inspired her to launch the National Indian Association in Britain to "enable Indian visitors to study the institutions of England, and to ripen English opinion respecting the wants of India." Her last visit to India was in the winter of 1875 to 1876; "she made careful reports to the authorities in India and at home, and saw many of her suggestions carried into law." She died in Bristol in 1877, aged seventy. The mourners included two Indian students "whose education she was superintending" (ibid:1070).

Mary Carpenter was clearly ahead of her time in hoping to influence the British government in India on the issue of social reform. It is, therefore, not surprising that Lord Napier, the Governor of Madras, advised her that she could "do more for the cause of female education by *staying at home and supporting those who are interested in it*" (quoted in Ramusack 1990:311, emphasis in original). Similarly, missionaries were not enthusiastic about Carpenter because her proposals for secular female normal schools went against the Christian project (ibid:311). Carpenter's goals, nevertheless, influenced Indians who had their own agenda for India's regeneration through a program of social reform. For them, she represented the Western woman who was more enlightened than the British rulers, more radical than the missionaries, and because of her feminist consciousness, more daring and persistent than her male compatriots in exposing the evils of the patriarchal social structures of both Britain and India.

ANNETTE ACKROYD'S SECULAR SCHOOL

Some of the contradictions that arose when British women reformers were involved in pioneering change in India are seen in the interesting life of Annette Ackroyd (1842–1929) who started a girls' school as a secular venture. Born in 1842, her family from Sturbridge, England, were Unitarians; she was educated from 1860 to 1863 at Bedford College, London, which had been founded in 1849 by a Unitarian, Miss Read, for the higher education of women. Here she studied English, mathematics, Greek and Latin. (Beveridge 1947:48). In 1871, Ackroyd began to teach at the Working Women's College in London, and during these years she became interested in social reform, one of her friends being the famous reformer Bessie Raynor Parkes, also of a radical Unitarian family. Ackroyd was also concerned about colonial issues, especially after meeting Indian students in London and attending a speech delivered in London in 1870 by Keshab Chandra Sen. Sen had called for "well trained, accomplished English ladies" to come to India and start schools for their "Indian sisters" that would be without religious bias, giving "an education free and liberal and comprehensive in character, calculated to make Indian women good wives, mothers, sisters and daughters" (Barr 1976:161).

After her father's death, Annette Ackroyd felt free of the usual family obligations of an unmarried daughter, and decided to leave for India. In preparation for her journey, she took lessons in Bengali and in teaching methods. After arriving in Calcutta, she stayed with the family of Mary Carpenter's friend, the lawyer Manomohan Ghose, whom she had known in England. Her decision to live with Indians and her strong views on secular education annoyed both the local British and the missionaries. In turn, she despised both groups. The intolerance and prejudices of the British led her to declare that she was "convinced of the falseness of our position here" (Beveridge 1947:88), and she dismissed the missionaries as "ignorant and conceited" (Barr 1976:162). On Ghose's death, Annette became the Secretary of a Memorial Fund for him, which donated 200 books to Bethune College in his memory.

Annette Ackroyd belonged to a very small minority of British liberal feminists in India who had sympathy with the locals and were keen on social and political reform. But like many liberal women who came to India with great hopes, she was disappointed to find that Indian reformers did not practice what they preached. She noted that her friend Keshab Chandra Sen's wife was illiterate and secluded, and played with jewels "like a foolish petted child." She was also annoyed that at one of Sen's public meetings, she was the only woman among around 2,000 men, which aroused a lot of curiosity and "impertinence" (ibid 1976:163–64). Adverse comments on her were also made in the local press that she was a danger to the morals of girls, because Western women in India "are utterly shameless," that she had been starving in England, was unmarried and therefore unfit to teach, and that she knew nothing of Indian social customs. Ackroyd was not too bothered, "I care no more for them than for the flies walking in the room below" she wrote, adding that, "I've got used to seeing my name in print, though at first I did think it very dreadful" (ibid:164–5). But she also had support, including a letter from "A Hundred and Ten Bengalee Gentlemen" who expressed gratitude "for the zealous interest…in our local institutions, and for the benevolent objects of your sojourn in our country generally" (ibid:165). Among Bengali admirers was an Anglophile, Dr. Ghose, whose son was born in December 1872 in the house of his friend Manomohan Ghose, Annette's host. In honor of Annette, the child was named Aravinda Ackroyd Ghose. He became a famous revolutionary and later the sage of Pondicherry, Sri Aurobindo (See Chapter 15).

In 1873, Annette Ackroyd started the Hindu Mahila Vidyalaya (Hindu Ladies School) in Calcutta with ten pupils and two teachers. The treasurer of the school and promoter of Bengali women's education was Emily Phear (1836–1897), wife of Sir John Phear, a judge in Calcutta. English, Bengali and basic subjects were taught in the school but strict religious neutrality was observed. Annette also took the pupils to art exhibitions, the botanical gardens and magic-lantern shows. But the caste inhibitions of the students, and the general lack of interest in female education left her disillusioned. Nevertheless, there was some support for her secular school from Britishers, such as Henry Beveridge of the Indian Colonial Service, who was on the school's managing committee. Beveridge was an agnostic, a humanitarian and a believer in women's emancipation, often citing the views on women's rights of John Stuart Mill and Harriet Taylor (Beveridge 1947:41). He proposed marriage to Annette and they daringly opted for a civil ceremony as opposed to the traditional church marriage. But in spite of Beveridge's ideas on women's rights, Annette had to close down the school in 1876 after her marriage, moving from Calcutta to be with her husband in other parts of India. Annette Beveridge, however, kept up her intellectual activities, learning Bengali and Persian. She had many Indian friends, which was unusual at that time, and also gave her child Laetitia a second Sanskrit name, Santamani. Another child, later Lord William Beveridge (born in 1879), was the author of the Beveridge report which ushered in the welfare state in Britain in 1945, and her younger daughter Annette Jeanie, in 1909, married the famous economic historian R.H. Tawney.

Annette and Henry Beveridge publicly disagreed on an important issue. This was the Ilbert Bill (1883) that amended the Criminal Procedure Code to allow Indian magistrates outside the large cities to try Europeans in court. There was an expected outcry against the bill among the local European community, including public meetings and a Ladies' Petition signed by 5,758 European women in India (Sinha 1992:108). The issue of white womanhood dominated the debate, and much was written of the dangers of white women being tried by local magistrates.[9] Liberals such as Henry Beveridge, publicly defended the bill, but writing to the papers under her name, Annette Beveridge opposed it, not on grounds of "pride of race," but "something far deeper" namely "the pride of womanhood." As she wrote,

> In this discussion the ignorant and neglected women of India rise up from their enslavement in evidence against their masters. They testify to the justice of the resentment which English women feel at Mr Ilbert's proposal to subject civilized women to the jurisdiction of men who have done little or nothing to redeem the women of their own races and whose social ideas are still on the outer verge of civilization. (Barr 1976:186)

This was a controversial view coming from a person known for her enlightened attitude to Indians, and whose mixed parties in her home had challenged accepted practice. As Barr writes, "It was an anomalous position and one that brought her into unusual public conflict with her husband" (ibid:187). In London, she was also reprimanded by Elizabeth Manning of the National Indian Association and by other friends. But she continued to defend her position and claimed she had no regrets. In later years her son, writing about his mother said, "she thought India uncivilized, not because she was English, but because she was a woman" (Beveridge 1947:248).

By 1893, Henry Beveridge—still a district Judge—had retired from the civil service, after being ignored for promotion because of his liberal opinions. In retirement in Britain, the Beveridges continued to study Persian, Annette Beveridge translating the Humayun-Nama composed in the 16th century by Gul-badan, one of the Emperor Babur's daughters, and also Babur-Nama in four sections, all of which were published. But although Annette Beveridge spent a full life in family and intellectual pursuits, Henry Beveridge always felt regret about her decision to marry and forego "a more brilliant career" (Barr 1976;188). But she comforted herself with the familiar story that the past was "far away and unregretted," adding that, "if then I might have drawn a few souls with me nearer to the light and have cheered a few workers with fellowship and sympathy," she was now content to live through the lives of her children (ibid:188–9). But during these years there were also educated women who were not content to live through their children, preeminent among them being the foreign women doctors in South Asia whose work and struggles will be considered in the next chapter.

5

THE MEDICINE WOMEN

The Struggles of Western and South Asian Women Doctors

Dr. Branfoot expressed himself as to the folly of educating women to be doctors. He told us that the Government had sent us to him, and he could not prevent us from walking round the wards, but that he was firmly determined that he would not teach us. I suggested that he could not help himself, and that if we were carefully observant of his methods of treatment we should do very well.

—Dr. Mary Scharlieb recalling her experiences as a student (1875) in a Madras hospital (Scharlieb 1924:41)

WOMEN MEDICAL DOCTORS IN SOUTH ASIA WERE DIRECTLY INOLVED IN "women's work for women," and in the many feminist struggles that such work entailed. The medical function of missionary women doctors had been inspired by Christianity and the ideal of spreading the gospel. But hospitals were curing rather than proselytizing institutions, and from the patient's point of view, the religion of the doctors mattered little; nevertheless, the missionary doctors occasionally had to remind themselves that they were not running secular institutions providing religion-free medical treatment. Concern with the health of the "natives" was a significant "burden" of colonial policy. Kipling, using a metaphor of imperialism's civilizing mission, had urged the British to,

Take up the White Man's Burden
The savage wars of peace
Fill full the mouth of Famine,
And bid the sickness cease

Bidding the sickness cease in the colonies became an important issue for women in Britain. When it was known that many women in South Asia refused to consult male doctors, the argument for admitting British and Indian women into medical colleges was strengthened. The line of division between missionary and secular doctors, however, was clear, the latter being interested less in Christianity and more in institutional and social reforms, especially in areas affecting women; these included female medical education, the training of midwives, nurses, and apothecaries, and the establishment of exclusive women's hospitals. In this struggle, women doctors from Britain and the United States were involved in fund-raising, starting dispensaries and women's hospitals and promoting medical training for women.

Women in Victorian Britain campaigned for equal educational opportunities so that they could break into the professions. By the 1840s, training colleges were established to produce teachers and governesses, and women's university colleges were first started in London (Bedford College, 1849) and Cambridge (Girton 1869 and Newnham 1873). The most bitter struggle, however, was that of medical women beginning in 1865 when Elizabeth Garrett Anderson, having passed the examinations held by the Society of Apothecaries, was refused admission to medical colleges in England. In 1870, seven women were admitted as medical students to the University of Edinburgh, but after opposition from a section of the faculty and students (and a court case) they were expelled.[1]

Nevertheless, several British women had qualified as doctors in France, Germany and Switzerland[2], but a bill in parliament to permit their registration in Britain was defeated (Lutzker 1964:44). In the face of this opposition the women students who had been rejected by the Edinburgh university (led by Sophia Jex-Blake, Edith Pechey and others) formed the London School of Medicine for Women in 1874, which enrolled twenty-three students in its first year, with visiting male lecturers from other faculties. Parliament finally passed legislation in 1876 that removed restrictions on medical education for women. In October 1877, Dr Edith Pechey gave the inaugural lecture, urging women students not to be tempted by "a large practice with a large income," but instead to be inspired by a "desire of leaving a world better and richer and wiser for your presence in it." She urged them to "do what in you lies...to further the prevention and cure of disease" (Lutzker 1973:60). Pechey herself and some of the early women doctors were to work in India.

This area of social reform in South Asia was also to attract the attention of

Western women doctors who campaigned especially against the horrors of child marriage and premature childbirth, which they came across in the course of their medical work in India. Some women doctors who worked in India and Sri Lanka were the products of the bitter struggle for higher education in the West and were also linked to the feminist suffrage struggles of the early 20th century. The burden of women doctors was often an ideological one, not merely concerned with day to day work in hospitals, but also with a process of social reform and modernization, bringing many ideas of "women's rights" into their work with Indian and Sri Lankan women. And because women doctors were involved in saving lives rather than souls, the local non-Christian population regarded them with great affection and respect. They were the "noble" foreigners of colonial society.

The early missionaries, though medically unqualified, had often provided some basic medical services to their converts and other locals. Medical attention, it was also felt, would be an important means for missionaries to get across to non-Christians. Female missionaries also had the added advantage of access to females, many of whom were reluctant to consult male physicians. Missionaries who worked in zenanas "saw women sinking into chronic ill-health and fatal disease unrelieved, but when advised to go to the hospital, holding up their hands with horror at the idea of consulting a man" (Balfour and Young 1929:14). Missionaries began to equip themselves with some medical knowledge, often using their vacations in the West to get hospital training. In a period before women had access to medical education in Europe and the United States, some institutions in the West gave short courses in medicine and midwifery to missionaries (ibid:14). Missionary women were never lacking in nerve. Fired by religious zeal, they expanded their medical work; "some bold spirits acquired pocket-cases and performed minor operations," and local Bible women were trained "as rough and ready assistants with girls from Christian schools and orphanages to help them." The medical work of a mission, started as a "side issue," sometimes became "the main purpose of the mission station, enjoying great success and resulting in the development of important hospitals" (ibid:15).

The first qualified woman doctor who came to India from the United States was Clara Swain (1834–1910), an MD from Pennsylvania who belonged to the Methodist Women's Foreign Missionary Society. Dr. Swain first trained fourteen girls from the mission orphanages as medical assistants. The Nawab of Rampur donated a site and a hospital was built, headed by Dr. Swain from 1874 to 1885. From 1885 to 1895 she was appointed physician to the Rani of Khetri and to women of the court; she accepted "on the understanding that she was allowed to carry on Christian work." This consisted of opening a dispensary and girls' school run by Miss Pannell, the only other Western woman in the state. Like many in similar positions, they "led very lonely lives, for which they were compensated," it was said, "by the opportunity of bringing lessons of the New Testament home to the Rani and others" (ibid:17). Dr. Swain left India in 1895, returning in 1906 for the jubilee of the Methodist Mission.[3]

An early intervention in the field of women's health was the training of midwives (dhais). In 1866, Dr. Aitchison, a Civil Surgeon started a class for dhais in Amritsar, which by the 1880's, was transformed into the Amritsar Dhais' School run by Miss Hewlett of the Zenana Missionary Society of the Church of England, who had come to India in 1877. She introduced new methods to local dhais and other Indian women to assist in hospitals run by missionaries (ibid:13, 17): the same society in 1880 sent out its first qualified woman doctor, Fanny Butler, who worked in Jhabhalpur, and in 1887 did pioneer medical work among Kashmiri women (ibid:18). Perhaps the most important of the early British women medical missionaries was Elizabeth Bielby, who arrived in India in 1875 with some basic medical training and opened a dispensary and a small hospital in Lucknow for the Zenana Missionary Society. Here she found that the great problems were ignorance and prejudice among women themselves, the lack of proper medical facilities and the absence of official concern (ibid:20).[4] Bielby was in charge of the Lady Aitchison Hospital for women in Lahore where she worked for fifteen years; she later continued in private practice, retiring in 1927 after fifty-two years in India (ibid:22).[5]

Missionary activity often ran in families, and this was true for several generations of the famous Scudder family who founded a notable dynasty of medical missionaries.[6] The pioneer was Dr. John Scudder whose son Dr. John Scudder, Jr. qualified in medicine and theology at Rutgers in New Jersey. He and his wife, Sophia, arrived for missionary work in South India in 1861 and founded the hospital of Vellore. Their daughter Ida followed the family tradition and became one of the leading women doctors in India. She was born in India in 1870, and in 1880 came to the United States for her education in Massachussetts at the Northfield Seminary for Girls. She returned to South India where she came across cases of women in childbirth who had died because male doctors were not permitted to intervene. She was asked to help in such a case, but being untrained, was unable to do so.[7] In 1895 Ida Scudder studied at the Women's Medical College of Philadelphia, and Cornell University. She then did fund-raising on behalf of the Women's Auxilary for a women's hospital in India, luckily obtaining a large donation of $10,000 from a banker named Schell (Jeffery 1938:59).[8] With another missionary, Annie Hancock, Ida Scudder came back to India in 1900 and settled in Vellore. By 1902 the Women's Hospital was completed, and in 1907 a nurses training school was begun, followed by a Women's Medical College in 1918. The Vellore group of hospitals was among the most advanced in India. Dr. Scudder was honored for her work by the

Dr. Ida Scudder visited by Gandhi. (From M.P. Jeffrey (1938), *Dr. Ida: India*; Schlesinger Library, Radcliffe College.)

British government, by American colleges, and by Mahatma Gandhi, who visited her in 1928 (ibid:113).

MEDICAL EDUCATION OF WOMEN IN SOUTH ASIA

By the 1870s there was an increasing demand in India for women doctors, foreign or local; but as in Britain, the medical profession in India refused to admit women students into the medical faculties. The urgent need for women doctors, however, led to successful pressures for medical training for women in India. In this field, Madras State led the way, the first developments being linked to the career of Mary Scharlieb, née Bird (1845–1930), the daughter of a Manchester merchant. She came to India in 1866 as the wife of a British lawyer, William Scharlieb, and her interest in medicine arose when she reviewed a work on medical jurisprudence in a law journal.[9] She also learned, through her contacts with Indians, of their health problems.[10] Being convinced that "some European women ought to qualify themselves," she started reading Churchill's *Midwifery,* but realized that a practical training was necessary. Dr. Cockerill of Madras was against Mary Scharlieb's proposal that she receive training as a midwife.[11] And in order to discourage her, he showed her a woman suffering from "the worst case of confluent smallpox he had ever seen" and asked if she would attend her. Scharlieb responded positively to such

Dr. Mary Scharlieb (From Mary Scharlieb (1924), *Reminiscences*, Schlesinger Library, Radcliffe College.)

questions, and received a year's training in midwifery at the hospital.[12] (Scharlieb 1924:32) Scharlieb put forward a scheme for medical training for selected women; in spite of some opposition, she and three other women made a historic breakthrough by being admitted to the Madras Medical College in 1875. They followed the lectures along with male students and did clinical work in the women's hospital under Dr. Branfoot, who was against women becoming doctors.[13] (ibid:41)

It is interesting that the opposition Mary Scharlieb encountered among male doctors was sometimes overcome when the case was made that women in India preferred to have women doctors. The Surgeon at Guy's Hospital, London (Dr. Bryant) whom Scharlieb met, said, "I entirely disapprove of women becoming doctors and will do nothing to further your wishes"; but after an "explanation of the situation" he changed his opinion "at any rate so far as it concerned the provision of women doctors for India" (ibid:48). Mary

Scharlieb entered the London School of Medicine for Women and in 1882 was awarded the M.B.B.S. with honors, a gold medal and a scholarship in obstetrics. She did post-graduate work in Vienna and returned in 1883 to Madras. Her endeavors had attracted attention, and before she left for India, Queen Victoria met her and showed interest in the work of women doctors there. In Madras, Dr. Scharlieb started a private practice, but feeling the need for a hospital, she started a fund, with support from both Indians and British officials, for a women's hospital named after Queen Victoria. She was in charge of this hospital and was also the first woman medical lecturer in India, teaching gynecology and obstetrics at the University of Madras. She returned to Britain in 1887 for health reasons. The struggle for medical education continued; in 1881–2 six more women in Madras (British, Anglo-Indian and Indian) were admitted for the LMS degree, making Madras State the fore-runner of female medical education.

DR. ANANDIBAI JOSHI——PIONEER OF MEDICAL STUDIES ABROAD

By the early 1880s, Indian women started to benefit from the opening of medical studies to women in Europe and the United States, the first being Anandibai Joshi (1865–1887), born in Pune to a Chitpavan Brahmin family. She was married (according to custom) when she was nine years old. In 1883, at age eighteen, she went to the United States (with her husband) and studied medicine at the Women's Medical College of Pennsylvania in Philadelphia where she graduated in medicine in 1886. While studying, she lived in the home of Dr. Rachel Bodley, Dean of the Women's Medical College. Pandita Ramabai came to Philadelphia for her graduation. Ramabai had come under the influence of missionaries and had converted, but Anandibai (a relative) remained a devout Hindu, defending child marriage as a "national custom" and strictly observing caste rules in eating, having claimed that "I will go [to America] as a Hindu, and come back and live among my people as a Hindu" (Ramabai 1887:iv).

Although she broke caste taboos by crossing the seas and took the bold step of studying medicine, the fact that she remained a Hindu made her a hero among orthodox circles. The *Kesari*, a journal of the traditionalists wrote:

> It is indeed wonderful that a Brahman lady has proved to the world that the great qualities—perseverance, unselfishness, undaunted courage and an eager desire to serve one's country—do exist in the so-called weaker sex. (ibid:v–vi)

In 1886, Anandibai was appointed Physician-in-Charge of the women's ward of the Albert Edward Hospital in Kolhapur. But by then she was ill with tuberculosis and died in Pune in 1887. An Indian journal, on her death, remarked, "although Anandibai was so young, her perseverance…and devotion to her husband were unparallelled" adding that "we think it will be long before we shall again see a woman like her in this country…. Dr Joshee is worthy of a high place on the roll of historic women who have striven to serve and to elevate their native land" (ibid:vi).

The other Indian woman pioneer was Annie Jaganathan, who began her medical studies in Madras in 1883 and then joined the Edinburgh School of Medicine for Women in 1888. In 1892, she qualified and returned to work at the Cama Hospital, but also died of tuberculosis in 1894 (Balfour & Young 1929:23). Numbers of Indian and Sri Lankan women in the early 20th century qualified at home and abroad as doctors, one notable instance being the case of Dr. Rukmabai, whose dramatic story is discussed in the following pages, and is linked to the career of Dr. Edith Pechey.

EDITH PECHEY IN INDIA

Edith Pechey (1845–1908) was one of the pioneers in the struggle for women's medical studies and women's rights in Britain and India. Her father was a Baptist minister who had an M.A. from Edinburgh and her mother had studied Greek. This background of learning and non-conformism was conducive to a life of dedicated work. As discussed earlier, Pechey had been in the campaign for women to enter the male-dominated medical faculties and hospitals.[14] The 1880s was a period of increased consciousness among Indians and British about the medical needs of Indian women. Criticism of the lack of medical facilities for women and prevalent harmful practices had already been made by Indians themselves.[15] Along with philanthropic Indians, the "Medical Women for India Fund" was launched in 1883 to bring women doctors from Europe to start a women's hospital. A major achievement occurred when an Indian Parsi businessman, Pestonji Hormusji Cama, financed the building of a hospital for women and children in Bombay, to be run entirely by women doctors, with the government providing the site and financing the maintenance of the facility. Edith Pechey was appointed senior medical officer, but until the hospital was completed she did private practice and worked in a dispensary started with a donation of Rs.20,000, by another Bombay businessman, Jaffer Sulleiman. In the first year, the women's dispensary had nearly 10,000 patients (Lutzker 1973:107).

Pechey also succeeded, in the face of some official oppositon, in starting a training school for nurses. She worked in the Cama Hospital until 1894, and after retirement continued to do private practice in Bombay. In 1891 she founded the Pechey-Phipson Sanatorium, 120 miles north of Bombay, with cottage units where "families without means of escaping from the insufferable Bombay summer were invited to come for a month's stay." Convalescent

Pioneer Women Doctors in India: top left, Dr. Edith Pechey; right, Dr. Elizabeth Bielby; middle, Dr. Clara Swain; bottom left, Dr. Annie Jaganathan; right, Dr. Rukhmabai. (From M. Balfour and R. Young (1929), *The Work of Medical Women in India*; Schlesinger Library, Radcliffe College.)

women and children were "encouraged to take advantage of a health-renewing sojourn at rent free, and only nominal cost" (Lutzker 1964:65). During the 1896 epidemic of plague and cholera, Pechey came out of retirement to work in Bombay hospitals and visit homes (ibid:66). Edith Pechey was not only involved directly in medical work but was also an active social reformer and fighter for women's social enfranchisement.

THE STRUGGLE FOR SOCIAL REFORM

The work by women doctors in India in the 1880s coincided with a period of increasing concern by reformers for the eradication of social evils affecting women, such as sati, enforced widowhood, polygamy and child marriage. The Western women doctors petitioned the Viceroy on the dire physical consequences of child marriage and childbirth in young girls, and pleaded for intervention to raise the age of consent (Mayo 1927:411–12). As medical education for women expanded—there being by 1889 over 220 female medical students in India—social issues came to the fore. Edith Pechey, for example, spoke out on the issue of child marriage in public. In 1890, during the "age of consent" agitation in India, she gave a public lecture on the subject.[16] She quoted from medical texts to prove that early marriage was injurious to women and children. Warning the Indians of physical degeneration, she said, "For centuries you have been children of children—and there is no surer way of becoming servants of servants"; she further claimed "all cruel customs relating to woman have been imposed upon her under the guise of religion" and stated that slavery and the burning of witches in Europe had been defended on religious grounds. She pleaded for freedom of choice in marriage, arguing that such marriages produced better children. She predicted that India would degenerate if attention was not paid to social reform, adding that if "England should one day have to retire from India" the country would "fall an easy prey to the first comer...you will be hewers of wood and drawers of water to any robust race who are the progeny of healthy adult men and women." The talk was well received by the Indian audience, one of whom had it translated into twenty Indian languages and "distributed in hundreds of thousands of copies throughout India" (Lutzker 1973:199).

Edith Pechey also campaigned for a government department for medical women that could supply staff "whenever native enterprise and liberality provided a suitable hospital and dispensary for women." She also fought for equal pay and pensions for women in the medical services and for the training of more local women as doctors, remarking that this would "help toward putting a stop to the very early marriages which are such a bane to the nation from every point of view" (ibid:88). In a period of social segregation between the British and Indians, Edith Pechey and her husband Herbert Phipson were also exceptional in their efforts to mix with Indians and join with them in efforts for social reform. Pechey also campaigned for female education in India, speaking frequently in public on the need for girls' schools. In a speech to the Alexandra Native Girls English Institution in Bombay, she stressed, "the paramount importance, the binding duty, of a perfect system of education for women" and made a special appeal to the women of India.[17] (ibid:186)

On her retirement in 1905, Edith Pechey traveled to Canada, Australia and

New Zealand where her time was "crowded with engagements." She was brought into contact with issues of "women's suffrage, medicine and education" (Lutzker 1964:66). The question of female suffrage occupied her last years. In 1906, she attended the International Conference of the Women's Suffrage Alliance in Copenhagen on behalf of the Leeds Women's Suffrage Association. Her last public appearance was in 1907, when, along with three other leading suffragists, she headed a demonstration in London organized by the Central Society for Women's Suffrage. They campaigned for funds and support for women's suffrage. She died in 1908 before the suffrage movement reached its peak. Pechey had fought many feminist battles—for women's medical studies, equal pay for women doctors and women's suffrage. She had worked for many years in hospitals in India and was at the forefront of campaigns for social reform. In these years perhaps the most sensational case in which Pechey was involved was that of Rukhmabai, which raised several fundamental issues of women's rights.

THE RUKHMABAI CASE——FROM CHILD MARRIAGE TO MEDICAL STUDIES

One dramatic instance that highlighted the joint struggle by South Asian and British medical women was that of Rukhmabai, the child bride who not only resisted forced married life but went on to qualify as a doctor in London. The case raised controversial issues of child marriage and female education and developed into a bitter tussle between Indian reformers, British women doctors and enlightened officials on the one side, and Indian orthodoxy and conservative British officialdom on the other.

Rukhmabai came from an affluent, high-caste family; after her father's death, her mother, who was seventeen, broke the custom that widows should not remarry, by marrying a doctor of the Grant Medical College. Rukhmabai was legally under the guardianship of her mother's father who influenced her mother and got Rukhmabai married at eleven to Dadaji Bhikaji, nineteen. However, Rukhmabai did not leave home, and during this time, she read her stepfather's books, visited the American Mission House and attended zenana parties given by the Governor's wife, where she met Dr. Edith Pechey. At seventeen, when Rukhmabai refused to live with her husband, he went to court for the "restoration of conjugal rights." In 1885, Justice Pinhey gave a judgment in favour of Rukhmabai (Lutzker 1973; 199–200).[18]

While the anti-reformists launched a campaign against this judgement, a Rukhmabai Defence Committee was formed to collect funds for the case. Opponents, however, alleged that this was an attempt to "shake the foundation upon which the family life of the Hindus rests" (ibid:203). The nationalist leader Tilak condemned Rukhmabai's refusal to live with her husband as an attempt to sow discontent in Hindu family life (Pradhan & Bhagwat 1959:50).[19] On appeal, in 1886, the Chief Justice sent the case back for retrial, but Rukhmabai lost and was ordered to live with her husband or undergo six months imprisonment for contempt of court. This judgment caused a furor among the reformers and among sections of the British community.[20] The Rukhmabai case thus raised the whole issue of British justice in a colonial situation where the authorities sometimes hesitated to interfere with local custom. Rukhmabai herself was very critical of the stand taken, and, in a letter to Pandita Ramabai said:

> Are we not living under the impartial British government, which boasts of giving equal justice to all, and are we not ruled by the Queen-Empress Victoria, herself a woman? (Ramabai 1901:92)

Both Rukhmabai and Ramabai were perceptive and realistic not only in their analysis of the situation of women, but also in their understanding of the foreign rulers' reluctance to interfere in local law. As Rukhmabai wrote:

> *There is no hope for women in India; whether they be under Hindu rule or British rule;* some are of the opinion that my case so cruelly decided, may bring about a better condition for woman by turning public opinion in her favour, but I fear it will be otherwise. The hard-hearted mothers-in-law will now be greatly strengthened, and will induce their sons, who...have been slow to enforce the conjugal rights to sue their wives in the British Courts, since they are now fully assured that under no circumstances can the British government act adversely to the Hindu law." (ibid:92, emphasis added)

Ramabai also commented sharply on the Rukhmabai case and used the occasion to condemn Hindu law while significantly drawing attention to this interesting instance of "male bonding" between the British and Indians:

> We are not at all surprised at this decision. Our only wonder is that a defenseless woman like Rukhmabai dared to raise her voice in the face of the powerful Hindu law, the mighty British government, the one hundred and twenty nine million men and the three hundred and thirty million gods of the Hindus, *all these having conspired together to crush her into nothingness.* We cannot blame the English govenment for not defending a helpless woman; *it is only fulfilling its agreement made with the male population of India.* (ibid:93, emphasis added)

The case became international news and even the distinguished Orientalist, Professor Max Müller, wrote a letter on this subject to the *London Times,* referring to the "sale and so-called marriage of children" and the punishment of those who "revolt against this degrading slavery"[21] (Lutzker 1973:206). Rukhmabai appealed to the Privy Council and the case became an international cause célèbre. In the face of this publicity, a settlement was reached by the husband not to continue litigation. In all this tumultuous period and later, Rukhmabai voiced her appreciation of Pechey's intervention. "When my trials began in 1884," wrote Rukhmabai, "Dr. Pechey took up my cause in real earnest, and worked very hard in interesting other people to form a committee in my defence.... She was my mainstay for sympathy and support all through the four long weary years of my trials, and she constantly urged me to proceed to England and study medicine." While Rukhmabai was keen on studying, her mother and grandfather, as good Hindus, were reluctant for her to cross the "black waters." It seems that Pechey's "tact and perseverance" overcame this obstacle (ibid:207–8).

Pechey also raised funds for Rukhmabai's further studies in London through Eva McLaren, a British suffragist. Rukhmabai did an intensive English language course, passed the Society of Apothecaries examination and graduated at the London School of Medicine. She also obtained qualifications in Edinburgh, Glasgow and Brussels (ibid:207). After Rukhmabai finished her studies in 1894, she obtained a position as Medical Officer at Surat in West India. The links between Pechey and Rukhmabai continued in later years and Rukhmabai recollected that when she devised a series of lectures for the women of Surat, Pechey "spared no trouble in writing to friends and collecting funds for my object," adding that "she was the great champion of women, and hundreds of grateful women in India can testify to her kind acts for their welfare" (ibid:208). Rukhmabai spent thirty-five years as chief medical officer in Surat and Rajkot Hospitals, living in Bombay after retirement, supporting movements of social reform and writing on the harmful effects of women's seclusion (parda). She retired in 1930 and died in 1955, aged ninety-one (ibid:209).

DR. MARY RUTNAM IN SRI LANKA

Like Edith Pechey, Sri Lanka too had an outstanding reformist woman doctor in Mary Rutnam. Following the Indian example, the Medical College in Colombo was opened to women in 1892 and local women also went abroad for medical studies from 1899 onward. Some foreign women doctors were in government service and in missionary hospitals, among them a Canadian from Toronto, Mary Rutnam née Irwin (1873–1962). She married a Tamil Christian, S.C.K. Rutnam, who was studying philosophy at Princeton University in the United States. Mary Rutnam came to Sri Lanka in 1897 as a missionary doctor, but her marriage was opposed by the missionaries and she left them to join government service and later to do private practice.

Dr. Rutnam not only worked in the field of gynecology all her life but also pioneered numerous women's groups including the Ceylon Women's Union (1904), the Tamil Women's Union (1909), the Lanka Mahila Samiti (1931), based on the Canadian Women's Institutes for rural women, and the Women's Franchise Union (1927), which spearheaded the movement for women's suffrage in Sri Lanka in defiance of conservative opinion. Her campaigns for maternal healthcare, childcare, hospital facilities for women, milk bars, female prisoner's rights, temperance and family planning were carried out through the organizations she had created. Mary Rutnam became a household word in the country; her school texts on health and hygiene were widely used and translated; in 1937 she was elected the first woman member of the Colombo Municipal Council, and was the recipient of honors and awards, locally and internationally (Jayawardena 1993).

THE FUND-RAISERS

While Indian opinion and British officials agreed in principle about the need for women doctors in India, government funds were subject to bureaucratic restrictions and were often not available for "special interests" such as women's medical training and facilities. There was thus a need for private funding for schemes to benefit women, and serious attempts were made from the 1880s onward to raise funds in Britain and India for such work. In Britian, the initiative seems to have come from the highest quarters. Dr. Elizabeth Bielby and Dr. Mary Scharlieb had met Queen Victoria and had spoken of the medical needs of Indian women, and when Lord Dufferin was appointed the Viceroy in 1883, the Queen asked Lady Dufferin to look into the question.

Lady Dufferin started to mobilize a network of British women in India, writing to the wives of the Governors of the various provinces, and in 1885 she inaugurated the National Association to Supply Female Medical Aid to the Women of India, known popularly as the Dufferin Fund. The objectives were to open women's hospitals staffed by women doctors from Britain and to train Indian women as doctors (Balfour and Young 1929:5–6). In the three years of Lady Dufferin's stay in India, around Rs.700,000 was collected locally, of which provincial branches and sub-branches collected Rs.300,000; funds were also collected in Britain. During this period five women doctors recruited from Britain and six from India were employed in eight cities in India. The branch and local associations also had their own activities. The Bombay section, for example, starting a nurses training school attached to the Cama Hospital, and other branches either built or supported hospitals or paid the salaries of women hospital assistants or midwives (ibid:37).

Another important development was the formation, in 1907, of the Association of Medical Women in India, with a branch in Britain. It's secretary was Dr. Emma Slater (one of the early women doctors in Bombay) who took "an active part in rousing public opinion in England on the need for proper organization of women's medical work in India." In 1910 a deputation of women doctors (Mary Scharlieb, May Thorne, Annette Benson and Emma Slater) met Lord Morley, Secretary of State for India, to explain the weaknesses of the Dufferin Fund. They gave him a scheme for a properly organized women's medical service. Although the government thought this scheme was impractical, the issue received publicity in the press, which highlighted the suffering of Indian women and the failure, in this respect, of the government of India. In 1912, a deputation of fifty-four persons brought the question again to the Secretary of State for India (Lord Crewe), Mary Scharlieb presented the case, and Sir Fredrick Lely, a former official in India, spoke of 119 million women in British India, "of whom roughly two thirds objected to treatment by men doctors" and also urged the need for Indian women to study medicine with women teachers (ibid:42–48).

As a result of this agitation, in 1913 the government announced a subsidy of £10,000 a year to the Dufferin Fund; and in 1914 a Women's Medical Service was established, giving women salary increases, permanency of service, a provident fund, regular home leave and study leave, the right to full professional control of the hospital and employment by the Central Committee of the Dufferin Fund (ibid:47–52). The enthusiasm of prominent individuals continued to be an important factor: for example, Lady Willingdon, President of the Bombay branch of the Dufferin Fund, pioneered large scale maternity and child welfare work in 1912; Lady Chelmsford continued this interest and formed an All-India League for Maternity and Child Welfare in 1920. Lady Reading became the Fund's President in 1921 and through her efforts a new women's section (the Dufferin Block) of the Ripon Hospital, run by a woman doctor, was opened in Simla, and by 1924 there was a separate hospital for women, the Lady Reading Hospital (ibid:62). A donation for a women's medical college was made by the Maharajah of Kotah, resulting in the opening in 1915 of the Lady Hardinge Medical College for Women in Delhi with teaching and administrative buildings, well-equipped library and laboratories, residential hostels, a students' common room and recreation grounds. Attached was a modern hospital with all departments, and a nurses hostel. This College gave a seven year medical training to women students from all parts of India (ibid:118–19).

Thus, in the forty years between the pioneer efforts of the Madras group and the full-fledged Delhi Women's Medical College, important strides had been made in promoting the training of women doctors. This movement had parallel links with the British women doctors' long and bitterly fought battles for acceptance, which were a crucial part of the movement for women's liberation in both India and Britain. The clamor for social reform however continued, with the controversy about child marriage becoming a site of contention between Indians and foreigners during a period of nationalist upsurge. This is discussed in the next chapter.

6

"CHILDREN OF CHILDREN"

The Child Marriage Controversies and India

And with Kipling goes Katherine Mayo and that whole crowd of foreign missionaries from civilized countries that have tried to portray India to the Indians.

—D.F. Karaka (1938), *I Go West* (1945:14)

Where suffering and injustices affecting women are concerned, I as an old suffragist cannot remember or bother about national distinction.

—Eleanor Rathbone, *Child Marriage: The Indian Minotaur* (1934:118)

THE AGE OF CONSENT AND CHILD MARRIAGE

Agitation on social problems in India went back to the days of the Baptist William Carey in the late 18th century and Rammohan Roy in the early 19th century, but with the awakening of a consciousness of national identity in India, issues of social and political reform came to the fore from the late 19th century onward. Indian nationalists argued that to be politically credible, social reform of unacceptable practices was necessary, while the British often found an excuse for the continuation of imperial rule in the "social evils" prevalent in India. Long before the movement for "Home Rule" there was agitation for social reforms relating to marriage, sexuality and the family. These became extremely contentious issues between ruler and ruled, and between the ruled themselves. And child marriage was the scandal that raised the most controversy.

In the late 19th century, sections of the British press kept up the campaign for reform, and articles depicting the plight of Indian child brides and widows increased concern about these issues.[1] The continuous pressure by social reformers on child marrige led to legislation in India in 1891, raising the age of consent to sexual intercourse for a female from the age of ten to twelve years, making the breach a criminal offense punishable by law. The bitter controversy over this legislation among Indians raised several crucial issues. The Parsi reformer Behramji Merwanji Malabari, submitted a memorandum entitled, "Notes on Infant Marriage and Enforced Widowhood" and called upon the government to raise the age of consent. And in his journal, *The Indian Spectator*, Malabari frequently discussed the treatment of women and children in India. In 1890, on a visit to Britain, he wrote an "Appeal on Behalf of the Daughters of India" that led to further debates in Britain on Indian family life (Farquhar 1915:87). Similarly, one of India's leading social reformers, M.G. Ranade (1842–1901), a high court judge in Bombay, also took up the issue. He had succeeded in bringing together social reformers from all parts of India into a National Social Conference that met annually from 1887 to 1895 as part of the Indian National Congress sessions. On these occasions, Ranade gave the keynote speech summarizing India's progress in social reform during the year (Wolpert 1962:39). As a liberal reformer, Ranade advocated changes involving child marriage, widow remarriage and female education; while these were issues on which many intellectuals agreed, there were differences of opinion on the way changes were to be made. Serious clashes also occurred between liberals and social conservatives over the role of the British government and Ranade's support of legislative intervention "stirred a hornet's nest of orthodox opposition" (ibid:45).

Leading the opposition was Bal Gangadhar Tilak (1856–1920), a Chitpavan Brahmin who combined extremism in politics with orthodoxy on questions of social reform. Tilak's brand of revivalist Hindu nationalism was to prove effective in mobilizing public opinion.[2] The appeal to mass sentiment enabled him to combine nationalist political demands with religious and populist fervor. Radicalism and social reaction proved to be a heady and potent mixture, and Tilak's political rhetoric made him a hero to those who found the liberalism of the social reformers politically tame. Tilak clashed with important reformers on the "Age of Consent" issue and continuously attacked state interference in social questions. Chatterjee notes that "the refusal of nationalism to make the women's question an issue of political negotiation with the colonial state" was due to the fact that it seemed to "deny the ability of the nation to act for itself even in a domain where it was sovereign" (1993:132). In contrast to Tilak, however, M.G. Ranade argued that,

> Wherever there is a large amount of unredressed evil suffered by a people who cannot adopt their own remedy, the state has a function to regulate and minimise the evil.... The regulation of marriageable age has in all countries...been a part of its national jurisprudence. (Wolpert 1962:48)

Replying to criticisms of foreign interference, Ranade claimed that social reform did not originate with foreign rulers who had "no interest to move of their own accord" and who would prefer to "let us remain as we are, disorganised and demoralised, stunted and deformed, with the curse of folly and wickedness paralysing all the...vital energies of our social body." He noted that social evils had "grown as excrescences upon the healthy system of ancient Hindu society" and could only be checked by "the strong arm of law" (ibid:49). Dr R.G. Bhandarkar, an outspoken social reformer and supporter of Ramabai, was also involved in acrimonious debates with Tilak. In "A Note on the Age of Marriage and its Consummation according to Hindu Religious Law" Bhandarkar claimed that post-puberty marriages, deferment of consummation for three years after puberty and postponement of childbirth until after sixteen years of age were compatible with the sacred laws. Bhandarkar was more daring than other reformers, often criticizing Ranade for his caution. He described Indian women as being "on a level with cattle" and sharply attacked educated men who married young girls of nine or ten, referring to such events as "cases of female human sacrifice" (American Ramabai Association 1901:18).[3]

The agitation over the Age of Consent Bill did not end in 1891, but became a perennial topic for social reformers, both local and foreign. Ramabai's book on child widows, went into numerous editions in the United States, Britain and Australia, and kept the issue alive. Cornelia Sorabji, (1866–1954) a Parsi from Bombay whose family had converted to Christianity, also wrote about these issues. She had graduated from Somerville College, Oxford and was called to the Bar in London, the first Indian woman to achieve such success. As a result, she became socially known in Britain and met the Queen, Gladstone, Florence Nightingale and numerous scholars such as Jowett and Max Müller. Sorabji returned to India in 1894 and took up legal work, appearing often in cases for Muslim women. In 1904 she was given a government appointment under the Court of Wards Act, which dealt with the property of minor heirs (Sorabji 1934:124). Her work brought her into contact with women and children and she became concerned with the issues of widows and child marriage. Her book *Between the Twilights* (1908) described many of the cases she came across in her legal and social work, for example, the murder of a child widow by her mother to save her from the tortures of widowhood (Sorabji 1908:163–64). Sorabji's book and her later writings were severely criticized by Indians, but were much quoted by missionaries and Western critics of Indian society.

AMY CARMICHAEL EXPOSES "DARK DEEDS IN A DARK LAND"

The issues of social evils affecting Indian women and children continued to be taken up in a bold way by missionary women. One of the most controversial of such foreign women who caused a stir among fellow missionaries was Amy Wilson Carmichael (1867–1951). She was born in Ireland to a middle-class Presbyterian family, educated in Yorkshire at a Methodist boarding school, where she heard talks given by missionaries. After being active in Christian circles, in 1893, Carmichael went as a missionary to Japan and subsequently to Sri Lanka and South India, where she lived until her death without returning to Britain. In India she was revolted by Hinduism as well as by the fashionable and nominal Christianity of the British residents; she described the "depressingly English" Anglican church in Ootacamund, which the Governor of Madras attended in frock coat and top hat accompanied by the ladies, but where Indians were only allowed in the back pews. She spoke out openly that she would rather be in a mud hut among the people, than live like the English (Elliot 1987:122). Contrary to practice, Amy Carmichael took to wearing a sari which was frowned upon by both British residents and missionaries; she also scorned any adornment or jewelery. Carmichael's attitudes to Hinduism also caused problems; by the 1890s many missionaries were trying to project a more liberal Christianity, which did not totally condemn other religions, and they were more cautious in using terms like "heathen." Amy Carmichael, however, spoke like an old-style missionary and wrote of the "dark deeds of this dark land" which for her involved mainly the sufferings of women (ibid:138). To her, the Indian gods, "as depicted by their aggressive or seductive images," were satanic, and they who made them were "like unto them." Hinduism was, in Carmichael's words, "slime, filth, sin." She adds that "books that whitewash Hinduism are turned out by the dozen now, and it's terribly unfashionable to feel as we do" (ibid:243).

Amy Carmichael worked in villages and small towns of South India, with a "band" of converts travelling in a bullock cart, visiting houses and preaching the Bible. Her experiences on these journeys provided the material for her book *Things as They Are* (1903) published in London. It created such a stir in Britain and India that there were six reprints by 1906. Carmichael had given details of caste, child marriage, ill-treatment of widows, and temple prostitution (devadasis), which shocked the readers, especially since she resorted to a sensational type of writing.[4] Some of the "horrors" and unthinkable things referred to by Carmichael led to doubts about their veracity and in subsequent editions of the book, the publishers included an endorsement of its contents by well-known Christians, including Pandita Ramabai, who wrote, "I can honestly corroborate everything said."[5]

Carmichael's center of activity was Dohnavur (Thirunelveli) where she started a refuge for children and babies "in peril," which included girls dedicated to temples and boys sold to temples to become musicians or adopted for "infamous purposes" (ibid:244). But during the early phase of Carmichael's work, there was a fairly strong "Get-Amy Carmichael-out-of-India" movement among missionaries and Indian Christians. She was accused of "going native," doing demeaning work, opposing marriage and using the issue of temple children as a stunt (ibid:198-201). Some of the young women rescued from temples were converted to Christianity and grew up in Dohnavur, calling Carmichael "amma" (mother); "We shaped ourselves into a group" wrote Carmichael and formed the "Sisters of the Common Life" consisting of those who worked with their hands, concentrating on "a pure and godly life" (ibid:240). Carmichael continued to write about her experiences and her books became known to a general public. In later years (1927) she was quoted by Katherine Mayo, who caused an even greater uproar than Carmichael. As Mayo wrote on child marriage:

> Anyone curious as to the fierceness with which it would be defended by the people…in the name of religion…will find answers in the extra-ordinary work and in the all-too-reticent books of Miss Amy Wilson-Carmichael. (Mayo 1927:48)

KATHERINE MAYO "RAKING MUCK"

In July 1927, Katherine Mayo published *Mother India*, which created such a sensation that it went into nine reprints in one year (1927–28) and forty-two by 1937. Thirty years after its publication, A.M. Rosenthal, in discussing the scandal the book caused, summarized the contents as follows:

> India is a country whose people are self-cursed. Their religion is degrading, their society leads them into ways of life even more degrading mentally, morally, socially and economically. Too-early marriage…has created an indolent, weakened, ineffectual people. Indians are mentally sterile, as well as bodily feeble and often sexually impotent. (Rosenthal 1957)

India's backwardness was attributed to social evils, which included "Temple prostitution, infanticide, child marriage, bitter isolation for widows, untouchability, ignorance, cow worship (and) a cow-crippled economy," as well as "cruelty and callousness, disease and a layer of filth over the country" (ibid).

Hindu culture was full of sexually explicit themes and sexual symbols. All the woes of the Hindu, "material and spiritual poverty, sickness, ignorance, political minority, melancholy, ineffectiveness," she argued, had a "rock-bottom physical base," namely, his "manner of getting into the world and his sex-life thence forward" (Mayo:1927:22). It was this "physical base" which preoccupied Mayo, and her book was full of accounts of the tortures of child marriage and early motherhood and horrifying childbirth and child-rearing practices. All these lurid and graphic accounts caused shock waves and accounted for both the rapid sales of the book and the outrage among Indian leaders and their Western friends. But Mayo was not the first to write about these topics; she was one of a line of women and men, both Western and Indian who had exposed social evils. Her predecessors among women, as we have noted, included Ramabai, Cornelia Sorabji and Amy Carmichael.

Katherine Mayo (1867–1940) was the daughter of James Henry Mayo and Harriet Ingraham, both from distinguished New England families. By 1892 she had begun her career as a writer for journals such as *Life* and *Atlantic Monthly*, and also became a research assistant for Osward Garrison Villard of the *New York Evening Post*. In 1910 she met an orphaned heiress, M. Moyca Newell; they traveled the world together collecting material for Mayo's books and built a house in Bedford Hills, New York, where Mayo lived until her death in 1940. Mayo was a strong proponent of British and American imperialism and her early writings show deeply-held beliefs in the Anglo-Saxon civilizing mission to bring law and order to the poor and the colonized. She was also concerned about the sexual exploitation of women,[6] and first achieved fame through her writings on the condition of women in the Philippines.[7] The book attracted the attention not only of Americans who opposed independence for the Philippines, but also of the British. In October 1925, when Mayo was in Britain to discuss a book on India, the Foreign Office and India Office in London gave her introductions to high officials in India. She visited India from December 1925 to early 1926 and in 1927 *Mother India*, which ran 400 pages, was published in America. Fame and notoriety came immediately to Mayo and she followed up the book by publishing more on the same issues—*Slaves of the Gods* (1929), *Volume Two* (1931), and *The Face of Mother India* (1935).

Mother India drew a virtual avalanche of protest and replies, especially from the leadership of the Indian national movement and those interested in India's struggle for independence. As the Indian historian S. Gopal has noted:

The publication...of *Mother India* in 1927 was at the time a cause célèbre. On the eve of the announcement of the all-white composition of the Simon Commission, the Raj and Indian nationalist forces were preparing for a fresh trial of strength. Just then was published this book, seeking to show with lurid detail, that India's social backwardness rendered her unfit for freedom. (Gopal, Foreword to Jha 1971)

While many Indian men were willing to acknowledge social evils in India, they were not prepared to hear such criticisms from a foreign woman—least of all one with racist and pro-imperialist attitudes. Running through Mayo's book was the theme that Indians were morally unfit for self-government and that British rule was the best thing that ever happened to them. She particularly targeted the Bengalis for indulging in political and sexual excesses.[8] Among those who replied to Mayo was the Bengali poet Rabindranath Tagore, who had been quoted in Mayo's book as idealizing early marriage; he protested about "the numerous lies mixed with facts that have been dexterously manipulated by her," and referred to Mayo's "shocking statements made by a casual tourist against a whole people" (Mukerjee 1928:105).[9] Gandhi, too, joined the fray and wrote a review of Mayo's book in *Young India* under the title, "Drain Inspector's Report";[10] and the nationalist leader Lala Lajpat Rai, in a book *Unhappy India*, refuted Mayo, also in the process exposing the seamier side of American life.[11] Typical of such books was *American Sex Problems* (1929) by an Indian Parsi, Dinshah Ghadiali of New Jersey. Calling Mayo "Baroness Munchausen," he counterposed Mayo's list of Indian horrors with accounts of rape, prostitution, venereal diseases in America, as well as descriptions of the lynching of blacks by the Ku Klux Klan, of practices in Chicago slaughter houses, of the American form of sati which roasts women murderers on the electric chair, and of the college co-ed from Denver who "sold her soul for a fraternity pin" (Ghadiali 1929:33–36). Another similar book was entitled, *Uncle Sham; Being the Strange Tale of a Civilization Run Amok*, published in Lahore in 1929 by Kanhaya Lal Gauba.

Other critics of Mayo included Western men and women who had lived and worked in India or who were supporters of the Indian national movement. Some missionaries also disassociated themselves from her views. The sharpest rebukes came, however, from Western women who lived in India or had worked for Indian freedom. Annie Besant called it a "wicked book slandering the whole Indian people." While claiming that she had "worked against child marriage, with the help and support of large numbers of Indians, men and women," she added that Mayo has "merely sought for filth.... Does she imagine that, if her presentation were an accurate picture of Hindu civilization, Hinduism could have produced a civilization dating from...some 9,000 years before the Christian era? It would have been smothered in its own putrefaction" (Natarajan 1928:113). Margaret Cousins, a theosophist and feminist who had lived in India from 1916, stated that while her experience "corroborates a large number of her facts and illustrations regarding sex, health, untouchability, and the treatment of animals," the impression conveyed "is cruelly and wickedly untrue" (ibid:118–19). In addition, those on the left, like Agnes Smedley, were particularly annoyed by Mayo's snide references to Bengali revolutionaries. "But she (Mayo) regards the British government with all its massacres and bomb-throwing against the Indian people as an admirable and valuable system" (1927:26–27). There were also several British women were speakers at the meeting of protest about *Mother India* held in London in November 1927.[12]

Many of Katherine Mayo's critics (including Gandhi, Lajpat Rai, Besant and Cousins) agreed that there was substance to some of her accounts of social evils. Reformers in India, including Ramabai, had spoken out against such practices in the 19th century, and in the 1920s almost all the horrors denounced by Mayo had been condemned in forceful language by Gandhi. In fact a year before Mayo's book, Gandhi had written several articles against child marriage and on the plight of widows. But Gandhi, by the mid-twenties, was the leader of the nationalist movement who had succeeded in mobilizing masses of Indian men and women in campaigns of passive resistance and non-co-operation with British rule. But who was Katherine Mayo? To her critics she was not only a pro-imperialist and a racist American, but was also an old, unmarried, childless woman who acted as an agent for the British; she was also from the United States, famous in the mid-1920's for unimagined social freedoms for women resulting in immodest dress and outrageous behavior.

During this debate, much was said by men on the theme of Indian "womanhood."[13] India, wrote K. Natarajan, "would not forgive Mayo for this cowardly assault on the honour of her mothers." (Natarajan 1928:vi) In September 1927 a meeting was held in Calcutta chaired by the Mayor "to express indignation against and to repudiate the scurrilous attacks and malicious allegations made against Indian womanhood" (ibid:10). Actually, the criticism in Mayo's book had been more of Indian men for oppressing their women, but Indian critics knew that the best way to arouse male public opinion was to claim that local "womanhood" was under attack from foreign females. In this campaign, the "modern" American woman thus became a popular target and Mayo's Indian critics contrasted Indian woman's "purity" to American women's "licentiousness." As Ghadiali exclaimed:

> God help the man who is married to one of the present-time American wives, with a cigarette in her mouth, cards in her hand, revolver in her pocket, whiskey flask on her hip, moving around with a string of admirers attached to her ultra-short skirt. (Ghadiali 1929:27)[14]

While this was one popular stereotype of the white woman, the other was that of the sex-starved spinster whose curiosity is served by obsessively seeking out and denouncing vice; Katherine Mayo was firmly placed in this category. That she was unmarried became a point frequently commented upon by her Indian critics.[15] While Indian men protested strongly, and many foreign women condemned Katherine Mayo's biased reporting, Indian womens' silence was noted. As Florence Wedgwood wrote:

> Many English women are feeling strong indignation at the way Indians have been misrepresented by Katherine Mayo.... Also tho' many protests have appeared, there has not yet been one from an Indian *woman*, tho' there must be hundreds well equipped to confute this false witness.... Who will do this? We need a Mrs. Sarojini Naidu or a Dr. Joshi to speak for her country. (Natarajan 1928:127)

It is true that on this issue the voice of women in India remained unheard abroad. Gandhi, however, tried to make amends by sending Mrs. Sarojini Naidu to the United States "to undo the effect of *Mother India* on the mind of the Americans." (Jha 1971:Preface). The Katherine Mayo "trauma" that Indian males continued to have long after the book was published can be understood in terms of Mayo's horror of all aspects of Hindu society, in contrast, for example, to foreign devotees of Kali like Sister Nivedita, who had written an eulogy called *Kali, the Mother*. Mayo, in the opening chapter of her book contrasted the "decorous, sophisticated people of all creeds," who go to the Calcutta Government House garden parties "to talk good English while they take tea and ices and listen to the regimental band," with a goat sacrificed simultaneously in a Kali temple nearby, "the blood gushes forth...the drums and the gongs...burst out wildly, 'Kali! Kali! Kali!' shout all the priests and the suppliants together, some flinging themselves face downward on the temple floor" (Mayo 1927:6).

As the writer A.M. Rosenthal, reflecting in 1957 on *Mother India Thirty Years After* stated, "there are few people more important in the relationship between India and the United States than Katherine Mayo, few books, if any, that contributed more violent coloring to the American mental image of India than "Mother India" ...the picture she drew of India is the picture that remains alive in the mind of the rest of the world" (Rosenthal 1957). It is not surprising that American feminists like Mary Daly have "discovered" Katherine Mayo and claimed her as a sister. Daly exposes the way Mayo "the just accuser becomes unjustly sentenced to erasure," and condemns the researchers' fears of criticizing other cultures "making the feminist open to accusations of imperialism, rationalism, racism, capitalism or any other "-ism" that can pose as more important than gynocidal patriarchy" (1978:129). Daly makes a strong point, but chooses herself to erase Mayo's politics and motives in exposing social evils in India. If Katherine Mayo had seriously wanted to improve the conditions of Indian women, rather than to justify British rule, the way she set about it was unhelpful to Indians and foreigners fighting for national liberation and women's rights.

ELEANOR RATHBONE——SLAYING THE MINOTAUR

As a result of the storm over Katherine Mayo's book, other women social reformers in Britain took up the issue, in a more serious and less sensational way, with the objective of prohibiting child marriage through legislation. One of the most notable of these reformers was Eleanor Rathbone (1872–1946) who came from an eminent Unitarian—Quaker family. One important event in the family history was the hospitality the Rathbones gave to Rammohan Roy, the Indian reformer, when he came to Britain in 1831 and stayed at the Rathbone estate. (Ramusack 1981a:110–11). Eleanor Rathbone was one of the early products of higher education for women; she went to Somerville College, Oxford, from 1893 to 1896, graduating in Philosophy. She became her father's assistant in 1896 and the next year was the Secretary of the Women's Suffrage Society of Liverpool. She was also involved in numerous welfare organizations and wrote on social issues.[16] In 1919, she became president of the National Union of Societies for Equal Citizenship (NUSEC), campaigning for equal pay, parliamentary representation, widows' allowances, family allowances, equal sexual morality, equal guardianship of children and for the appointment of women magistrates (ibid:112–13). She argued for a "new feminism" that sought to give women independence (Banks 1985:167).

The extension of Rathbone's interests to the condition of women in India was provoked in 1927 by Mayo's book; she called a conference of British women's groups to discuss the issue, and NUSEC decided to send a questionnaire on Indian women's conditions to Indian groups. This caused criticism from Indian women who had not been consulted. Commenting on a meeting Rathbone chaired in 1929 of British women interested in India, Dhanwanthi Rama Rau, an Indian woman visiting London, spoke out in protest.

> I disputed the right of British women to arrange a conference on Indian social evils in London, when all the speakers were British and many of them had never even visited India.... We were already assuming the responsibility ourselves, and we were sure we could be more successful than any outsiders, especially those who were ignorant of the cultural patterns of our social group and therefore could not be as effective as our own social reformers. (Ramusack 1981a:115–16)

In 1929, Rathbone entered parliament as an independent from the Universities constituency and used her position to carry on a campaign against child marriage in India, lobbying the British government for support for the Child Marriage Restraint Act (known by the name of its sponsor as the Sarada Act), which raised the age of marriage to fourteen. It was a period of political unrest in India, when Gandhi (in 1930) launched his civil disobedience movement and the British authorities did not want to further inflame the situation with controversial legislation on child marriage. As Ramusack writes, "Rathbone did not want reforms improving the condition of women to be delayed by British or Indian concerns for self-rule. She continued to badger Samuel Hoare at the India Office for firmer government implementation" (1981a:117).

Rathbone visited India in 1932, making contacts with Indian women, who by this date were organized in several important associations; the object of her visit also being to find out how the legislation to prevent child marriage in India was being implemented. She met women's organizations in the main cities of India and there was disagreement on tactics between Rathbone and some Indian women; Rathbone had opposed Gandhi's civil disobedience in favor of gradual reforms, both political and social. As a pragmatist she argued for "working to get what we can as we can and making it the basis for more," while Rajkumari Amrit Kaur, President of the All India Women's Conference, said Rathbone's strategy might work in a free country but not in "a subject country" because a start on the wrong basis means disaster...and can never lead to the ultimate true goals" (ibid:121–23). Nevertheless, Rathbone continued her campaign and formed the British Committee for Indian Women's Franchise, which lobbied for greater franchise and reserved seats for women in the Indian legislatures, arguing that if women were represented, there would be better social legislation for women.

On her return from India, Rathbone's attention was again focused on social issues and in 1934 she published *Child Marriage: The Indian Minotaur*. She described the Minotaur as a symbol of evil, the mythical animal, "to whom the Athenians were compelled to pay a tribute of seven youth and seven maidens till Theseus slew the monster," adding that she hoped Indian women would "play the part of Theseus" (1934:10). In this book Rathbone recounted the long battle to legislate the age of marriage and the age of consent and, unlike Mayo, she was critical of the British authorities. As a feminist she argued that there could be no doubt of the attitudes of the all-male British administration, whose advice openly tendered to its new recruits was "keep off the woman question," because this was delicate ground likely to cause trouble and bring odium on the government (ibid:16).

Ramusack notes that Rathbone's book was "a harsh, polemical work intended to stimulate people to action" which, in contrast to Mayo, did not put all the blame on the Hindus, but also exposed the prevalence of child mar-

riage among the Muslims. Rathbone claimed that her criticisms of the British
government were important and this task was her particular responsibility as
an English woman (1981a:117). Like Mayo, she went into all the details of child
marriage, quoting medical reports and the testimony of doctors, but in a non-
sensational way. And she did this without alleging, like Mayo, that the Indians
were unfit for self-government. She also made several suggestions, including
the establishment of an All-India Society for the Abolition of Child Marriage
which was to educate public opinion, enforce the Sarada Act and try and
strengthen it by amendment; she stated that "the orderly presentation of
accumulated facts" was not enough, and urged that "some Indian woman
capable of kindling the flame" should use sensational methods of publicizing
the issue (ibid:109–11). To the argument that Indian women had a more immediate task to free the country from the British, she replied that, "a general
uprising of Indian women against child marriage and its sister evils would do
more to forward the cause of Indian self-government and raise the repute of
India in the eyes of the world" (ibid:114). And to the other argument that suggestions from British women were unacceptable, she replied in an
internationalist feminist spirit that she would not bother about national distinction (ibid:118).

Rathbone's campaigns for Indian women were appreciated by many of her
Indian women contacts, and the All-Indian Women's Conference in 1934 discussed her proposal and offer of financial aid for a new organization to combat
child marriage. But the time was certainly inauspicious for such an approach.
The Women's Conference refused to take foreign funds and said that they did
not have the personnel for such an organization; some members disagreed,
including a lawyer, Lakshmi Menon, who argued that if Indians appealed
abroad for help during earthquakes, she did not see "any reason why we
should reject the offer of voluntary help from one sister abroad." Menon took
over the task of heading an All-India Sarada Sub-Committee appointed by the
Women's Conference (ibid:118).

Rathbone was perhaps the last of the liberal women who were able to use
their class position to lobby for Indian and other women with British politicians and officials.[17] But like other foreign women activists in India in the 1930s,
she was faced with the fact that the new generation of Indian nationalist,
socialist and communist women leaders did not need the advice of old British
suffragists. Times had changed and the fierce struggles for Indian independence eclipsed the well-meaning efforts of British liberals seeking reform on
single issues, while avoiding the main issue of India's freedom.[18]

But there were many other British women—Unitarians, Quakers, Liberals
and Socialists—who supported the cause of Indian independence, and campaigned in Britain on this issue. Some had close links with Indian leaders and

kept in touch with all questions concerning Indian politics and social reform. Others who were more concerned with Indian religion and culture in a political context, became closely associated with spiritual movements, theosophy, Orientalist scholarship as well as issues of Indian independence, cultural nationalism and "national" education, which will be considered in the next section.

III

"CONSOLATION IN AN ALIEN SOCIETY"
Women Theosophists and Orientalists

7

"THE LIGHT OF ASIA" OR "HOOEY FROM THE ORIENT"?

While most religious groups viewed the existing order of gender, race and class relations as ordained by God, ardent Spiritualists appeared not only in the women's rights movement, but throughout the most radical reform movements of the 19th century...the abolition of slavery, reform of marriage...labour reform, vegetarianism, dress reform, health reform, temperance and anti-sabbatarianism.

—Ann Brande, *Radical Spirits* (1989:3)

We regard (Madame Blavatsky) neither as the mouthpiece of hidden seers, nor as a mere vulgar adventuress: we think she has achieved a title to permanent remembrance as one of the most accomplished, ingenious, and interesting imposters in history.

—Richard Hodgson (1885), report to the Society for Psychical Research (Taylor 1992:239)

THE TASKS OF "CIVILIZING THE NATIVES" IN THE COLONIES—CONVERTING them to Christianity and reforming their social structures and practices—was the necessary accompaniment to the spread of imperialism. This opened up opportunities for Western women in the public domain—in missionary activities, in hospitals and schools, in social reform, and in fund-raising. In terms of women's freedom, this was a significant advance: women were able to travel, work outside the home and fight for "good" causes. But the causes were well within the framework of imperialism and were often supported by its power. This set of activities was discussed in Parts I and II of this book. Part III of this book concerns Western women who had a sharply different impact on South Asia. They came out of anti-systemic and heterodox movements that emerged in the West in the 19th century, which questioned the social and ideological orthodoxies of the day and rejected the notion of Christianity as the only true religion. The view of the East and of its spirituality as constructed by European scholars, writers, artists and travelers played a distinct role in the formation of these movements. It was in a sense the discovery of the "East" that led some Western women to travel to South Asia and help in the conservation or regeneration of "Eastern" ideals that they felt were under attack by the rapacious and materialistic West. Some of them achieved international fame if not notoriety, as female gurus, holy mothers and high priestesses of theosophy and various esoteric sects, while others branched off into educational activities or into social and political movements. They too were independent women, who traveled abroad for a cause, but they also entered into a second level of protest by undermining the sacred beliefs of the Christian patriarchs and critiquing colonialism. Their own examples of female leadership, rebellion and independence as women, and their freedom from domestic ties influenced local people who were able to relate to the "new women" from the West, who sympathized with the political aspirations of the colonized. But in their anxiety to promote local culture and traditions, some of these women questioned the benefits of the modernizing process the missionaries had begun, especially in the education of women.

The rejection of orthodox Christianity was basic to many movements of dissent. The French philosophers of the Enlightenment, Montesquieu, Voltaire, Rousseau and others, had made the great historic challenge to the institutions of feudalism and to Christian ideology; God was declared to be dead and Man rather than God became the center of debate. It was a period, as Friedrich Engels remarked, when philosophers "recognized no external authority of any kind" whether religious or political, and when "every old traditional notion was flung into the lumber room as irrational" (Engels (1882), 1972:31). While Darwin's *Origin of Species* (1859) cast doubt on the biblical story of creation, many of the attacks on orthodox beliefs came from the more radical sections of the church itself. Bishop Colenso of Natal, South Africa, for instance, caused a scandal in 1862, with his *Pentateuch and Book of Joshua*, which challenged the literal interpretation of the Bible; in France, Renan's iconoclastic *La Vie de Jésus* (1863) had the same effect. Scientific advances in this period led to new waves of skepticism, rationalism and atheism in Europe and America, and William Lecky's *History of the Rise and Influence of the Spirit of Rationalism in Europe* (1865) celebrated its humanitarian effects. Engels noted with amusement "the fatal spread of continental scepticism in matters religious" in mid-19th century Britain, where "agnosticism, though not yet considered the "thing" quite as much as the Church of England, is very nearly on a par, as far as respectability goes, with Baptism and decidedly ranks above the Salvation Army" (1972:13). This ideological challenge also expanded into a questioning of the powers of the church and of the clergy.

At a popular and more sensationalist level, were the small but aggressive groups of atheists, free-thinkers and "blasphemers" who ridiculed Christianity at home, and missionary activity abroad, challenging the church and state on religious issues. For example, the National Secular Society in Britain associated with Annie Besant and Charles Bradlaugh, published pamphlets on atheism that were popular among the Hindu and Buddhist intelligentsia in India and Sri Lanka. Also in demand were G.W. Foote's journal, *The Free-Thinker*, his "Crimes of Christianity," ribald pamphlets such as *Bible Romancings*, and *Bible and Beer*, in which the Bible was called the "drunkard's text book." He was prosecuted but acquitted on charges of blasphemy, further popularizing his work at home and abroad (Jayawardena 1972:52).

Many Christians reacted to this "wave of unbelief" by rejecting fundamentalist, old style Christianity for a more modern, less literal version of the Bible. Some interpreted the message of Christ as a liberating call for equality and social justice, while others (including Charles Kingsley, the writer of novels on working-class conditions in the "hungry" 1840s) called themselves Christian Socialists. As G.D.H. Cole has noted, they believed that "the Kingdom of Christ...must be of this world, not merely of the next" and that there was "a Christian ideal of society, which it was incumbent upon Christians to strive to make real here on earth" (1947:157). In Britain, the Christian Socialists promoted workers' associations, self-governing workshops and successfully helped to revive the co-operative movement (ibid:158). Various denominations of Christians, both in Britain and the United States, were influenced by the concept of the social gospel with Christ as the symbol of the liberation of the oppressed, and by the possibilities of dialogue with other religions.

Challenges to Christianity also induced a critical reassessment of the role of missionaries in the colonies and their naive "civilizing" and christianizing campaigns. The more intellectually sophisticated Christians preferred to distinguish themselves from the crude evangelism of missionaries abroad and their funders at home and began to regard other religions not as heathen idolatry, but as systems of knowledge and belief worthy of study; as Webb notes, there was also in England, "a direct line of romantic adventurers who have sought consolation in an alien society, and who have been idolized for it" (1988a:57). This attitude was fostered by the Orientalists in the West who translated the religious texts of Islam, Hinduism and Buddhism, by travelers' accounts of other cultures and religions, and by the theosophists who denied the exclusive role of Christianity in favor of finding "truth" in all religions. The bigoted missionary view of non-Christian religions was seen as dangerous and misleading, and attempts were made by concerned Christians to acquire a knowledge of Asian religions and cultures. Many Westerners traveled to Asia and there was also a reverse flow of Asian intellectuals and religious leaders to Europe and the United States, where they found receptive audiences eager for a deeper knowledge of the East.

THE ORIENTAL RENAISSANCE

Early Western missionaries to South Asia had denounced its religions as idol worship and condemned temple art as obscene. Rev. Miron Winslow, for example, describing the Hindu temple at Nallur in Jaffna, referred to "the roof…ornamented with hideous and grotesque figures in sculpture" (1840:293–94). As Mitter has noted, in the 19th century, when "classical ideals of order and rationality were especially favoured by art critics, Indian gods… were regarded as monsters because they defied all ideals of rationality" (1977:8). However, in contrast to the negative images of Asia projected by early travelers and missionaries, there was also a serious attempt by British, French and German Orientalists to study the texts and learn more about Asian religions and civilizations. An important area of study was linguistics and William Jones (1746–1794), a British civil servant in India, wrote about the relationship of Sanskrit to the Latin and Greek languages (Schwab 1984:36). He was followed by a long line of British Orientalists.[1]

Germany also became an important center for Oriental scholarship from the 1790s onward. Numerous texts were translated into German, and in 1808 Friedrich Schlegel published a study of linguistics and Hindu philosophy that was to influence Oriental studies of the 19th century. Schlegel made India into "the cradle of all primitive purity, especially religious purity," and at the same time reanimated the idea of a relationship between Asia and Germany (ibid:53, 76). One of the later German Indologists, Max Müller, developed the idea that the affinity of Sanskrit and European languages indicated a common origin. Linguistic affinity was expanded into racial affinity and the concept of the Aryan race was popularized and efforts were made, in Müller's words, to locate "the cradle of our race." Origins in a common racial stock meant that Europeans and Indians had the same "blood," and although in later life Müller denied that the category of Aryan was applicable to race, the "Aryan myth" had been launched and became a powerful political force after it was picked up by white supremacists and racists (Gunawardana 1984:88–89). The "Aryan myth" also influenced nationalists and chauvinists in India and Sri Lanka, as well as Western theosophists and Orientalists who idealized an ancient society in India where a superior Aryan way of life was said to have prevailed, with freedom for women.

France too became an important center of Oriental studies. Many French Orientalists and art historians were products of the French revolutionary tradition and of the anti-clericalism, atheism and rationalism of the Enlightenment. They were thus more receptive to other cultures and religions. Some even spoke of a universal religion, tracing, like Charles Dupuis in 1795, "all religions back to a common source" (Mitter 1977:86). French scholars also wrote of the bisexual divinities in Hinduism, and analyzed sexual imagery and fertility symbolism. Some like Pierre Sylvian Marechal, projected paganism as a "natural, noble, ancient religion at once dignified and appealing to the senses" (ibid).

The interest in the Orient spread to America. Ralph Waldo Emerson (1803–1882), the American writer and philosopher, created a scandal in 1833 by expressing a "belief in the divine in man akin to the concept of the Soul, Atman-Brahman" (Rolland 1984:48). Emerson influenced Henry David Thoreau, whose vision was of a "joint Bible" of Asian scriptures (Chinese, Hindu, Persian and Hebrew) with the motto "The Light from the East" (*ex Oriente lux*). Thoreau rejected both church and state in the United States and in 1849, wrote an essay, *Civil Disobedience,* urging people to recognize "higher laws" where civil laws were unjust, claiming that where a government imprisons a person unjustly, the true place for a just man was in prison. Gandhi and Tolstoy were influenced by Thoreau's ideas on civil disobedience[2]. His other seminal book that influenced radicals all over the world was *Walden* (1854), an account of his life as a semi-hermit in a cabin by Walden Pond, in which he criticized materialist society and called for a return to simplicity in living. Just as renowned was the author of *Leaves of Grass*, Walt Whitman (1819–1892); according to Romain Rolland, "the spirit of Whitman" attested to the willingness of Americans to listen to Indian thought, and to the teachings of Vivekananda. And Whitman in his poem *Passage to India* "solemnly announced the arrival of India" (ibid:67).

Europe was no longer the sole locus of true religion and high culture, surrounded by barbarism and heathenism. Curiosity about the Orient also fed into the wave of romanticism that swept Germany, France and Britain in the late 18th and mid-19th centuries and influenced all forms of cultural expression. The Romantic movement, a revolt against the earlier classical traditions, created a new interest in the emotional, supernatural and creative side of life. In this melange, notions of the East, of its culture and of its art forms played a significant part. This influence manifested itself in various ways. The exotic "Other" and the male and female "noble savages" were sought after by European travelers and writers and became objects of fiction, poetry, art and opera.

Schwab states that "literary appetite for mystery was completely revived" adding that "the arrival of India in Europe coincided with the birth of Romanticism" since India "resembled the romantic half of the human spirit" (1984:225). In Germany, the philosophers Schelling, Fichte, Hegel and Schopenheur, as well as poets and writers such as Heine, Goethe and Schiller and scholars like J.G. Von Herder "spread among the Romantics an idea of placing the cradle of the divine infancy of the human race in India" (ibid:53, 58).Oriental influences imbued the work of British romantic poets—Wordsworth, Coleridge, Keats, Shelley, and Byron—and Asian themes were continually used by writers and poets in the 19th century, one of the most popular books being Edwin Arnold's, *The Light of Asia* (1879), a compilation in verse of "Buddhist legend and doctrine…which was to enjoy a boundless success in English-speaking countries" (ibid:198). Romanticism also had an impact on the appreciation of Indian art and architecture and the beauties of Elephanta, Ellora, Ajanta and other cave temples and buildings.[3] Museums in Europe acquired and collected Asian art treasures and the famous "Grand Tour" was extended to Asia, with many western travelers visiting the famous monuments of South Asia.

By the late 19th century, Japanese, Chinese, and Indian art was influencing contemporary artists in Europe and books like E.B. Havell's *Indian Sculpture and Painting* (1908), and *The Ideals of Indian Art* (1911), had an important influence on the art world. He argued that Indian art should not be judged by European standards. These influences created an environment of opinion in which notions of European superiority in culture and in religion came under serious questioning. An opening into other religions, cultures, and art forms was made possible; and orthodox belief in Christianity and in its civilizing mission began to erode. From the late 19th century onward, swamis, gurus, philosophers, poets, orientalists, scientists and nationalists from South Asia became known in intellectual circles in Europe and the United States; the names of Swami Vivekananda, Aurobindo, Lala Lajpat Rai, Mohini Chatterjee, Jagdish Bose, Ananda Coomaraswamy, Gandhi, Nehru, Sarojini Naidu, Anagarika Dharmapala and Rabindranath Tagore, among others, appeared in the Western press and their ideas entered the popular discourse. They also became personal friends of dissidents in the West, including many Western women who were to move to India and Sri Lanka to serve religious, educational or political causes.

WOMEN AND SPIRITUALISM—THE FLIGHT FROM REASON

Disillusionment with the materialism of the 19th century and the principles of rationality that had been its original basis also led to what James Webb has called, "A Flight from Reason." The earlier optimism of the Enlightenment, the rejection of religion, the advances of science and the homocentric view that the "universe revolved round man," created its own reaction, causing a "sense of insecurity" that was made worse "by the need to accept personal responsibility in the society which was evolving." This anxiety and loss of faith led to a revival of interest in earlier forms of belief—in arcane knowledge, in the occult, magic, spiritualism, astrology and in "a multitude of similar topics of doubtful intellectual respectability" (Webb 1988a 10–11). It also led to curiosity about religions of the non-Christian world.

One of the manifestations of this reaction was spiritualism, earlier linked with Swedenborg and Mesmer, which had its hey-day in the 1870s, attracting a large number of women as leaders and followers in both Britain and the United States.[4] Alex Owen has emphasized the link between feminism and spiritualism, and has stated that "the discourse of spirit has long been a means of articulating subversive ideas," since "spiritualist culture held possibilities for attention, opportunity and status denied elsewhere" (1989:4). She notes also that feminists have often "sought a spiritual dimension to the political struggle" (ibid:242). Similarly, Ann Brande claims that in the United States, though not all feminists were spiritualists, all spiritualists advocated women's rights and women were "in fact equal to men within Spiritualist practice, polity and ideology" (1989:3).

Spiritualists operated at several levels; séances in semi-darkness involved communication with the dead, the posing of specific questions to the spirits (who replied through raps or moving tables), the actual materialization of spirits as well as spirit healing. Owen has noted that some mediums were from "theatrical backgrounds" and that " the entire business of mediumship was…superb theatre with young girls in the starring roles" (1989:54). Several upper-class women were involved in private séances to an elite clientele, but spiritualism also provided a vocation for young women of lower-class origin, who gave public performances. Mediums were inevitably women, in the belief not only that spirits favored women, but also that women were "particularly gifted" in such spheres, possessing "not only genuine spiritual power, but also the right to exercise it" (ibid:6). There was thus a "meteoric rise and then decline of the famous female spiritualist mediums…some of whom were able to make a good living from their talents" (ibid:1–3).

Because spiritualism was "intimately concerned with the unfolding of a vision of human fulfillment," many of the spiritualists' organizations and journals supported social change, dietary reform and temperance. Moreover, spiritualists also advocated women's rights. The British National Association of Spiritualists called for the "rights of women to be recognized to the full," and urged that the "wrongs of women be redressed" (ibid:27). Some spiritualists argued for women's rights on the grounds of women's spiritual superiority, while others came to spiritualism after being earlier involved in social and religious movements that advocated women's equality. Owen also remarks that there was a "strong feminist presence among American mediums and believers," adding that many leading feminists of the period went in for spiritualism, "attracted by other worldly promises of a new age which would see the development of women's full potential" (ibid:31). Thus most spiritualists were for women's rights. Some—especially the Americans—caused a scandal by going as far as advocating "free love" and the abolition of marriage.[5] Victoria Woodhull not only spoke out for free love and women's suffrage, but was also closely linked with Socialist causes and the formation of the International Working Men's Association (the First International), and was even a candidate for the United States presidency (Brande 1989:17).

Victorian mediumship was "a form of protest and dissent which pre-dated political awareness" of a later period (Owen 1989:240). Spiritualists were also a link with the earlier millenarian movements. The androgynous deity and belief in female messiahs, which were ancient heresies, formed part of movements challenging religious and political orthodoxy. However, the movement was also riddled with frauds, and their exposure contributed to the decline of the spiritualist fad toward the end of the 1880s, after which many prominent spiritualists went into other dissident movements—such as theosophy and the women's franchise movement. For as Brande points out, those who had practice in speaking in a trance could speak on other issues "in a conscious state as well"[6] (1989:193). One important point that emerges is that the origins of spiritualism lay in social protest, religious heresy and various forms of radical challenge to political and religious orthodoxies. It was not so much that disillusioned feminists turned to spiritualism, but that spiritualism itself originated from dissenting currents of opinion, which included a strong component of feminism.

HELENA BLAVATSKY AND THE APPEAL OF THEOSOPHY

The spiritualist, occult and theosophical movements of the late 19th century produced women leaders of international renown, the most outstanding examples being Helena Blavatsky and Annie Besant. The following chapters will attempt to distill some of the feminist and political content of their work and examine how they coped with the contradictions arising from their sharp break with Western traditions and their absorption with Eastern cultures and religions. Blavatsky and Besant were in fact among the two most outstanding women rebels of their period. Abandoning family life for the free life of the independent woman, rejecting personal domination by men and becoming forceful leaders themselves, they deliberately flouted bourgeois morality, discarding all prevalent creeds, beliefs, social conventions and political orthodoxies for the ideal of political, social and spiritual freedom. It is not an exaggeration to say that the "scandals" they caused reverberated around the world to the disgust of the Victorian establishment and the delight of dissenters in the West and the East.

The Theosophical Society was started in New York in 1875 by Helena Petrovna Blavatsky (1831–1891), a Russian, and Colonel Henry Olcott, an

Helena Petrovna Blavatsky (From *Annie Besant: An
Autobiography* (1893). By permission from the Theosophical
Society, Madras.)

American of liberal opinions who had earlier dabbled in spiritualism.
Theosophy basically was a critique of modern science, religion and philosophy, all of which were held to be distorted forms of ancient thought and
wisdom. The objects of the Theosophical Society were to acquire "a knowledge of natural law, especially its occult manifestations" and to "oppose the
materialism of science and every form of dogmatic theology, especially the
Christian, which the chiefs of the Society regard as particularly pernicious";
the Society further aimed at counteracting missionary propaganda by making known "among Western nations the long-suppressed *facts* about Oriental
religious philosophies" (Jinarajadasa 1925:26). The movement attracted some
members of the intelligentsia in Europe and the United States, including many
women who had been earlier interested in the occult, in spiritualism and in
dissenting political and social movements.

Richard Ellmann, explaining the popularity among certain 19th-century
intellectuals of "the treacherous currents of semi-mystical thought" argued

that, "science had disproved orthodox conceptions of the making of the world (and) Darwin had husked the world of meaning"; Christianity had been discarded and science offered little solace, and so "a new doctrine purporting to be an ancient and non-European one was evolved by a strange Russian lady" (1988:58). The new doctrine was theosophy and the strange lady was the charismatic Helena Blavatsky. Born in 1831 in the Ukraine, her father was Captain von Hahn, an artillery officer of German origin, and her mother was a popular novelist. At sixteen she married N.V. Blavatsky, whom she left soon after. There is no reliable account of her life from this period to 1872 and she herself gave various versions of her travels and adventures. Farquhar, writing in 1915, claims that "for many years she lived a very wild and evil life," quoting one of Blavatsky's letters stating that "the devil got me into trouble in my youth" (1915:211–12). By the 1870s, she was back in the United States and was well-known in spiritualist circles; in 1874, she attended séances held in Vermont by the Eddy brothers, where she met Colonel Henry Olcott (Symonds 1960).

All of Blavatsky's biographers and contemporaries have commented on her powerful personality. She was described as "a woman of unusual temperament, possessing the powers of the medium, the clairvoyant, ...and probably the automatic writer" (Farquhar 1915:220). Blavatsky's mesmerizing eyes were an important part of her personality; according to Princess Von Racowitza, she had "a pair of eyes the like of which I have never seen; pale blue, grey as water but with a glance deep and penetrating and as compelling as if it beheld the inner heart of things" (Nethercot 1961:321). Nethercot notes that "almost every commentator who knew her remarked on the maleness of her personality."[7] Blavatsky used her skills to mesmerize others, through demonstrating "occult phenomena" to audiences in both the West and in Asia; her repertoire was reminiscent of spiritualists, including table raps, tinkling bells and the materialization of objects. While her opponents debunked these phenomena as magician's tricks, and alleged that she used sliding panels and secret doors to obtain such effects, devotees like Olcott described Blavatsky as a "wondrous woman, made the channel for great teachings, the agent for the doing of a mighty work" (1954:vii). Drawing on contemporary interest in comparative mythology and religion, Blavatsky, in 1877, wrote *Isis Unveiled*, described as "a master key to the mysteries of ancient and modern science and theology;"[8] Webb claims that this book put together "magpie-like accumulations of mysticism, tall stories and archeology" and that Blavatsky's theosophy consisted of "romantic nostalgia for a more "spiritual" and less taxing past, the determination to answer...the question of life after death" (1988a:82, 84).

Soon after its formation, the Theosophical Society developed links with those Hindus, Buddhists and free-thinkers in India and Sri Lanka who were opposing Christianity and the proselytizing and educational activities of missionaries. Arriving in India in 1879, Blavatsky and Olcott established the Society's headquarters in Adyar, Madras, and also helped in 1880 to form the Buddhist Theosophical Society in Sri Lanka. The theosophist influence was politically important in the years of cultural revivalism and incipient nationalism in India and Sri Lanka. In India by 1884 there were over 100 branches of the Theosophical Society, and its ideology proved attractive to many Indians. As Farquhar noted,

> Theosophy provided a new defence of Hinduism for the thousands of educated men whose Western education had filled them with doubts about their religion. It condemned Christian missionaries as impudent and ignorant intruders, who dared to criticise Hinduism and Buddhism, the two faiths which still taught clearly the truths of the Ancient Wisdom. (1915:233)

The influence of the theosophists spread with their establishment of Hindu and Buddhist schools in India and Sri Lanka, respectively. These schools not only promoted a Buddhist or Hindu education, but also exposed students to liberal thought from the West and encouraged feelings of patriotism, national identity and self-esteem, laying the foundations for later political movements for independence. Many of the theosophist schools had European and American teachers, women and men with radical opinions, sympathetic not only to liberation struggles but also (as in Sri Lanka) to working-class actions against employers (Jayawardena 1972:56–57). In the late 19th and early 20th centuries, theosophy also exerted a strong influence on some nationalist leaders in Asia. For example, Gandhi, on his arrival in London for studies in the 1880s, moved in theosophist circles. Jawaharlal Nehru, aged twelve, had been tutored at home by a European theosophist; in 1901 he attended Annie Besant's lectures, and the next year, he became a member of the Theosophical Society, the initiation ceremony being performed by Besant (Nethercot 1963:75–76).

Theosophy also had a great appeal to those European intellectuals who were against imperialism and hostile to the claims of superiority made for Christianity and Western civilization. While denying the ideological superiority of the West, theosophy spoke of universal brotherhood "without distinction of race, creed, sex, caste or colour." Blavatsky's achievement was to make the theosophical movement not merely an occult society, but a part of "progressive" thought of the late 19th century. Webb surmises that the "doctrine of the occult destinies of races...may well account for the influence that theosophy has exercised on several nationalist movements" (Webb 1988a:92). The importance of a non-Eurocentric and non-racist view of the world was further emphasized in Blavatsky's major work *The Secret Doctrine*, published in 1888, which outlined a theory of spiritual evolution, and "made huge generalizations about man and the cosmos" (Ellman 1988:60).

Theosophy came under attack from many quarters—from Christians and missionaries, who condemned it as a fraud, and from Socialists and liberals who were fiercely hostile to any "mumbo-jumbo." The *National Reformer* (in Britain) said many theosophists were "very good, very respectable and very mad" (Taylor 1992:238) and the liberal American journal, the *Springfield Republican* called *Isis Unveiled* "a large dish of hash" (Symonds 1960:90). Theosophists were also denounced by some scholars, including T.W. Rhys Davids, who said they were "lamentably ignorant of the literatures of the East. They know nothing of Pali...their ideas are based on the medieval alchemists which they mix up with a little misunderstood Indian thought." Indian spiritual leaders like Aurobindo were equally skeptical; making a distinction between magic tricks, occultism and real spiritual practice, he claimed that Blavatsky was "an occultist, not a spiritual personality" (Aurobindo Vol.22:483). H.L. Mencken, the American iconoclastic journalist, in 1919 raised the question of the growing popularity among women of the "thin incense of mysticism" (1919:240–45); to him and many others, theosophy was another example of Oriental hooey (Mencken 1949:355).

Nevertheless, inspite of all these criticisms, theosophy attracted a number of European and American women, some of whom were to spend their lives in India and Sri Lanka as teachers, social reformers and propagators of the new faith. What was, then, the attraction of theosophy for the "new woman"? James Webb has suggested that it had a particular appeal to leisured upper-class women, "those generally concerned by the crisis of consciousness; hosts of women, on whose hands time hung heavy"; he admitted, however, that in Britain the movement for women's suffrage and the theosophical movement "ran...simultaneous courses" (Webb 1988a:105). But many "new women" were skeptical. Beatrice Webb called theosophy "a wonderful fairy tale" (Taylor 1992:221).

While it is true that some of the leading theosophist women were from titled families, there were also many women professionals, scholars and political activists. Among eminent theosophists were Annie Besant, Henrietta Muller, Charlotte Despard, Margaret Cousins and Florence Farr, all suffragists, Esther Bright (daughter of the radical M.P., Jacob Bright) and Isabel Cooper-Oakley. who opened a restaurant in London for working girls. According to Burfield, "a number of theosophical ladies owed their freedom of action to...private incomes"; quoting Eric Hobsbawm, she notes that in Britain in 1871, there were "170,000 'persons of rank and property' without visible occupation—almost all women...a surprising number of them unmarried" (1983:30). But many theosophist women, like Besant, Cousins and Farr had no private wealth or regular employment, but nevertheless man-

aged to live full and independent lives. Theosophists themselves were an interesting group; "A dilletante circle of spiritualists, freemasons, occultists and
bohemians" as well as "intellectuals and socialists" (ibid:31–33). Because
theosophists differed from the diehard patriarchs and puritans of the Victorian
period, they attracted support from independent, educated women.

The other possible appeal of theosophy for women was that it meant equal
rights in both the spiritual and secular spheres. Henrietta Muller in 1893
remarked that "no religion and no philosophy…would be welcomed…
which did not accord to women *a place of perfect equality with man….*
Theosophy…accords to women the place which the thinking and advanced
minds of today require that it should accord her." Muller had earlier asked
Helena Blavatsky if women in the Society enjoyed equal rights; "*the whole way
along the line, with men,*" Blavstsky replied, also stating that recognition was given
by theosophists for work, whether done by a man or a woman, and that there
had been "women adepts in ancient India from time immemorial" (Muller
1893:168–69, emphasis added). Twenty years later in *Theosophy and the Women's
Movement*, Charlotte Despard, the Irish suffragist and Home Rule agitator,
claimed that "there are moments in the world's history when ideas that have
been moving in the world of thought, realized by the few and dreaded by
many, enter into manifestation. This is such a moment"[9] (1913:35).

One important aspect of theosophy was its acceptance of "difference" in
culture and religion, and rejection of the universalist claims of Christianity
and Western civilization. Theosophy thus offered a non-Christian view of the
world, and a non-racist, humane approach to older religions, to arcane knowledge and to non-European cultures. As noted earlier, it also offered a prospect
of a break-through in terms of women's spiritual, intellectual and political
freedom. To throw off the shackles and constraints imposed on them as
daughters and wives of Christians (and often of Christian clergymen) was
exhilarating, as was the link-up with dissident social and political movements.
To be able to cause further scandal by espousing Asian religions and associating
with Asian men as gurus, philosophers, friends and sometimes husbands, was
also a way of expressing the rejection of their own society, of its religion, values, culture—and, very significantly, of its men. The attraction of the "Other"
was strong and an idealization and romanticization of the East, its way of life,
religions and peoples was prevalent among women of the Theosophical
Society. Spiritualism and theosophy, which had roots in various earlier utopian, democratic and dissident religious and secular movements, also led to
women's interest not only in new methods of education pioneered by
Pestalozzi, Froebel and Montessori, which challenged the rigid school system,
but also to modernism and experimentation in the creative arts and a rejection of conformity.

In dismissing Western society, its ideology, culture, economic structures and class system, many of the women influenced by theosophy became interested in looking to Asian societies for alternative beliefs and ways of life. The enemies at home—the church and state—had been exported to the colonies; as a result many who opposed the British state and Christian church also identified with the colonized peoples who were being subjected to Christian evangelical influences and domination by British imperialism. And many theosophists, including Blavatsky, gravitated to South Asia.

BLAVATSKY AND INDIAN WOMEN

When Helena Blavatsky and Olcott visited India and Sri Lanka in 1879 and 1880, they used the occasion to meet Hindu and Buddhist leaders and monks, to form theosophical societies, and to study the local social and political scene. One of the most extreme representatives of the 19th century "new woman," Blavatsky kept a sharp eye on the situation of women in India and Sri Lanka. From the outset, theosophy had emphasized the absence of any distinction of race, creed, sex, caste or color in its theory and practice; and gender equality was therefore one of its distinctive features. In 1879 Blavatsky, using the Indian name Radda-bai, wrote several travel articles for Russian publications under the title "From the Caves and Jungles of Hindustan," in which her concern for the condition of Indian women was very sharply expressed.

Blavatsky had attended a Hindu wedding of a girl age ten to a boy age fourteen, and describes the "endlessly drawn out rites and rigmaroles" [1975 (1879):228]. She also reported on a Brahmin wedding where a boy age seven was marrying a girl age five, and a Parsi wedding between a boy age five and an infant aged two and a half.[10] Blavatsky wrote: "But what a strange and incredibly unjust fate has befallen the women of India, in all that concerns their living conditions," giving further details of Brahmin marriages where there was "no love or free choice." She also described "the terrible custom" of female infanticide (ibid:232). Blavatsky wrote of the right of some Hindus to have more than one wife and the remarriage of widowers which was encouraged, contrasting this with the "complete, unconditional social death…in cases of widowhood, even if this occurs when she is but a five or three year old girl, and even in cases of betrothal" (ibid:239). Blavatsky condemned the disfigurement of the widow who must "shave her head…is not allowed to wear…adornments, …must wear nothing but white"; temples and religious and social occasions were "closed to her forever" and the widow "sleeps, eats and works separately, her touch is considered impure for seven years" (ibid:239).

Missionaries had made similar condemnations of such social practices, blaming them on Hinduism. Blavatsky offered a different interpretation and traced these social evils to corruptions of Hinduism perpetrated by the

Brahmins who, to preserve their power and wealth, had distorted the original teachings of the Vedas. She alleged that the Brahmins had even prohibited others from reading the Vedas, "these parasites disfigured their ancient scriptures to suit themselves...burdened the Hindus with an endless series of rites, non-existent feasts, and the silliest of ceremonies." In contrast to the missionaries, Blavatsky believed that child marriage, female infanticide and sati were not central to Hinduism. She wrote that in the Aryan society of ancient India "women enjoyed the same rights as men, including remarriage. Her voice was listened to in the state councils; she was free in the choice of her husband and was at liberty to stay single if she so chose." She noted that "many a woman's name plays a prominent part in the chronicles of the ancient Aryan land and has come down to posterity as that of eminent poets, astronomers, philosophers, and even sages and lawgivers" (ibid:232). Foreign invasions by Persians and Muslims were alleged to have changed this situation: "Woman became a slave and the Brahmins took this opportunity of placing additional shackles on her" (ibid:223). Writing on the practice of sati, Blavatsky alleges that the Brahmins falsely doctored the ancient religious texts (ibid:241).

It must be noted that Blavatsky was writing in 1879, when Indian reformers were taking up the issue of women's rights, and when liberal circles in the West were joining in the clamor for the eradication of glaring social evils. Blavatsky had been forthright in her views. For example, when she met the Chief Justice of Baroda in 1879, who introduced her to his child wife, Blavatsky exclaimed, "Your *wife*? You old beast! You ought to ashamed of yourself" (Symonds 1960:123). Blavatsky was also supportive of the Indian reformers and in the same year noted, "As I write these lines, agitators and opponents of the Brahamanas have initiated a reform movement in Bombay, in regard to the remarriage of widows, and this is bound to shake the whole of orthodox India to its very foundation" (1975:239).

But events in the 1880s were to change the attitude of theosophists. The crucial factor was the campaign launched by orthodox Hindus against foreign interference by missionaries and bureaucrats in the domestic life of Hindus. This real resentment was not confined to a few intellectuals, but became an explosive popular issue based on nationalist sentiment against imperialism. In this clash, foreign theosophists certainly did not want to appear to side with British officials, missionaries or those Indians who were labeled traitors. In 1879, Blavatsky could write that, "If the English ever did any good in India, it is undoubtedly that they succeeded in suppressing...infanticide" (ibid:232). But in later years, the theosophists took care not to be seen as supporters of the British in their attacks on Hindu social life. Blavatsky also found nothing critical to say about the status of Buddhist women in Sri Lanka. Writing in 1889, attacking missionary efforts to convert women, she denounced Christianity as a misogynist religion, and stated, "woman in Ceylon, like any other Buddhist woman, has always been free and even on a par with man.... The Buddhist woman owes her position to Buddha's noble and just law, and the Christian to her intolerant and despotic Church" (Blavatsky 1973:449–51).

Although Blavatsky had spoken out on the situation of Hindu women, while idealizing ancient Indian society, by the 1890s and the early years of the 20th century, theosophists like Annie Besant—herself a strong advocate of women's rights in Britain—continued the glowing romanticization of early Indian society, but deemed it tactically prudent not to press too much for women's rights or women's education. This will be discussed in the next chapter.

"SANDALS IN INDIA AND SHOES IN THE WEST"

Annie Besant's "Passage to India"

We must decline to concur in Mrs. Besant's wholesale condemnation of Western civilization...but if nothing else, it is superior to that of the East in being able to produce women of the courage of conviction which have made Mrs. Besant and many others of her sex a power for good.... Hindu civilization is yet to produce a woman of the stamp of the talented lady...and until it does...we...cannot appropriate for Hinduism the praises which Mrs Besant so generously lavished on our ancestors.

—Subramania Aiyar (1893), editor of the *Hindu*, in R. Parthasarathy (ed.), *A Hundred Years of the Hindu* (1978 :134)

Things go on as usual, and they are marrying off little girls.... I am sending you the pictures of a child wife and a child widow...sometimes it looks as if the world is going backwards, when one hears an English woman, like Mrs. Besant, declaring that the Hindu widows should never marry again.

—Pandita Ramabai, quoted in the *American Ramabai Association Report* (1904:21)

THE DENIAL OF CHRISTIAN UNIVERSALISM BY THEOSOPHISTS AND THEIR criticism of the pretensions of Christianity to be the one true religion delighted and inspired the South Asian religious and nationalist intelligentsia. But it was Annie Besant (1847–1933), the leader of the Theosophical Society after Blavatsky's death in 1891, who made the sharpest impact. She used the argument of cultural relativism and asserted that Western models were unsuitable for India. Limiting her feminism to the West, she advocated orthodoxy and traditional education for Indian women. How was this possible? According to her friend George Bernard Shaw, Besant played many roles and like all great public speakers, was a born actress:

She was successively a Puseyite Evangelical and Atheist Bible smasher, a Darwinian secularist, a Fabian socialist, strike leader and a Theosophist exactly as Mrs. Siddons was a Lady Macbeth, Lady Randolph, Beatrice, Rosamund and Volumnia." (Taylor 1992:261–62)

One of Besant's biographers, Nethercot, describes her "nine lives" which included her extraordinary Indian phase as president of the Indian National Congress and promoter of the "World Leader" Krishnamurti. Besant's praise for Hinduism and Indian culture and her advocacy of Home Rule for India also made her the scourge of both the British and the missionaries. She became a national and international symbol of women's revolt, challenging the patriarchs of church and state in her personal struggles; she was also a critic of capitalism and colonial rule, both in their heyday in the 19th century. The Fabian Socialist Sidney Webb called her "one of the 19th century's most remarkable women" (Taylor 1992:261); to Beatrice Webb, she was "the most wonderful woman of her century" (Holroyd 1988:170), and to Indian leftist Kamaladevi Chattopadyaya, Besant was "one of the most outstanding world figures of her time" (1986:32–33).

Annie Besant was born in London in 1847. Her father, William Wood, of English-Irish origin, was educated at Trinity College, Dublin, and was a mathematician and classical scholar. He died when Annie was a child, leaving the family without an income (Besant 1984:11). Her Irish mother ran a boarding house in Harrow for school children, which enabled her son to be educated free at the famous school, Harrow. The limited family savings were used to send her brother to the university while Annie attended a small school run by Ellen Marryat, where she received a liberal education—including French, German and music, in a strictly religious background. At twenty, she married an Anglican priest, Frank Besant, and had a son and daughter. Besant faced all the constraints of Victorian marriage, where women had to be good mothers and wives, subject to the prevalent religious and sexual morality. Although a Vicar's wife, she developed serious doubts about Christianity and bourgeois marriage and, taking her daughter with her, left Besant in 1873 to live the life of an independent woman in London. She began to read about religion and philosophy, and to move around in "progressive" circles where new interpretations were being given to Christianity. She attended the famous Unitarian Chapel of the dissident Rev. Moncure Conway, who widened her views "on deeper religious problems" (ibid:112). Deprived of money and fighting child custody battles after leaving her husband, she experienced all the hazards of branching out as a "new woman." In addition, she compounded this scandal later by publicly advocating atheism, which was anathema to the ruling classes of the era.

Besant joined the National Secular Society and attended meetings at the Hall of Science to hear Britain's foremost exponent of atheism, Charles Bradlaugh, an elected M.P. who could not take his seat in the House of Commons because he refused to take the oath on the Bible. She then began traveling around the country and addressing meetings with Charles Bradlaugh, both of them propagating atheism and free-thought, and writing a *Freethinkers Text-Book* in 1876. In a pamphlet "The Gospel of Atheism" (1876) Besant wrote that "atheists are the vanguard of the army of Free-thought."[1] She gave up the use of prayer "as blasphemous absurdity, since an all-wise God would not need my suggestions nor an all-good God require my promptings" (ibid:113). In 1877 Besant and Bradlaugh were involved in public scandal when they republished a pamphlet on birth control by Dr. Charles Knowton, which had been earlier declared obscene. They were prosecuted and won the case, making birth control a topic of public discussion in Britain. Annie Besant wrote her own popular pamphlet on the subject, *Law of Population*, which "cited India as an example of what might occur in the future" (Taylor 1992:122). She dropped the issue in 1891 on joining the theosophists, feeling that, as Taylor notes, "artificially to interfere with the act of procreation was incompatible with the idea of reincarnation" (ibid:251)[2].

Annie Besant's feminism was expressed through her revolt against her own marriage in particular and her concern for women's subordination in general. She had been influenced by John Stuart Mill's writings on women, and her first public lecture in 1874 was on "The Political Status of Women." During the tussle with her husband over their daughter's custody, Annie Besant wrote a pamphlet, *Marriage As It Was, As It Is and As It Should Be*, (1879) reviewing marriage laws from Hebrew and Roman times up to contemporary Britain, where woman was legally a chattel. She criticized the laws regulating child custody, urged that marriage should not change a woman's civil status and that there be equal rights in divorce for adultery, cruelty or drunkenness. (Nethercot 1961 :142–43). During her case for child custody heard in 1878, Besant appeared in court "with a cohort of her closest women friends—Mrs. Conway, Mrs. Parris, the Misses Bradlaugh, and a dozen other Secularist members and wives" (ibid:144). The judge objected to Besant defending herself without counsel, and was "especially perturbed about a woman thus exposing herself before lawyers, journalists, and the nation" (ibid:145). Although she lost custody on grounds of her atheism, the issue became a topic of debate. All radical groups and their journals publicized the trial, which had combined the issues of free-thought and women's rights.[3] The case also drew attention to certain anomalies of English law, under which a wife had no legal claim to her children, whereas (as Besant wrote), "if legally you are your husband's mistress, your rights as a mother are secure." Besant's confrontational stand on these issues led to changes in the British law (ibid:153).[4]

Annie Besant also attempted to get a degree in Science at the London University, which had admitted women in 1878. By 1880, she had taken top honors in botany, advanced physiology, mathematics and advanced chemistry (ibid:186). In 1881, she obtained honors in the botany examination, being the only student in England to achieve this distinction, but she had to face a great deal of petty harassment. The curator of the Regent's Park botanical gardens refused her permission to enter the gardens for her studies, on the grounds that his daughters who used them might be corrupted and the Birkbeck Institute omitted her name from the result sheets of a class in electricity, as her name might offend potential contributors to the building fund. Besant retaliated by distributing a circular on this issue to the press (ibid:186–91). She was, however, unable to get her degree because, even though she had passed the First B.Sc., and Preliminary Science examinations, she kept failing in practical chemistry because of one examiner who "told her beforehand that however brilliantly she might do…he would not pass her, because he had a strong antipathy toward atheism and to certain of her activities for the masses, which he considered immoral" (ibid:192–93).[5] As "immoral," no doubt, was her Socialism.

Annie Besant was an active socialist on the executive committee of the Fabian Society along with Bernard Shaw and Sidney Webb; she joined their lecture circuit, giving talks: "Why We Work for Socialism," "Socialism and Political Action" and "The Trade Union Movement" (ibid:248–49).[6] During these years she also spoke out against war, capital punishment, flogging, the cost of royalty and the "obstructive power" of the House of Lords:

> I was a Home Ruler, too…and a passionate opponent of all injustice to nations weaker than ourselves, so that I found myself always in opposition to the Government of the day, against our aggressive and oppressive policy in Ireland, in the Transvaal, in India, in Afghanistan, in Burma, in Egypt. I lifted up my voice in all our great towns, trying to touch the conscience of the people, and to make them feel the immorality of a landstealing, piratical policy…no wonder I was denounced as an agitator, a firebrand, and orthodox society turned up at me its most respectable nose. (Besant 1984 (1883):153–54)

Another spectacular campaign by Annie Besant was her leadership of the women workers in the match factories of Bryant and May, who suffered from low wages and bad conditions of work, including health hazards caused by chemicals. A strike in 1885 had failed because of lack of support from the trade union movement which then only organized male workers. In 1888, Besant published an article on *White Slavery in London*, detailing the atrocious conditions of these workers and distributed it to them, with some roses, as a present. The subsequent strike of the match workers, led by Besant, achieved publicity in the national press and was supported by contributions from the public, lead-

Annie Besant in 1892. (From *Annie Besant: An Autobiography* (1893). By permission from the Theosophical Society, Madras.)

ing intellectuals and Socialists. The employers granted a small wage increase and significant improvements in working conditions. This success led to the Match Workers' Union formed on "the most advanced modern methods," with 600 members and Annie Besant as its secretary. The women unionists gained the right to be represented at the International Trade Union Conference in London, which included delegates from Europe (Nethercot 1961:270–74). The match women's strike, which the historian Trevelyan referred to as the "first skirmish of the new unionism," was followed by a wave of industrial unrest and unionization, in which Besant was very active (ibid:275).[7]

But in 1889 there occurred a sharp break in Annie Besant's life; after reviewing Blavatsky's *Secret Doctrine* for a socialist journal, she came under Blavatsky's hypnotic influence. Blavatsky made her renounce the advocacy of any type of family limitation and instead promote self-restraint. In 1890, Besant bought all copies of her *Law of Population* and had the plates destroyed (Taylor 1992:251–52).

This renunciation of what was, in fact, one of the key issues of feminism of the time, marked the beginning of Annie Besant's abandonment of the "woman question." The rupture with atheism, secularism, and militant Socialism was also swift and by 1891 she was totally absorbed in theosophy, becoming the President of the Theosophical Society after Blavatsky's death that year. Her Socialist and rationalist friends were appalled; when she resigned from the Fabian Society, its secretary cut off her name with a note—"Gone to Theosophy" (ibid:255). G.W. Foote, the editor of the *Freethinker,* expressed concern how "at one leap she left atheism and materialism and plunged into the depths of the wildest pantheism and spiritualism" (Foote 1889:3). She also plunged into work in India for the next thirty years—promoting theosophy, Indian Home Rule and Hindu boys' education.

ANNIE BESANT AND INDIAN WOMEN'S EDUCATION—
AN INTERESTING PARADOX

In 1893, Annie Besant made her first journey to India and Sri Lanka and claimed that one of her priorities in India was the education of girls. But her enthusiasm was dampened; "many thoughtful Indians" she wrote, "begged us to wait until we had secured the confidence of the Hindu community, so that no suspicion could arise with regard to our objects" (Besant 1913:318). Suspicion of foreign and Christian women interfering in Hindu domestic practices had been aroused by missionary agitation, by the uproar surrounding the government's Age of Consent Bill in 1891, and perhaps most of all by the example of Pandita Ramabai, the Brahmin woman who had not only done the unthinkable by converting to Christianity, but had also started a home for young widows where they came under Christian influence, some even converting. As Besant wrote in 1904, referring to Ramabai, "the unhappy perversion of an Indian lady had shaken the confidence of the Hindu public with respect to girls' education, and they feared Christian proselytizing under the garb of interest in education." But instead of resisting the specious arguments of "thoughtful Indians," Besant noted that the advice on this issue "seemed sound and we accepted it" (ibid:318). In Sri Lanka, in contrast, theosophists had started Buddhist schools for girls with foreign women as principals from 1889 onward.[8]

Annie Besant turned to boys' education and stressed the need for a correct national education for Indians. She urged wealthy Indians to start a modern school for Hindu boys, based on Hindu religious culture and traditions, with the emphasis on Sanskrit and the teaching of science. This was achieved in 1898, when the Central Hindu College was opened in Benares with Dr. Arthur Richardson, a science graduate from England, as principal, and with another English staff member to teach mathematics and science, and three Indians to teach Sanskrit, logic and history. Besant's continuous fund-raising for the school in India and Europe was successful and included a generous gift of land and a building from the Maharaja of Benares. The school magazine, subsidized by two English women theosophists, was edited by Besant and aimed at a broad audience of Hindu youth, achieving a circulation of 15,000. The boys of the Hindu College, whom Besant referred to as "the natural leaders of young Hinduism," included many who in later years became important education-alists and political leaders (Nethercot 1963:68–69).

The boys' school had been in existence three years when Besant (in 1901) remarked that "as soon as the Hindu College is secure, I am going to open one for girls and try to raise the women." The same year she tried out her ideas in a short article for the *Indian Ladies' Magazine* entitled "The Education of Women." It was not until 1904, however, that Besant "felt safe in going on with her plan" (ibid:73). The time seemed propitious for testing the waters with a pamphlet on *The Education of Indian Girls*. Besant claimed that "the confidence of the Hindu public in the purity of our aims and the straightforwardness of our actions has been won. The appeals to me to take up the education of girls have been many and urgent" (Besant 1904:318). She insisted that "the national movement for girls' education must be on national lines: it must accept the general Hindu conceptions of women's place in the national life, *not the dwarfed modern view but the ancient ideal*" (ibid:319 emphasis added).

In a talk on "Womanhood," she propagated the Hindu view that the "Creator divided himself into two...both sexes are equally divine, each is one half of God." Besant argued that the "ideal Hindu husband and the ideal Hindu wife make the most perfect picture of the marriage union that has ever inspired practice in right living" (Besant 1901:113–16). Besant selectively quoted from the laws of Manu that women should be "honoured and adorned" by their fathers, brothers, husbands and other male relatives, discussed the role of the unmarried *brahmavadini*—teacher of the Veda—and gave examples of learned women and women spiritual teachers in ancient India. Besant regret-ted the decline of the woman religious leader and urged the need for female education, but she insisted that this should not be a Western education:

That is not the kind of education you need. It would not build up women of the ancient Aryan type.... I presume that no Hindus...desire to educate their daughters, and then send them out into the world to struggle with men for gain-ing a livelihood. (ibid:126–28)

Much was made of this distinction between the "modern view" and the "ancient ideal." This was not merely a question of tactics, but was linked to the basic tenets of theosophy, and the search for lost formulas for the good life that had allegedly existed in the ancient world. What is surprising is that thirty years earlier the first Indian woman had gone to the United States for medical studies and that by the turn of the century Indian women doctors, graduates and lawyers had already made their mark. But Besant in 1904 held that Western education was "not suitable for the education of Eastern girls"; she made allowances for exceptional cases, and urged that:

> the *national* movement for the education of girls must be one which meets the national needs, and India needs nobly trained wives and mothers, wise and tender rulers of the household, educated teachers of the young, helpful counsellors of their husbands, skilled nurses of the sick rather than girl graduates, educated for the learned professions. (Besant 1904:319–20)

Education for girls, said Besant, should include a "sound literary knowledge of the vernacular, both in reading and writing" and a classical language "according to the girl's religion should be learned sufficiently to read with pleasure the noble literature contained therein"; this would not only give her "never-failing delight," but also enable her to "listen with intelligent pleasure *to the reading of her husband as he enjoys the masterpieces of the great writers.*" The emphasis should be on Indian history and geography, using examples of the "sweetest and strongest women in Indian history" to give students a "splendid... model," freeing them from the "very narrowness of their present lives, their triviality and frivolity." Girls should learn English because "English thought is *dominating the minds of men,*" and also because women should be exposed to "the world of thought outside India." However, Besant cautioned that if "Westernizing in a bad sense of Indian men is undesirable, still more undesirable is such Westernizing of Indian women," adding a warning that "the world cannot afford to lose the pure, lofty, tender and yet strong type of Indian womanhood." Yet she suggests that a knowledge of English may enable women to travel abroad *"in the company of their husbands,"* on the ground that "the larger horizons will interest without injuring" (ibid:323–24, emphases added).

Besant, though herself in revolt against all the constraints of Victorian patriarchy, was to use the "ancient ideal" of the Hindus to propose a traditional education for women. It was the "good wives and mothers" syndrome based on the argument that Hindu women had a role to play in the redemption of India, because "the wife inspires or retards the husband; the mother makes or mars the child." She also argued that "the power of woman to uplift or debase man is practically unlimited," and urged that "man and woman must walk hand in hand to the raising of India, else she will never be raised at all." The one-time atheist ended her article on women's education with the plea: "May Ishvara bless those who are the vanguard, and all beneficient Powers enlighten

their minds and make strong their hearts" (ibid:328). Having made her objectives clear, and allaying the fears of traditional Hindus, a Girls' College was
begun with the main finances coming from the British theosophist, Francesca
Arundale (who became the school's first Principal).[9]

While continuing to champion a restricted, traditional female education
for Indian women, Annie Besant simultaneously spoke in support of the militant movement for women's rights in the West. In 1913, she claimed that "the
only live movement in the world today is the women's movement," and in
1914, in a lecture in London on "Women and Politics," she spoke out as a radical,
recalling the first public lecture she had given four decades earlier on women's
suffrage; she protested that "for forty years and more women have been
claiming justice: for forty years and more justice has been denied." Speaking in
support of higher education for women she said, "you can never keep people
in a condition of subjection when you...educate them," and described the
courageous struggle of women in England to get medical education in spite of
"the bitter opposition of the medical profession" (Besant 1914:1–5).

On feminist issues in India, however, she moved cautiously: she called for
female education, late marriage for girls, an end to women's seclusion and
female franchise, but took care to put the interests of nationalism above feminist demands, feeling that "Home Rule was the more expedient cause"; she
preferred for example, "to work for women's suffrage and better education
separately through the Women's Indian Association," rather than include
such demands in the platform of the Home Rule League that she formed
(Paxton 1990:344).

FROM HOME RULE TO THE NEW MESSIAH

Annie Besant is mainly honored in India today not for her theosophy, or her
early Socialism and feminism, but for her activities for Home Rule for India,
even before Gandhi and Nehru had emerged on the political stage. In 1914 Besant
was part of a deputation to Britain (with some Indians) to present the case for
political reform (Nethercot 1963:215–19). In Britain, Besant launched a Home
Rule League for India. On her return to India, she acquired the *Madras Standard*
and turned it into the *New India*, a daily paper promoting ideas on self-government. After Gandhi's arrival in India from South Africa in 1915, she acknowledged his leadership, but was to have several disagreements with him on
political issues. Besant started the Home Rule League in India in 1915 (as an auxiliary to the Indian National Congress); its leading officials included Besant and
other theosophists.[10] The tone of the articles in *New India* roused the government's anger and she and two others were interned for three months. This
created a sensation and public meetings in protest were held all over the country; in Britain and the United States, too, her internment was condemned. In

1917, Annie Besant made history with her election as President of the Indian National Congress, the first woman to achieve that position. But in following years she had problems with Congress leaders about the non-cooperation and civil disobedience campaigns to which she only gave qualified support. Tilak was critical of her claim to be guided by supernatural Mahatmas: "in democratic politics we must go by the decisions of the majority," he wrote. "Congress recognises no Mahatma to rule over it except the Mahatma of the majority" (Taylor 1992:315). Disillusioned with Congress politics, Besant decided to devote her time to the coming messiah, J. Krishnamurti, to the relief, no doubt, of her Congress opponents and the British authorities in India.

For all its much vaunted religious universalism, however, theosophy tended to privilege Hinduism in India and Buddhism in Sri Lanka. As Taylor notes, Besant believed that "Hinduism, not Islam, came closer to the universal religion that was Theosophy and therefore tended to neglect the Muslim section of the population" (ibid:312). To Annie Besant, Hindu practices and India's Aryan heritage, with its caste hierachies and attitudes to women, were to be celebrated rather than criticized. "Those who, like myself, desire the maintenance of the caste system," she wrote in 1895, should reform the system of subdivisions of the same caste and thereby strengthen "the caste system against its assailants" (Besant 1913:111–12). In Britain, Besant had identified with workers, women, secularists and dissidents; but in India she took an elitist attitude, concentrating on upper-caste Hindu male society as being representative of the "nation," thereby neglecting many issues pertaining to minorities, the "low" castes and women.

MAHATMAS AND MESSIAHS

The theosophists in confronting Christianity, in associating with Hinduism or Buddhism, in extolling Eastern society, and eventually in sponsoring a new messiah, inevitably attracted the derision if not the hostility of some sections of the British in India and Britain. The missionaries were particularly appalled by the "treachery" of Westerners "going native." They denounced Besant for saying that Indian civilization was the "oldest, truest and best in the world," and gave warnings that such fallacies and materialist thinking led to Nihilism, as in Russia, "no God...no government, no marriage" (Jayawardena 1972:56).[11] In addition, some Westernized local social reformers also thought it hilarious that white women were espousing local superstitions and picking up phony world messiahs on the beaches of Madras. Dr. Nanjunda Rao stated that it would be "very silly" to "deify an English woman, be she ever so clever, ever so eloquent...more especially when she...offers as an object of worship the little Hindu boy...." (Nethercot 1963:159).

While Hindus were happy to see Besant and the theosophists condemn

Christianity and vilify the missionaries, not all appreciated her denunciations of Western materialism, and her belief in mahatmas and messiahs. After a lecture tour in Madras in 1893, where she proceeded to condemn the West and extol Hinduism, Besant was attacked by the *Hindu*—the leading English newspaper in Madras. Subramania Aiyar, its editor and founder, was a keen social reformer and critic of child marriage, women's seclusion and the caste system. He constantly wrote about the "new women" in the West, their education and freedom in contrast to Indian women who were imprisoned at home: "we are unable to see that…it can be consonant with eternal justice," he wrote, "that one half of the human race should be condemned to a perpetual life of drudgery and mental darkness" (Parthasarathy 1978:134). Ironically, Besant would have agreed with this sentiment in a Western context and it is clear that Subramania Aiyar had been influenced by Besant's social reform and radical activities in Britain. Other educated Hindus, especially the Westernized doctors, lawyers and writers, thought that Besant's claims that she was a Brahmin pandit in her previous life and that she communicated with spirits known as mahatmas in Tibet were ludicrous. They also thought it totally unacceptable that she was promoting Krishnamurti as the new World Teacher and Messiah of the Order of the Star in the East.

Jeddu Krishnamurti, the Indian male in Annie Besant's life, was born in 1896 to a poor Brahmin family of Andhra. His father was a clerk, and Krishnamurti and his brother Nityananda had been pupils at a school in Adyar where the former Bishop turned theosophist, C.W. Leadbeater, was on the look-out for the coming World Teacher; he had spotted the boys on the beach and Annie Besant and Leadbeater thereafter supervised their spiritual initiation and secular education. An Order of the Star in the East was formed with Krishnamurti as its nominal head, which by 1913 claimed 12,000 members who awaited the "New Messiah and World Teacher" (Nethercot 1963:214). When the youthful Krishnamurti allegedly wrote the book *At the Feet of the Master* in 1910, inspired by the "masters," there was sharp criticism of him in the Madras press.[12] More scandal was to follow when the boys' father initiated legal action in court for the recovery of the children. The columns of the *Hindu* were filled with protests on these issues. The custody case by Krishnamurthi's father was lost by Besant in the local courts and went on appeal to the Privy Council in London. Besant took her two wards with her to London, and after she won the case, the boys stayed on there. They studied and took part in sports, especially tennis and golf, but failed their matriculation examinations. They were, however, lionized by theosophists and traveled widely in Europe and the United States. In 1921, a Dutch Baron gave Krishnamurti a large estate and castle near Ommen in Holland for meetings and several "Star Camps" were held there.[13]

By 1929, however, the tide had turned and Krishnamurti felt he had enough of the whole show. To the amazement of the devotees at the Holland summer gathering of that year, he "slowly, deliberately told them that, after careful consideration for over two years…he had resolved to disband the Order of which he was the Head" (ibid:425). Traveling back to India in 1929, Krishnamurti was in Adyar with Besant when she spoke of the dissolution of the Order before a large gathering of theosophists. Krishnamurti also broke with the Theosophical Society, and renounced any claim to be World Teacher or Messiah; he continued, however, to pursue a long and fruitful career for the rest of his life as an important independent thinker, surrounded by many Western women admirers. Annie Besant was deeply upset by the debacle of 1929; her health declined in the early 1930s and she died at eighty-six in 1933.

The question arises whether Besant and the theosophists had two standards—one for Europe and one for the East, or in the words of Nethercot, whether Annie Besant knew how "to wear sandals in India and shoes in the rest of the world" (ibid:469). The Sri Lankan Buddhist leader Anagarika Dharmapala had noticed this difference and remarked that Besant was preaching "gentleness and obedience" to Indians, while supporting the militant suffragettes in England (Guruge 1965:513). From the theosophists' point of view, of course, there was no inconsistency. They believed that each country works out its own destiny and evolves a religious culture suitable to its needs; therefore, what is relevant and good for Europe could be harmful in India and Sri Lanka. In a colonial situation this could be a daring thesis—namely, that Europe had no civilizing mission to impose on others. Where women were concerned, however, such a view could also legitimize existing repressive structures and lead to a glorification of practices that many South Asian women and men reformers were trying to change. From the local women's point of view, the foreign women's idealization of Indian patriarchy was harmful, while to traditional Hindu males, it was a godsend. No wonder, therefore, that the white goddess found her place in Indian society and that a suburb of Madras is named Besant Nagar.

FROM LONDON'S WEST END TO JAFFNA

Florence Farr as George Bernard Shaw's "New Woman"

This is to be the Woman's Century. In it she is to awake from her long sleep…there is to be a revaluation of all values, old rubbish is to be burnt up, the social world is to be melted down and remoulded "nearer to the heart's desire"; but the old lies are in our blood—we still believe in Eve and her shame…*it remains for white women to fight now and at last rid their sex all over the world of the ignominy of this false doctrine.*

—Florence Farr, *Modern Woman: Her Intentions* (London 1910: Preface—emphasis added)

And they wanted more from their women,
Wanted 'em jacked up a little
And sent over for teachers (Ceylon)
So Loica went out and died there
After her time in the post-Ibsen movement.

—Ezra Pound on Florence Farr (Canto xxviii)

Florence Farr's (1860–1917) career provides another fascinating example of the life of a liberated woman of the period who was considered "outrageously advanced," and part of the modernist movement, but was steeped in the occult, theosophy and Hinduism. She was a famous actress who moved in Socialist and feminist circles in Britain. Bernard Shaw wrote *Arms and the Man* for her; she pioneered new art forms with W.B. Yeats, and inspired Ezra Pound. Her multi-faceted life included many lovers, and according to Shaw "she attached no more importance to her love affairs than Casanova. I think she was rather proud of her Leperello list [of lovers] which contained fourteen names in 1894" (Bax 1946:55–56). Farr lived out her life in Sri Lanka as the principal of a new school for Hindu girls in Jaffna—the people of Jaffna, of course, were kept unaware that the respectable "Lady Principal," Mrs.

Florence Emery, was Florence Farr, the actress with a lively past. But even if they knew, they might have accepted her as a "good" woman because she was involved in Hindu girls' education.

In a social context Florence Farr belongs to a category hard to place; her parents born into one class, moved up the social ladder, but she became a declassé bohemian, breaking all the rules of the patriarchal establishment, opposing both church and state, defying Victorian morality, rejecting traditional family life and leading the independent life of the turn of the century "new woman."[1] Florence Farr was born in 1860 and at the age of thirteen was sent to one of the most prestigious girls' schools in England—Cheltenham Ladies' College in Gloucestershire—run by the famous educationist Dorothea Beale. It was an era of advance in women's education; girls' schools adopted the same curricula as the boys' and trained their students to aim at equality in education through competitive examinations and admission to universities (see Chapter 2). Farr, however, rebelled against this type of formal education and in later years recalled that, "it took me quite six years to get out of the shell my education had hardened around me. I don't suppose I would ever have spread my own wings if the beak of my destiny had not been stronger than my overwhelming education, so that it succeeded in hammering through that shell at last" (Farr 1910:68). From 1877 to 1880 she joined Queen's College, London. But although she attended classes, she abstained from examinations which she held were "really damaging to the vital apparatus…" (Johnson 1975:18).

While being intellectually keen on a variety of subjects and spending her leisure hours reading in the British Museum, Farr was in revolt against the institutionalized, narrow system of education. She had the artist's belief in a full, creative life, rather than a rigid, competitive one, and was to respond in later years to modern systems of education, including the Montessori method of teaching children. She was exposed at an early age to the cultural world of London, when her sister Henrietta married Henry Marriot Paget, a romantic painter of the late 19th century. Their home was an artistic center, and the activities included play-acting in which Florence participated. In 1882 she became a pupil of J.L. Toole, an actor-manager who had his own theatre, and by 1883 she had appeared in several light plays. In 1884, she married an actor, Edward Emery (of a well-known acting family) who had been in a play with her, but the marriage was not a success; Emery migrated to the United States in 1888 and Florence Farr divorced him in 1894 on the advice of Bernard Shaw (Holroyd 1988:308).

Florence Farr met Shaw around 1889 at the house of the Socialist William Morris, whose daughter, Mary Morris, was a mutual friend. At this time Shaw was an impecunious writer, active in socialist circles in London, and Farr was a minor actress, whom Shaw had seen in *A Sicilian Idyll*, which he described as "an hour's transparent Arcadian make-believe." He had also commented on Florence Farr's striking good looks (ibid:246). Shaw had "optimistically invented" the "New Woman" in his early novels, especially Madge Brailsford in *Love among the Artists* who defies her father and becomes a successful actress. As Holroyd notes, "this had been one of Shaw's earliest portraits of the 'New Woman,' and in Florence Farr he appeared to have met a 'New Woman' after his own prescription" (ibid:246). Shaw and Farr became lovers although he had several other women friends at the time, including Mary Morris, Annie Besant, and an actress, Jenny Patterson; many of the complicated dramas that arose as a result would be depicted in Shaw's future plays.

But by the 1880s, there emerged the beginnings of a "New Drama" in reaction to the narrowly conventional theatre of the period. Influenced by Ibsen, Shaw was to move on to a new dramatic mode with its harsh critiques and mockery of the bourgeoisie and British economic and social institutions; he exposed the evils of slum landlordism, prostitution and the armaments industry, and attacked middle-class morality. Ibsen's "new women" were all the rage and in 1891 Florence Farr appeared in the English premiere of Ibsen's drama *Rosmersholm,* coached by Bernard Shaw for the part of the emancipated woman, Rebecca West. Soon after her success, Farr appeared in 1892 in Shaw's first play, *Widowers' Houses*, a problem play based on a socialist critique of unconscionable profits. She played the leading role of Blanche (daughter of a slum landlord) whose fiancé, an idealistic young man, breaks off the engagement when he finds that the heroine's money comes from slum property[2] (ibid:283). Soon after, financed by Annie Horniman of the wealthy Quaker family, Florence Farr organized a modern theatre season in London.[3] For this, Shaw wrote *Arms and the Man,* in which Farr played the part of the servant, Louka; Yeats' wrote *The Land of Heart's Desire,* in which Farr portrayed "a wife who escapes domestic drudgery, through death, into fairyland" (ibid:300). As du Cann pointed out, "few actresses or women can have extorted such a double tribute"; this event was described by Shaw as a "startling" success (du Cann 1963:88).[4]

FLORENCE FARR AND THE GOLDEN DAWN

Like some middle-class women of the late 19th century, Florence Farr, in escaping from the constraints of Victorian patriarchy and asserting her independence, also rejected Christianity. These were also years when spiritual, occult practices, theosophy and modernism in art and literature were beginning to make their mark by provoking the "Establishment." As Noel Annan has said, to cause outrage "you created a scandal, you proclaimed your belief in nothing; or in something absurd that would be scorned by the scientific—for instance, alchemy or the occult" (1990:53). Florence Farr, influenced by Yeats, joined the Order of the Golden Dawn, an organization devoted to occult studies. Yeats described her lack of interest in the real world, "actual things" being spoken of with "cold wit or under the strain of paradox." He refers to the long hours she spent in the British Museum becoming "erudite in many heterogeous studies" and moved by "an insatiable curiosity." The walls of her rooms were "covered with musical instruments, pieces of Oriental drapery, and Egyptian gods and goddesses painted by herself" (Johnson 1975:70). In 1894, Farr published her first work, *A Short Enquiry Concerning the Hermetic Art by a Lover of Philalethes,* and by 1895 she had risen to become "Praemonstratrix" of the Golden Dawn. She wrote two texts in 1896, *A Commentary on Euphrates or The Waters of the East* and *Egyptian Magic.* But many quarrels broke out when Farr tried to assert her authority in disciplining members. More troubles with Annie Horniman, the founder of the Golden Dawn, led to Farr's break from the Order in 1902, the same year she joined the Theosophical Society.

Shaw had hoped to make Florence Farr into the leading Shavian actress of the era, but her life was dominated by the Golden Dawn and theosophy. Shaw was incensed that Farr was wasting her time on the occult and writing a small book, *Esoteric Egyptology,* rather than working to change society:

> I hereby warn mankind to beware of women with large eyes, and crescent eyebrows, and a smile, and a love of miracles and moonshees.... I warn them against all who like intellectual pastimes...who live for and in themselves instead of for and in the world. (Bax 1946:12)

Having made a complete break with Christianity himself, it was galling for Shaw to see his dynamic Socialist and artistic women friends (Annie Besant and Florence Farr) move into the sphere of "miracles and moonshees." He was unhappy that Farr, instead of working at "some reality every day," was working hard at her "unreality". He particularly regretted that all his attempts (in the style of Professor Higgins) to make her into the ideal "New Woman" were wasted. "And now you think to undo the work of all these years by a phrase and a shilling's worth of esoteric Egyptology" he wrote to her, with some bitterness, in 1896 (ibid:10).

By 1894, W.B. Yeats had replaced Shaw as Florence Farr's favorite.[5] Under the guidance of Arnold Dolmetsch, who performed old English music, Yeats and Florence Farr developed the techniques of mixing words and music. By 1898, Yeats had introduced Farr to the new Irish Literary Theatre movement. Yeat's play, *Countess Cathleen* was produced by the group in London, with Farr taking part in it, using the new combination of music and poetry. The play was successful, and by 1902 Yeats and Farr were giving lectures and demonstrations on the music of speech, at which Yeats would talk about his theories, and Farr would chant poems to music; one critic, William Archer, claimed that Farr had possibly "hit on something very like a new art" (Holroyd 1988:108). In 1909, Florence Farr's book, *The Music of Speech*, dedicated to Yeats and Dolmetsch, contained illustrations and accounts of the new art, which was influenced by the "mysteries of the East" (Johnson 1975:122). Florence Farr's other extraordinary friendship was with the poet Ezra Pound, who was impressed by the experiments of Yeats and Farr with music and poetry. Farr was a frequent visitor, and one of Ezra Pound's recollections of around 1909 was, "in the front room, Florence Farr reading Tagore." Johnson notes that "Pound knew Florence well enough to write her biography in a poem *Portrait d'Une Femme* (1913), which ends as follows:

You are a person of some interest, one comes to you
And takes strange gain away:
Trophies fished up: some curious suggestion;
Fact that leads nowhere; and a tale or two,
Pregnant with mandrakes, or with something else
That might prove useful and yet never proves,
That never fits a corner or shows use,
Or finds its hour upon the loom of days;
The tarnished, gaudy, wonderful old work;
Idols and ambergris and rare inlays,
These are your riches, your great store; and yet
For all this sea-hoard of decidious things,
Strange woods half-sodden, and new brighter stuff:
In the slow float of differing light and deep,
No! There is nothing! In the whole and all,
Nothing that's quite your own.
Yet this is you.
(Pound 1928:74–5)

WOMEN'S RIGHTS

While Pound is somewhat dismissive of Florence Farr for her dilletantism, not surprisingly, he fails to note or value her feminism, her challenge to patriarchal attitudes and her approach to education. Farr's vision of education went beyond the narrow field of formal learning and competitive examinations; in this respect her attitude was more iconoclastic than that of women who only aimed at equalling men in educational excellence and the professions. Farr, as a journalist, also wrote frequently for *The New Age* on issues affecting women, including publicizing and championing "the cause of prostitutes and

Florence Farr on the London stage. (From M.
Holroyd's *Bernard Shaw*, Victoria and Albert
Museum, London.)

other unpopular persons" (Bax 1946:vi). Moreover, she was in the thick of the
struggle for women's franchise. Writing a pamphlet in 1910 on "Modern
Woman," she replied to all the current arguments against women's rights:

> They say the vote is the thin end of the wedge; and I reply gladly...that the
> wedge is being driven every day...delay in giving women the vote gives them a
> power far more deadly...the power of standing up for themselves, freed from
> the belief in the protection of men. It gives them hope in each other. It teaches
> them to speak for themselves and discover the force of their eloquence and the
> ingenuity of their resources. (Farr 1910:17)

Farr was optimistic for the future of the women's movement, declaring in
1910 that this was "the Woman's Century" (ibid:Preface). But to her, the vote
alone was not enough; what women need, she wrote, "is strength to hammer
through the prisons which have kept them for many centuries packed away
conveniently for use on occasion. They are coming out into the daylight for
the first time within our memory, and now the real movement of life begins"
(ibid:93). To Farr, feminism meant more than obtaining a few equal rights in a
patriarchal society. She celebrated the "splendid uncivilized women immortalized for all time—Medea, Elektra, the Roman Empresses, Queen Maeve of

Connaught," and the Russian bomb-throwing heroines, who were the strong defiant women, whether "as noble savages or as gloriously barbaric haters of ordered life." In fact, her own enthusiasms stemmed from her challenge to many aspects of the "ordered life" of Victorian Britain and she wrote with fervor of the "quickly spreading passion of enthusiasm which is moving the women of all nations" to make a fight against patriarchy (ibid:92).

VENTURING TO THE EAST

The last phase of Farr's life was linked to female education in North Sri Lanka. She had already become disappointed with her life in England, and her declining influence as an actress, musician and writer. The break came in 1912, when Florence Farr left for Sri Lanka (at fifty-two) where she had been offered the post of principal of Ramanathan College, Jaffna, a Hindu Girls' school. She was disillusioned by her British lovers and friends and bitterly remarked that, "half-baked people like Yeats and Shaw have tremendous influence and yet they only tell half-truths" (ibid:97). The whole truth, she began to feel, was in the East and she sought the company of Indians and Sri Lankans. There were, by the early 20th century, many Asians in London who as students, travelers or gurus were popular in intellectual, political and spiritualist circles. One of Florence Farr's friends was a theosophist, Mohini Mohan Chatterjee, a lawyer from Calcutta; he was wellknown among theosophists and occultists in the 1880s and had been a "social hit in England and America" (Nethercot 1961:303). Yeats had even written a poem entitled *Mohini Chatterjee*. Farr possibly had also met Tagore because Yeats was closely associated with him.

The other important Asian influence on Farr was Ponnambalam Ramanathan from Sri Lanka. Ramanathan had visited London in 1902 and had addressed a meeting of persons interested in Eastern philosophy, where Farr was present. She was impressed by the speaker and his plans for education in Sri Lanka and promsied to help him in such a venture. Farr herself made the strange pronouncement that "The Being they call Christ arises at certain intervals from the age-long trance. He is Mamanakaja which has been active during the last three years or so. He is working through Ramanathan and many others" (Johnson 1975:92). Farr then immersed herself "in Eastern meditations and the study of pamphlets written by Ramanathan" (ibid:93). Ramanathan returned the compliment by inviting Farr to Jaffna. It is interesting that for all their allegiance to Hindu Tamil traditions, members of Ramanathan's family had a history of being influenced by the West and more unusually, of marrying Western women (Ramanathan's uncle Sir Mutu Coomaraswamy married an English woman as early as 1874, and their son Ananda Coomaraswamy married four times—all Westerners. Ramanathan and his elder brother P. Coomaraswamy also had Western women as their second wives).

Ponnambalam Ramanathan (1851–1930) came from a family of merchants who had migrated early in the century from Jaffna, in the north of Sri Lanka to the capital, Colombo. The family produced some noted intellectuals—especially Ramanathan's brother, Ponnambalam Arunachalam and their cousin Ananda Coomaraswamy (see Chapter 11). Ramanathan was a lawyer, and from 1879 to 1892, he was appointed by the Governor to the Legislative Council. He was liberal in his politics, clashing with officials, taking on unpopular causes, and championing the rights of Buddhists and Hindus against the missionaries. In 1905 and 1906, Ramanathan visited the United States, lecturing in New York, Boston, Washington and other cities; his lecture in Brooklyn was on "The Spirit of the East contrasted with the Spirit of the West," which concerned the "materialism" of the one, and the "spirituality" of the other, a popular topic at that time (Vythilingam 1971:525).[6]

Ramanathan, after his return from the United States, devoted much of his time to Hindu education. He had over the years frequently clashed with the missionaries on this issue. "There is a great deal too much of hypocrisy in Jaffna in the matter of religion," he wrote because "the love of the Missionaries for proselytes is as boundless as the love of the Jaffnese to obtain some knowledge of English at any cost" (ibid:250). Female education in Jaffna had become a preserve of Christian missionaries, who from the 1820s onward had established a network of English schools in the region, including the first girls' boarding school at Uduvil, Jaffna, in 1824 (see Chapter 2).[7]

The reasons behind Florence Farr's decision to leave for Sri Lanka were a source of much debate. W.B. Yeats wrongly believed it was because of her fear of old age and loss of beauty, expressed in some lines of his poem *All Souls Night,* in which he commemorated Farr and other lost friends "who had shared his love for strange thought:"

On Florence Emery I call the next,
Who finding the first wrinkles on a face
Admired and beautiful,
And knowing that the future would be vexed
With 'minished beauty, multiplied commonplace,
Preferred to teach a school
Away from neighbour or friend,
Among dark skins, and there
Permit foul years to wear
Hidden from eyesight to the unnoticed end.

Before that end much had she revelled out
From a discourse in figurative speech

By some learned Indian
On the soul's journey. How it is whirled about
Wherever the orbit of the moon can reach
Until it plunge into the sun;
And there, free and yet fast,
Being both Chance and Choice,
Forget its broken toys
And sink into its own delight at last.
(Hone 1942)

Jayantha Padmanabha (Ramanathan's nephew) claimed that "these magnificent lines are likely to preserve the memory of Florence Farr long after her
admired and beautiful person is forgotten" and also surmised that the
"learned Indian" of the poem was Ramanathan; he referred to "the effect of
his spell-binding eloquence on a mind susceptible to occult influences and
mysterious ways of thought" (Padmanabha 1947a). Bernard Shaw was not
impressed by Farr's enthusiasm for the Vedas, and in 1903, a year after Farr had
met Ramanathan, he poured scorn on "people who have taken up this particular craze," urging her not to be "misled by sloppy-minded lunatics" (ibid).
Shaw, in later years in his play *On the Rocks,* created a pompous character, partly based on Ramanathan, called Sir Jaffna Pandranath.

Another view of Farr's journey to Sri Lanka was that she knew she had cancer and had come to Jaffna to make a "brave end." What is more likely,
however, is that by this date she felt that she had reached the end of a phase,
and was prepared to embark on a new venture; in a letter to an American
lawyer friend, John Quinn, she wrote of her plans, "to end my days in the
'society of the wise,' as the Vedantist books say one should." Quinn replied
that it sounded "romantic" and would "read well in a book," but inquired anx-
iously about insects, neighbors, cooking, doctors and whether the local
English were "sane and comfortable" (Johnson 1975:181–82). Farr herself also
wondered about the twenty Europeans in Jaffna and thought that her work
among the Tamils might lead them to suspect that she was "upsetting the
Empire" (ibid:187).

In preparation for her work in Sri Lanka, Farr went back to her old school,
Cheltenham Ladies' College, to spend a month finding out about new educational methods and was excited to hear of the Montessori system, which
she hoped to introduce to Jaffna. Farr arrived in Colombo in October 1912 and
stayed in Ramanathan's house, discussing "the nature of the soul" with the
host, studying Tamil and meeting officials of the Department of Education.
She then moved to Jaffna to prepare for the opening, in 1913, of Ramanathan
College. The parents of the young girls of Jaffna, who referred to the new prin-

cipal as Mrs. Florence Emery, did not know of her socialist, feminist past and her acting career. Instead, without actually telling untruths, a formula was adopted whereby Florence Farr's earlier life experiences were made to sound like just what the Jaffna Tamils needed in their "Lady Principal."[8] Writing on Florence Farr in 1947, under the subtitle, *The Life and Death of a Victorian Cleopatra*, Padmanabha states that the generation of Hindu girls who were her pupils, "would perhaps be surprised and a little shocked if they knew the full story of her early life." In those days, she was, in Shaw's words, "In violent reaction against Victorian morals, especially sexual and domestic morals," setting no bounds "to her relations with the men she liked" (Padmanabha 1947b). It was, however, her reaction against Christianity and not her morals that interested the Hindus.

Ramanathan College, which was opened in 1913 on a site of thirty acres, consisted of several large buildings around an open courtyard with dormitories, classrooms and a large hall. In its first year there were seventy pupils in residence.[9] Ramanathan stressed the need for a traditional education in a modern context; a good grounding in the religious texts, "the precepts of right conduct; ancient legends...national stories of famous dynasties," combined with success in the Cambridge school leaving examinations conducted by the government. He also had been impressed by modern methods of education in the West, and hoped that the children in his school would have "a combination of the ancient Tamil system" with new methods including the Montessori system (Vythilingam 1971:550–1). Ramanathan also started a Training School for teachers on the premises, with teachers from India to impart South Indian vocal and instrumental music, and including courses in home science. As a teacher of the school wrote:

> Ramanathan attended personally to all details.... He was in the temple with the girls to direct them in worship.... He was in the dining hall to supervise the...meals.... He was keen about their personal cleanliness and their dress and deportment. Ramanathan wanted the girls to be *brought up as Hindu girls in every respect, so that they might become good Hindu wives and mothers.* (ibid:555, emphasis added)

It is, of course, interesting to note the limitations of Ramanathan's vision. In the words of his biographer, he quite clearly was "out of sympathy with the modern concept of women's place in society and clung tenaciously to the view that the legitimate sphere of a woman's activity was the home, not the tumultuous and competitive world, for which he believed, God designed man" (ibid:556). Moreover, in the late 1920s, when the suffrage issue was debated in the legislature, Ramanathan opposed universal franchise for women (Jayawardena 1972:267). One may also add that while Ramanathan College was meant to strengthen the Hindu Tamil family by producing good wives and mothers, Florence Farr had already rejected the family as the ultimate goal for women. "I think the object of our life," she wrote in 1910, "is to make experiments…. I quarrel with absorption in the family because family jealousy is a bar to that kind of social intercourse which is the only education worth having," adding that "family love cannot absorb us if we wish to survive…we are greatly indebted for our culture to individuals who do not desire to be parents" (Farr 1910:93–94). As Ezra Pound observed, Farr preferred her bohemian existence to "the usual thing:"

> One dull man, dulling and uxorious.
> One average mind—with one thought less each year.
> (Pound (1913) in 1928:74)

But Florence Farr, who was principal of Ramanathan College from 1913 to 1916, had escaped from Europe only to get entangled in the administrative and bureaucratic details such as (in her words), supervising "gardens—stores—servants—teachers—sick children—money." She wrote to Yeats, describing the Tamils and their culture, sending him translations of Tamil poetry and speaking of her recitals of poetry using the vina, a stringed musical instrument. The role of school principal, however, made her restive; it was, she said, like being Queen Elizabeth, "the children who have fever…who steal…who are so naughty no one else can manage them are brought to me. I hear evidence and give decisions." Moreover, as her biographer noted, "the daily rituals at Ramanathan were not really dissimilar to the Victorianism she rebelled against at Cheltenham and at Queens" (Johnson 1975:192–3). During her Jaffna years, Farr was also exposed to British officialdom. The Governor attended the school prize-giving in 1915 and was amazed at her good diction when reading out the school report; at a subsequent display of fireworks she had to sit on the Governor's right, which she found comparable to sitting on the right hand of God. She became "unenthusiastic in her role of Lady Principal" and resigned in 1916, but not wanting to leave Jaffna, she decided to stay on in the College as bursar, with a salary of Rs.60 (£6) a month. In 1916 she discovered she had cancer and was operated on in Colombo, but died in April 1917, at 57, and was cremated according to Hindu rites (ibid:211).

The drama of Florence Farr's life and her multiple identities reflect the many disjunctures of the time, when, as Yeats said, "things fall apart." What is more, the many roles she played in her lifetime led to misidentification. As a suffragist, socialist, actress and a "new woman" she appealed to Shaw, but then she transformed herself into an occultist, spiritualist, and theosophist, much to Shaw's annoyance and Yeat's delight. But rejecting them both, she turned towards Ramanathan, the Hindu guru, only to find that his ideal role for Hindu woman was only that of wife and mother. In Europe, she disappointed her admirers one after another; one of them, Ezra Pound, wrote a poem about her varied interests and lack of success:

> Your mind and you are our Sargasso Sea,
> London has swept about you this score years,
> And bright ships left you this or that in fee:
> Ideas, old gossip, oddments of all things,
> Strange spars of knowledge and dimmed wares of price.
> Great minds have sought you—lacking someone else.
> You have been second always.
> (Pound (1913) in 1928:74)

Some of the "great men" in her life, like Pound, patronizingly put her "second always," ignoring her important feminist and other contributions. And in Sri Lanka she was again badly misrepresented; Ramanathan deliberately erased her past and she had to act the role of respectable lady principal and school administrator. But rejecting this burden and overtaken by illness, she died in Colombo, treated by a local doctor (Dr. Lucian de Zilwa) who recognized her as the actress on the London stage he had ardently admired when he was a student. The wheel had come full cycle.

"BLAZING THE TRAIL FOR
INDIAN WOMEN'S FREEDOM"

Margaret Cousins in India

Amongst astrologers and psychical researchers and spirit mediums, past and
future seemed to come near us. But amongst the theosophists, suffragettes and
vegetarians we felt on the *terra firma* of the present, with its insistence on work to
be done today.

—Margaret Cousins (around 1910) in *We Two Together* (1950:131)

We in India, look upon Margaret Cousins as our dear sister of service, a citizen
of the world—a messenger of love and goodwill between women and between
nations…the active and enterprising women of the West have been a source of
inspiration to us, many are our friends and co-workers in the same cause.

—Dr. Muttulakshmi Reddy (1931), in the *All-Asian Women's Conference Proceedings*
(1931:166–67)

SOCIAL AND POLITICAL CHANGES IN EUROPE IN THE FIRST DECADES OF THE
20th century led to certain ideological changes.[1] One major result was to push
the concern with the occult and the spiritual onto the fringes of the European
"progressive" movement; instead, attention was focused on secular issues such
as Socialism, modernism and feminism. It is in such a context of political
upheaval and social change that this chapter considers the life of an Irish
woman, who came from a background of theosophy, alternative politics and
women's rights, to work in similar fields in India and Britain. Margaret
Cousins née Gillespie (1878–1954), born to a Protestant family in Ireland, was
part of the Irish Home Rule agitation, the Irish literary awakening, suffragist
militancy and Socialist politics.[2] She was also a theosophist who, in India,
devoted her life to education and also to forming women's organizations and

supporting Gandhi's agitation in the 1930s. She went to jail several times—in London and Ireland for suffragist protests, and in India for being in a nationalist demonstration. Her activism went further than Annie Besant's on the women's issue in India, and unlike Besant, who had disagreements with Gandhi, Margaret Cousins was to work closely with him. Her political and feminist consciousness outweighed her theosophical preoccupations and she took a step forward in actually organizing Indian women in both national associations and in promoting the first Asian Women's Conference in 1931.

From 1898 to 1902, Margaret Gillespie studied and obtained a Bachelor of Music degree from the Royal University of Ireland, Dublin. There she met James Cousins who was involved in the dramatic and literary revival in Ireland, and married him in 1903. They continued to take part in literary work, James Cousins publishing poetry, and teaching at a school in Dublin. Like many other Socialists in Britain at that time, he was "a devotee of Robert Blatchford with his spicy weekly paper, *The Clarion*—a paper devoted not only to radical politics, but also to feminism and modernism in art and literature." The Cousins were also interested in exploring psychical phenomena, including trances, and even had a seance in their home with Yeats and his friend Maud Gonne[3] (Cousins & Cousins 1950:352, 121).

At the end of 1906, Margaret spoke at a vegetarian conference in Manchester, and on the same trip, attended a session of the National Conference of Women:

> The latter was to prove itself a turning-point in my life. It was the first large gathering of women I had contacted.... It made me aware of the injustices and grievances which were taken for granted as the natural fate of my sex.... I had never, in my insular life in Ireland, heard of the movement till I went to Manchester. (ibid:128–29)

Returning to Ireland, she joined the Irish branch of the National Conference of Women and organized a meeting on the issue of women's suffrage in 1907. That year the Cousins' attended the Convention of the Theosophical Society, held in London and presided over by Annie Besant. London at the turn of the century was full of intellectual and political excitement, and the Cousins experienced the exhilaration of being involved in dissident movements and ideologies. Besant's message to Margaret Cousins was "Go back to Ireland, my dear, and form a lodge of the Theosophical Society, and when it is formed I will come and lecture for you" (ibid:126). This was the beginning of her formal link with the theosophists. During her stay in London in 1907, Margaret Cousins was also in touch with the suffragists, joined their demonstrations, and was present when Christabel Pankhurst, Mrs Pethick-Lawrence and Charlotte Despard of the Women's Social and Political

Margaret Cousins as a Magistrate in India. (From J. H. & Margaret Cousins, *We Two Together* (1950); Schlesinger Library, Radcliffe College.)

Union were arrested. She also forged links in London with the vegetarians, the anti-vivisection movement and those interested in the occult.

Returning to Ireland, the Cousins were very active; an Irish branch of the Theosophical Society was formed in 1908, and the same year, the Irish Women's Franchise League was begun, with Margaret Cousins as its treasurer. The aim was to link the Home Rule struggle to the women's suffrage issue and "to start a new women's suffrage society on militant lines." Another task was to obtain pledges from Irish MPs to vote for women's suffrage bills in the British Parliament, and to push for the inclusion of women's suffrage in any Home Rule Bill. The League published a paper, *The Irish Citizen*, and much of its work involved traveling around Ireland and speaking in small towns. In 1918 Margaret organized a visit to Ireland by Christabel Pankhurst. In November 1910, she was one of six Dublin women to attend the Parliament of Women in London, which drew up a resolution on women's suffrage, and in groups of twelve proceeded to the House of Commons to attempt to hand it over to the Prime Minister. Home Secretary Winston Churchill ordered the police to break up the procession, and 119 women were arrested, fifty requiring medical care. The next day more women marched on Downing Street, but police turned them back. Cousins writes that the women then decided to break the windows of the houses of Cabinet Ministers, which were "the property of taxpayers of whom thousands were women" (ibid:177). The Irish women along with several English women went to the house of the Chief Secretary for Ireland, and broke the windows by throwing potatoes. In all, over 200 were arrested. That night Cousins went with a group to Downing Street and broke windows; she was arrested and sentenced to one month in Holloway Jail, the largest women's prison in Britain, and served the sentence in early 1911, spending the time reading, including books by Vivekananda (ibid:180).[4]

During these years, James and Margaret Cousins kept their links with literary circles in Ireland and England, and in 1912, vacationed with W.B. Yeats in France. On this occasion, translations of poems of Rabindranath Tagore were read by Yeats; James Cousins states that when Yeats first obtained the poems he "had gone on fire with the fullness in them that told that the renaissance of poetry had appeared in India" (ibid:161). Margaret Cousins continued suffrage work in Ireland, with open air and indoor meetings. When the Home Rule Bill omitted the question of women's suffrage, she went to London to lobby Irish MPs, whose general line was that women's suffrage could be considered after Ireland had achieved Home Rule. Back in Ireland, with the second reading of the Home Rule Bill, Margaret Cousins and others broke the windows of Dublin Castle and were arrested and sentenced to one month in jail. They demanded to be classed as political prisoners, went on a hunger strike and after public pressure the demand was met. In 1913 the Cousins moved to Liverpool, where James Cousins had a job in a vegetarian food factory (Ramusack 1981a:125). They continued their interest in theosophy, and in 1915 they accepted an offer to go to India. From then onward, India was their permanent home. James Cousins became the literary sub-editor of *New India,* the newspaper started by Annie Besant in 1914, which had a large circulation, and became a "national institution"[5] (Nethercot 1963:227). As Taylor records, it was "hypercritical of the Raj, often strident" and to many British "down right poisonous." In 1916 an article in *New India* by James Cousins praising the Easter uprising in Dublin "caused such a storm of rage Besant was obliged to dismiss him" (Taylor 1992:302). He was then appointed the Vice-Principal of Madanapalle College, where Margaret got a job teaching English.

INDIAN WOMEN'S RIGHTS

Margaret Cousins' main interest, however, remained women's issues, and after discussions with groups in India, she formed a society that became the Women's Indian Association in 1917. The first president was Annie Besant, and Dorothy Jinarajadasa, an English theosophist, was the secretary. Cousins, who edited its journal, *Sthri Dharma,* was outspoken on the question of women's rights:

Centuries of social degeneration lay between the superb marriage ideals and practice of Vedantic India and the railway platform at the pilgrimage station of
Tirupati where I saw a big man beat his little wife. The inhumanity, the un-
Indianness of it, hauled me like a streak of red lightning out of my compartment
into a protest that was a mixture of indignation on behalf of outraged womanhood and a lecture on the Vedantic relationship of man and woman. (Cousins
& Cousins 1950:301–310)

She claimed that she was "sane enough to expect no nearer an approach to
the Upanishads on the Mount Road in Madras than to the Sermon on the
Mount in the tenement streets of Dublin"; but, as she said, her ideal view of
Indian philosophy and life persisted, leading her sometimes "into queer corners." Again, in contrast to Sister Nivedita and other foreigners who preferred
to turn a blind eye to the issue of child marriage, Margaret Cousins was openly critical[6] (ibid:331).

The Women's Indian Association, soon after its formation, was active in
organizing a deputation of women to interview Lord Chelmsford (the
Viceroy) and Edwin Montague (the Secretary of State for India) who were
inquiring into constitutional reforms for India. Sarojini Naidu led the delegation and was its spokeswoman; Cousins drew up the delegation's address calling for the vote for women, for women's education, teacher training schools,
women's medical colleges and maternity courses, for compulsory and free
education, and for an equal number of schools for girls and boys. In the
Montague-Chelmsford reforms of 1919, female franchise was left to the dis-
cretion of each provincial legislature. Using her fund of experience in the
women's suffrage movement in Britain, Margaret Cousins "organized campaigns in key provinces, beginning in Madras and proceeding to Bombay and
Bengal, arranged public meetings, produced resolutions, lobbied Indian leg-
islators, and solicited funds from Indians and foreign suffrage groups"
(Ramusack 1981a:127–28).

But Cousins and Besant disagreed on tactics. Cousins wrote, "The antipathy of the Irish Parliamentary party to the claim of votes for women, on the
ground that it would go against the main cause of freedom, was paralleled by
the refusal of Mrs. Besant to make votes for Indian women a plank in the platform of her Home Rule League" (Cousins & Cousins 1950:331). Besant, in 1917,
had been elected President of the Indian National Congress and was disinclined
to mix Home Rule politics and women's suffrage; Cousins and Indian women,
however, pressed on with the campaign, which achieved early success. By 1921,
for example, the Madras Legislative Council gave a limited female franchise,
and in 1929 all the other provinces of India, as well as some of the princely
states, followed suit. The next stage of the struggle was for women to enter

the legislature, and Cousins, who was by then the General Secretary of the Women's Indian Association, helped to organize two women candidates for the 1926 Madras State elections.[7]

One of the other achievements of Margaret Cousins was her appointment in 1921, as the first woman magistrate in India; she served at the Saidapet courthouse for five years. After her return from a visit to Britain in 1925, she plunged into activity to form the All-India Women's Conference, also urging women to "form local Committees and organise Constituent Conferences in the Provinces and the States." The first national conference was held in Pune in January 1927, with fifty-eight delegates representing twenty-two Constituent Conferences with a total membership of 5,492. Resolutions were passed on female education, including higher education, that marriage under the age of sixteen be made a penal offense, that proper facilities be provided for girls in parda educational institutions, and that women's schools for law, medicine, social science and the fine arts be established.

The most important event organized by Margaret Cousins, however, was the historic All-Asian Women's Conference held in 1931 in Lahore from January 19th to 25th, which included delegates from Afghanistan, Burma (Myanmar), Ceylon (Sri Lanka), Japan, Persia (Iran), with observers from Britain, New Zealand, the United States and Java (Indonesia).[8] The key resolutions of the conference were concerned with equality of status for women through equal opportunities, equal education, the abolition of polygamy, equal rights of guardianship of children and rights of property, divorce and adult franchise.[9] An important resolution on labor asked for the regulation of hours of women's work and wages, and the provision of illness, old age and maternity benefits as well as proper housing, medical inspection, adult education and the prohibition of child labor; equal moral standards were urged for men and women in dealing with prostitution. It was indeed an impressive list of demands, way ahead of the times, but reflecting the major concerns of Asian women.

Disagreements on the presence of European women as conference organizers came up when the two observers from Java said they had come to the conference with the intention of being delegates, but with "a mandate to refrain from participating as delegates…in the eventuality of co-operation and help from Europeans." On arrival in Lahore they found that "the Conference had among its body of helpers some European women," and therefore, opted to be observers (All-Asian Women's Conference Proceedings 1931:21). The problem arose because the conference had been Margaret Cousins' idea and she bore the brunt of its organization. Other delegates did not have the same problem and cheered when the Secretary, Lakshmibai Rajwade, declared "the proposal to hold an All-Asian Women's Conference was originated by Mrs. Cousins… after her world tour during which she came in touch with other

women's organizations and brought back messages of sympathy and co-operation from the women of many lands" (ibid:25–6). In the final vote of thanks,
the delegate from Persia said the success of the conference was "to a very great
measure due to the untiring zeal and to the great organizing abilities of our
dear Mrs. Cousins" (ibid:172). Dr. Muttulakshmi Reddy also referred to the
conference as "the dream of one woman," Margaret Cousins, which had
"become a reality," creating "an indissoluble bond among Asian women."
(ibid:166).

Appreciation of Margaret Cousins' work has also been recorded by
Kamaladevi Chattopadyaya, who became one of the leading Socialist women
in the Indian national movement. Cousins had been at the Mangalore girls'
school in Kamaladevi's home town and they had both been involved, in 1920, in
producing a drama where males and females acted together. This led to opposition in the town, even resulting in intervention by Annie Besant. "We felt
very let down," recalled Kamaladevi when the play was banned. Subsequently,
Cousins urged Kamaladevi to run for the Madras legislature and organized
her campaign. "Her entry into my life was of tremendous import," wrote
Kamaladevi, "my vague yearnings to serve society, especially women, ...took
concrete shape. For she was a seasoned and practical worker who qualified to
blaze the trail for Indian women's freedom...[she was] like a Guru to me."
(Chattopadyaya 1986:65, 80, 84).

Involvement in Indian women's issues led Cousins to recognize the importance of political struggle. In the 1930s she became active in nationalist politics,
participated in the 1930 civil disobedience movement and "briefly skirmished
with the British authorities." In 1932, she challenged the ban on free speech by
speaking at a public meeting in Madras and was arrested; her trial and sentence of one year in prison caused an outcry in India and abroad (Ramusack
1981a:120–23). In a "speech from the dock" Cousins boldly criticized British rule,
claiming that her trial was the result of years of living and working with her
"Indian sisters and brothers," during which time she learned how "exploitation and injustice through foreign rule" was crushing the Indians. Calling
upon people to persist in non-violent defiance, she added: "I am proud to
stand here in support of free speech and Indian national freedom and I am
ashamed that English idealism has fallen to the present depths of oppression
and suppression" (Cousins & Cousins 1950:582–83).

Margaret Cousins spent a year in the women's prison in Vellore, where she
was put with other women political prisoners; she spent her time there
teaching inmates and reading and writing. Her release was an occasion for
celebrations:

From the entrance to the old town there was a rush of welcoming people...

doors, windows, and roofs were crowded. At street corners the car was held up
while speeches were made, fruits and sweets presented. I was smothered in gar-
lands and flowers. (ibid:591)

Margaret Cousins resumed her active life in politics, in the women's move-
ment and the work of the Theosophical Society. She presided over the
Women's Indian Association in 1933, and in 1936 became the President of the
All-India Women's Conference "in recognition of her previous work for the
organization." She was also a neutral candidate at a time of tension between
Indian women of the Association about the issue of political involvement
(Ramusack 1981a:130). The late 1930s was a period of heightened political activity when the presence of militant Indian women leaders made the role of.
foreign women seem less necessary. "I longed to be in the struggle," Cousins
wrote, "but I had the feeling that direct participation by me was no longer
required, or even desired by the leaders of India womanhood who were now
coming to the front" (Cousins & Cousins 1950:746). Her health declined after
1943; but before her death, she and James Cousins produced a remarkable joint
autobiography in 1950 called *We Two-Together*, which covered the exciting period
through which they lived—the years from the Irish Home Rule agitation to
Indian independence. She died in 1954 at 76.

During the years when Margaret Cousins was active on women's rights and
in the Gandhian movement, numerous other foreign women were also
involved in educational work in theosophist schools and political work in the
national movement. Some of them are remembered by an older generation
in South Asia, but few details about their lives are available. One interesting
case is that of Dorothy Jinarajadasa, née Graham, an English woman who was
the first secretary of the Women's Indian Association in 1917. She was married
to C. Jinarajadasa, a leading Sri Lankan theosophist who lived in India and
worked with Annie Besant at the Theosophical Society headquarters in Madras.

Another remarkable case was that of Nellie Grey, an English woman who,
in 1909, married Jatindra Mohan Sen Gupta, a Cambridge graduate and barris-
ter. Returning to Bengal they were both in trade union and nationalist
politics. In 1921 they were involved in the railway strike in Chittagong and in
the campaign for the boycott of foreign goods. Gandhi praised her for having
the courage to go to the "cloth bazaar in Chittagong to tell the consumers to
buy khadi and avoid foreign cloth" (Sen Gupta 1985). By the late 1920s, J.M. Sen
Gupta was Mayor of Calcutta and leader of the Bengali section of the Indian
National Congress. He and Nellie were arrested and jailed in 1930 for participation in the civil disobedience movement. In 1933, a year of intense political
unrest, the annual sessions of the Indian National Congress were held in
Calcutta, but the President-designate and others were arrested on their way

to the meeting. Nevertheless, other delegates assembled and Nellie Sen Gupta presided at the meeting and read the address; resolutions on independence for India, civil disobedience as a legitimate weapon of resistance, a boycott of British goods and a denunciation of the White Paper on reforms were adopted. One writer states, "She read out her presidential address confidently, as if nothing was going to happen" (Gopal 1967:404). Soon after, the police charged the meeting and made numerous arrests, including Nellie Sen Gupta, who was tried and sentenced to six months in jail (Zaidi & Zaidi 1980:278–79, 281, and Sitaramayya 1946:557). After J.M. Sen Gupta's death she continued to be active in Congress politics. Between 1933 and 1939 she was elected to the Calcutta Municipal Corporation, and after independence stayed on in East Pakistan (now Bangladesh). As an elected member of the legislature (1940 and 1946) for the Chittagong constituency, she spoke out for minority rights and women's rights (Sen Gupta 1975:151).

From Blavatsky's visit to India and Sri Lanka in 1879 to the period of the late 1930s, the role of Western women committed to Indian nationalist causes, women's rights and female education became an accepted feature of the local scene. Besant could become the President of the Indian National Congress and Nellie Sen Gupta could read the Presidential Address of the Congress under conditions of illegality. Moreover, actresses like Florence Farr could end up as the principal of a Hindu girls' school and Margaret Cousins could lead women's organizations and go to jail for supporting Gandhi. It was clearly an era where gender roles of Western women in a colonial situation were no longer merely those of missionaries and "maternal" social reformers. Foreign women's active intervention in education and politics in South Asia coincided with the appearance of women scholars of the Orient, as well as writers and travelers who made significant intellectual contributions to an understanding of South Asian cultures. There were also foreign women philanthropists whose monetary contributions to local causes were extremely generous. The next chapter discusses some cases of such intellectual input and financial munificence.

II

"O FREE INDEED! O GLORIOUSLY FREE"

Women Orientalists, Writers and Funders

The contrast existing between our habitual opinions and those expressed by
philosophers belonging to other ages and to other countries ought to help us to
see more clearly whatever is worth preserving in our ideas and principles and
what we should do well to reject.

—Alexandra David-Néel, *Buddhism: its Doctrine and its Method* (1978:12)

APART FROM FOREIGN WOMEN DIRECTLY INVOLVED IN POLITICS AND
alternative education projects, by the turn of the century the Oriental
Renaissance had produced numerous Western women imbued with great
enthusiasm to study, travel and write about South Asia. The expansion of university education for women in Europe together with their greater freedom
and mobility gave rise to women scholars and writers with an interest in the
study of texts and societies other than their own. Some of them concentrated
their attention on India and South Asia. Their efforts also contributed to the
growing interest in the Orient and fed into spiritualist and other heterodox
currents. Curiosity about Asian societies also produced women travelers and
concerned women philanthropists who funded religious causes in South Asia.
From the earliest years of British colonialism, numerous foreign women

had recorded their impressions of South Asia in travelers tales, diaries and memoirs.[1] The range they covered was wide: Marian Postan's *Cutch, Random Sketches* (1839) and Fanny Park's *Wanderings of a Pilgrim in Search of the Picturesque* (1850) are traveler's stories; Maria Graham's *Journal of a Residence in India* (1812), Julia Maitland's *Letters from Madras* (1843) and Lady Dufferin's *Our Viceregal Life* describe the experience of living in India. *The Manners and Customs of Society in India* (1841) was an early attempt at an ethnographic study by Mrs. Major Clements. Accounts of Indian family life by British women married to Indians form another part of this genre. Typical is the two volume *Observations on the Mussulmans of India, Descriptive of their Manners, Customs and Habits and Religious Opinions* (1832) written by Mrs Meer Hassan Ali, the British wife of a member of an upper class Lucknow family (MacMillan 1988:215). Most of their writings contain a great deal of interesting ethnographic source material.

WOMEN ORIENTALISTS

There were two types of women Orientalist scholars: those who were for social reform and found a liberating message for women in the early texts and highlighted their "feminist" content and those who celebrated tradition and were, as Uma Chakravarti has noted, "unabashedly romantic" (1989:43). Among the romanticists who accepted current notions about the Aryan culture of India and its superiority over Western materialism, was Charlotte Speir, who in 1856 wrote *Life in Ancient India*, which referred to India as a "land of gold and sunshine" with "luxurious scents, gay with flowers and sparkling with precious gems and fabrics" (1973:2). She wrote of the civilizing influence of the Aryans and the high status of their women and extolled the learned females of ancient India. A similar romanticization of India's past and the status of women was made by a French woman Orientalist, Clarisse Bader, who in 1867 wrote *Women in Ancient India*. The time was ripe, she wrote, for Europeans to refresh themselves "from more life-giving and generous sources." Even sati inspired respect rather than horror (Bader quoted in Chakravarti 1989:45–6).[2] Such glorifications of the myths of Aryan superiority and Aryan womanhood found much support among Indian nationalists.

In later years there developed a more serious interest in the East and its religious and cultural systems. Among the women Orientalists were Dr. Mabel Bode, who did translations for the Pali Text Society; Jessie Weston, who in 1913 wrote *Quest for the Holy Grail*, a study in comparative legends; and Jessie Duncan Westbrook, translator from the Persian of the *Diwan of Zeb-un-Missa* (1913), the mystic verses of the daughter of the 17th-century Emperor Aurangazeb, and the *Diwan of Inayat Khan* (printed in 1915 by the Women's Printing Society); this was a rendering from Persian into English verse of "some of the different aspects of Sufic thought and feeling." Westbrook's husband was a theosophist and their daughter Hilda, a graduate of Cambridge (who married a Sri Lankan, Patrick Kularatne), became the principal of several Buddhist theosophical schools for girls in Sri Lanka from the 1920s onward (see Chapter 18).

CAROLINE RHYS DAVIDS——A FEMINIST LOOK AT BUDDHISM

The most eminent of the women Orientalists was Caroline Foley Rhys Davids, daughter of Rev. John Foley, a Bachelor of Divinity from Oxford, and his wife Caroline Windham. Caroline Foley studied at home before joining University College, London, where she did a degree in philosophy, and in 1894 married the Orientalist and Pali scholar Thomas William Rhys Davids (1843–1922).[3] Caroline Rhys Davids' career as an Orientalist was, in the early years, closely linked to her husband's interests. She took on work in the Pali Text Society in 1900, becoming its Secretary in 1907; she helped in the publication of numerous texts translated into English, and also in keeping the society financially viable. She taught Indian philosophy at the University of Manchester from 1910 to 1913, and from 1918 to 1933 was lecturer in the History of Buddhism at the School of Oriental Studies in London. After her husband's death in 1922 she succeeded him as president of the Pali Text Society.

Caroline Rhys Davids was also a committed feminist. From 1890 to 1894 she worked in societies concerned with the welfare of working women and children, and from 1896 to 1914 was active in the women's suffrage movement. The Buddhist Society, under her influence, spoke out for women's rights (during the period when the suffrage movement was at its height), upholding the view that Buddhism was more advanced than other religions on the women's issue (Wickremeratne 1985:199). She was a typical "new woman" of the period, moving in feminist circles, involving herself in women's struggles, doing academic work, raising three children, and writing about Buddhism up to her death in 1942.

One of Caroline Rhys Davids' best-known books was *The Psalms of the Sisters* (1909), a translation into English of the verses of the Theri-Bhikkunis of the Buddhist Order, the sisters or nuns of Buddhism. A religion of reform posited against the Vedic religions of the period, Buddhism allowed some social space for women, most notably through the creation of an Order of Nuns. The *Psalms of the Sisters* consists of the writings of seventy one nuns, written around 80 B.C., describing hardships endured in domestic life under patriarchal control and the freedom achieved by entering into the religious life. As one of them wrote:

O free indeed! O gloriously free
Am I in freedom from three crooked things—
From quern, from mortar, from my crookback'd lord!

Ay, but I'm free from rebirth and death,
And all that dragged me back is hurled away.
(Rhys Davids 1909:15)

Rhys Davids clearly was more than a translator; her two main interests, Oriental studies and feminism, combined to imbue these translations with a deeply symbolic content and to give them a feminist perspective. In the introduction to her book she allies herself with the aspirations of the "sisters" whom she calls "these dear and revered ladies" (ibid:xiii). "All who are capable of a historical sympathy," she writes, "will be glad to see somewhat of the age-long traditions in which these rare and remarkable utterances have been set and fostered in so venerable a literature as that of the Pali manuscripts" (ibid:xix). She refers, for example, to "the fine summary of woman's 'woeful lot'" as experienced by Kisagotami, who is "set at liberty" on becoming a nun.

Woeful is woman's lot! hath he declared
Tamer and driver of the hearts of men:
Woeful when sharing home with hostile wives
Woeful when giving birth in bitter pain, ...
Woe too when mother murdering embryo
Comes not to birth, and both alike find death.

As Rhys Davids noted, entering the Order of Nuns provided relief from painful situations that affected all women, cutting across class and age.[4] The theme of freedom runs through the verses; they had "won the status of an individual in place of being adjunct" (ibid:xxv–vi). The Buddhist nuns, "these notable women of long ago," as Rhys Davids calls them, were not confined to a life of introspection, but were active educators, propagators of the faith, and eloquent itinerant preachers, like Dhammadinna and her pupil Sukka. Significantly, Rhys Davids refers to Sukka's audience as "stirred to enthusiasm by this new woman's eloquence" (ibid:xxxvi). When Dr. Neumann, a German translator of these verses, refused to accept this ascription to nuns and said that they "must have been shaped by…a man," Rhys Davids retorted sharply and wittily:

Not often since the patriarchal age set in has woman succeeded in so breaking through her barriers as to set on lasting record the expression of herself and of things as they appeared to her. But to assume that, because this happened seldom, therefore, this collection of documents, though ascribed to her, are necessarily not by her, is to carry over far the truth… "she that hath not, from her shall be taken even that which she hath."

Writing like a spirited feminist, Rhys Davids says, "I make no counter-assumption that gifted Theris had a hand in the compilation of the Brothers' Psalms" (ibid:xxiii). In this way the feminist analysis Rhys Davids brought to her Pali scholarship gave fresh meaning to the old texts and made known the "new women" of the past to audiences in the East and West.

I. B. HORNER AND EARLY BUDDHIST WOMEN

Inspired by Rhys Davids, another outstanding woman Orientalist highlight-ed the role of women in early Buddhism; she was Isaline Blew Horner (1896–1940), born in 1896 at Walthamstow, Essex and educated at Prior's Field, a progressive school in Surrey. While visiting relatives in Kent around age twelve, she met Professor Rhys Davids and Caroline Rhys Davids and discussed Buddhism with them. In 1917, she graduated from Newnham College in Cambridge, with a degree in Moral Sciences, and in 1918, took a job at the Newnham library (Iggledon 1974:1). In 1921, Horner made her first visit to Sri Lanka and India and stayed in Mysore for two years with the sister of the prin-cipal of Newnham College. She also visited Pagan, the ancient capital of Burma, and returned to Britain via Kenya and South Africa. She then contacted Caroline Rhys Davids about possible areas of research and began to concen-trate on Pali studies. From 1923 to 1936 Horner was a Fellow of Newnham and its librarian. She visited Sri Lanka and India again in 1929, and in 1930 her first major work, *Women under Primitive Buddhism*, was published in London.

The first half of Horner's book deals with Buddhist laywomen in their roles as mother, daughter, wife, widow and worker; the second part is concerned with the almswomen (nuns), their conditions of admission into the Order, the rules of the Order, the life they led, including details of their daily activi-ties, the training of novices and the relationship between the almswomen and the laity. In the preface to the book, Caroline Rhys Davids especially com-mends Horner's treatment of Buddhist women's place in society as a whole, paying attention to lay society in order to understand "what women left and why they left" and "what they gained...by going forth" into a religious life. (Horner 1930:xiii). In 1938, Horner visited Sri Lanka again, keeping in touch with scholars in that country. When Caroline Rhys Davids died in 1942, Horner became Secretary of the Pali Text Society, and in 1959 was appointed its presi-dent. She continued translating Buddhist texts, such as the *Vinaya Pitaka* (The Book of Discipline of the Monks and Nuns) and also published *The Living Thoughts of Gotama the Buddha—An Anthology* (1948), co-authored with Dr. Ananda Coomaraswamy.

Horner visited India, Burma and Sri Lanka regularly in the years after the Second World War, and was awarded a honorary doctorate by the University of Ceylon in 1964, in recognition of her work in Pali translation and indefatigable support of Pali studies (ibid:6). Apart from all her international contacts, Horner, who was not married, derived support from her network of women friends who were scholars. These included the archaeologist Winifred Lamb, whom she visited in 1933 and 1934 during her excavations in Troy. She moved to Manchester in 1936 to join her friend Eliza M. Butler, the first woman professor of German at the Manchester University. While Horner's work was valued by her learned women friends, she is also remembered in Sri Lanka with affection as an exemplary woman, making Buddhism known in the West, and writing scholarly works that discussed the status of early Buddhist women.

ALEXANDRA DAVID-NÉEL'S MAGIC AND MYSTERY

The expansion of imperialism in the 19th century had led to the era of great male explorers "discovering" Asia and Africa. The travel writings of Burton, Baker and Livingstone were, as Kabbani notes, "an aggressive racist exploration of the colonised…a frenzied attempt to know the world…it was in the process of conquering…serving to forge the imperial representation of the world" (1986:6–7). She also notes the element of sexism in their accounts; especially in the case of Burton, where "the articulation of sexism in his narrative went hand in hand with the articulation of racism, for women were a subgroup in patriarchal Victorian society just as other races were sub-groups within the colonial enterprises" (ibid:7). This distinction becomes important when we consider the significant group of women travelers. The famous "lady adventurers" of the 19th and early 20th centuries were women in revolt against their lack of mobility and domestic bondage in Victorian society. Women like Isabel Bird, Gertrude Bell, Freya Stark, Mary Kingsley, Hester Stanhope and Alexandra David-Néel proved their equality with men by undertaking arduous and hazardous journeys. Some of their writings reflect a concern with indigenous societies and the condition of their women and children usually absent in the writings of male travelers.

A particularly interesting case of a woman scholar and traveler was Alexandra David-Néel (1869–1969). Her French father Louis David (a nephew of the famous painter David) was a republican socialist, and her mother was Belgian. Though educated in a convent, she became interested in spiritualism and theosophy and joined a group with similar interests; one of this group was Mirra Richard, the future "Mother" of Pondicherry. David-Néel studied Sanskrit and Buddhism at the Sorbonne University and made her first journey alone to India and Sri Lanka when she was twenty-one. Back in France she was active in feminist and Socialist groups and went to Britain in 1910 to participate in demonstrations for women's suffrage.

In 1911, at forty-two, she traveled again to India. She visited Sikkim, went to many monasteries and met the Dalai Lama of Tibet, then in exile.

Alexandra David-Néel, circa 1914, in lama's robes. (From Alexandra David-Néel, *Journal de Voyage*, 1975, Paris; Widener Library, Harvard.)

Accompanied by a Tibetan fifteen year-old called Yongden, she went into Tibet illegally in 1914, then forbidden territory. On this journey, she lived in Tibet for three years in a cave, and as the student of a famous lama, became proficient in the Tibetan language and Buddhist texts. After a short stay in Sikkim, she and Yongden made the perilous journey through China to Lhasa, the "forbidden city." Disguised as a Tibetan beggar and son, they traveled for months over mountain terrain and stayed in Tibet undiscovered for two months before returning to India. Her journey became internationally known through her writings; it was a voyage, her biographer states, "the qualities of which far surpassed those invented by Jules Verne, traversing regions never before visited by a European" (Middleton 1989:173). She was much sought after all over Europe as a lecturer and became quite a celebrity. She wrote extensively on Buddhism and Tibet, her best known works being *My Journey to Lhasa* (1927), and *Magic and Mystery in Tibet* (1932).

David-Néel frequently expressed the need for understanding the "Other" in order to understand oneself. Her feminist awareness is evident in her writings. She claims that the Sikkimese attitude to her, a woman student, was one of great respect, unlike the University of Paris where women students were reviled and sometimes even needed police protection. She also described the courage of scattered bands of nuns in Tibet, who were sometimes snow-bound for half the year, and of women pilgrims who traveled alone across Tibet.[5] David-Néel's feminist awareness thus enabled her to go further than "magic and mystery" and probe the lives of independent women in Tibet and South Asia.

MARY FOSTER, DHARMAPALA'S "FOSTER MOTHER"

Apart from women writers, scholars and travelers who helped in making the East known to the West, there were others whose inputs were more material. These were the rich heiresses who made lavish donations without which the "noble causes" could not function. Similar to the Christian missions, the theosophists in India and Buddhists in Sri Lanka had a good source of support from rich women sympathizers in Europe and the United States. The women who financially helped Annie Besant's ventures in India have been discussed in Chapter 8. The most generous of the women funders however, was Mary Elizabeth Foster, an American theosophist from Hawaii who, over a period of thirty years, financed Buddhist activities in India, Sri Lanka and Europe.

The activities of reviving Buddhism, establishing Buddhist schools and institutions and translating and publishing Buddhist texts and journals required extensive funds, which the local Buddhist bourgeoisie in Sri Lanka could not raise on its own. Foreign well-wishers were thus an important source of money. Mary Foster was the daughter of James Robinson and Rebecca Prever. Robinson, a native of London and carpenter on the ship Hermes, had come to Hawaii in 1820 and became a pioneer of its shipbuilding industry (Hackler 1986:34–35). Mary married Thomas R. Foster, the owner of a shipyard, a shipping agency and a number of schooners. When Foster died in 1889 a Honolulu newspaper wrote that he was a "far-seeing and keen business-man…reputed to have left a fortune of about a quarter million dollars" (ibid).

Mary Foster's interest in Buddhism dates from her meeting with Anagarika Dharmapala in October 1893. She was one of "two lady theosophists" who met Dharmapala on board the ship in which he was returning to Sri Lanka after participating in the Parliament of Religions in Chicago. From then on she became a great benefactor of Dharmapala and of Buddhist causes. Anagarika

Dharmapala (1864–1933) was born Don David Hewavitarna, to a Sinhala Buddhist family who had a prosperous furniture business. Though educated in English at local Christian schools, he was involved with the Buddhist revivalist agitation led by militant monks and the founders of the Theosophical Society, Helena Blavatsky and Colonel Olcott, who visited Sri Lanka in 1880. He dropped his Europeanized first name, joined the theosophists and accompanied Blavatsky to Madras, becoming active in Buddhist educational matters and in the campaign to assert the ethnic and cultural identity of the Sinhala Buddhists. In 1891 he formed the Maha Bodhi Society in Calcutta for the promotion of Buddhism in the land of its birth, and for the protection of historic sites in India sacred to the Buddhists. In Calcutta he moved with Bengali nationalists and intellectuals including Swami Vivekananda, and was an admirer of Annie Besant, although in later years he denounced the theosophists as "perfect fools"; (Pieris 1980:16). He also formed the Maha Bodhi Society in Sri Lanka, and wrote and lectured extensively on Buddhism until his death in 1933.

Anagarika Dharmapala's work for Buddhist revival through the Maha Bodhi societies and through his Buddhist organization in London were dependent on the generous funding he received from Mary Foster. In 1903 she sent him $4,000 to start an educational publication of the Maha Bodhi societies of Sri Lanka and India. Further contributions of $1,000 each in 1905 and 1906 were used by Dharmapala for the English-Sinhala free school in her name in Rajagiriya, near Colombo.[6] "On behalf of the Buddhists of Asia," said Dharmapala in 1908, "we render Mrs. Foster our grateful thanks. May she live long in peace, happiness and prosperity" (Guruge 1965:727–30). During this period, she also helped in several Buddhist publication ventures including the Maha Bodhi press in Colombo, and its journals in Sinhala and English (ibid:748).

In 1913, Dharmapala visited Honolulu to thank Mary Foster for her donations. She gave him a further £4,000 for the building of the Foster Robinson Hospital in Colombo. In 1915, the Calcutta Maha Bodhi Society bought a house in the heart of the city for a Buddhist temple at a total cost of Rs. 123,800 (£12,380), of which Rs. 87,800 was provided by Mary Foster, and in 1919, Mary Foster sent Dharmapala $50,000 worth of US Government Victory Bonds. Another donation in 1923 of $100,000 worth of bonds was used to buy a house in Kandy, Sri Lanka, which later became the Foster Buddhist Seminary (*The Maha Bodhi*, 1931). Dharmapala was in Britain in 1925 and from there he again visited Mary Foster in San Francisco. She subsequently helped the Maha Bodhi Society in London to buy a house for £2,500 in Ealing, London, to start a library and to publish a journal, *The British Buddhist*, contributing £61 a month towards its work for a period of two years (Guruge 1965:666, 672, 740, and Maha Bodhi

Society Report 1928). The numerous large donations were kept in the Foster Fund, or in special purpose funds, with Dharmapala as trustee, and were invested in lands and securities (Ratnatunga 1991:29).[7]

Mary Foster is probably best known in Hawaii for the bequest to Honolulu of her home and lands, including a large botanical garden. In a report on Mary Foster's will, the *Honolulu Star Bulletin* (December 29, 1930) stated that she bequeathed $400,000 to various philanthropic organizations. Of this, $50,000 was given to Anagarika Dharmapala for hospitals and schools. Such large sums of money inevitbly attracted attention and Mary Foster's bequest to Dharmapala was challenged by the executor of her estate, who wrote to the Governor's Secretary in Colombo questioning Dharmapala's use of previous donations (Pieris 1980:17).

Dharmapala's relationship to Mary Foster was close and has been described as "enigmatic" (ibid:16). She was to him either the all-giving Mother, or Visakha, the benefactor of the Buddha. Foster was always ready with large donations to enable Dharmapala to launch ambitious projects in Sri Lanka, India and Britain. She also provided him moral support in times of personal loss and is constantly referred to by Dharmapala as his "foster mother." When his father died, in 1906, Dharmapala wrote to Foster of the "great loss" of his "best supporter." She replied that "she would help me to carry on the work and that she would be a foster parent to me" (Guruge 1965:739). One of his publications was dedicated to his parents and "to my dear 'Foster Mother', the noble lady, Mrs. Foster of Honolulu, to whose unfailing kindness and munificent donations, the construction of the first Buddhist vihara in Calcutta...has been made possible" (ibid:247, 155). Dharmapala also dubbed Foster the "queen of the empire of righteousness," and a British Buddhist, G. R. S. Mead, at a meeting in London of the Maha Bodhi Society, called Mary Foster's benefactions a "romance of unparalleled generosity" (ibid:741). To the Buddhists of Sri Lanka she was certainly the white goddess of plenty.

But not all Dharmapala's foreign women supporters were "goddesses." There had been an American Buddhist who turned out to be a "devil," having started out as a "goddess." Following the trend among South Asian spiritual leaders (like Vivekananda) to have foreign women as soul mates, Dharmapala became the guru to an American woman, Countess Miranda de Souza Canavarro, the wife of a Portugese Count. According to Bartholomeusz, she was "a colorful socialite" who professed Buddhism. Dharmapala had met her in San Francisco in 1897 and had hopes that she would come to Sri Lanka and pioneer a religious order among Buddhist women. She arrived in Sri Lanka in 1897, took on the name Sister Sanghamitta and became a Buddhist *upasika* or lay devotee (1994:47).

But by the following year the relationship had soured. Dharmapala complained of Canavarro's "strange behavior" and predatory manner, while she "resented his involvement" in the running of the Sanghamitta Buddhist women's school and cloister of nuns (ibid:63, 71). By 1899, much to Dharmapala's relief, Canavarro had returned to the United States. "The woman is a she-devil," he noted in his diary, "Unhappy is the man who falls into her clutches. She tempted me; but she failed in her diabolical efforts" (ibid:64). This was a far cry from his experiences with the noble Mary Foster, and it is not surprising that Carnavarro was erased from the history of the Buddhist revival in Sri Lanka.

ETHEL COOMARASWAMY——REVIVING THE ARTS AND CRAFTS

One of the long forgotten but interesting British women who married a Sri Lankan was Ethel Coomaraswamy née Partridge (1872–1952), who lived in Sri Lanka for a few years, studying, translating, traveling and promoting ideas of cultural revival, and like Annie Besant, advocating traditional education for women. Born in 1872 in Barnstaple, North Devon where her father had a chemist's shop, she studied music, design and drawing in London, and later became a Licentiate of the Royal Academy of Music. She also studied science and geology, and met Ananda Coomaraswamy (1877–1947) during a student expedition to Devon. He was the product of two cultures; his father, Sir Mutu Coomaraswamy, a Tamil Hindu, had been called to the Bar in London in 1863, and was knighted in 1874. He married an English woman from Kent, Elizabeth Clay Beeby (1854–1939), whose family was in the "India trade." She used to attend Coomaraswamy's lectures on Indian religions at the chapel of the Unitarian Minister Rev. Moncure Conway, and was also interested in spiritualism. Their son Ananda was born in Colombo in 1877, but after Mutu Coomaraswamy's death in 1879, the mother and child made their home in Kent, England. Ananda studied geology at the University of London, returning to Sri Lanka, after his marriage to Ethel Partridge in 1902, to take up the post of Director of Geology.

Between the years 1903–6, the Coomaraswamys were involved in studying the arts and crafts of Sri Lanka and its folklore. Ethel Coomaraswamy worked in the Kandy School of Art and accompanied her husband all over the island "studying not only rocks and minerals, but also the people, their arts...history and their legends" (Durai Raja Singham 1977:4). Ananda and Ethel Coomaraswamy, during this period of national awakening in India and Sri Lanka, made an important contribution to the appreciation of South Asian arts, starting a campaign for cultural revival and for the preservation of traditional crafts. He was the first President in 1905 of the Ceylon Social Reform Society, whose aim was to "discourage thoughtless imitation of unsuitable European habits and customs," and included the promotion of vegetarianism, temperance, and cremation, and opposition to capital punishment. The members were local theosophists, Buddhists and social reformers who associated themselves with cultural and national revival and with liberal causes (Jayawardena 1972:112). While in Sri Lanka, Ethel Coomaraswamy wrote articles on "Old Sinhalese Embroidery" (1906), "Music in Ceylon" (1907) and did a translation (from German) of William Geiger's book *The Dipavamsa and Mahavamsa and their Historical Development in Ceylon* (1908), and helped found the Kandy Arts and Crafts Society.

Both Ethel and Ananda Coomaraswamy deplored the westernization taking place in India and Sri Lanka. In 1903, Ethel commented in her diary that "the most incongruous and unsightly thing to see is a native in European dress, women especially with badly shaped shoes and no taste in dress or colours. They walk clumsily and heavily, whereas with bare feet they are generally graceful" (Durai Rajasingham 1977:10). Ananda agreed, and in 1905 wrote "Borrowed Plumes," an article in which he especially decried the European clothes worn by local women; "I think it quite impossible for a native lady to look anything but vulgar in European dress, or anything but a lady in her own" (Coomaraswamy 1905:6).

Such attitudes naturally strengthened their views that women needed traditional rather than modern education. Ethel Coomaraswamy spoke out in public on women's education, urging that Sri Lankan women did not need to imitate the West. In 1906 at the opening of the Kotahena Girl's Free School by a Buddhist Siamese prince, she condemned the Western education given to girls. Remarking on the "shoddy" products of the system based on the cramming of useless subjects for the Cambridge examinations, she asked "Of what use or profit is it to a girl to learn French" and "why do girls learn Latin instead of Sanskrit?" Speaking of the "shams of a pseudo-English education in the East," she said "we hear of mothers begging that their children may learn…just a few strokes on the violin…and of children being taught the piano…to play "Home Sweet Home." She warned that in the meantime "the culture and beauty of the East" were slowly vanishing (E. Coomaraswamy 1906:210).

Like Annie Besant, Ethel Coomaraswamy argued that while Sri Lankan girls may need a knowledge of English, cooking, hygiene and physiology, there was certainly no need for English history or geography. Local history, geography and literature should be taught instead; the teaching of art should be based on Eastern or indigenous forms, not on those derived from the West. She advised parents to demand a proper education for their daughters that would equip them to fulfil their traditional roles:

> If you know your girls are being crammed with false knowledge instead of what
> will fit them to become good mothers—loyal mothers to their country—then it

is time…to insist on a true education for them (ibid:212).

The Coomaraswamys returned to Britain in 1906 and lived in Broad Campden, Gloucestershire, in the Norman Chapel restored by the famous designer and architect C. R. Ashbee of the Arts and Crafts Movement, a follower of William Morris and John Ruskin. Ashbee had in 1888 started the Guild of Handicraft—which in 1902 moved to Chipping Campden as a part of the "Back to the Land" movement—where furniture and metalwork were made and books printed by seventy workers, including Ethel's brother, a silversmith (Durai Raja Singham 1977:15). Many were attracted to this experiment and visited Campden, and the Norman Chapel became a center for discussion. Ashbee's wife Janet described Ethel as a "strange…figure…by day dressed in…gaunt sack-frocks…and by night coming out like a brilliant moth in Eastern plum cherry and orange colours, with strange Singhalese jewels." And her account of Ananda refers to his "pale olive skin, deepest dark eyes and thick black hair," adding that "both of them live in their enchanted chapel, which glows rose colour with linen and Morris hangings and Oriental crimsons" (Crawford 1985:147). It was certainly a taste of the good life in the midst of the best of Asian and European arts and crafts. The Coomaraswamys also used the Chapel to organize meetings with interesting visitors; Sister Nivedita (the Irish devotee of Swami Vivekananda) for example, spoke on Indian women, and the invitees included many "average English folk of Campden" as well as the Guildsmen and their wives (Durai Rajasingham 1977:8).

During this idyllic period at Campden, Ananda Coomaraswamy wrote his seminal book *Medieval Sinhalese Art* (1908), and the next year he left for India. He became absorbed in Indian culture and along with Rabindranath Tagore and others provided the cultural revivalist movement with an intellectual input. But by this time the Coomaraswamy marriage broke up and they divorced in 1910, the Norman Chapel was sold to the Ashbees, and in 1913 Ethel married Philip Mairet who was also in the crafts movement. She set up a weaving shop near Stratford-on-Avon, becoming well-known in later years as "one of the leaders of the 20th-century revival of English hand-weaving" (Crawford 1985:158); Gandhi consulted her on weaving and dyeing in 1913 while in London on a visit (Durai Raja Singham 1977:20). In the 1930s Ethel Mairet "gained a national reputation as a designer for weaving" and her publications, which included *A Book on Vegetable Dyes* and several books on handweaving, went into many editions (ibid 1977:17).

Ananda Coomaraswamy, in the meantime, became a world renowned scholar. He also spent time in India building up a priceless collection of Indian art (particularly painting), which later became the nucleus of the Indian collection of the Boston Museum of Fine Arts, with Coomaraswamy himself in charge of the Asian section. Coomaraswamy is a person of interest in the whole East-West debate, because of his confrontation with feminism during the years of the suffragist struggles. In spite of his enlightenment on cultural issues, he remained utterly conservative on women's role in society. In 1910 he wrote a pamphlet on *The Oriental View of Women* where he not only claimed that, "women in the East...are happier than Western women," but also added that it was a tragedy that only half of the women between the ages fifteen and fifty in Britain were married, since women should be "primarily concerned with the making of children." The West, he added, had much to learn from the East on the question of reverence to women. "The Western view of sex is degraded and material...sex for the Oriental is a sacrament. For the European it is a pleasure" (Coomaraswamy 1910:17–22).

Coomaraswamy's anti-feminism increased in the 1920s when the condition of Indian women was a matter of public discussion. In *The Dance of Shiva* (1924), Coomaraswamy idealizes the Indian woman, and because of his culturally defensive position he praises various traditional practices; arranged marriage was doing one's social duty, while free choice in marriage was "individualistic"; woman's role in India was to "realise herself" as wife and mother, rather than "express herself"; education for women was often "little more than parlor tricks," and nothing was gained, he said, "by communicating this condition to Asia" (Coomaraswamy 1957 (1924):105–106). In finding excuses for sati, Coomaraswamy is at his most tortuous; giving selected examples of "willing satis," who showed "devotion beyond the grave"; he said, "We think of our satis not with pity, but with understanding, respect and love...like the tenderness which our children's children may some day feel for those of their race who were willing to throw away their lives for their country right or wrong" (ibid:109). It would be worthwhile to pause, says Coomaraswamy, "before we make haste to emancipate, that is to say, reform and industrialize the Oriental woman," and he predicted that "there might come a time when it could not be believed that such women had ever lived as the ancient poets describe; it would be forgotten that women had ever been unselfish, sensuous and shy" (ibid:122). Whatever his views on feminism and sati, in his personal life Coomaraswamy was married four times to emancipated and talented Western women.[8]

This chapter, which has highlighted some women Orientalists, travelers and funders in South Asia, has a common thread linking all these women: a profound sympathy for local cultures and religions, a desire to make them known to the world, and support of efforts to revive or sustain such cultures in their indigenous environments in the face of the perceived destructive effects of imperialism and westernization. They sought to take part in this process in various ways: through reinterpretations of religious texts, through publications at both scholarly and popular levels, and through financing such activities.

Rhys Davids and Horner, as Western women influenced by the women's struggles of their time, brought a fresh understanding of women's roles in early Buddhist society in India; in doing so, they also influenced Buddhist revivalist and reformist trends. These two women scholars are still quoted and honored in Asia. David-Néel, traveler and scholar, made an arduous journey and brought a sympathetic view of Tibet and of its religion to both European and Asian readers. Ethel Coomaraswamy helped in the revival of arts and crafts of Sri Lanka, some of which were dying in the face of competition from Western manufactures. Mary Foster, a philanthropist, was far ahead of South Asians of the period in munificence, supporting with generous grants both Buddhist revivalist activities in Sri Lanka as well as propagandist efforts in India and in the West. These women did not live for long in Asia or attach themselves to local nationalist movements or to local gurus. There were, however, other Western women who chose to live in South Asia and to become the close collaborators of leading sages and political leaders, their roles making them the most revered white women in colonial India. The next chapter deals with the most famous of such women.

IV

WHITE WOMEN IN SEARCH OF
BLACK GODS

WESTERN HOLY MOTHERS AS SOUL MATES OF INDIAN GURUS

Let me tell you frankly that I am now convinced that you have a great future in the work for India. What was wanted was no man, but a woman; a real lioness, to work for the Indians, women specially; India cannot produce yet great women, she must borrow from other nations. Your education, sincerity, purity, immense love, determination and above all the Celtic blood make you just the woman wanted.

—Vivekananda to Margaret Noble (1895) quoted in Chatterjee (1968: 207)

Of course, a woman can never be a Sannyasee...but a memsahib in the garb of a Sannyasee is a spectacle that is not always seen.

—Amrita Bazaar Patrika (28 May 1899) cited in H. French (1974:111)

SOUTH ASIANS HAVE OFTEN BEEN WARY, AS WE HAVE INDICATED EARLIER, OF "foreign women devils" bearing gifts of Christianity and "civilization" and using education and health as a means of approaching the people; but many have had a special affection for white women ready to identify with Hindu religious culture and spirituality, and have indeed been ready to turn them into Holy Mothers and cult figures. The memsahib (master's woman) as sannyasi (Hindu ascetic) was of course more than an unusual sight; to some she was a figure of fun, to others a symbol of defiance. At a time when white males were dominant and Britannia ruled the waves, white women who rejected their own religion and culture and accepted those of the colonized were a challenge to the "civilizing mission" and concepts of the superior "master race." They could also be a threat to the British, because they inspired local patriotism and nationalism. In some cases, white female spiritual figures attained more prominence than any of their Indian women counterparts and were treated with great deference almost as saints and divine mothers, and are commemorated even today. These foreign women were not only spiritual figures, they also performed the role of organizer, manager, confidante, secretary and fund-raiser to the "great man." For all their spirituality they were also Western "new women" and brought to their work daring and innovation on the one hand and a sense of order, efficiency and discipline on the other; they were educated and cultured and able to introduce dialogue and intellectual debate into their relationship with the guru. But they also had a romantic view of India and of Hinduism, playing down social evils as aberrations from the ancient Vedic ideal society. And while asserting more equality and familiarity with the gurus, they also idolized these men over whom they had a special "claim."

The belief that India in 1895, needed (in Vivekananda's words) a "real lioness" from abroad to work for Indian women was based on the understanding that India did not at that time have "great women." Earlier in 1893, the editor of the Madras *Hindu* had praised Western civilization for producing great women like Annie Besant and had regretted that India had yet to produce such a woman leader. But in fact India, a decade earlier, did have a courageous woman leader, but one whom Indians could not acknowledge, namely Pandita Ramabai; she had attacked Indian patriarchy, blaming all the social evils affecting Hindu women on the Hindu family system. And since Hinduism was, to her, the cause of women's misery, she renounced it in favor of Christianity. But her conversion to the religion of the imperial masters shocked Hindu opinion, both orthodox and reformist. And Ramabai's denunciation of women under Hinduism was particularly shameful and offensive to Hindus as she not only aired these views abroad, but also published a book on the subject in America that got world-wide publicity. She was therefore never given the status of a national figure by Indians; nor did she even achieve the homage paid by Indians to Blavatsky, Besant and Nivedita.

Moreover, Ramabai was reviled by Tilak, the leading nationalist of the time, and was criticized by Vivekananda and Besant; because of her conversion, she remains, even today, half-forgotten in India (see Chapter 3). Ramabai, in becoming a Christian and obstinately pursuing her Christian proselytizing work, in spite of the advice of her funders, had lost the chance of leadership. But were there no other Hindu women at the turn of the century who could speak out on the rights of women? The Indian women devotees of Ramakrishna and Vivekananda might have filled this role but they remained at the level of religious women and did not emerge as independent figures active on social and political issues or on women's rights. For example, one person who had the advantage of charisma was Sarada Devi, widow of Ramakrishna; after his death, she played a purely religious role as a Holy Mother, as did other notable women devotees, such as Golap Ma, Yogin Ma, and Gouri Ma.

But several foreign women, such as Margaret Noble (Sister Nivedita), Mirra Richard (the Mother) and Madeleine Slade (Mira Behn) were the disciples if not co-partners of three of India's most revered figures, Swami Vivekananda, Sri Aurobindo and Mahatma Gandhi respectively. All these women and their gurus were born in the latter decades of the 19th century; Vivekananda in 1863, Margaret Noble in 1867, Gandhi in 1869, Aurobindo in 1872, Mirra Richard in 1878, and Madeleine Slade in 1892. They were all products of the spiritual and intellectual curiosity and reformist influences of the late 19th and early 20th centuries that posed challenges to established institutions, beliefs and traditions, and were inspired by the vision of a future new age and a new species of politically and spiritually liberated human beings. The common themes that formed their outlook were those of the unity and universality of all religions, the perfectibility of humans, and consequently an optimistic view of humanity. These views had been popular in 19th-century Europe where theorizing on a universal level had become prevalent; moreover, the ideologues of France and America had spoken of universal human rights, Darwin had shown the common origin of all living things, Marx had projected a "world view" of history and political economy, Nietzsche had written of the "superman," and "Universal Exhibitions" were held in Paris and London.

But spiritualists, occultists and theosophists also acknowledged differences. They were at the forefront of evolving alternatives to orthodox religion, holding that truth was not exclusive to Christianity. They propagated the common truths in all beliefs and therefore the "brotherhood" of all, based on an elaborate theory of stages of spiritual growth from lower to higher levels. While universality was in the air, difference was recognized and the opening up of the world through imperial conquest had the unexpected result of making ancient civilizations and religions of Asia known to Europe, and also in loosening the hold of national boundaries and exclusivist doctrines. In India too, the concept of the universality of religions was also particularly popular among reformists like Rammohan Roy, Keshab Chandra Sen and members of the Brahmo Samaj were eager to move away from sectarianism in religion. The catalyst who successfully challenged orthodoxy was Ramakrishna Paramahamsa; from his vantage point in the popular Kali temple of Calcutta, he reclaimed the unity and universality of all religions, passing the message on to his most notable disciple, Swami Vivekananda, who in the 1890s traveled to Europe and the United States and developed a following that included several Western women.

EAST-WEST DIALOGUE

One of the most important East-West exchanges in the field of religion occurred in Chicago in 1893 when (as part of the Chicago World's Fair) a Parliament of Religions was held, with representatives of all the world's religions meeting at this unique gathering. Among the Indians was Swami Vivekananda, "the most popular and influential man in the Parliament," who spoke on several occasions, dressed in an orange robe and turban, a "commanding presence and...an electrifying figure" (French 1974:54–55). Other Indians also included theosophist, Hindu, Jain, Brahmo Samaj and Parsi representatives. The Buddhist delegate was Anagarika Dharmapala, a leader of Buddhist revivalism in Sri Lanka, and Annie Besant, former atheist and socialist also attended as president of the Theosophical Society. According to Harold French, there were hopes,

> That a large measure of fellow feeling would emerge from the lifting up of the
> noblest aspirations of the world's religions. Some sense of a world community,
> with a humanitarian imperative to respond to the rising demand for education,
> economic justice, and political freedom, lay at the heart of those who now gazed
> in hope towards Chicago. (ibid:53–54)

There was an interesting congruence between "advanced" Christians like the Unitarians and the reformist Hindu movements. The new thinking of the Unitarians, known for biblical criticism, had been compared to the Brahmo Samaj in Bengal which under Keshab Chandra Sen had been influenced by Christianity. The Indian theosophist G. Chakravarty, who attended the Chicago Conference, also remarked on the new trend in the West, namely that,

> There is something to be learned of religion outside of the circle of the church,
> that the Hindoos and Buddhists are not quite the heathens that they have been
> represented by the American missionaries sent to India and Ceylon. (Nethercot
> 1961:408)

While in Boston in 1893, Vivekananda met many liberal Christians, giving talks in Greenacre, Maine, a well-known center of religious discussion at that time. At the Parliament of Religions, Vivekananda had suggested that missionaries should be sent to India "to teach them how better to earn a piece of bread, and not to teach them metaphysical nonsense," and in a lecture in Detroit on "Christian Missions in India," he attacked missionaries for their ignorance, incompetence and methods of conversion by offering money during famines and also for their links with the British administration. "When you come to us as missionaries, you ought to throw over all idea of nationality. Jesus did not go about among the English officials attending champagne suppers. If your missionary does not follow Christ what right has he to call himself a Christian?" (Pathak 1967:227). A similar view had earlier been expressed by Keshab Chandra Sen who wrote, "The Christ that has come to us is an Englishman, with English manners and customs...hence...Hindu people shrink back" (ibid:214). These views led to interesting debates among Christians in America; the *New York Herald* wrote that after hearing Vivekananda, "we feel how foolish it is to send missionaries to this learned nation," and similarly the *Critic* spoke of "the impertinence of sending half-educated theological students to instruct the wise and erudite Orientals" (ibid:223–24).

The theme of universality pervaded all Vivekananda's speeches and writings in India and abroad and attracted many foreign disciples, including Margaret Noble (Nivedita). That all religions, cults and folk beliefs were manifestations of the unity of the same Divine force, that each country had its own approach to the Divine, that the duty of the religious was not to concentrate on the next life but to work towards perfection in this life, that India had to shake off its lethargy and assert its own identity, were the common features in the religio-political messages of Vivekananda, Nivedita, Aurobindo and Mirra Richard (The Mother) as well as of Gandhi and Mira Behn. However, these sentiments, claiming to be "universal," were often articulated within a Hindu context and represented Hindu culture as superior to others; this alienated the Muslims and tended to distort future nationalist struggles (Choudhuri 1979:2).

In the case of Vivekananda and Nivedita, although their ultimate vision was one of universal religion, they saw their immediate task as the awakening of Hindus, the renewal of India's lost strength through the freedom of the country from the political, economic and spiritual shackles responsible for India's debasement and lethargy. It was a message compounded with the blood and thunder of Kali, of aggressive confrontation and opposition to stagnation at all levels, and a strong belief in the emergence of a free Indian nation. While the fire of Vivekananda and Nivedita found an initial response in Aurobindo, the young Bengali revolutionary, he became less involved in the growing political agitation after the 1920s and more absorbed in Hindu forms of meditation and ritual. With Mirra Richard he prepared a blueprint for the future, in which would rise a species of new men and women. In contrast, however, to speculation by Nietszche and others in the 19th century on the "superman," the Aurobindo-Mother ideal was not based on the supremacy of force and aggrandizement, but on their vision of a truly liberated being.

Gandhi had been influenced by Vivekananda's book *Rajayoga* and had met

Sister Nivedita in Bengal in 1902. His feelings were mixed: "In spite of my failure to find any agreement with her, I could not but notice and admire her over-flowing love for Hinduism," he wrote in his autobiography, adding, "I came to know her books later" (Gandhi 1985:223). His own approach was in contrast to the aggressive militancy of the Hinduism of Vivekananda and Nivedita, which was referred to as "muscular Hinduism" (Bose 1982:2). Gandhi's main teaching was the assertion of moral principles and truth through non-vio-lence (*ahimsa*). "I shall not submit to injustice from anyone. I shall conquer untruth by truth and in resisting untruth I shall put up with all suffering," he stated, challenging foreign rule and asserting India's right to freedom. Gandhi also coined the word satyagraha (truth force) to give non-violence an activist and positive content. The idea gripped the masses who rallied to his call for resistance but often went against his mandate of non-violence. In pro-claiming universality, however, Gandhi's views were generally expressed with the language and concepts of Hinduism.

In a country where kinship links were a vital element of the social struc-ture, these foreigners assumed roles of fictive kinship with the gurus as mother/sister/daughter. In a colonial situation, to come out openly and pro-claim ones kinship with Indians was a bold move. Thus Sister Nivedita saw herself as Vivekananda's "daughter," Mira Behn always acknowledged Gandhi in the role of "bapu" (father) and Mirra Richard was a universal "Mother." Nevertheless some Indians were ambivalent about such claims and about the white woman as sannyasi, in love with India, proclaiming the glories of Hinduism and allying with local gurus. Critics of Gandhi discounted Mira Behn, some Calcutta intellectuals were horrified at Nivedita's celebration of Kali, and not all the Bengali devotees of Aurobindo showed equal respect for the Mother.

The phenomenon of the white "sisters" and "holy mothers" was extraordi-nary. While they were absorbed into Indian society and culture, outliving their gurus and making India their home, they also introduced modern European methods of education, modernism in art, and an appreciation of Western music and culture. They were not only white women "appropriating the Other" in religion and culture, but were persons with a vision of a politically independent new India. A change of persona was symbolized by their change of name and life style; they moved from being rebels in Europe to nationally honored persons in India. The revolutionary, independent, Irish woman Margaret Noble emerges as Sister Nivedita, the devotee of the important sage Vivekananda; the cosmopolitan, Jewish-French "new woman," Mirra Richard, transforms herself into the "divine" Mother, partner of Aurobindo; and the upper-class English rebel, Madeleine Slade, becomes Mira Behn, the devoted follower of Gandhi, Britain's greatest political adversary of that period. They did not become recluses or renounce the secular life, but introduced a certain dynamism into their work, a product of their earlier rebellion. Their commitment—especially in the case of Nivedita and Mira Behn—took them among the poor and into political activities with the masses. They all shared a desire for an India free of colonial rule, and for this reason they continue to be revered and honored by many Indians as the ultimate "white goddesses." The following sections discuss the phenomena of these extraordinary white female devotees and the roles they played in the lives of three of India's greatest spiritual and political leaders during the British colonial period.

13

IRISH REBELLION AND "MUSCULAR HINDUISM"

Margaret Noble As Vivekananda's "Lioness"

Here a brown baby with black lines under his eyes, and a gold chain round his waist, carried in triumph by his mother…and above it all, the tall palm trees, with little brown villages and freshwater tanks nestling at their feet, while all kinds of birds flew about fearlessly…. *The golden glow of ones first sensation suffuses it still. It was all like a birth into a new world.*

—Sister Nivedita on her first impressions of India (1896) in *The Web of Indian Life* (Nivedita 1988:14, emphasis added)

As BEFITS A LEGENDARY FIGURE, THERE IS MORE THAN ONE VERSION OF THE life of Margaret Noble. To devout Hindus she was the famous disciple of Swami Vivekananda and devotee of the Goddess Kali; to Indian nationalists and revolutionaries she was the Irish revolutionary, promoting Indian nationalism through political and cultural awareness and inspiring violent and non-violent actions against British rule. To some she was the defender of the indefensible—Kali worship, and traditional Hindu family practices; to others she was the great modernist influence in local art, women's education, and the appreciation and acceptance of difference in culture. Was it possible she played these dual roles of both "goddess" and "devil"? An examination of her life and work will help in attempting to resolve this question and to understand why, over eighty years after her death, she is celebrated as one of the

Sister Nivedita (left) with Mrs. Sevier, Sister Christine, and Mrs. Abela Bose. (From *The Complete Works of Sister Nivedita*, Vol. 3 (1967); Widener Library, Harvard.)

pantheon of "Great Women of India," and is reviled as a supporter of armed struggle and a friend of the anarchist Kropotkin.

Margaret Noble (1867–1911) was born in Ireland to Protestant clergyman Samuel Noble and his wife Mary Hamilton. Her parents and grandparents, with whom she spent a part of her childhood, were supporters of the agitation for Irish Home Rule.[1] As a student she turned to alternative movements in education and politics, moved away from orthodox Christianity and studied Buddhism. "I became more and more convinced that the salvation preached was decidedly more consistent with the Truth than the preachings of the Christian religion" (Foxe 1975:16). She developed an interest in new methods of education, opposing, what her biographer Barbara Foxe calls the "stifling idiocy of formal Victorian education." She put these new ideals into practice by opening a school in Wimbledon, London, based on the free methods of Froebel and Pestalozzi, to "liberate the children" (ibid:17). She also became a member of the Sesame Club where Bernard Shaw, Thomas Huxley and W.B. Yeats lectured, and began to move in socialist and anarchist intellectual circles.

Some Indian writers have stressed Margaret Noble's contacts in London with

Irish leaders and Russian anarchists, from whom she allegedly received "a complete training in the techniques of terrorism and armed revolution" (Burman 1968:195). While there is no proof of this, it is true she knew the anarchist Peter Kropotkin and was influenced by his book *Doctrine of Mutual Aid*; as Noble herself wrote "Kropotkin knows, more than any other man, what India needs. What I specially dwell upon is the utter needlessness of governments" (Foxe 1975:125). He also convinced her of the "futility of constitutional agitation and the need for armed revolution for gaining the freedom of the motherland" (Mitra 1968:281). Apart from anarchist sympathies, Margaret Noble also had feminist tendencies, being herself, in many ways, a new independent woman of the 1890s. As Foxe writes:

> The battles that were being fought out within her, showed themselves in an aggressiveness that was often directed against men, for the bitterness of a brilliant woman trying to fight her way through a masculine dominated society tended to make her champion the rights (and break her heart over the wrongs) of women, almost to an excess. (1975:27)

Like many other politically and socially conscious women, Noble was also attracted to other cultures, religions and their leaders. In November 1895 she met Swami Vivekananda at the house of Lady Isabel Margesson in London.

SWAMI VIVEKANANDA

Vivekananda (1863–1902) a middle-class Bengali, was a product of European and Indian culture. The course of his life was changed by his meeting with Swami Ramakrishna Parmahamsa (1836–1886) of the Dakshineshwar Kali temple of Calcutta with his message of the universalism of religion. The mantle of Ramakrishna fell on Vivekananda after the guru's death in 1886. As part of his mission Vivekananda traveled all over India, and during this period the misery of India filled his mind "to the exclusion of every other thought." Recalling Ramakrishna's words that, "religion is not for empty bellies," Vivekananda began to urge that the country needed "a religion which would give us faith in ourselves, national self-respect, and the power to feed and educate the poor and relieve misery.... If you want to find God, serve Man!" (Rolland 1984:26, 10). By 1892, Vivekananda strongly felt that he had to travel to the West not only to make India's plight known, but also to give India's spiritual message to the world before it was wiped out in India itself: "The time is ripe. The faith of the Rishis must become dynamic" (ibid:29).

It was with this intention that he participated in the Parliament of Religions in Chicago in 1893. This event—the first international gathering of representatives of all religions—was sensational because of the dialogue and debate that took place between Christians and those of other religions. By all accounts Vivekananda dominated the proceedings both intellectually and physically. As Romain Rolland noted, while the other orators spoke of their own version of God, Vivekananda alone "spoke of all their Gods, and embraced them all in the Universal Being." He argued for "a universal religion without limit of time or space, uniting the whole *credo* of the human spirit, from the enslaved fetishism of the savage to the most liberal creative affirmation of modern science" (1984:40). In the West, where Christianity had been regarded as the only true faith, and from where missionaries had been sent to enlighten the "heathens," such words had a sharp impact. His fame spread and Vivekananda was invited to tour the United States. He visited Britain in 1895 and again in 1896, also traveling in Europe.[2]

Vivekananda attracted several Western disciples among whom were many women, some of them of independent means. They included Ellen Waldo, who produced books based on Vivekananda's talks, Marie Louise, who later became Swami Abhayananda and Christine Grenstidel and Josephine McCleod who came to India to work for the cause. Funding came from Sarah Bull and Henrietta Muller, while Minnie Boock gifted 160 acres of land in California to Vivekananda (French 1974:74). But the most devoted of the women disciples was Margaret Noble, who had attended his public lectures and had discussions with him in London in 1895 and 1896. In a letter to Noble, Vivekananda said, "the earth's bravest and best will have to sacrifice themselves for the good of many," and added, "I am sure *you have the making in you of a world-mover, and others will also come.*" (ibid:26, emphasis added).

The news of Vivekananda's successes in Europe and America was reported in the press in India. His message was one of national awakening, emphasizing the need for spiritual revival to restore the cultural and political life of India. He warned of the dangers both of Western materialism and of Asian obscurantism. India had to improve its economic conditions by learning from the West, without losing its own identity.[3] The message was also one of activity and strength, as well as of conscious action for the masses, rather than of renunciation. Vivekananda stressed the need for work among the poor: "the first Gods we have to worship are our own countrymen," he exclaimed. He visualized the creation of institutions to train "strong, vigorous, believing young men" as activists to preach the Hindu scriptural truths "in and outside India." And long before Gandhi, Vivekananda raised the issue of caste and Indian "untouchables" (ibid:111–12).[4]

Vivekananda arranged for Margaret Noble to help in his work in India; he also warned her of the difficulties she would face, not only in understanding Indian society, but also in confronting opposition from both Indians and the British:

You will be in the midst of half-naked men and women with quaint ideas of caste and isolation, shunning the white skin through fear or hatred.... On the other hand, you will be looked on by the whites as a crank, and every one of your moves will be watched with suspicion. (Foxe 1975:36)

Noble arrived in Calcutta in January 1898, declaring in her diary, "Victory! I am in India!" (Reymond 1953:6), and very soon falling "utterly and irrevocably in love…with India" (Foxe 1975:37). Soon after her arrival she visited the Himalayas and Kashmir with Vivekananda, his fellow monks and several foreign disciples. Margaret Noble was initiated as a brahmacharini (celibate novice) of Vivekananda's Order of Ramakrishna, a non-political organization with religious, social and humanitarian objectives; she was given the name Nivedita (the Dedicated), but never became a sannyasini (nun), retaining her lay status, which enabled her to lecture, teach and be involved in public life. Vivekananda's disciples were mobilized to combat the plague in Calcutta in 1898–1899. Vivekananda supervised the relief work and Sister Nivedita undertook the nursing of the sick, fund raising and the overall management of activities, because it was felt that she would bring order and discipline, and inspire courage in others.[5]

NIVEDITA AND FEMALE EDUCATION

Nivedita's main preoccupation, however, was the school she started in 1899 in Calcutta, which had about thirty girls, with four classes of two hours each, taught in relays by Nivedita herself. She used new kindergarten methods of teaching, especially in art and handwork. The public exhibition of the children's art work attracted many women and children of the neighborhood. In June 1899, she left with Vivekananda for Britain and the United States to collect funds for her school and lecture against the prevalent false accounts of India and Hinduism given by missionaries. Returning to Calcutta in 1902, Nivedita re-opened her school with another Vivekananda disciple, Sister Christine Grenstidel. The school, which soon had forty-five girls, was based on the new idea that "knowledge is supposed to receive a foundation in concrete experience, and all work to appear to the child in play."[6] The school was also innovative in that it had a women's section between the hours twelve noon and four p.m. where neighborhood married women learned reading, writing, religion and sewing.[7] The school also became a center of discussion, "men, women and children—and, later, statesmen, writers and thinkers of many nationalities—called, and talked, and discussed" (Foxe 1975:158–64). It was, in fact, a nucleus of political debate and activity during a period of emergent Bengali nationalism.

In the sphere of art appreciation and criticism, Nivedita influenced the new wave of Bengali artists. "Art must be reborn," she said, deploring the "miserable travesty of would-be Europeanism that we at present know." She was optimistic that local art would develop, for India "has found a new subject—India herself" (Chatterjee 1968:227). She also wrote several important articles on Indian art, one entitled "The Function of Art in Shaping Nationality," and together with Ananda Coomaraswamy, she co-authored *Myths of the Hindus and Buddhists* (1913).

VIVEKANANDA, NIVEDITA AND THE ISSUE OF INDIAN WOMEN

A question that inevitably arises is the personal relationship between Nivedita and Vivekananda. The standard literature of the devotees always describe it in terms of the guru and the disciple, where Nivedita emerges as the selfless, loyal, utterly dedicated disciple owing allegiance only to Vivekananda, the Master. But their writings and letters show a deeper personal relationship, based on mutual dependence. As a liberated and outspoken woman of the 20th century, Nivedita could not only talk frankly and even disagree with Vivekananda, but could also advise him, help in drafting and writing, and assist him in his travels in the West. Vivekananda had a freedom in inter-acting with Nivedita, which would have been impossible with Indian women, who would have treated him only with the utmost deference, as a swami. Calling Nivedita by her nickname Margot, Vivekananda would alternately praise, tease and scold her and also frankly express the anguish he felt about the political apathy and cultural and religious decline in India.[8]

But although Vivekananda believed strongly in women's education as the key to the awakening of India, he was often involved (while abroad) in controversy on the question of Hindu women's rights. In 1894, Vivekananda had been challenged by the Brooklyn Ramabai Association and in 1900, at a lecture in California, he asked his audience to choose the topic. But when the suggestion came, "Will you tell us about your women, their customs and education and the position they hold in the family?" Vivekananda caustically replied, "So you want to know about Indian women tonight, and not about philosophy and other things?" and proceeded to give his views on the subject of the ideal Indian woman. Making distinctions between practices in the East and West, he argued that what was allowed in the West, like cousin-marriage, was taboo in India, and widow re-marriage, which was practiced in the West, was considered the "greatest degradation" among the higher castes of India; therefore, "to judge our people by others standards would be neither just, nor practicable. We must know what the ideal is that a nation has raised before itself. We should not assume that there is one code of ethics and the same kind of ideals for all races," or think that "what is good for us must be good for everybody." As an example, he stated that Western women who denounce the practice of foot-binding in China do not think of the "injury to the human form that the corset has done" (Vivekananda 1986:5–6).

Vivekananda took a defensive stand, making a distinction between the West, where "the woman is wife," and India, where the "woman is mother first and the mother last." In an Indian home, the mother rules. If a mother comes into a Western home, she has to be subordinate to the wife. He added that the word "woman" signifies, in the mind of the Hindu, "Mother-hood"; and God is called *Mother.* He also contrasted the individualistic Westerners who marry whom they choose with the "socialistic" Hindu whose marriage is decided by the family. "So I have no choice in my marriage, nor my sister. It is the caste that determines all that" (ibid:16–17). In this speech, Vivekananda found devious arguments for child marriage and enforced widowhood, even quipping that foreign women "are always crying over the hardship of the Hindu woman and never care for the hardships of the Hindu man" (ibid:29). Nivedita's view of Indian women was influenced not only by Vivekananda's defensive position, but also by her own vision of India through a "golden glow." Rather than babies thrown to crocodiles, Calcutta, as seen by Nivedita, was, from the beginning a city of romance and excitement. Referring to the familiar horror stories told about India by missionaries, she exclaimed "And the reality was so different!" (Nivedita 1988, Vol.II:14).

Nivedita, like Annie Besant and the theosophists, idealized the Hindu wife and mother and all those aspects of Hindu family life that had come under sharp attack. Yet as Ramusack notes, "Nivedita wanted to spread a positive image of India, including its women, abroad." Given this difficult objective, she defended and sought reasons for the customs and institutions of Hindu society. Being herself a celibate novice, she used religious categories and "compared the Hindu household and women's roles and relationships within it to a Christian convent" (Ramusack 1987:5).[9] At a time when the practice of child marriage was a matter of public controversy in India and Britain, Nivedita offered no word of criticism and even attempted a justification.[10] She also remarked that the Hindu theory is "that a long vista of common memory adds sweetness to the marriage tie" (Nivedita 1988 Vol.II:35–36). Even the "Laws of Manu," which to Pandita Ramabai were the source of Hindu women's oppression, were seen by Nivedita in a positive light.[11]

The Hindu wife's characteristic emotion was "passive reverence" while the husband offered "measureless protection." Moreover, the wife prostrates herself before him, touching his feet with her head before receiving his blessing. This pattern of behavior, Nivedita archly asserts, "is not equality. No. But who talks of a vulgar equality, asks the Hindu wife, when she may have instead the unspeakable blessedness of offering worship?" (ibid:44–45). Nivedita's "most exuberant rhetoric," says Ramusack "was lavished on the role of the Indian woman as mother" (1987:7).[12] The mother in India, says Nivedita, is a "goddess enthroned in her son's worship—she is the bringer of sanctity and peace" (Nivedita 1982b, Vol.I:464).[13] The fidelity of the wife had to extend beyond death, and Nivedita found no difficulty in justifying enforced widowhood. "A widow remarried is no better in Hindu eyes than a woman of no character, and this is the case even where the marriage was only a betrothal and the young fiancee has become...a child widow" (Nivedita 1988, Vol.II:25). What critics, including Ramabai, called the disfigurement and torture of widows was again given a different interpretation by Nivedita, who describes a widow, "her white sari, unbordered, her short hair, her bareness of jewels, her scant food and long prayers, her refusal to meet guests and join in festivities" giving her a vocation similar to that of a nun (ibid:44). Even sati could be explained away.[14] Her acceptance of Indian social practices as justified by historical circumstances evoked a sympathetic reaction from many Indian men who were trying to develop a sense of cultural self-confidence.

Nevertheless, in many of her public speeches, she stressed the need for women's education in the national cause. In a speech in Calcutta in 1904 she spoke of "the goal...to be sought in the great word, *nationality* and emphasised the obligation for Indian men to educate the women of their households so that they would be a dynamic force in the struggle for Indian nationality (Reymond 1953:301). Nivedita rejected the purely "Western" type of education for Indian women, and asked, "Shall we, after centuries of an Indian womanhood, fashioned on the pattern of Sita or Savitri...descend to the creation of coquettes and *divorcees*?" (Nivedita 1973, Vol.III:4). Yet she was very forthright on women's rights and reportedly said:

> I am sorry to find one more Indian who considers women no better than slaves. What is the value of your education if it does not help you to bring up your women folk to your own level? Don't you realise that the country would never advance or prosper if one half of it is ignorant, backward and superstitious? (Mahadevan 1957:44)

She also influenced the Tamil poet S. Bharathi; his well-known essays on women's rights, which were "marked by a crusader's zeal," were "traced to his abiding admiration for Sister Nivedita" (ibid:171).[15]

NIVEDITA AS KALI DEVOTEE

Nivedita's book, *Kali, the Mother*, published in 1900 in London, was a collection of essays written in emotive language on aspects of Kali worship. To Nivedita, a strong-willed questioner of Victorian religious orthodoxy, the discovery of the female aspects of the Divine was an exciting contrast to the patriarchal representation of God the Father in Christianity. Kali was "a terrible...extra-ordinary figure," wrote Nivedita, and "those who call it horrible may well be forgiven" since the image of Kali was intended to strike terror in the heart of the viewer. Nivedita noted, however, that the image "so fearful to the Western mind, is perhaps dearer than any other to the heart of India" and it was through this confrontation with the Terrible that one experienced God (1982b, Vol.I:465). Nivedita explained the Kali image in terms of the Hindu mind: "the wail of all the creatures, the moan of pain...and the pitiful cry of little things in fear." To the Hindu, "Death is greater than life.... Though thou slay me, *yet* will I trust in Thee!" (ibid:472–73). Kali was also projected, in Nivedita's words, as "strong, fearless, resolute" at a time in India's history when the issue of national identity had appeared in Bengal (ibid:494). Ramakrishna and Vivekananda, and, later, Aurobindo—all Bengalis—chose Kali as the symbol of the awakening of Hindu-biased nationalism and spoke frequently of shakthi (power) associated with Kali. Nivedita, who was as politically conscious, also chose Kali to fire Indians into action, and to arouse them out of their political stupor and lethargy.[16] The British intelligence services were alert to the dangers of anti-British political mobilization in Bengal through Kali worship. According to Payne, a popular euphemism for killing a Britisher at the time was "sacrificing a goat to Kali" (1933:104).[17]

It was inevitable that reformist Indians and those who were non-religious and rationalist would take exception to Nivedita's views on Kali worship. The Brahmos, who were monotheistic and against idol worship, resented her defense of "idolatry" and her idealization of Hindu society. Significantly, a group of Brahmo Samaj women who were social workers, opposed Nivedita, one of them claiming that Nivedita's writings were like "pages of Browning, full of human sentiments," adding that the renunciation she preached "only produced the spinelessness and cowardice from which we suffer. The source of all this is the blindness which lies in the teaching of Ramakrishna" (Reymond 1953:172). It is interesting that there was also disagreement on Kali worship and its symbol-ism, Kali representing "for some, the goddess of orgies; for others, the Mother of the Universe" (ibid:178). Surendranath Tagore is reported to have asked Nivedita, "If you have to adore an image, why that hideous Kali?" To which Nivedita replied, "I adore no image.... Kali is in me as She is in you" (ibid:148).

REVOLUTIONARY POLITICS

Soon after Vivekananda's death in July 1902, Nivedita broke with the Order of Ramakrishna and declared that her work would be "free and entirely inde-pendent of the sanction and authority of the Order" (ibid:150). This gave her the freedom to move into broader areas of activity aimed at arousing Indian national consciousness in both men and women.

We talk of "woman making"; but the great stream of Oriental women's life flows on. Who am I that I should in any way seek to change it? Suppose even I could add my impress to ten or twelve girls, would it be so much gain? Is it not rather by taking the *national consciousness of the women,* like that of the men, and setting it towards greater problems and responsibilities that one can help?... *I think my task is to awaken the nation, not to influence a few women.*" (ibid:150–51, emphasis added)

In 1902, at a time of incipient Indian nationalism, Nivedita began a lecture tour of the main cities of India, addressing large public meetings and private gatherings, speaking of her hopes for Indian unity and a national awakening. She spoke in emotional language couched in a religious form, but with a clear political content.[18] In 1904, Nivedita toured India again, lecturing against Lord Curzon's Universities Act which brought higher education under government control; she also spoke on the need for Hindu-Muslim unity (Foxe 1975:164–65). She was in touch with many Bengali activist religious and political groups, speaking at their meetings, giving them books on the Irish struggles, the American Revolution and the lives of Garibaldi and Mazzini.

The years 1904–1907 were turbulent in the political history of Bengal. The campaigns for swaraj (home rule) and swadeshi (local produce) came at a time when there was outrage in 1905 over the partition of Bengal. The swadeshi campaign to produce all necessities locally and to boycott British goods, received the total support of Nivedita, on both political and aesthetic grounds. Self-sufficiency, training in new techniques and trades, and challenging the dependency on foreign imports were politically important, as was the growth of a class of local entrepreneurs; but pride in the beauty and quality of Indian goods was a crucial aspect of the campaign. Nivedita wrote on the attractiveness of local products; "her descriptions emphasised the elegance of simple lines, and established canons of taste. She revealed beauties which the Hindus themselves had failed to see" (Reymond 1953:315).

One of Nivedita's close associates at this time was Aurobindo Ghosh, who regarded the policies of the Indian National Congress as too moderate, and favored armed resistance. He tried to unite the scattered Bengali revolutionary groups and formed a "Central Council" of five, which included Nivedita. She was not only a guru in practical matters to the young revolutionaries, but was also regarded idealistically as a "Mother of the Revolution." She had doubts as to whether passive resistance alone would be enough, and she made no secret of the fact that if this tactic failed, Aurobindo's ideas might be needed (ibid:169–70). Nivedita was in Benares at the time of the 1905 sessions of the Indian National Congress and many political discussions took place in her house. By this date she supported the extreme faction of Congress against the moderates. Her anger at the partition of Bengal and her experience in working with the rural poor during the famine in Bengal in 1906 made her more open-ly hostile to British rule. In 1907, when Vivekananda's brother, Bhupendranath Dutt, a young revolutionary, was arrested for writing a seditious article, she stood bail for him. She was probably kept under surveillance by the police, and on the advice of friends, left for England in 1907.[19]

In India, however, there was increased violence, with bomb attacks, assassinations, arrests and deportations. Some writers allege that Nivedita helped in publishing Indian revolutionary journals in Europe, especially *Bande Mataram* (from Geneva) linked to extemists like Krishnavarma (Burman 1968:202). She also did a lecture tour of America, collecting funds and contacting revolutionary Indians in exile, and in 1909, she returned to India after the violent movement in Bengal had been crushed. Nivedita continued to be politically involved; for example, Aurobindo, who had been released after a year in jail, started two journals, *Karma Yogin* in English and *Dharma* in Bengali. After a violent incident when he faced a threat of deportation, Nivedita is said to have advised Aurobindo to leave Calcutta; she also took over and edited the *Karma Yogin* until it was banned in 1910. With her as editor, the journal's tone was nationalistic.

Nivedita's actual involvement in helping Bengali extremists are matters of debate even today. As Foxe cautiously notes, "the extent to which fervour, anger and a passion for nationalism might have forced her, at last, to move in the direction of the insurrection which she had helped to arouse, can never be answered. Some of her statements suggest that she saw little hope in the end, for any other method" (1975:208–209).[20] Her French biographer, Lizelle Reymond, describes Nivedita as being "swept along like some great stormy wind bringing life to everything it touched" and "her boundless love for Ireland" was transformed into a "fervent Indian patriotism which provided the vitality that radiated from her" (1953:279, 282). She also claims that around 1907 Nivedita's activities were "so inextricably mingled with those of the nationalists that they cannot now be isolated...her house was a refuge with food, money and maps for those who had to escape." Reymond even goes to the extent of saying that Nivedita "did not remain unimplicated in the manufacture of bombs" (ibid:336–37).

Foreigners like Nivedita, however "Indian" they became, also brought a whiff of the Protestant ethic into their work. From all accounts, Nivedita was dynamic and efficient, pushing herself to work not only in the religious, political, educational and artistic fields, but also in fund-raising, lecture tours, writing and in more mundane things like packing Swami Vivekananda's bags and sorting his papers and books (ibid:211). Nivedita's vitality was to inspire many others—Indian politicians, artists, poets and scientists. But she died at forty four in 1911, after a short illness. She is commemorated in many ways;

her school still survives, a road is named for her in Calcutta, and in 1967 the centenary of her birth was celebrated in India. Her name is linked with some of the important political currents of her time—Irish rebellion, Indian nationalism, anarchism and socialism as well as modernism and feminism. Yet over-determining all this was her devotion to Vivekananda, to India and to traditional Hindu social practice. The brew was a heady one, inspiring Indian nationalist males, but from a feminist perspective, bringing a more questionable message to the women of India.

14

FROM ADMIRAL'S HOUSE
TO GANDHI'S ASHRAM

Madeleine Slade in India

The "Gandhi-Mira" episode was one of the great idyllic stories of human life reminiscent of the high-minded and heroic women who clustered around Jesus

—John Haynes Holmes, *Gandhi's Letters to a Disciple* (1950:3)

Gandhi's fast in 1942 "burned like hot iron into the flesh of the nation, and gave the last touch to the people's detestation of British oppression"

—Mira Behn (Madeleine Slade), *The Spirits Pilgrimage* (1960:252)

ALTHOUGH SISTER NIVEDITA'S POLITICAL ACTIVITIES IN BENGAL HAD STRONG revolutionary undertones, she died in 1911 before the generalized mass struggles for Indian independence had developed. Her guru Vivekananda died nine years earlier. This chapter focuses on a later "sister," Madeleine Slade, a British devotee of Gandhi, the political leader of the Indian national movement. Madeleine Slade was not as politically militant as Nivedita, but she stood by Gandhi for over two decades, during the peak years of mass resistance to British rule. She became nationally and internationally known for her daring political stand and subversion of gender, class and racial expectations of white women in a colonial context.

Mohandas Karamchand Gandhi (1869–1948) shared with other Indian leaders and gurus an admiration for the independence and courage of the unconventional "new women" and feminists of the West. Born in Gujerat, Western India, Gandhi studied law in London between 1888 and 1891. In heterodox London he came into contact with people in diverse movements including theosophists, liberal Christians, free thinkers, socialists and vegetarians; ironically, it was the theosophists who first inspired him to read the Hindu texts. He returned to India and practiced law until 1893 when he went to South Africa and made new contacts with theosophists and liberals. There he also began his campaign for the rights of the Indian community, and formed the Natal Indian Congress, using the tactics of passive resistance (satyagraha) against discriminatory laws. He also served in the Indian Ambulance Corps on the side of the British during the Boer War.[1]

Returning to India in 1915, Gandhi became active in the Indian National Congress and in the early 1920s launched protests against British rule, which took the form of non-violent mass civil disobedience. By the mid-1920s, Gandhi was promoting hand spinning and weaving; he adopted the peasants' attire of dhoti and shawl, and started a community (ashram) to promote a new way of living. Gandhi's leadership of the national struggle, combined with his philosophy of non-violence, advocacy of self-sufficiency, and a return to the simplest possible way of life, attracted interest abroad, and by the mid-1920s he had become a world figure. Many Western intellectuals were sympathetic to his approach to life and to the Indian political struggle.

Among Gandhi's admirers and co-workers there had always been a group of women supporters, including many Western women involved in religious and political controversy. In his student days in London, he was a frequent guest at the home of Elizabeth Manning (1828–1905), the general secretary of the National Indian Association from 1877 to 1905. One of the first women graduates from Cambridge, she was for active thirty-five years in events concerning India, especially Indian women's education and the training of women doctors. She visited India twice, inspecting schools and colleges (Beveridge 1947:407). In London, Gandhi also met Madame Blavatsky, and read her *Key to Theosophy*. In Gandhi's words this "stimulated in me the desire to read books on Hinduism, and disabused me of the notion fostered by missionaries that Hinduism was rife with superstition" (1985:77). Gandhi, at that time, had a great admiration for British legal and political systems and was amazed by British dissidents who defied the law, and questioned the accepted social and religious shibboleths. He was even more impressed by the leadership of women. In 1887, Gandhi met Annie Besant, then at the height of her fame as a free-thinker, socialist, critic of colonialism and champion of the rights of women and the working-class. As Morton writes, in Annie Besant, Gandhi met "a woman who changed his whole concept of her sex, she defied law, religion, tradition, yet she was honoured, even revered. There were indeed few men who had her

Mira Behn with Gandhi in 1931. (From Mira Behn (1960), *The Spirit's Pilgrimage*; Widener Library, Harvard.)

high status" (1953:37). Gandhi eagerly read Besant's pamphlet, *How I Became a Theosophist* and followed, "with great interest the controversy about her conversion" (1985:77); in his later years in South Africa, Gandhi had her picture on the wall of his office (Morton 1953:39); and on a visit to India from South Africa in 1902, he went to Benares "to pay my respects to Mrs. Besant" (Gandhi 1985:224).

In his South African phase, Gandhi had many women friends, including Olive Schreiner, the celebrated feminist author of *The Story of an African Farm* (1883), who championed the rights of the non-whites and supported Gandhi's satyagraha movement. "To Gandhi, distinguished and successful lawyer, it was sustaining to have her friendship" (Morton 1953:77). But there were disagreements too. When Schreiner met Gandhi in London in 1914 she opposed his support for Britain during the war and his efforts to recruit Indians in London for the war effort.[2] In South Africa, Gandhi's home became a community; although his wife Kasturbai showed no enthusiasm for having to cope with a house full of supporters, including foreign men and women, Gandhi nevertheless persisted in surrounding himself with guests. Among the Western women in the house were Minnie Graham Polak of Scotland and a Mrs. West, from Leicestershire, wives of two of his keenest followers. He also relied on foreign women secretaries because he needed persons who were good in both English and typing. One of his secretaries was Miss Dick from Scotland. As Gandhi recounted:

She became more a daughter or a sister to me than a mere steno-typist. She was often entrusted with the management of funds amounting to thousands of pounds. She won my complete confidence, but what was perhaps more, she confided to me her innermost thoughts and feelings…in the final choice of her husband. (1985:260)

Miss Dick was succeeded by Sonya Schlesin, of Russian Jewish origin, also from Scotland, who worked as Gandhi's secretary and typist and expressed a commitment to the causes he was fighting for. "Between Sonya and Gandhi arose a friendship wholly impersonal, yet profoundly deep…at the service of his cause" (Morton 1953:87). Gandhi wrote:

She is one of the few women I have been privileged to come across, with a character as clear as crystal and courage that would shame a warrior. Thousands of stalwart Indians looked up to her for guidance. When during the Satyagraha days almost every one of the leaders was in jail, she led the movement single-handed. (1985:261)

Gandhi continued to attract strong, independent foreign women who had the courage to risk political opposition from the rulers and social ostracism from others. The most famous of Gandhi's female foreign devotees, however, was Madeleine Slade, who until his death remained his loyal devotee.

MADELEINE SLADE (1892–1982) BECOMES SISTER MIRA

Madeleine Slade, born to an upper-class English family, was the daughter of Admiral Sir Edmund Slade. Her mother was also from a similar class background and Madeleine's early years were spent at her maternal grandfather's country home, Milton Heath, until the family moved to London where she was taught by a governess. In 1903, her father became Captain of the Royal Naval College at Greenwich and later was posted to India as Commander-in-Chief of the East Indies Station. Here she participated in the social round of Bombay official life, with family holidays in the naval camp in the hills of Sri Lanka. Madeleine later recalled that, "India had meant nothing to me but a life of social functions and formalities in a very restricted society which did not appeal to me at all. The real India…I had neither seen nor even sensed" (Mira Behn 1960:40).

Returning to Europe, Madeleine lived a life of privilege, traveling to Germany and Austria and studying French in Paris. She was at this time absorbed in Beethoven's music and read Romain Rolland's life of Beethoven. She met the author and read his latest book *Mahatma Gandhi* (1924) and then decided to visit India to meet Gandhi. She spent a year in preparation, reading about India, learning spinning and weaving and practicing sitting and sleeping on the floor; she also became a vegetarian and a teetotaller. On hearing about Gandhi's fast in 1924, she sold a diamond brooch and sent Gandhi a cheque for £ 20, receiving a reply from him that her money would be used for "popularizing the spinning wheel" and adding that "if a year's test still impels you to come, you will probably be right in coming to India" (ibid:62). In 1925, Slade sent samples of her spinning to Gandhi and asked if she could join his ashram.[3]

In preparation for India, Slade spent the summer in Switzerland "working with the peasants in their fields in order to be in as good physical trim as possible." She even sent to Delhi for homespun cloth (khadi) and had clothes specially made, and with two trunks of books and some jewelery ("for presentation to the Cause"), she left for India. Her family made no objections and did not try to dissuade her. "Everyone seemed to realise that it was a spiritual necessity and accepted it." Her father, however, said "Be careful," and as Slade writes, "It was not an easy thing for a man connected with the highest British officials and ministers to have a daughter going to join the arch-revolutionary of the British Empire!" (ibid:63–64).

On arrival at the ashram near Ahmedabad, Slade fell on her knees on meeting Gandhi; "You shall be my daughter," he said and allocated her tasks of carding and spinning cotton, learning Hindi, sweeping, and washing latrines. The ashram consisted of several hundred people "men, women and children of all ages and all degrees of faith," drawn to the place by political, social or religious aspects of Gandhi's work (ibid:66, 70). Slade was accepted into the life of the ashram and Gandhi, known as bapu (father) changed her name to Mira Behn (Sister Mira); on her insistence she adopted local dress, took a vow of celibacy and had her hair cut. "There was no ceremony or solemn taking of a vow. Bapu quite simply cut off my hair with his own hands, and gave me a loving slap on the back when I bowed down at his feet for blessing" (ibid:80–81). Her reactions to Gandhi were those of the religious devotee:

> By God's infinite blessing I had arrived, not at the outer edge of Bapu's activities, but right in the intimate heart of his daily life. The impact on my emotions was tremendous. From early morning to the last thing at night I lived for the moments when I could set eyes on Bapu. (ibid:69)

Mira Behn from that time onward lived through some of the most tumultuous periods of Indian history in which Gandhi was involved—the civil disobedience movements of 1930 and 1934, including the Salt March in 1930, the political agitation of the Indian National Congress of the late 1930s, and the war years. But through these hectic years, Mira's main role was that of devotee and secretary, rather than that of colleague in political activity; her loyalty was at all stages a purely personal one, although her actions led her into opposition to the government and to British rule in India. Mira accompanied Gandhi to public functions and to sessions of the Indian National Congress held all over India; she looked after his food and made arrangements for his travel and accommodation.[4] At public meetings, Mira hovered around till she heard the sounds of "Mahatma Gandhi Ki Jai". She then knew the meeting was over and would fly to the host's house "to see if the seat in the room was covered with pure khadi and not mill cloth—but once it was not, and I got a scolding" she recalled. When she attended Gandhi's meetings, her task was also to collect donations of money and jewelry from the crowd (ibid:104–106). Gandhi also had Mira's help in editing and proof-reading his autobiography (1927) and in helping to correct articles (ibid:87). Whenever Gandhi traveled without her, they corresponded regularly; 351 of his 650 letters to her (in reply to what Gandhi playfully referred to as her "love letters") were published after his death (Holmes:1950). As Gandhi's biographer Louis Fischer remarked, "Miss Slade became physically ill on a number of occasions when she was separated from Bapu or...worried about his health. Her bond with him was one of the remarkable platonic associations of our age" (1982:545).

The relationship between them was not without tension because Mira's devotion was very personal, while Gandhi's concerns were political. When Mira once left the ashram after a scolding over "trifling matters" in 1931, Gandhi wrote:

> You have left your home, your people and all that people prize most, not to serve me personally, but to serve the cause I stand for. All the time you were squandering your love on me personally. I feel guilty of misappropriation. And I exploded on the slightest pretext...my anger turns itself upon me for having given you all those terrible scoldings. But I was on a bed of hot ashes all the while I was accepting your service. (Mira Behn 1960:127)

But Mira was serving the cause through serving the man who led the cause. When questioned about her religion she replied, "I follow Gandhi's religion of service. But I am not a Hindu. I think it is very difficult to describe the God of the Hindus.... There was Christ and Buddha, and now there is Gandhi" (Morton 1953:210). While her devotion and service were considered a normal part of the disciple's work at the ashram, her services extended into a wider area. She accompanied Gandhi when he led the Indian delegation to Britain for the Round Table Conference on Indian constitutional reforms in 1931. In London, Gandhi and Mira stayed at Kingsley Hall in the East End, a community house for the poor, run by Muriel Lester, who sympathized with India's struggle for freedom. They were also looked after by Quaker sympathizers.

During this visit to Britain, Gandhi traveled with Mira to Oxford, Cambridge, Birmingham and Lancashire, where the mill workers gave him a rousing reception. In Britain, Gandhi's presence was an important media event that was flashed around the world. As Morton notes, Gandhi had become "the most publicized man on earth," but with him "Mira had become the most publicized woman living" (ibid:189). She was pestered and followed by reporters and asked questions about herself, her father and her role in India. She replied that she was not part of Gandhi's political work adding that "I am in England only because I have to come. To me, it is like coming to a foreign country. India is my home" (ibid:190). Mira's tasks in London were to look after Gandhi. As she wrote "I had to heat Bapu's bath water and provide his breakfast...then see Bapu off promptly at 8 o'clock.... After that, I swept the rooms, made up a bundle of clothes and attended to the washing—fetched provisions, cooked Bapu's midday meal, packed it up and hurried off...to serve him the meal." On his return late at night after discussions, Mira would, "rub his feet hard to try to bring some warmth to them," then wake him for the early morning prayer, and at four forty-five prepare a drink for him of hot water, honey and lemon (Mira Behn 1960:135–36). The sight of a six foot, angular, upper-class English woman, dressed in a long homespun garment and sandals, cooking, sweeping and washing clothes for Gandhi, certainly caused much comment. In serving Gandhi, she was crossing class and race boundaries, challenging the established gender roles for white women and also "betraying" the Empire. She was frequently ridiculed as a typical eccentric spinster of the British upper class.

> All that (Madeleine Slade) said, all that she did for Gandhi, became subjects of amused scrutiny, of mocking conversation in the high and low places of London...sometimes the accounts became all but hilarious. (Morton 1953:190)

To give one example, Robert Bernays, who wrote a critical book on Gandhi in 1931 called *Naked Fakir*, describes Mira's voice as having "the clear unmistakable accents of the English governing class" and added, "She appeared with the Holy Man's meal, and bending down on one knee, held it in front of him like a serving maid before Pharaoh" (1931:94).[5]

The political discussions in London were not successful and Gandhi and Mira returned to India making stop-overs in Paris (where he addressed a public meeting), Switzerland (to meet Romain Rolland) and Rome (where he met Mussolini). By the time he returned to India, the mood of conciliation, which had occasioned the London conference, had changed, and the British launched a policy of repression, arresting Congress leaders, including Gandhi

and Nehru. At this point Mira Behn went to Bombay to start a news information service on events in India for dissemination abroad. She "sorted and
sifted" material and prepared a "Weekly Report." Her move from the ashram
to political journalism led to her arrest and imprisonment for three months,
which she spent among women political prisoners. After her release, she continued to be active and was arrested again and sentenced to one year's imprisonment (Mira Behn 1960:155–65). While in jail, on Gandhi's advice, she read the
Upanishads, the Ramayana and the Mahabharata, and was impressed by the
tales of women's devotion and dedication (ibid:170–71). Released again, Mira
joined Gandhi on a tour of India to eradicate "untouchability" and she was
"again in charge of Bapu's personal requirements." The campaign was frequently on foot, addressing meetings in villages and being confronted with
the opposition of high-caste Hindus.

Mira decided to return to the West to combat the misrepresentation of
Gandhi. Her upper-class connections also helped her to have access to politicians and officials. In London, she met Sir Samuel Hoare and got his consent
for a lecture tour of England and Scotland. She also visited Lloyd George (a
former Prime Minister) at his country home, and had discussions with Lord
Halifax, General Smuts and Winston Churchill. She concentrated on working-class audiences, lecturing in many towns, staying in the homes of workers, and meeting groups of pacifists and socialists (ibid:180–85). She was again
followed by reporters wherever she went. She spoke of Gandhi's work for the
down-trodden and the "untouchables" and described the routine of the
ashram. From Britain, Mira Behn traveled to the United States where her
tour was arranged by Dr. John Haynes Holmes, the liberal clergyman who
supported many radical causes, including the struggles of colonial peoples
and the rights of African-Americans. She stayed at the Henry Street House
Settlement, gave five broadcasts and spoke at twenty-two meetings in New
York, Boston, Philadelphia and Washington, where Eleanor Roosevelt welcomed her at the White House.[6]

In the mid-1930s, Gandhi had several differences of opinion with the more
militant left-wing sections of the Indian National Congress and even withdrew from the organization for a period. He concentrated on work with the
"untouchables" whom he named harijans (children of God) and persuaded
one of his financiers (Birla) to start a Harijan Colony in Delhi for their education and training. Another businessman, S.J. Bajaj, donated a large house and
grounds to Gandhi, which became the headquarters of the Village Industries
Association. Making this his base, Gandhi urged Mira to undertake work in
the nearby villages, among the harijans. Here Mira with her sense of organization and discipline—not unlike Nivedita before her—proceeded to help in
cleaning, disinfecting and looking into the sanitary problems of the village.

She helped in a cholera epidemic, bringing medicine, and obtaining an inoculating squad from the nearby hospital. "Never had I realized more clearly" she wrote, "the meaning of Bapu's insistence on sanitation. The best medical aid was to overcome insanitation and malnutrition" (ibid:195–96). When Mira fell ill with typhoid, Gandhi undertook to look after and nurse her.

> I protested…but Bapu said he enjoyed nursing…. As I was rapidly becoming helpless, I gave in and allowed myself to reap the infinite blessing of Bapu's gentle, loving care. With perfect regularity he saw to my every need. (ibid:206)

Elections were held in 1936 and the Congress took office in nine out of eleven provinces of India. Gandhi did not participate in the legislature, but remained behind the scenes as a key political figure, meeting the Viceroy on several occasions, as the international situation worsened and world war seemed imminent. In the meantime, the old ashram had been disbanded and by the mid-1930s a new ashram, Sewagram, was started. There were numerous activities, including the production of cloth, sugar, handicrafts and the launching of an education center. This period was one of uncertainty for Mira Behn. Like other Western women who, in an earlier period, had been at the center of activity on Indian issues, she was marginalized by the emergence in the mid-1930s of competent and politicized Indian women.[7] "The result was that I had nothing whatever to do beyond the teaching of spinning to two or three village boys," wrote Mira, who tried to interest herself in animal husbandry. But "inner misery and outer aimlessness" began to affect her health, and in 1937 she went to the Himalayas to recuperate (ibid:209–10). Mira Behn's restlessness during this period prompted Gandhi to suggest that she live an independent life outside the ashram and even get married. She, however, decided to live alone in silence and read, spin and meditate for a period, instead of staying in the ashram where "I could find no place and felt myself useless" (ibid:219). Gandhi agreed and arranged for her to stay in a hut in the forests of a friend's estate where she spent five months before returning to the ashram; Gandhi then sent her to another rich friend who had a fruit garden on the coast, where she lived alone in a mud cottage for several months in 1941 with birds, peacocks, toads and some harmless snakes for company. Her period of silence lasted fifteen months, but events forced her back into active work.

The first task she was involved in during this period was the organization, with Kamaladevi Chattopadhyaya, of a women's camp in Bombay.[8] By 1942, when the threat of Japanese invasion was being discussed, Mira went to the ashram and expressed her views to Gandhi on "nation-wide non-violent resistance" to the Japanese and asked permission to attend the Congress Working Committee in Allahabad to discuss this with other Congress leaders; she was given a statement of Gandhi's views which she carried to Allahabad. "It was Bapu's original draft of the now-famous "Quit India" resolution. Of course, it appealed to me" (ibid:227). Mira Behn now became an important messenger for Gandhi, not only to the Congress leadership, but also to provincial Congress politicians and to British officials. To the Allahabad Congress group she had to explain Gandhi's draft resolution (which led to differences of opinion) and carry back a compromise resolution to him. Gandhi then sent her to Orissa to contact local Congress leaders and discuss strategies in the event of a Japanese invasion, and to urge them to resist the Japanese. From there she went to Delhi, where the Viceroy, Lord Linlithgow, refused to meet her; she was allowed to speak to his private secretary and explained the need for the British to understand the mood of the country.[9]

But stormy days were ahead. The Indian National Congress in August 1942 adopted the "Quit India" resolution and the same night Gandhi, Nehru, Mira and others were arrested and confined in the Agha Khan's palace in Pune. There were violent and non-violent demonstrations of protest all over the country and after a few weeks Gandhi began a protest fast of twenty-one days. While protests and repression continued, Gandhi was kept in house detention for two years. But Mira was released and decided to leave Gandhi and start an ashram in 1944 on ten acres of land in a village near the Himalayan range. It was named Kisan (Farmer) Ashram and included a cowshed, some cottages, and a kitchen. In the meantime, the question of Hindu-Muslim relations had arisen and efforts at approachment between Jinnah's Muslim League and the Congress failed. With the end of World War II in 1945, talks were held in Simla by the British, to which all parties were invited, including the released Congress leaders. With Gandhi's permission, Mira joined him in Simla. The conference failed and Mira returned to her ashram (ibid:263). After elections in 1946, which resulted in the formation of Congress governments in the Provinces, Mira began to take an interest in the drive for food production and the restoration of agricultural land that had been requisitioned by the military to civilian hands. Gandhi intervened to get her appointed a special adviser to the United Provinces government in Lucknow for the "Grow More Food" campaign.

By 1947, when India was in the throes of Hindu-Muslim clashes and Gandhi was busy trying to quell the disturbances, Mira was involved in work in the rural areas. The government asked her to supervise the establishment of two large cattle projects near Rishikesh at the foot of the Himalayas. She explored the area on horseback and chose a site—naming the new venture Pashulok (Animal World) because of the wildlife in the area. Giving the Kisan Ashram to the Department of Rural Development, Mira put all her efforts into developing Pashulok, only coming to Delhi for a medical check up, and staying at

Birla House with Gandhi for three months at the end of 1947. She left Delhi in December of that year to return to her work. Gandhi began a fast in January when violence between Hindus and Muslims broke out again in Delhi. He wrote, "Don't rush here because I'm fasting.... Trust God and be where you are " (ibid:291). But the tension grew, and on January 30th, 1948, Gandhi was assassinated. Mira wrote:

> I stood silent and still. A vast emotion held me as in a trance. The only thought that came to me was, "Bapu, Bapu, so it has come!" I looked up into the heavens and through the boughs of the trees, the stars were shining in peaceful splendour.... They told of Bapu's spirit released and at peace, and as I gazed on them it was as if Bapu was there—yes, there and with me too. It all became one. (ibid:292)

Following Gandhi's earlier advice to "stay where you are," she chose not to go to Delhi for the cremation, but a part of his ashes was sent to her for immersion in the river near the Kisan Ashram area (ibid:292–5). She went the next month to Delhi for a brief visit to meet Nehru and other Congress leaders, and to visit Gandhi's cremation site. She decided to go back to Pashulok, "to the life and light of the fields and forests, where nature knows no such thing as mourning for the dead," adding that, "Bapu is there, not here" (ibid). But after discussions in Lucknow and Delhi, the Pashulok scheme was wound up by the government and the Pashulok Seva Mandal was formed, "to develop an area...where men and animals combine with Nature in the formation of a decentralized society demonstrative of Bapu's ideals for World Peace, where man in his own village, will, along with his cattle, be self-sufficient, healthy and happy" (ibid:300).

The idea was to start a village co-operative on 700 acres, upgrading local cattle and developing village industries. The scheme was inaugurated by the first President of the Republic of India. But funds were not forthcoming and speculators attempted to control the land, resulting in Mira having to request the government to take the land under its protection. She moved away "with three or four companions and some pack animals," and on her devoted horse, she went for about 200 miles looking for a suitable place in the Himalayan valley. She leased two acres of forest land, constructed cottages and cowsheds from pinewood and called the place Gopal Ashram. Mira had a young typist, and two assistants for the animals and garden. She started the monthly paper, *Bapu Raj Patrika*, in five languages, to urge the adoption of a self-reliant economy as envisaged by Gandhi, but again "it never paid its way and ultimately left me penniless" (ibid:306). She toured the nearby villages on horseback to see what the possibilities were of starting community projects. Mira met Nehru and suggested that Gopal Ashram could be such a project and with his approval obtained funds from the government. A formal opening was held and work started but "the same thing began all over again." Instead of a decentralized project, she was restricted by bureaucratic interference and decided to hand it over to the government and move away, distributing the animals.

Next she went to Kashmir and established Gaobal, a cattle development scheme. But Mira's plans to import a Jersey herd was canceled because the Kashmir government decided to stop the import of foreign cattle. Once more she had to succumb to official interference and decided to leave. "But what to do? I had no place to live, and very little money left. Kisan Ashram, Pashulok, Gopal Ashram and Gaobal had all passed out of my life like dreams" (ibid:313). She wandered around and found an "extraordinarily beautiful" place with a "glorious view" where she had a small cottage and cowshed constructed. In 1958, Mira Behn left India to live in a farmhouse in the forests near Vienna and write her memoirs, published in 1960 entitled, *The Spirit's Pilgrimage.* In 1981, she was awarded a high honor of the Indian government, the *Padma Vibhushan,* and died at ninety in Vienna in 1982.

Madeleine Slade was among the last of the Western women devoted to Indian religious-cum-political gurus. In subsequent years many foreign women joined religious movements in India and became acolytes of various holy men. However, with the end of colonialism, such conversions became drained of any nationalist or political content and acquired significance only within a purely religious context. One Holy Mother who lived through the colonial and post-colonial period as more the equal partner (than the devotee) of the guru was Mirra Alfassa, who is discussed in the next chapter. Though regarded as the Divine Mother, she was nevertheless able to use religious discourse to promote radical views on politics, education and women's rights.

THE "JEWISH MOTHER" OF PONDICHERRY

Mirra Alfassa Joins Aurobindo

Woman is the slave of man because of the attraction she feels for the male...
because of the desire for a "home" and...security (and) because of the attach-
ment to maternity. That is why no law can liberate women unless they free
themselves...the best...is to treat the two sexes on a footing of perfect equality,
to give both the same education.

—The Mother, *On Women* (1984:4, 7)

Mother and I are one but in two bodies.

—Aurobindo, *Mother or the Divine Materialiasm* (Satprem 1979:1)

A FOREIGN WOMAN WHO WAS TREATED BY SOME AS DIVINE DURING HER LIFE
time but was a proponent of "advanced" feminism was La Mère, the "Mother"
of Pondicherry, Blanche Rachel Mirra Alfassa (1878–1973), soul-mate of one of
India's most famous sages, Sri Aurobindo. She was born in Paris, not of French
origin as is commonly believed, but of a Sephardic Jewish family from Cairo.
Her father, Maurice Alfassa, was a banker originally from Turkey, and her
mother, Mathilde Ismaloun, was from Egypt. In Cairo, French influence was
strong in elite circles and Mirra Alfassa's mother and grandmother, who were
both very independent women, were closely linked with the cultural and
social life of France. Her mother took the family to Paris after being forced to
leave Egypt because she had allegedly snubbed the Khedive (Nahar 1985:29).
Mathilde, it seems, was a positivist and an atheist. Satprem claims that she was

also "a Communist at a time when well-raised young ladies were busy knitting their trousseaux, adding that "she would remain a communist until she left this world at the age of eighty eight" (1979:16). Her daughter, Mirra, however, from an early age showed interest in occultism and spiritual matters while retaining radical attitudes, and being modernist and feminist, a not unusual combination among some of the "new women" of that time.

Mirra Alfassa was an art student at the Ecole des Beaux Arts and was part of the artistic avant-garde of Paris at the turn of the century; she knew the painters Monet, Degas, Renoir, and the writer Anatole France (Wilfried 1986:8, 15). In 1897 she married and had a son by the artist Henri Morisset. He was a pupil of the painter Gustav Moreau, who used Indian themes in his paintings, and whose other pupils included Georges Rouault and Henri Matisse. Her interest in spiritualism also developed during this period when there was an increase of such groups in France; writing of her early years, Alfassa said: "Between the ages of eighteen and twenty I had attained a conscious and constant union with the divine presence." She had read Vivekananda's *Rajayoga* and was given a copy of the *Bhagavad Gita* by an Indian who advised her to "envisage Krishna as the immanent Godhead, as the Divine within ourselves" (ibid:10). By 1906, Mirra Alfassa was a part of a group called *Idéa* which met regularly to discuss occult experiences and spiritual realization.

Alexandra David-Néel, known for her travels and writings on Tibet, was a member of the group, and wrote of her friendship with Mirra Alfassa. "We spent marvellous evenings together with friends, believing in a great future.... I remember her elegance, her accomplishments, her intellect endowed with mystical tendencies" (Srinivasa Iyengar 1978:30). Alfassa also knew Max Théon, a "Polish Jew who was highly advanced in occultism," who had worked with Blavatsky and had started an occult society in Egypt before moving to Algeria (Joshi 1989:30). Alfassa spent some time in occult studies with him and his British wife Alma, also a "gifted occultist," in Tlemcen, Algeria. In 1912, she formed another group of twelve members in Paris, named *Cosmique*, to study Eastern spirituality and to promote, in Alfassa's words, "the advent of a progressive universal harmony...and, collectively, to found the ideal society in a place suited to the flowering of the new race, that of the "Sons of God" (Wilfried 1986:14–15). At this time she was also a close associate of Abdul Baha, son and successor of the founder of the Bahai religion (Sethna 1978:105). Alfassa divorced Morisset in 1910 and married Paul Richard, a lawyer and politician interested in religion. In 1910, he had visited Pondicherry, the French enclave in India for electoral purposes. There he met the political exile Aurobindo; on his return to Paris with news of Aurobindo, Mirra began to feel "irresistibly drawn towards India, the one country which she had always felt to be her true mother country" (Wilfried 1986:18). She and Richard returned to Pondicherry

Mirra Alfassa—The Mother. (By permission from the
Ashram, Pondicherry.)

in 1914, where Mirra recognized Aurobindo as the "Krishna" she had been
looking for.

Aurobindo (1872–1950), born Aravinda Ackroyd Ghose in Calcutta in 1872,
was the son of Swarnalata Devi and Dr. Krishnadham Ghose, a civil surgeon
who had done his higher medical studies in Britain and brought up his children in European style. Aurobindo was born in the house of his father's friend,
Manmohan Ghose, where Annette Ackroyd was also staying (see Chapter 4).
She had come to Calcutta to start a secular school for girls and Dr. Ghose gave
Aurobindo the middle name of Ackroyd in her honor. At the age of five,
Aurobindo was sent to the Loreto convent run by Irish nuns in Darjeeling,
and in 1879, along with his brothers, was taken to England to study at the pres-
tigious St. Paul's Day School in London. Here Aurobindo received a classical
literary education from 1884 to 1889 and spent time reading English and French
literature, learning other European languages and writing poetry. In 1890
Aurobindo won a scholarship to King's College, Cambridge, where he did the
Classics Tripos. While in Cambridge, Aurobindo was the secretary of the

Indian Majlis, a student group, and was a member of a secret society of Indians called "The Lotus and the Dagger," which was committed to Indian independence. Like many Indians he was influenced by the Irish struggle, and in 1891 wrote a poem on the death of the Irish hero Parnell. After spending fourteen years continuously in Britain, Aurobindo returned to India in 1893, joining the Baroda State Service as a bureaucrat, (Karan Singh 1963:43–44). From 1893 unitl 1907 Aurobindo also taught English and French at the Baroda College, becoming a Professor of English in 1900. Aurobindo made his mark in nationalist circles with a series of articles (in 1893 and 1894) entitled *New Lamps for Old*, which attacked the Indian National Congress policy of gradual constitutional reform. By the later 1890s Aurobindo had become convinced that constitutional methods would not lead to independence and that an armed uprising was necessary.

In the early 20th century there was rising nationalism in Bengal, aggravated by the partition of Bengal in 1905. New methods of passive resistance to British rule developed, and extremist groups using violent means were also active. Aurobindo returned from Baroda to Calcutta in 1906 and became the Principal of the National College. He started a paper in English, *Bande Mataram,* which was described as "a flaming newspaper which struck a ringing new note in Indian daily journalism." The policy was to "use violence against violence, to return blow for blow...and awaken manhood in the nation" through various methods including the boycott of foreign goods, national education and resistance to foreign rule. (Sarkar 1977:90). There were also many secret societies of young revolutionaries aimed at violent actions against the British using Hinduism for mobilizing support; many were influenced by the patriotic and religious fervor of Vivekananda, and by Nivedita's book *Kali, the Mother,* which gave a "startling interpretation of the goddess as incarnated in the sword" (ibid:486).

Aurobindo's uncompromising opposition to British rule was couched in the language of the cult of the Mother. Deprived of his own mother (who was insane), while in Britain for fourteen years, Aurobindo, in the political and spiritual phases of his life, constantly invoked the divine mother who would make India strong again. This emotional juxtaposing of Mother Goddess and Mother Country is seen in his revolutionary tract *Bhawani Mandhir*, written in 1905, which the British authorities produced as evidence against Aurobindo in later years.[1]

Aurobindo emerged as a leading "extremist" working in both legal and illegal organizations.[2] In 1908, he and other revolutionaries were arrested after a bomb intended for the District Magistrate of Muzaffarpur had killed two British women. He was in Alipur jail for a year under conditions of great hardship but found solace in meditation and became absorbed in spiritual matters.

After his acquittal, he began two journals, *Dharma* and *Karma Yogin*, in Bengali and English respectively; but the period was one of police repression and Aurobindo was in constant danger of re-arrest, especially after the publication of an article, "An Open Letter to My Countrymen," which gave a plan of activity for nationalists in case of his arrest. He escaped to Chandernagore, a French enclave in Bengal, and from there to Pondicherry, another French possession in South India, leaving Sister Nivedita to take over the editorial work at *Karma Yogin*, until the paper was banned.

The French enclaves in India gave Indian nationalists and revolutionaries some protection, because British laws did not apply on French territory and the French upheld the right of political asylum. While in Pondicherry, Aurobindo became involved in fasting, meditation and yoga, establishing a core group of disciples, ostensibly renouncing all interest in nationalist politics. Of course, the question arises whether or not Aurobindo deliberately did this to convince the British and French authorities that he was non-political and only interested in spiritual matters. The meeting, in 1914, of Paul and Mirra Richard and Aurobindo was to change their lives. At first there was a strong common interest in spiritualism and philosophy and together they started a journal, *Arya*, for "the formation of a vast synthesis of knowledge, harmonizing the diverse religious traditions of humanity, occidental as well as oriental."[3] The First World War led to more changes in their plans; Paul Richard had to return to France and Mirra accompanied him reluctantly, lamenting that "He (Sri Aurobindo) did not keep me, what could I do? I had to go. But I left my psychic being with him" (Wilfried 1986:21). From 1916 the Richards spent four years in Tokyo and Kyoto, making contact with Japanese intellectuals and those interested in the occult and in theosophy. In Japan, Mirra also met Rabindranath Tagore, who invited her to work at his educational institute, Santiniketan (ibid:29). What is also interesting is that Mirra moved in socialist circles in Japan.[4] Meanwhile, Paul Richard gave lectures excitedly proclaiming the advent of the leader, Aurobindo:

> For the hour is coming…of great events and also of great men, the divine men of Asia…it is in Asia that I have found the greatest among them, the leader, the hero of tomorrow…Aurobindo Ghose…this name signifies Asia free and one- Asia resurgent. (Richard 1920:81–82, 87)

SPIRITUAL FEMINISM

During the years spent in Japan, Mirra Richard made known some of her radical views on political and social questions. As a remarkable "new woman" of her age, she also defined her attitude towards feminism in a talk on "Woman and the War," in 1916 in Japan. She claimed that the war "would give quite a new aspect to the question," especially because "women were replacing men in most of the posts they occupied before." Those who had earlier looked upon woman as an "object of pleasure and distraction" or, at best, as "the guardian of their hearth and the mother of their children," would be surprised by these changes (The Mother 1978:143). Mirra Richard attacked male aggression, putting forward alternative politics, which in some aspects prefigured radical feminism of later decades:

> It is certain that purely masculine politics have given proof of incapacity; they have foundered too often in their search of strictly personal interest, and in their arbitrary and violent action. Doubtless, women's politics would bring about a tendency to disinterestedness and more humanitarian solutions. (ibid:145)

She, however, also visualized mutual perfection of the sexes. "To reduce woman's part to solely interior and domestic occupations and the man's part to exclusively exterior and social occupations...would be to perpetuate the present sad state of things." But she concluded that "the problem of feminism, as all the problems of the world, come back to a spiritual problem." Some of Mirra Richard's later interests are reflected in this article where she states that the solution to the problem of the relations between the sexes is in spiritual equality and refers to the "new life" around which will be constructed the future "Temple of Humanity" (ibid:145–6). In "A Talk to the Women of Japan" (1916), Mirra Richard spoke of the period as an "exceptional turning point of the world's history," where "hatred, bloodshed and confusion" had led to an "ardent hope" for a "new reign of justice, of beauty, of harmonious goodwill and fraternity." She, however, noted that,

> as soon as great events and work are in question the custom is to relegate women to a corner with a smile of patronizing contempt which means—this is not your business, poor, feeble, futile creatures.. and women, submissive, child-like, have accepted...in many countries, this deplorable state of things.(The Mother 1978:154–55)

She predicted that in the future there would be no such "disequilibrium between the masculine and the feminine" and asserted that the "true relation of the two sexes is an equal footing of mutual help and close collaboration" (ibid:155). She also anticipated some of her future work, speaking of the appearance of "a new species...a new plane of consciousness, a new force or power" that would be a leap forward to "the superman," just as there had been a transition from ape to man (ibid:159). In later years in her role as the Mother, she consistently advocated women's rights. Her secretary called her "one of those

outstanding women who have worked for women's eventual liberation."
According to Mirra, a woman had to liberate herself and not "depend on a
man to liberate her"; speaking of a Charter for Women's Freedom, she said a
woman should liberate herself from slavery to the three attractions of "masculine strength, security of home and motherhood" (Pandit 1983:53–54).

On the question of women's role in society, Aurobindo at this time had also
developed ideas that were in many ways in advance of his contemporaries. He
had been exposed to life in the West at a period when women's issues and the
"new woman" were being hotly discussed; women played a significant role in
nationalist and revolutionary politics in Bengal, and, of course, Aurobindo
was influenced by strong female personalities like Sister Nivedita and Mirra
Richard. In 1919, for example, in an article on the self-determination of nations,
he wrote critically that:

> Just as the glorious possession of liberty by the community has been held to be
> consistent with the oppression of four-fifths or three-quarters of the population
> by the remaining fraction, so it has lately been held to be quite consistent with
> the complete subjection of one half of mankind, the woman half, to the physi-
> cally stronger male. (Sri Aurobindo, Vol.15:600)

Aurobindo, describing the effective challenge to male supremacy, supported the claims of women to be regarded as free individuals and deplored the
"many strong tentacles of old legislation.. (and) persistence of traditional
ideas" (ibid). This "break" Aurobindo made with the "traditional" and his
search for a "new," society, sets him apart from other spiritual nationalists and
elite Indians of the time.

MINDING THE ASHRAM

In 1920, the Richards returned to Pondicherry. According to one account of
events, "it was probably clear to Paul that the Mother was completely giving
herself to Sri Aurobindo and that there was a kind of collaboration and development in the relationship which he could not follow any more" (Wilfried
1986:30). Richard left Pondicherry, breaking with his wife, who remained for
the rest of her days in India, moving into Aurobindo's house and being referred
to as The Mother. Here she began to build up an ashram, taking charge of
Aurobindo's household, establishing order among the disciples, organizing
meditations and re-arranging everything, "books were nicely stacked up
in cupboards and everything found its right place." Not surprisingly, these
changes caused some problems with the disciples, who were used to a more
relaxed life, and resented the intrusion of a foreign woman. They began to
revolt and grumble but, in deference to Aurobindo, they gradually accepted

her authority and her insistence on hierarchy; as one disciple said, "The Mother...showed us in actual practice what was the meaning of Disciple and Master" (ibid:32—33). In 1926, Aurobindo withdrew from mundane activities, leaving all organizational matters to the Mother. The ashram had twenty-four disciples in 1926, the number rising to 100 in 1930; they lived in twenty-one houses, had five cars and twelve bicycles, as well as a library, reading room, dairy, bakery and workshops. In 1933, the Mother reported that "The life we lead here is as far from ascetic abstinence as from an enervating comfort. Simplicity is the rule here, but a simplicity full of variety...of occupations, tastes, tendencies, natures; each one is free to organise his life as he pleases" (ibid:39—40). The disciples were provided every month with clothes and stationery and could request other requirements.[5]

Not surprisingly, as India's struggle for independence gained momentum, many efforts were made to attract Aurobindo away from spiritual activity (which many deplored) to political involvement, especially because he had been such a charismatic political figure in his time. The ashram, where Aurobindo and the Mother lived, became a center for discussion and spiritual activity and a meeting place for local and foreign intellectuals, political figures and those interested in spiritual matters. Although Aurobindo kept out of Indian politics, he and the Mother could not be oblivious to the rise of fascism Europe in the 1930s, and especially (because the Mother was Jewish), to the persecution of the Jews. After war broke out in 1939, Aurobindo and the Mother publicly declared themselves in support of the Allied war effort, donating money to War Funds in Britain and France; this was in marked contrast to the stand taken by the Indian National Congress leaders who rejected the idea of a wartime truce and launched the "Quit India" movement in 1942 (Purani 1987:228). It is interesting to speculate why Aurobindo took this line. It could have been because he was not only more "internationalist" than the Congress leaders, but also because he was not enthusiastic about the replacement of the British by the politicians of the Indian bourgeoisie.

In the meantime, the "deification" and transformation of Mirra Richard into "The Mother" pervades the writings of Aurobindo, who identified "Four Great Aspects of the Mother" as "Wisdom (Maheshwari), Strength (Maha Kali), Harmony (Maha Lakshmi) and Perfection (Maha Sarasvati)." While clearly one had to be a devotee to believe in all such spiritual explanations of Mirra Richard's charisma, there were strong secular reasons for admiring her talent and dynamism, especially in her innovative contributions to education.

THE MOTHER AND AUROBINDO ON EDUCATION
When Aurobindo returned to India from Cambridge in the 1890s to teach in Baroda, he was horrified at the prevalent system of colonial education; "the

most ingeniously complete machine for murder that human stupidity ever invented," he called it, "murder of both body and soul."[6] One of the important messages of the Mother and Aurobindo was the need for a new system of "integral education," and they wrote extensively on this issue. When, in the early 1940s, disciples began entering the ashram with their families, a practical problem arose about the education of children. In response to this need, the Mother, in 1943, opened the Ashram School for twenty children. In 1959 it was renamed the Sri Aurobindo International Centre of Education, with students enrolled from kindergarten level to the higher classes. It pioneered new methods of education and became famous for its "free progress system" which the Mother described as a "progress guided by the soul and not subject to habits, conventions or preconceived ideas." The school was co-educational and gave girls an equal place with boys in all activities (Patel 1986:85–86).[7]

Emphasis was placed on aesthetic training and the development of the senses. The Mother urged that the children should "learn to add artistic refinement to power and precision…be made to…love beautiful, lofty, healthy and noble things, whether in nature or in human creation." The Mother corresponded with Maria Montessori and in the kindergarten, the Montessori system of "sense-training" was used. In the higher classes much emphasis was put on art, art history, dramatics, dance and Indian and Western music. The school also emphasized sports activities. Because the Mother was a very keen tennis player right up to the age of eighty, she took a personal interest in the physical education programs of the school, insisting on girls and boys participating equally. She introduced sports activities for girls, including the wearing of shorts, which "shocked many elderly devotees" (Wilfried 1986:63). Even today women devotees of all ages in Pondicherry can be seen, riding bicycles, wearing shorts, with their hair in nets, as worn by the Mother. The subjects taught at the International Centre were the same as in other schools, with the addition of the teachings of Aurobindo and the Mother in the higher classes. Students were encouraged to do their own research as part of the process of learning, while also being exposed to collective teaching. In such an atmosphere, free of drudgery, regimentation, punishments and homework, the students were told to "open the mind upward to receive inspiration and intuition and inwards to have psychic influences and promptings" (Prasad 1976:106). The school charged no fees and students and visitors came from all over India (including Nehru and Indira Gandhi) attracted by this novel system of education. The school discouraged competition among students and awarded prizes of equal value to all those who achieved the required level. There were no diplomas or degrees and the usual goals of passing examinations, getting jobs and making money were discouraged in favor of studying "for the sake of knowledge and perfection" (ibid:125).

Aurobindo's death in 1950 did not mean the eclipse of the Mother, for as she wrote:

Sri Aurobindo...with whom I lived physically for thirty years...has not left me, not for a moment—for He is still with me, day and night, thinking through my brain, writing through my pen, speaking through my mouth and acting through my organizing power. (Wilfried 1986:69)

Thus inspired, she continued for over two decades to give leadership to the ashram and to the International Centre of Education. But her main interest was the creation of Auroville, a "city of dawn," which was to be a creative international experiment in living, "a universal town where men and women of all countries are able to live in peace and progressive harmony, above all creeds, all politics and all nationalities." The city was near Pondicherry, on fifteen square miles, and was inaugurated in 1968, when the Mother declared that Auroville was "for all those who thirst for progress and aspire to a higher and truer life" (ibid:88–89). There were 124 nations and twenty-four Indian states represented at this ceremony and the first article of the Auroville charter was read out in sixteen languages: "Auroville belongs to nobody in particular. Auroville belongs to humanity as a whole. But to live in Auroville, one must be the willing servitor of the Divine Consciousness" (ibid:89).

It was to be a model for the future and those who lived there were expected to have "the simple goodwill to make a collective experiment for the progress of humanity" (ibid:89).[8] Many foreigners were attracted to Auroville, but like all experiments in community living, serious problems arose about the running of the venture in addition to financial, climatic and logistic difficulties. After the Mother's death in 1973, at ninety-five, there were more problems resulting in a split between Auroville and the ashram, which generated considerable tension. Nevertheless, Pondicherry continues today to be dominated by the institutions created by Aurobindo and the Mother. Many devotees from India and abroad live in Auroville, the ashram and in the town, fervently believing that "the Mother is present among us and Her work continues" (ibid:97).

The Mother, who settled in India in 1920, remained there without going abroad until her death fifty-three years later. She was respected by Indians for her commitment to India and to an Indian savant, as was Sister Nivedita; however, there was a marked contrast in their attitudes and practice. Concentrating on the vision the Mother and Aurobindo had of the future, they did not involve themselves in controversies over contemporary Indian social and political problems; although their political sympathies were radical, they consciously and carefully steered clear of pronouncements on such topics, including Hindu social practices. These silences were strategic and not based on acquiescence. She had to play the role of Mother and be pragmatic, while no doubt conscious that she was a foreign Mother. Yet she never condoned social evils or traditional practices, preferring to take an "enlightened" line on education and women's role in society. Her work for the ashram, the school and the model city of the future singled her out as an unusual woman. Indians, even when they dismissed her divinity, were nevertheless willing to praise the Mother for her other work, for her internationalism and her innovative ideas.

Mirra Richard had been in radical circles; apart from the influence of her communist mother, Mirra moved with socialists in Japan, and in Pondicherry joined the revolutionary exiles linked to Aurobindo. But due to the political and social constraints of the time, Mirra's radicalism and feminism were overdetermined by her spiritual role as Divine Mother. There was, however, another group of Socialist women with no spiritual mission or other constraints, whose cause was left-wing revolutionary politics in South Asia. The final section of this book discusses their role in nationalist and Socialist movements as partners or wives of some of the key Marxist leaders of South Asia.

COMRADES IN ARMS

Western Socialist Women Fight Imperialism

16

WOMEN AND REVOLUTION

(Women) who did not live up to the ideal were perceived as a menace to society
and the nation, threatening the established order they were intended to uphold.
Hence the deep hatred for women as revolutionary figures, almost surpassing
the disdain which established society reserved for male revolutionaries. Woman
as a symbol of liberty and revolution...contradicted the "feminine" values of
respectability and rootedness.
—George L. Mosse, *Nationalism and Sexuality* (1985:90)

DRAMATIC CHANGES HAD TAKEN PLACE IN THE LIVES OF WESTERN WOMEN IN
the fifty years between 1875 and 1925, in terms of education, employment, franchise, property rights and sexual freedom. While some rights could be realized under capitalism, there was also another view that real equality between
women and men could only be achieved in a Socialist society. Hence, the left
movement of these years attracted many who were concerned with women's
liberation and social change. The earlier women missionaries and social
reformers had asserted their rights as women to travel, lead missions and work
for other women—all important advances in their time. The theosophists
who rejected orthodox religion and appropriated Eastern religions and cultures were part of another "feminist" breakthrough, opting out of patriarchal
Victorian society and disassociating themselves from Judeo-Christian culture

and Western traditions. But it was the Socialist women who were to take the battles further. While accepting all the earlier rights won by women and agreeing with critiques of religious orthodoxy, they opposed capitalism, imperialism and patriarchal structures, advocating instead secularism, national liberation, women's rights and revolutionary change. The women who worked in anti-colonial movements were making a clearly subversive challenge to important institutions and ideologies of the West. And, what is more, several Western women were actively involved in the Marxist parties of India and Sri Lanka, some even being associated with their formation.

These women were products of their age, influenced by Socialist movements in Europe and America and by famous and controversial women revolutionary theoreticians and activists. Socialist ideas had drawn sustenance from millenarian and Utopian visions of a new society—movements idealizing the pre-industrial past, dreaming of the advent of the new man and woman, and the liberation of the individual from puritan morality. Groups that were critical of capitalist society, private property, bourgeois marriage, and orthodox religion attracted women members. Some of these formations in Britain were the forerunners of Socialist parties and trade unions of the late 19th century. For example, the "Fellowship of the New Life" (1883), which was dedicated to the "cultivation of a perfect character in each and all" split into two groups; as Bernard Shaw quipped, "the one to sit among the dandelions, the other to organize the docks" (Burfield 1983:33). The latter group eventually became the Fabian Society, which had Bernard Shaw, Sidney Webb and Annie Besant among the leaders. One quarter of its members were women.

As Hobsbawm has noted, the emergence in the late 19th century of Socialist and labor movements urging "the emancipation of the underprivileged unquestionably encouraged women seeking their own freedom"; it also "provided much the most favourable public environment for women...to develop their personalities and talents" (1987:202, 209). Some of the outstanding Socialist women of the era included Beatrice Webb, who was active in the Fabian Society and with her husband Sidney Webb, wrote extensively on trade unionism and the condition of life among workers; Annie Besant who outraged Victorian England with her views on atheism and birth control; Eleanor Marx, who was active in Socialist politics and in organizing workers, and Olive Schreiner, the South African feminist who lived partly in Britain, and in 1883 created a sensation by publishing *The Story of an African Farm*, about an unrepentant unmarried mother. Among the activist Socialist women were Katherine Conway and Enid Stacey who as "itinerant propagandists" helped in the forming of the Independent Labour Party in 1892 (ibid:212), and Alice Dax whose feminism and Socialism were portrayed in the character of Clara Dawes in D.H. Lawrence's novel *Sons and Lovers* (Delaveney 1971:21). In 1906, several trade unions, Socialist groups and co-operative societies joined together to form the Labour Party, and by 1924 Ramsay Macdonald was Prime Minister of a short-lived Labour government, with the first woman cabinet minister— Margaret Bondfield. Other movements in this period included Syndicalism, which was popular briefly during the years of industrial militancy (1910–1913), and Communism, which gained some support among sections of the working-class, leading to the formation of the Communist Party in Britain in 1921, and the election of an Indian Parsi (S. Saklatvala), as the first Communist member of parliament.

Significantly, many women revolutionary leaders of the West came to prominence by their oppositional positions within the left movements; these were no doubt heightened by their experience of subordination as women and their struggle to break free from all forms of patriarchal restraint, choosing revolutionary alternatives in their personal as well as political lives. From the 1870s onward, there were many women revolutionaries in Russia; some joined the populist Narodnik movements and achieved international notoriety through their involvement in political assassinations.[1] Others were anarchist, one of the most famous of their leaders being Emma Goldman (1859–1940), who migrated from Russia to the United States and became a labor organizer and supporter of women's sexual freedom; she was known as Red Emma, "the enemy of God, law, marriage and the state" (Shulman 1979:12)[2]. The Communists in Russia also had numerous important women leaders, such as Nadezhda Krupskaya (1869–1939) who, as Lenin's wife, was at the heart of politics while in exile, and after the 1917 Revolution. More controversial was Alexandra Kollontai (1872–1952) who not only opposed many of Lenin's policies but also made demands for sexual freedom and the abolition of marriage[3].

But it was Clara Zetkin (1857–1933), one of the leaders of the German Social Democratic Party (SDP), who brought women's issues to the fore in internationalist Socialist circles. The SDP, formed in 1869, expanded and by 1912 had won thirty-five percent of the votes and 110 seats, becoming the largest party in Parliament; female membership rose from 4,000 in 1905 to 206,000 in 1919, with women forming twenty percent of party members. It became the "strongest womens' mass movement in Europe" (Mies 1981:143). On two crucial issues, Zetkin clashed with the SDP. Against Zetkin's wishes, the autonomous organization of women within the SDP was ended in 1908 and women were integrated into the party. She also opposed the right-wing drift in the SDP and its support for the war in 1914 and left the party in 1917 to join the German Communist Party, becoming one of its leaders (Foner 1984:39). In 1910, on her suggestion, March 8th had been adopted as International Women's Day and in the 1920s Zetkin kept the women's issue alive in the Third International by forming a Communist Women's International (1920), which brought together women of the left from around the world (ibid:39). Through her work in such organizations, Clara Zetkin became well-known among European and American Socialist women.[4] A close collaborator of Clara Zetkin was Rosa Luxemburg (1871–1919)[5] who contributed to Marxist theory on the accumulation of capital, political revisionism, the mass strike and imperialism, and also made important critiques of nationalism and of the Bolshevik revolution.

In the United States, small radical groups of Socialists, abolitionists and feminists had been active in the first half of the 19th century, and their influence was to grow with the expansion of popular movements of protest in later years. By the early 20th century Socialist ideas were popularized by writers like Jack London and Upton Sinclair, and intellectuals and working people were drawn into the Socialist Party formed in 1901. In 1910 the first member of the party was elected to Congress, and by 1911 there were seventy-three elected Socialist mayors; in the 1912 presidential election, the socialist leader, Eugene Debs, polled 900,000 votes (Zinn 1980:333, 346). There were many militant women leaders—among the best-known being the legendary "Mother Jones" (1830–1930), the organizer of mine and textile workers.[6] The 'Rebel Girl' Elizabeth Gurley Flynn, was a union organizer from 1906 onward and spent her life fighting for workers' rights. Other women who supported the Socialists included the famous blind, deaf and mute Helen Keller, and feminists such as Charlotte Perkins Gilman, Margaret Sanger, Frances Willard and Agnes Smedley.

While women often became Socialist because of their concern for the exploited and the oppressed, there were many Socialist women who gave some priority to questions of Home Rule and anti-colonialism. In the 19th century, many Irish women joined the struggle for Home Rule, while also being involved in feminist and anti-colonial causes.[7] From the 19th century onward, Indian and Sri Lankan scholars, writers, religious activists and nationalists traveled abroad and made their views known to wide audiences of Westerners. As a result, European and American Socialist women joined in protests against imperialism; they included many Jewish women, whose consciousness of colonial oppression was heightened by their own experiences of anti-Semitism and racism. Thus, many women were involved in anti-colonial activities in the West and supported Asians abroad who were openly or clandestinely collecting funds and organizing groups to oppose imperial rule. In addition, the struggle for social change in the colonies meant an attack on foreign and local vested interests. Merely replacing the "white sahibs" with the "brown sahibs" was not enough. Hence, reformist Asian nationalists were discounted by Socialist Western women in favor of revolutionaries who had the dual goals of political independence and Socialism. In so doing, foreign women were not only confronting Western imperialism and its ideologues, but also rejecting orthodox Asian reformers, religious gurus, and leaders whose nationalism lacked a Socialist vision of the future. In a sense these women had the formidable task of taking on and fighting a whole array of patriarchs, both Western and Asian, who were hostile to Western Communist "she-devils" and embarrassed by their presence.

What was this hostility and embarrassment based upon? Foreign women who confined their activities to charity, education, health and social reform were following the accepted pattern of female behavior, namely concern for the deprived. British rulers and most locals were not unduly worried by their activities as long as there was no breach of the law and accepted norms of conduct. White women as theosophists or Holy Mothers were more daring in their questioning of accepted ethnic and gender roles; hence, the British were not happy seeing women of their race and class wandering around behind Indian gurus and proclaiming the greatness of India or the coming of a New Messiah. It was strange and sometimes potentially subversive. To most Indians, however, such women, though startling in their attempts to "go native," were nevertheless admired for their courage in undermining Britain's own "sacred cows"—Christianity and colonialism.

But Western women Socialists and Communists in the colonies were anathema to British rulers, and of course, the ultimate shame in terms of race, class and gender. Because they were regarded as dangerous threats to colonial rule, the severe punishment of deportation could be imposed, and in some cases they were prevented from entering the colony. Foreign women Communists legally married to Indian or Sri Lankan men were difficult to deport. If they worked in the West, they could be closely watched and arrested for violating the law. Many Western women of the left were middle-class and University educated, and did not fall into the category of "undesirable, low-class Europeans" who could be deported under archaic colonial laws; but in race terms they were traitors, and the treachery was compounded by their betrayal of "white womanhood." Instead of helping the white man bear his burden in the colonies, these women were undermining the system, both by their "unspeakable" Socialist views and their "scandalous" marriages or liaisons with Asian men.

The anti-imperialist movements of the early 20th century, and especially the ferment in India in the 1920s, led some women in the West to commit themselves to this struggle. And after the Russian revolution of 1917, there was also a vision of a new social order in Asia combining national liberation with Socialist revolution. The foreign wives and companions of South Asian revolutionaries who joined these movements are a group almost lost to history because very little data about them is available. To give some examples, Philip Gunawardena (1900–1977), one of the founders of the first leftist party in 1935 in

Sri Lanka, studied at Wisconsin State University, and at Illinois University, between 1922 and 1925; during this time, his companion was a radical American fellow student at Wisconsin, Esther Bilstad (born in 1903). They were both active in the Wisconsin University International Club. She visited the Soviet Union (possibly with Gunewardena) and in the 1930s qualified as a pilot.[8] But when she tried to join Gunewardena in Sri Lanka she was refused permission to land by the British authorities. One of the most prominent of the Indian National Congress leaders of the 1930s, Subhas Chandra Bose, secretly married Austrian Emilie Schenkl during the 1940s when he was residing in Germany. Hoping to destabilize the British in India, he allied with the Germans and Japanese during the Second World War. His marriage was kept a secret since he thought it would damage his political career, and was only revealed after his death in 1945 (Bose 1982).

British intelligence kept track of Indian revolutionaries and their activities abroad, providing a few glimpses of some of the foreign wives. Abani Mukherjee, who was in M.N. Roy's communist group, was married to Rosa Fitingof, of Russian Jewish origin; she had joined the Communist Party in 1918, and was assistant to Lydia Fotieva, Lenin's private secretary when Mukherjee met her in 1920; Fitingof was one of the founding members of the Indian Communist group (formed in Tashkent by M.N. Roy), and was Roy's interpreter (Haithcox 1971:22). Also a member of M.N. Roy's group in Berlin was Dr. Anadi Bhaduri, who was studying for a doctorate in chemistry; his wife Irmgard (born in 1907) of German Jewish origin from Berlin, continued to live in Calcutta after Bhaduri's death. Another early associate of M.N. Roy was Brajesh Singh, who financed Roy's convalescence in Switzerland and his trip to India; Singh, who had access to money, being the brother of a wealthy Raja, was for a time the common-law husband of Stalin's daughter Svetlana. Also in the Berlin Indian Communist Party was Saiyid Abdul Wahid Abai, who married a German Jewish woman, Kaethe Hulda Wolf. In the rival Chattopadyaya Communist group in Moscow in 1921, was Pandurang Khankhoje (1884–1966) from Maharashtra, who was in the Ghadr movement in California and had fled to Mexico in the early 1920s. He worked in the Ministry of Agriculture in Mexico, and in 1936 married a Belgian, Jeanne Alexandrine Sindic (born 1913), both returning to India only after independence.

Mention has been made of the opposition of the British community to foreign women leftists, who were breaking the rules of the colonial game and "tarnishing" the British image. But the local bourgeoisie was also embarrassed by these women who not only attacked local class, caste and gender oppression but also took part in political demonstrations, strikes and other types of activism or used their skills as writers and journalists. Punjabi Communist leader B.P. Bedi's English wife Freda (from Derbyshire) was active with him in

leftist politics in the 1930s and 1940s in Lahore; she was jailed in 1930 for participating in the Gandhian movement. The Bedis published several books and
edited *India Analysed* (1934). Another couple in left politics was the famous Urdu
poet Faiz Ahmad Faiz of Lahore and his wife Alys George of London. She and
her sister Christobel had worked with Krishna Menon in the India League. Her
sister married Mohamed Din Taseer of Lahore (also in the left movement).
On a visit to India, Alys met and married Faiz and worked in politics and journalism and was a founding member of the Democratic Women's Association.
He died in 1984; she still lives in Pakistan, active in human rights work.[9]

After Sri Lanka achieved Independence (in 1948) the new government used
the old colonial laws to deport foreign women of the left who did not have
citizenship. One case was that of an American journalist of Jewish origin,
Rhoda Miller de Silva (1911–1980) of New York. In the late 1930s and early 1940s,
she was a writer for *Time* magazine, and later for leftist journals and the *London
Economist*. She was a first cousin of Howard Fast (a famous one-time
Communist writer), and married a Sri Lankan, Joseph de Silva, who had been
a student in Britain, and was linked to leftist politics.[10] In the early 1950s they
lived in Vienna, and in 1953 returned to Sri Lanka where they were actively
associated with the Communist party. In March 1954, just before she obtained
local citizenship, Rhoda was deported on grounds that she was an alien sus-
pected of subversive activities. Ironically, she was also unjustly reviled by
sections of the local Communist Party which turned against her, alleging that
she was an American spy.[11] She later returned to live in Sri Lanka. Rhoda de
Silva was an excellent journalist, writing a widely-read weekly column in the
Ceylon Daily News, called "An Outsider Comments," on issues relating to politics
and economic development in the 1960s. Another foreign wife of a leftist leader
who was also nearly deported at this time was Jeanne Moonesinghe, née
Hoban, a law graduate of the University of London, who in 1948 married Anil
Moonesinghe, a Sri Lankan Trotskyist.[12] In 1952, the Moonesinghes came to Sri
Lanka, where Jeanne began working in the Lanka Estate Workers Union
(among plantation labor), causing much annoyance to the British planters
and their wives who were still living in Sri Lanka. When Rhoda de Silva was
deported in 1954, Jeanne Moonesinghe, fearing arrest after a visit by the police,
went into hiding.[13] She escaped deportation and stayed on to work as a journalist (from 1954–1959) at the *Lake House* group of newspapers.[14]

The following chapters deal in more detail with selected American and
European women Socialists who were linked to revolutionary struggles in
India and Sri Lanka, and were part of the process of the formation of the Left;
they include Agnes Smedley and Evelyn Trent of the United States, who
worked with pioneer Indian Communist leaders abroad, Doreen Young of
Britain, and Hedi Simon of Austria, who with their husbands were connected

with the founding, in Sri Lanka, of the Communist Party. All these women were demonized in their time by the authorities in South Asia and sometimes in their own countries, but are remembered with affection by many in South Asia as true internationalists and revolutionaries who chose to work for political freedom and social change for colonial peoples.

COMRADE OR EVIL TEMPTRESS?

American Socialist Women and Indian Left Leaders

The tired intellectuals of Europe may look to the East in search of a new Messiah.... But to all honest revolutionaries who understand...great movements as the Russian and Indian revolutions, all talk about "spiritual welfare" and the triumph of non-violence, is...the babble of children or the fevered eloquence of intellectual degeneration in search of new illusions.

—Evelyn Roy, "Mahatma Gandhi: Revolutionary or Counter-Revolutionary?" (1923b:158)

We to whom a free India—social, economic and political—is precious, hate the social horrors that exist today (and) hate the economic and political system of British rule which harbours and perpetuates these horrors.

—Agnes Smedley, "'Bootlickers' Handbook of India"(1927:27)

WESTERN WOMEN REVOLUTIONARIES PRESENTED THE EXTREME CASES OF subversion of imperialism, local capitalism and moderate nationalism, and in doing so they crossed sensitive race and gender barriers. They inevitably aroused the hostility of the British and also provoked opposition from some Indian nationalists. Revolutionary attitudes meant being critical of the whole of Indian society, including the status of its women and in this, foreign women were treading on contentious ground. The line between acceptance by Indians as "comrade" in the movement and their demonization as spy or "evil temptress" was also often a thin one. The British and American authorities treated these women as Communist agents, trailing their movements and intercepting their correspondence; and when Indian revolutionary groups had factional fights, they often denounced the foreign women of the rival group as spies for the British.

The interweaving lives of M.N. Roy, Evelyn Trent, Virendranath

Chattopadyaya and Agnes Smedley form a dramatic story to illustrate some of these issues. The two best-known pioneers of Indian Communism, Roy and Chattopadyaya, were both born in the 1880s to Bengali Brahmin middle-class families. Exposed as schoolboys to the dynamic nationalism of Vivekananda, Nivedita and Aurobindo, they were influenced by the militant politics of Bengal and the early armed resistance. They both became ardent nationalists, participated in the extreme-wing of the nationalist struggle and were involved with the Germans in trying to promote revolutionary activities in India during the First World War. By the early 1920s, they were operating on the same terrain and came into bitter conflict over which one was to be accepted by the Communist International as the leader of the Indian Communist movement.

There are interesting parallel developments in the stories of two American women. Both Evelyn Trent and Agnes Smedley were born in 1892 in the United States, and were radicalized by the labor, feminist and anti-imperialist struggles of the period. Both were politically active in California around 1915–1916 and met briefly in New York before their dramatic confrontation in Moscow in 1921 as the consorts of the two rival Indian revolutionaries vying for the attentions of Lenin and the Communist International. They both had stressful lives in addition to the strain of living with Indian revolutionaries who were lionized in the context of the Communist movement, but often forced to live the lives of fugitives on the run to avoid arrest or deportation by American and European governments. The dedication and commitment of these two women to Indian causes was remarkable, although neither of them visited India. But in 1925, both couples separated, the women never again to be directly involved in Indian nationalism or the Indian Communist movement. Agnes Smedley became an internationally-known writer because of her subsequent links with the Chinese revolution. In contrast, Evelyn Trent, from the mid-1920s, went into oblivion as far as Indian Communism was concerned. In the following section, the "Indian" phase of the lives of Smedley and Trent are pieced together to try and reconstruct not only their commitment to national liberation and Communism but also the extent of their feminist awareness.

EVELYN TRENT AND M.N. ROY

Leonore Evelyn Trent (1892–1970), born in Salt Lake City, Utah, was the youngest of eight children of an English-born mining engineer, Lamartine Charles Trent of California, and Mary McLeod of Florida. Evelyn attended high school in Auburn, California and also the Polytechnic High School in Los Angeles before joining Stanford University, California in 1912, graduating with a degree in English.[1] At Stanford, she met M.N. Roy, who was visiting other Indians there. He was, she later recalled, a remarkable figure like "John

Evelyn Roy in 1924. (From Sibnarayan Ray,
ed., *Selected Works of M.N. Roy* Vol. II. Picture
courtesy of Professor Sibnarayan Ray.)

the Baptist coming out of the wilderness."[2] Roy went to New York with Evelyn
and they were married there in 1917. In New York, the Roys were closely associated with leading Indian nationalists and American Socialists.

Manabendra Nath Roy (1887–1954), a Bengali Brahmin, son of the head pandit of a school, attended the Bengal National College where Aurobindo was
principal, and became a militant nationalist. He was also influenced by the
writer Bankim Chandra Chatterjee, and by Swami Vivekananda, and joined
the Anushilan Samiti, a revolutionary group. In 1907 and 1908 he was involved
in political robberies, and in 1910, along with forty-four others, he was tried for
conspiracy and discharged (Ray 1988 Vol.II:4–12). With the start of the First
World War in 1914, the Germans tried to destabilize the British in India by
fomenting armed revolution and shipping arms from California.[3] Roy was
involved in these dealings and arrived in California in 1916. The American
authorities were well aware of the movements of Indian revolutionaries, and
Germans and Indians were tried in the famous Hindu Conspiracy Case in
California in 1917, which lead to M.N. and Evelyn Roy's escape over the border
to Mexico. Roy was a founder of the Communist party of Mexico in 1919, and
in 1920 he published *An Indian Communist Manifesto*. The Roys went to Moscow in
1921 as delegates to the Second Congress of the Communist International. Roy

played an important role at the Congress, opposing Lenin's view that in a colonial situation, the "bourgeois democratic" liberation movements had to be supported by Communists.[4]

When the Central Asiatic Bureau was set up in Tashkent to train Asian revolutionaries, the Roys worked there among Indians in exile, mainly Indian Muslims who had left India to join the struggle in Turkey, and Pathans who had deserted the Indian Army. Roy started the Indian Communist Party and also a training school at "India House" in Tashkent. The school did not last long, because of factionalism and disagreements. The Roys returned to Moscow where a "University of the Toiling Masses of the Eastern Autonomous Republics" was set up in 1921 "to harmonise the nationalist sentiments of the former subject peoples of the Russian Empire with the internationalist proletarian ideology of the Communist government." There were 713 students that year studying history, economics and political theory in ten languages. An American woman journalist has described Evelyn Roy teaching a class of eighteen Indians using Raymond Postgate's *Revolution from 1789 to 1906* as a text. (Evans 1922:972) Meanwhile, in Moscow in 1921, the Communist International called a meeting of the Indian revolutionary groups abroad—M.N. Roy's Communist group and the Berlin revolutionary nationalists led by Virendranath Chattopadyaya, who was living with Agnes Smedley and organizing Indians in Europe.

AGNES SMEDLEY AND VIRENDRANATH CHATTOPADYAYA

Agnes Smedley (1892–1950) was born to a poor white family of tenant farmers in Missouri. Unable to survive, the family moved to a mining town in Colorado. The low wages of the time led to many strikes, including the famous incident of the shooting of mine workers by the police in nearby Ludlow. It was in such a harsh milieu that Agnes grew up, attending the school run by the mine-owning company, where she studied up to the eighth grade, before taking up a job as a teacher in 1908 in New Mexico (MacKinnon & MacKinnon 1988:8–13). She moved to Denver and became a magazine agent traveling in the region, before entering a Teachers' Training School in Arizona, where she edited the school weekly. In 1912, she married Ernest Brundin, a Swedish immigrant who was a Socialist, and in 1913 joined the San Diego Normal School. She was influenced by Emma Goldman, the anarchist, who gave lectures on Ibsen and Nietzsche in San Diego, and by Margaret Sanger's birth control movement. She also became aware of India's struggle against imperialism after attending a lecture on the subject. (ibid:24).

In 1916, Smedley joined the Socialist Party and moved to New York in 1917, where she associated with Socialists, feminists and artists in Greenwich Village and attended night classes at New York University (ibid:33–34). In New York

Agnes Smedley (in a sari) in New York, circa 1919. (From Janice MacKinnon and Stephen MacKinnon (1988), *Agnes Smedley. The Life and Times of an American Radical*. Picture courtesy of Janice and Stephen MacKinnon.)

she met the noted Indian nationalist Lala Lajpat Rai and, impressed by his call for Americans to support the Indian struggle, became his secretary.[5] As Smedley wrote:

> He introduced me to the movement for the freedom of his people and showed me that…it was part of an international struggle for emancipation…. Because I loved him as I might have loved my father, I learned more than I could have learned from any other source. (ibid:35)

Through Lajpat Rai, Smedley met other Indian nationalists, including M.N. Roy and Evelyn Roy, who "introduced Smedley to the more radical ideas advocated by members of the Ghadr Party in California (whose members had been arrested by the US government for being allegedly part of a German conspiracy). Smedley, inspired by events of the Russian Revolution in 1917, was attracted to this strand of Indian nationalism although Lajpat Rai warned her of its romanticism (ibid:40). She began to work with some members of this group to start a radical Indian National Party. Her correspondence with them was intercepted, and in 1918 she was arrested and charged not only with helping the Germans (by stirring up rebellion against British rule in India), but also with disseminating information on birth control (ibid:46). A campaign for her release was launched by Margaret Sanger and other New York liberals and Socialists, and after eight months she was released on bail. Soon after, Smedley got a job on Sanger's *Birth Control Review* and also wrote articles about India in other journals; but during the years 1919 and 1920 an increase in state repression against political dissidents led to the deportation of foreign Socialists, anarchists and Indian "agitators." Anxious to move away from this hostile environment, Smedley traveled to Berlin in 1920 and contacted Chattopadyaya, who was the leader of the Indian revolutionaries in Germany.

Virendranath Chattopadyaya (1880–1941) came from a politicized Bengali Brahmin family.[6] He went to Britain in 1901 for studies and became involved with Indian extremists in London and revolutionaries from Ireland, Egypt and Europe. Faced with possible arrest, he escaped to France in 1910, where he worked with French Socialists, and with the Indian revolutionary Madame Bhikaiji Cama and other Indians in Europe. He edited an Indian revolutionary journal *Bande Mataram* and was in contact with anti-imperialist groups in Europe. At the outbreak of the First World War, he left for Germany.[7] Chattopadyaya married several foreigners; an English woman (up to 1910) and then, from 1912 to 1914 an Irish woman. From 1920 to 1925 he lived with Agnes Smedley, and in the 1930's married a Russian. As Smedley wrote, he was "the epitome of the secret Indian revolutionary movement and perhaps its most brilliant protagonist abroad…with a mind as sharp and ruthless as a saber. He was thin and dark…to me he seemed like thunder, lightning and rain." When they began their life together, she recalled, it was the meeting of two eras and two cultures:

> I was an American working woman, the product of a distorted commercial civilization, he a high-caste Indian with a cultivated labyrinthine Brahmin mind and a British classical education. Though he hated everything British, he had an even deeper contempt for American capitalism which judged all things by their money value. His mind was modern, but his emotional roots were in Hinduism and Islam. (ibid:70-71)

At this point the lives of the Roys, Agnes Smedley, and Chattopadyaya, converge in extraordinary circumstances in Moscow. It was a period when events in India were gathering momentum; the All-India Trade Union Congress had been formed in 1920 with Lala Lajpat Rai (who had returned to India) as president; moreover, Gandhi's first large civil disobedience campaign had attracted the masses, erupting in violence, which led Gandhi to call off the massive protest "at a moment when it might have become a full-scale revolution." This act led to much controversy and discussion on the merits of non-violence over revolutionary violence. It was also a period when Marxism was discussed in India and the tactics of Gandhi and Lenin were being compared (Overstreet & Windmiller 1959:37–38). When groups led by Roy and Chattopadyaya met in Moscow in 1921, their main political difference was based on conflicting assessments of the Indian scene. Chattopadyaya was in favor of a united front of all anti-imperialist forces, whether Communist or not, to overthrow British rule. Roy's thesis was that rather than losing its identity by joining Indian nationalists, the building-up of the Indian Communist party should have priority in order to give the anti-imperialist movement a Socialist direction.

The theoretical and political differences also degenerated into personal abuse, including attacks on Agnes Smedley.[8] In his memoirs, Roy describes Smedley in New York as "an anarchist of the Bohemian type" and in Moscow as "the driving force of the delegation" and its "evil genius"; he believed that she and Chattopadyaya had prepared the long thesis against the Roy group (M.N. Roy 1964:93, 479, 488). The Chattopadyaya camp no doubt replied that another American woman—Evelyn Roy—was running the opposing show, that she was more efficient than Roy and was the brains behind the scene. As M.N. Roy's biographer has noted, Evelyn, "a very dedicated and competent person," suffered from the "unconcealed distrust and hostility shown to her personally by Roy's jealous opponents among Indian revolutionaries in Europe" (Ray Vol. II 1988:339–40). In this Moscow confrontation, M.N. Roy was victorious and the Communist Party that Roy had started in Tashkent was recognized by the Communist International.

In the meantime, Evelyn Roy's life was also eventful. From Moscow in 1922 the Roys went to Berlin, where M.N. Roy's "An Indian Communist Manifesto" and a book, *India in Transition*, were published. Attacking Gandhi's strategy and predicting that he would compromise with the British, M.N. Roy also started a journal, *The Vanguard of Indian Independence*, which, along with Comintern publications, were smuggled to Indian Communist groups. Evelyn Roy wrote numerous articles to *The Vanguard* (later called *Masses of India*) under the name Santi Devi; her articles on Gandhian politics and economics were referred to as "the best-argued critiques of Gandhi ever published in Communist literature" (Overstreet & Windmiller 1959:510). Some of these were reproduced in 1923 in a book by the Roys, *One Year of Non-Cooperation from Ahmedabad to Gaya*. In 1923, she wrote for the *Labour Monthly*, attacking the Indian Congress sessions at Gaya in 1922, making a detailed criticism of the reformist programs presented to the Congress by C.R. Das, whom she called "a humanitarian bourgeois liberal intellectual fallen among orthodox Gandhians" (E. Roy 1923a:372). The same year, her article "Mahatma Gandhi: Revolutionary or Counter-

Revolutionary?" critiqued both Romain Rolland, who saw Gandhi as the apostle of love and non-violence, and Henri Barbusse, who saw him as a revolutionary like Lenin who was only using non-violence as a tactic (E. Roy 1923b:158). In 1924, Evelyn Roy also wrote in the *Labour Monthly* about the militant strike of 150,000 textile mill workers in Bombay, urging the British Labour government to save the Bombay workers from death by starvation, adding that "the international proletariat must hang together, or they will hang separately" (E. Roy 1924a:209–210).

In 1923, the German government issued an order for M.N. Roy's arrest, but he and Evelyn fled to Switzerland and from there to France in 1924; in January 1925 Roy was arrested and sent to Luxembourg where he escaped. Meanwhile, Evelyn Roy stayed in Paris, writing protests about Roy's arrest, publishing the journal *Masses of India*, and working with French leftist intellectuals on the Comité Pro-Hindou. In July 1925, the Roys attended a small meeting of European and Indian Communists to plan the Congress of Oppressed Nationalities; here they had strong disagreements with the British Communist Party over its interference in Indian party matters. Around this time, the Roy's marriage broke up, and from 1925 onward, Evelyn Roy's name did not appear "in any of the documents or the literature relating to Indian communism," (Overstreet & Windmiller 1959:80). The vanishing act was complete as far as Indian leftist circles were concerned; British intelligence lost track of Evelyn Roy in 1927, yet all reports suggest that Evelyn Roy was not only politically and intellectually an important figure in the early history of Indian Communism, but also was one of its founding members.[9]

THE ISSUE OF FEMINISM

In the early 20th century there had been militant struggles by women in Britain and the United States, and the Socialist and Communist movements of the period had to face issues of women's rights and feminism. Moreover, the "responsibility" that Westerners felt about social evils in the colonies became a topic of bitter controversy in the 1920s and 1930s. Indian Communist men in Europe, who were mobilizing against British imperialism, had to come to terms with several gender issues, including their personal relationships with foreign women and their attitude to the oppression and exploitation of Indian women by their own men.

Both Evelyn Roy and Agnes Smedley were influenced by the feminist movements of their time in America and Europe and they brought these concerns into their work for India. One of Evelyn Roy's Indian students at Tashkent recalled that Evelyn was "very enthusiastic" about such subjects as the fuller emancipation of the women of India, and in this context she looked forward eagerly to a revolution in that country (ibid:1959:36). While teaching in Moscow, Evelyn got an American journalist, Bessie Beatty, to give a lecture to her students on the moderate and militant struggles for women's suffrage (Evans 1922:973). Evelyn Roy also wrote two articles (in 1924) on the revolution in the Central Asian regions, commenting upon the struggle in Bokhara against the Emir and the resulting reforms, including schools for girls; she commented on Bokharan students in Russia, Germany and Turkey, "among them twenty-five young Bokharan women, emancipated from their semi-slavery by the experiences of the revolution" (E. Roy 1924b:564). Evelyn Roy also kept her links with the Communist women's network.[10]

Agnes Smedley, however, was more aggressive in her feminism.[11] In 1919 in an article entitled "Sidelights on Women in India," she described the role of women in the Indian struggle and argued that women would only gain equality when India was free (MacKinnon & MacKinnon 1988:359). But her personal experiences with Indian nationalists and Communists, many of whom were male chauvinists, made her bitter and her feminism made it difficult for her to tolerate "feudal Indian customs" and the way Indian men sometimes treated her and their own women. She found life with Chattopadyaya ultimately impossible because there was little equality in the relationship. She complained of having to do all the household chores, not only for Chattopadyaya and other revolutionaries, but also for non-political Indians who passed through Berlin.[12]

> There were days when I did not have enough to eat, because Indian hospitality demands that a man must be fed. But I had to cook for these men…who had never raised a hand to free India…and I would sit and listen to them talk about (how) "all European women are prostitutes." (ibid:81)

Chattopadyaya and Smedley broke up in 1925; their life together had been turbulent, due mainly to a clash of class and cultural background and differences of approach to the role of women: "The Indian work has completely ruined my health…. The Indians here harbour harsh prejudices against women and against foreigners" she remarked (ibid:76). In 1923 she wrote "We make a merry hell for each other," but later recalled that the years with Chattopadyaya had been "the most formative of her life" and that he was her teacher (ibid:73, 290). In the year of her break-up with Chattopadyaya, however, Agnes Smedley felt sufficiently confident to speak out critically on aspects of Indian society and the need for change. One aspect was the touchy issue of birth control.[13] Smedley argued that in the absence of birth control, India produced "droves of weak slaves" and that Indians and those sympathetic to India would be in a stronger position if they acknowledged "India's evils"; "we are the ones who recognize them and are willing to change them," she wrote, adding that "We don't need the British government or Christian missionaries" (ibid:114–15).

In 1925, Smedley began to write critically of India; up to that date she had "followed the unwritten rule of keeping the movement's public face intact by not revealing weaknesses to outsiders." According to the MacKinnons, she felt she had "more than paid her dues and deserved to be treated as an equal member of the Indian nationalist family, fully entitled to criticize...aspects of the movement"; and she wrote several articles in 1925, published in Europe and India deploring the lack of birth control campaigns in India (ibid:116).[14] Smedley was also very critical of Indian nationalists; she believed they should openly come out in favor of the Soviet Union and Communism and abandon their upper-class ways of life.[15] Smedley was rebuked by Indians for such comments but regained favor by her trenchant criticism in 1927 of Katherine Mayo (ibid 123–26); she alleged that Mayo "could not have done better, had she been bought and paid for by the British" (Smedley 1927:26).[16]

What of Roy, Chattopadyaya and the "woman question"? In spite of the difficult nature of their relationships with Western women, as Socialists they had to take what was called a "progressive stand" on women's equality. But as in the case of many men of the left, there was often a divergence between theory and practice. The years Roy and Chattopadyaya spent abroad in the United States and Europe coincided with a militant phase of feminism and many revolutionary feminists were personally known to them. Moreover, Chattopadyaya's mother had been, in Smedley's words, "an advocate of the emancipation of women" (MacKinnon & MacKinnon 1988:71); and his sister Sarojini Naidu was a leading fighter for women's rights in India. The women Roy and Chattopadyaya chose as partners had strong views on women's liberation in both the West and India. But yet there was always some ambiguity among Indians on the issue of foreign women as "political comrades." To Indian Communists, the Western women in their lives were a "sign" of progress and a badge of modernity in defiance of the traditional society they were trying to change. But there were problems, as vividly described in Smedley's autobiographical novel, *Daughters of Earth*, where the foreign wife (Smedley) opposes the political line of one of the Indians (who had earlier tried to rape her). When the husband (Chattopadyaya) supports her, the Indian bursts out, "I object to foreigners influencing our movement, (and) I object to women and to wives influencing our members," to which the wife replies: "Foreigners! You do not object to foreigners who help save the lives of your men! Wives! Don't you insult me! I am not here as a wife, but as a comrade and co-worker, and I demand to be treated as such!" (ibid:75)[17]

However, even if M.N. Roy had personal problems with individual foreign women and especially with Smedley, his theoretical and public position on the issue of women's rights was clearly more radical than any of the other

Indian nationalists and reformers of the 1920s and 1930s. In his years with the Comintern, Roy had been close to Clara Zetkin, the German Communist and feminist who was active in the International Women's Secretariat and from 1921–1925 edited its paper.[18] Roy had serious disagreements with the Comintern, returned to Berlin and left for India in 1930; he was arrested and jailed from 1931 to 1936 and while in jail he wrote about a number of issues, including a very long pro-feminist essay of seventy-five pages on "The Ideal of Indian Womanhood" (1934) in which he spoke out clearly for women's equality and denounced the Hindu family system. He wrote:

> Many fables have been fabricated about the exalted position of the woman in Hindu society.... This fiction of a spiritual union gilds the galling chains of chattel—slavery.... The codes of Manu deprive women of all independence. (Roy 1957:124)

Roy condemned India's "feudal-patriarchal society" as an "ugly ghost of the past," criticized Gandhi's views on celibacy and his opposition to birth control and wrote about the reactionary content of "traditional ideals put forward by nationalist leaders" (ibid:128, 122, 142). For Roy, the modernization of Indian society was "a historic necessity" to transform traditional institutions "which deprive women of elementary human rights" (ibid:145–46). Rejecting the argument then in fashion that women's rights were "modern ideas imported from the benighted West," Roy trenchantly replied,

> We no longer need to dig into...ancient wisdom to find the Indian ideal of womanhood. We can find it in the accursed West itself; as represented, for example, by the Germany of the Kaiser or of Hitler. The imperial lord of the Germans placed before women the ideals of...kirche, kuche, kinder (church, housekeeping, children).... The ideal of Indian womanhood can fit into the scheme of a social philosophy which incorporates the worst features of Western culture (ibid:154-55).

Roy's view was that modern women were rebelling "not against men," but against "certain social codes and economic disabilities which place them under the domination of the male" (ibid:158). Clearly Roy was, in theory, many decades ahead of his time in his proclamations, but in his personal relationships and his attitude to Western women of rival political groups, he did not differ much from contemporary male left culture.

THE LATER YEARS

What eventually happened to the "Left Quartet" of Roy, Trent, Chattopadyaya and Smedley? The subsequent lives of Roy and Smedley are well-documented in their own writings and by their biographers. Like Roy, Smedley's involvement in the late 1920s was with the Chinese revolution and India, which she had never visited. India became a distant cause, though she kept up friendships with Nehru and Chattopadyaya's relatives. Smedley became interested in the tumultuous revolutionary upsurges in China, and at the end of 1928 left for China to write about events there. Unlike Evelyn Roy, Smedley did not "disappear from history," but became internationally famous as one of the few foreign writers reporting on events in China (where she lived off and on from 1928 to 1941). On her return to the United States she continued to write and support radical causes up to the time of her death in 1950. In the case of Chattopadyaya, his life became more linked with European Communists in the late 1920s. He joined the German Communist party and helped, through the Comintern, to promote the League Against Imperialism, which held its inaugural meeting in Brussels in 1927.[19] With the rise of Fascism in Germany in the early 1930s, Chattopadyaya felt that he was in danger, and in 1933 he moved to Leningrad and found work in the Institute of Ethnography. He married a Russian woman, but during Stalin's purges in 1938 he mysteriously disappeared. His wife, L.E. Karunovakaia, was informed in 1941 that he had died (MacKinnon & MacKinnon 1988:160, 291, 369).

Evelyn Roy, after her break with M.N. Roy, returned to her parents' home in Auburn, California in 1927. She was a columnist on international affairs for the *San Francisco Chronicle*, writing articles on a variety of contemporary topics, such as events in Afghanistan, Japan, China and other parts of Asia; she later moved to New York City where she worked as a freelance journalist and was the aviation writer for the *Herald Tribune*, flying all over Europe and the United States for material on commercial aviation. She kept in touch with the "Opposition Communists" in the United States led by Jay Lovestone.[20] In 1931 Evelyn wrote an article to their journal, *Revolutionary Age*, on M.N. Roy's arrest in India, giving details about his early history and describing how he had returned to India after a long exile "daring to brave British imperialism and to challenge it face to face"; she called upon "American liberal intellectuals, radicals and workers" to protest at Roy's arrest.[21] In 1935, Evelyn moved back to California and wrote for Sacramento papers, and in 1936 she married a writer, Dewitt Jones.[22] After his death in 1949, she returned to live in the family house in Auburn. In 1956, she worked for the Placer Country Welfare Department. She retired in 1962 and died in 1970 (Trent Jones Collection, Hoover Institute Stanford).[23]

Sibnarayan Ray, Roy's biographer, met Evelyn in 1957–1958 when she stated that the parting from Roy was friendly, but "on her part…quite sad," and she "retained…her admiration for Roy and…interest in his writings and activities." In defence of Roy's failure to acknowledge Evelyn in his memoirs, Ray states that the climate of witch-hunting in the United States in the early 1950s meant that "any recollection of her communist past would have caused her much harassment" (Ray, Vol. 1 1987:27). Ray also writes, "she told me she cherished her life as a revolutionary with Roy in Mexico, Moscow and Berlin, but she did not wish her Communist past to be made known" (Personal communication from Professor S. Ray, October 28, 1990).

M.N. Roy's career after the late 1920s was as eventful as his earlier years. In 1926 he was re-elected to the Presidium and Secretariat of the Comintern, and in 1927 he headed a Comintern delegation to China to sort out the problems arising from the alliance of the Guomintang and the Chinese Communist party. The failure of this mission led to his serious differences of opinion with Moscow and he turned away from both the movement and its ideology; he allied himself with the Communist Opposition, and in later years became a radical humanist and started a group and journal devoted to these ends. This period of his life has been fairly thoroughly documented both by Professor Sibnarayan Ray, who has edited four volumes of M.N. Roy's *Selected Works*, and by Roy's second wife Ellen Gottschalk.

POSTSCRIPT: M.N. ROY AND ELLEN GOTTSCHALK

From 1928 to 1930, M.N. Roy lived in Berlin with a German woman, Louise Geissler (1899–1973), who helped him in his political work and was his "devoted companion" (Ray Vol. 1:1987:28). In 1929 they shared the apartment of Willi Munzenberg, the Communist leader. Geissler had in 1919 joined the Spartacus Bund, the militant Communist group (of Rosa Luxemburg and Karl Liebknecht) and after its defeat, joined the German Communist Party. She was a staff member in the Communist International from 1920 and accompanied Roy on the Comintern mission to China in 1927.[24] Roy had in the meantime developed a new friendship with another German, Ellen Gottschalk (1904–1960). Born in Paris to a Jewish family, she went to school in Cologne, excelling in music and singing. Events in Europe, especially the First World War, aroused her anger against social injustice, militarization and what she later called, "the absurdity of hostile patriotisms" (Ray 1979:374). In Berlin she was involved in radical politics, joining the German Communist Party for a year (1927–1928) and working from 1925 in Berlin for the Peasant International established by the Comintern; she was in touch with many Communist intellectuals and the Opposition Communists and Trotskyists who disagreed with Comintern policies.

M.N. Roy had been expelled from the Comintern in 1929 for his critical articles; by 1930 he decided to return to India, where after a short period underground establishing the "Roy group" and contacting trade union and political leaders, he was arrested in 1931 and jailed. Ellen made a precarious living as a secretary and campaigned for Roy's release and kept him supplied with books and journals. After Hitler's rise to power and the harassment of Communists, Ellen fled to France; she came to know André Malraux, Arthur Koestler, Henri Barbusse and Paul Robeson, and urged well-known people including Romain Rolland, Stafford Cripps and Einstein to speak out on behalf of Roy. She traveled to Britain to see Labour Party leaders on this issue, and had discussions in Paris with Jawaharlal Nehru who was a member of the Roy Defence Committee. In the period 1935–1936, Willi Munzenberg, who was in France, gave Ellen work organizing an association of refugee German writers in Paris; she also helped Franco-Soviet friendship groups and was an organizer in 1935 of the International Congress on Defence of Culture, held in Paris. Since this was an era of the Popular Front government in France, her stay in that country was politically comfortable (ibid:32–35).

M.N. Roy was released from jail in 1936, and Ellen Gottschalk arrived in Bombay in 1937. They married and went to live in Dehradun where they edited a journal *Independent India*, the name being changed to *The Radical Humanist* in 1949. They also published Roy's *Letters From Jail*. Both the Roys, who earlier had links with opposition Communists in Europe, moved away from Communism and developed a concept of Radical Democracy, starting the Indian Radical Humanist Movement and the Indian Renaissance Institute (1946).

According to Ray, the "Royists" consisted of old anarchists, revolutionary nationalists (especially from Bengal), dissident Communists, as well as others "who were influenced by his philosophy of cosmopolitan humanism, which was made all the more attractive by (Roy's) exceptional personality" (ibid:6). The attitude of the Royists to Ellen Roy was also positive. As Ray notes,

> to some she was important, because she was the person closest to Roy and because in a self-effacing way she dedicated herself completely to Roy's work. To others…she was…a magnificent person in her own right, with gifts, perceptions and interests which were in their combination almost as rich and unique as those of her much more illustrious husband. (ibid:6)

M.N. Roy died in 1954 and his work was carried on by Ellen Roy until her death in 1960. She corresponded with Evelyn Roy, and in 1958 referred to "the experience we both have had with researchers from Berkeley." However, she recommended Sibnarayan Ray to Evelyn as a researcher of M.N. Roy's life, adding, "he will once again impress on you the work of historical reminiscences which only you can do," urging her that, "if this work is not done, it will do incalculable harm, leaving the field open to biased and ill-informed chroniclers" (Letter of February 28, 1958, in Trent Jones Collection, Hoover Institute). Ellen Roy created the M.N. Roy Archives and continued the annual study camps and meetings of the Radical Humanists, traveling around India and speaking to groups. Her views on India were not romantic or idealized. "I am not one of those who have gone East and come back with a message of a mystic light from the Orient," she wrote in 1955. Her internationalism came not only from her Socialism, but also from her life experience:

> When you are born in one country and your mother belongs to another, and your father to a third, and endowed with his citizenship, you are a foreigner in every country where you have grown up and studied and...lived and worked, and yet you feel at home in all of them; if then you marry an alien from a different continent...and become at home there too...you see the good and bad in all countries and peoples. (Roy 1979:374)

While Ellen Roy was able "to see the good and bad" because she lived in India for twenty-three years, Evelyn Roy, Agnes Smedley and many other wives and partners of Indian revolutionaries were unable to live and work with the left movement in India; they contributed to the movement from abroad. Evelyn Roy and Rosa Fitingof were founding members in Tashkent of the Indian Communist Party. But in contrast, foreign wives of leftists in Sri Lanka succeeded in being politically active in the Ceylon Communist Party, also becoming important in their own right and not merely as wives of left leaders. The next chapter discusses two important cases of European women who became nationally known in Sri Lanka for their activities in the left movement.

RED FLAGS IN THE EMERALD ISLE

European Socialist Women Intervene in Sri Lanka

> To a people in steadily worsening conditions, (Ceylon's) Prime Minister calls for patriotism, sacrifice, austerity...that the Government fresh from its callous festivity and rejoicing, should dare to give lip to such an appeal is enough...to condemn it out of hand.
>
> —Doreen Wickremasinghe, "They Preach Austerity to the Starving," *Ceylon Daily News* (5 March 1948)—one month after the country's independence

> The racial discrimination suffered by the Jews in Austria made me feel specially sympathetic to the victims of colonial rule and strengthened my determination to identify with the fight for the freedom and independence of colonial peoples.
>
> —Hedi Stadlen, Personal communication (December 1990)

As in India, leftist politics in Sri Lanka included significant contributions by foreign wives of party leaders. These women had to face the general opposition of both the local British community and the Sri Lanka bourgeoisie because they were not only transgressing the accepted rules of race, class and gender, but also confronting local social and political structures. They were not merely "political wives" but contributed in their own right to political, social, educational and women's projects of their time, thereby raising important issues of nationalism, leftist politics and incipient Socialist feminism. This chapter discusses the lives of two European women married to leaders of the Communist Party of Sri Lanka—Doreen Wickremasinghe, née Young, who was born in England and has lived in Sri Lanka since 1930, and Hedi Stadlen, née Simon, from Vienna, who lived in Sri Lanka from 1940 to 1945.

DOREEN WICKREMASINGHE——THE EARLY YEARS

Many of the religious and ideological strands discussed in earlier sections of this book come together in the life and background of Doreen Wickremasinghe; these included theosophy, Indian nationalism, the leftist movement, progressive education and feminism. Her mother's father, Robert Weare (whose house was called "Walden" after Thoreau's famous book), was a well-known Socialist of his time and a part of the famous Bristol Socialist Society.[1] Doreen's father, William Young, was active in the Labour Party and trade union movement; her mother, Lily Weare, was the daughter of Robert Weare.[2] According to Rowbotham, the Bristol Socialists had a "Whitmanic love of comrades which was an important aspect of the movement." It was a period when "ethical socialism" was popular, and Socialism also meant a return to the good, simple life (1977:67).[3]

Doreen was born in "Walden" in 1907 and lived there until she was twelve. She was strongly influenced by Weare's ideas, and met his friends and comrades of the Socialist movement; she recalls that "Walden" was a center of Socialist activity.[4] Doreen Young at sixteen (at the suggestion of the Socialist poet Edward Carpenter) was sent to St. Christopher's at Letchworth, a boarding school run by theosophists, one of the famous "progressive" schools in Britain. The school was co-educational and the relationship between the staff and students was a free one, some teachers being called by their first names. The teachers included the Indian nationalist, V.K. Krishna Menon who, while studying in London, taught history for a term. The students also had contact with other interesting personalities, and Annie Besant's visit to the school in 1924 was an important event.

Doreen's close friend at St. Christopher's School was Charlotte Jonas, from Germany, who after leaving school had studied at the Academy of Art in Berlin. Doreen graduated in economics and politics from the London School of Economics (LSE) famous for its left ambiance, the guru of the socialists being Harold Laski. At university, Doreen was politically active, becoming the Secretary of the Student Union. Doreen also worked at the India League in London during this period, and met many Indians and Sri Lankans who were active in anti-imperialist causes. A student friend, Consuelo Oppenheim (a theosophist) took Doreen to the Theosophical Society's premises where she met Dr. S.A. Wickremasinghe, a Sri Lankan doctor. Doreen and Charlotte Jonas attended a summer school in Sweden, and by 1930 were looking for opportunities to travel and work in India and especially to help in India's freedom struggle. They failed to get to India but when Dr. Wickremasinghe offered to find Doreen a job in Sri Lanka, she accepted the chance to go East.

Dr. Wickremasinghe (1901–1981), who was from an influential family in South Sri Lanka, had studied at Mahinda College, a Buddhist theosophist school.[5]

Doreen Wickremasinghe in the 1930s. (Picture
courtesy of Doreen Wickremasinghe.)

After qualifying as a doctor he did post-graduate studies in London from 1926
to 1929. There he moved with radical Sri Lankan and Indian students,
theosophists, British Communists and revolutionaries from many countries.
Doreen Young and Charlotte Jonas left for Sri Lanka in 1930. While these two
women, one British, the other German Jewish, were on their way to Sri Lanka,
the forces of anti-Semitism and Fascism were gathering strength in Europe.
These forces were to affect the life of Hedi Simon, another Jewish woman
linked to the Sri Lankan left movement.

HEDI SIMON——FROM VIENNA TO CAMBRIDGE
Just as the Socialist and Communist movements of the West have had a history of Jewish participation—both at the levels of leadership and activists,
anti-imperialist movements in the West also had Jewish supporters, including many Jewish women who worked for the national independence of the
colonies. The increasing anti-Semitism in Europe made them aware of the
realities of racial oppression—an awareness that in many cases increased their

Hedi and Pieter Keuneman (second and fourth from right) with two Indian communists in Colombo in the 1940s. (Picture courtesy of Hedi Stadlen.)

sympathy for colonial peoples. During the late 1930's, some Jewish refugees from Fascism found their way to India and Sri Lanka. They included many professionals (especially doctors), several Jewish women who had links with theosophist or Socialist circles, and others who married Indians and Sri Lankans.[6] One of the them was Hedi Simon, born in Vienna in 1916 to an assimilated Jewish family; her father was Dr. Hans Simon, an economist and lawyer, and her mother was Else Reis, a well-educated Viennese. The family was part of the sophisticated intellectual and cultural milieu of Vienna; Dr. Simon's great-uncle was Johann Strauss, the famous composer of "The Blue Danube." Hedi went to a leading girls' school (gymnasium) in Vienna, whose principal, Dr. Eugenia Schwarzwald was known for her advanced views; some of the teachers who influenced Hedi were Socialists. On leaving school, she studied philosophy for two years (1934–1935) at the university in Vienna.

During these years, Hedi Simon lived under the shadow of the Fascist menace, attacks on the Austrian Socialists, growing anti-Semitism, and continuous economic and political crises.[7] Repressive measures against Jews increased in Germany after Hitler's advent to power in 1933. In 1935 they were deprived of their citizenship and forbidden to inter-marry with non-Jews, and by the late 1930s, synagogues were destroyed and Jews deported to concentration camps. With the annexation of Austria by the Nazis, anti-Jewish laws were also introduced in that country and Jews were rounded up and deported to concentration camps. Before this the Simon family had moved to Switzerland, and then eventually to the United States, and Hedi's father, who had contacts in Britain, sent her to Newnham College, Cambridge where she obtained a degree in Moral Sciences. Studying in Cambridge at the same time was Pieter

Keuneman. Born in 1917, he was of the Dutch Burgher community of Sri Lanka (descendants of the Dutch), the son of A.E. Keuneman, a Supreme Court judge. While in school, Pieter had done a six month tour of Europe in 1933; in 1935 he spent a year at the Ceylon University College where he came into contact with local Socialists. In 1936 he entered Pembroke College, Cambridge (his father's old college) and graduated with a degree in English; he was successively secretary and president of the Cambridge Union Society and also editor of *Granta,* the student journal. Pembroke College at the time had a very active Communist group, including two Communist dons.

Cambridge in the 1920s and 1930s was an intellectually and politically exciting place. The university had produced dissidents and famous teachers—Bertrand Russell, Wittgenstein and M.G. Moore in Philosophy; E.M. Forster and F.R. Leavis in English; J.D. Bernal and J.B.S. Haldane in science, and Maynard Keynes and Richard Kahn in economics. The background events of the 1930s—the economic depression, the rise of Fascism in Germany, the Reichstag fire trial, the Spanish civil war and Mussolini's aggression in Abyssinia politicized the students. The Marxists, in particular, were active; they captured the labor and Socialist societies in the university as well as the Majlis, an organization of Indian students that was strongly socialist and anti-imperialist. There were numerous issues in local British politics that influenced students to join leftist movements. These included the rising numbers of unemployed, the hunger marches and the agitation against the inequities based on class differences in Britain. Students were also inspired by young British Communists and others of the International Brigade who died in Spain fighting against Franco's regime. There was also great admiration for the Soviet Union, and Communism seemed, to some, to be the answer to Fascism.

One important issue that mobilized leftist students was that of anti-imperialism, and during the 1930s there was a coming together of Asian nationalists and British Communists—many of the Asians also becoming active in the British Communist Party. Hedi Simon and Pieter Keuneman were in the Cambridge Union Socialist Club, and joined the Communist Party. They were in the campaign of support for Republican Spain during the civil war, and Pieter Keuneman visited Spain during this time. He was friends of the poet John Cornford and the writer Christopher Cauldwell, both of whom died in battle in Spain (Perera:1967). In 1937, Keuneman made a six week visit to the Soviet Union and returned via Poland and Nazi Germany, obtaining a first-hand view of the realities of Fascism. Keuneman and Hedi Simon also participated in anti-colonial activities, being in close touch with the colonial wing of the British Communist Party and especially its theoretician R. Palme Dutt (an Indian whose Swedish mother was the great aunt of Olaf Palme, former Swedish Prime Minister). Keuneman and Hedi Simon used to also travel to London during weekends and holidays to work in the India League, along with Krishna Menon, Indira Nehru and her future husband Firoze Gandhi. Doreen Young had also been very active in its work a few years earlier, but did not overlap with Hedi Simon, only meeting her in 1940 in Sri Lanka, after Hedi's marriage to Pieter Keuneman.

DOREEN IN EDUCATIONAL ACTIVITY IN THE 1930s

Life for Doreen Young was also very eventful in the 1930s. She and Charlotte Jonas arrived in Colombo in November 1930 where they were met by Dr. Wickremasinghe, Patrick Kularatne—the principal of the leading Buddhist boys' school, Ananda College—and Hilda Kularatne, his British wife. She was a Cambridge graduate (whose father was a theosophist and mother was an Oriental scholar Jessie Duncan Westbrook, translator of sufi poetry from the Persian). Soon after her arrival, Doreen (23), was appointed the principal of Sujatha Vidyalaya in Matara in the South of Sri Lanka. This girls' school had been started in 1925 by local Buddhists of Matara, where the only other good girls' school was the Catholic convent.

The history of girls' education in schools run by the Buddhist Theosophical Society dated back to 1889, when a Women's Education Society was formed and the Sanghamitta School opened in 1890 with Austrian theosophist Kate Pickett as first principal; a second school (Museaus College) was started in 1893 with a German, Marie Musaeus Higgins, as principal. In 1917, Visakha Vidyalaya became the leading Buddhist girls' high school (with a series of British and American principals), and many other schools for Buddhist girls were opened in the 1920s. It was Doreen Young, however, who radicalized Buddhist girls' education, taking it away from the Buddhist "wives and mothers" syndrome of the other schools. Doreen was amazed to find that Sujatha Vidyalaya was teaching British history, but no Sri Lankan history. There was no music or dancing, the kindergarten was an old-style one, and the only pictures on the walls were of British royalty.

Doreen Young was principal of Sujatha Vidyalaya from November 1930 until December 1932 and made many innovations. She visited Museaus College, Colombo, to look at their modern kindergarten, and inspected Alethea School, Colombo, run by Elizabeth Preston, a British theosophist and member of the Ceylon Labour Party; Doreen introduced local history and world history into the syllabus; she also got teachers to qualify themselves, since the school had only one qualified teacher. Charlotte Jonas taught art at the school for two years. While in Matara, Doreen was involved in activities outside the school. She and Charlotte wore saris and identified themselves with local issues. Doreen gave a rousing lecture to Matara lawyers in the Law Courts on the independence movement in India; this was reported in newspapers and she was invited to give a lecture at the Law College, Colombo. She and the teachers at Sujatha also caused a stir by marching through Matara in support of latrine workers and local residents who were protesting the demolition of the public latrines.

Doreen was asked if she would take a job at the leading Colombo Buddhist girls' school, Visakha Vidyalaya, but the offer was withdrawn when the selection committee found that she intended to marry Dr. S.A. Wickremasinghe. The marriage took place in April 1933, and soon after Doreen Wickremasinghe was invited by Patrick Kularatne to be the principal of Ananda Balika, a Buddhist girls' secondary school started in 1925 by Hilda Kularatne, teaching in English, with a hostel for thirty to forty girls from outside Colombo. Doreen Wickremasinghe was the principal of the school from June 1933 to December 1935; she reorganized it with great enthusiasm, and created a democratic awareness among the students. The usual barriers between teachers and students were broken and they joined together in many activities. Doreen emphasized cleanliness, and one day each term was a staff holiday when the students themselves would teach and clean up the school. The staff and Doreen were like friends, calling each other by nicknames, taking holidays together and going on a trip to India. The links were reinforced by the political involvement of some of these teachers in the leftist movement.[8]

The students and teachers of Ananda Balika were also exposed to Indian politics and culture.[9] Doreen was enthusiastic about the promotion of Indian and Sri Lankan arts and crafts; she popularized the use of traditional designs for furniture, clothes and book covers, and strengthened her cultural identification with local society by learning to speak Sinhala and wearing a sari on all occasions. Doreen also compiled a book, *Poems of East and West* (1937) dedicated to her students, which became popular because for the first time in Sri Lanka students were introduced to poems by Asian poets along with Western poetry.

THE EARLY LEFT MOVEMENT

Doreen Wickremasinghe was also active in leftist politics. In 1931, constitutional reforms ushered in universal adult franchise, and elections that year gave enhanced prominence in government to the Ceylon National Congress, which campaigned for self-government within the existing imperial system. Nationalist agitation, however, was taken up by the Youth Leagues, which were involved in several areas of activity; in the early 1930s the key campaigns were the 1933 strike of textile workers and political agitation against British rule. By the mid-1930s, the most active Youth League members saw the need to form a political party to carry on the anti-imperialist movement and political and trade union agitation. The new party, the LSSP, Lanka Sama Samaja

Party (formed in 1935) issued a manifesto calling for measures relating to economic reform, relief to the peasantry, child welfare, labor legislation and the official use of Sinhala and Tamil languages. The most dramatic event preceding the formation of the LSSP, however, was the Suriya Mal movement, in which Doreen Wickremasinghe played a key role.

As Socialists and pacifists, Doreen Wickremasinghe's family members had been against all manifestations of imperialism and militarism, and her grandfather Robert Weare had opposed Armistice Day (on November 11th) when poppies were sold and funds collected for disabled servicemen. At Sujatha Vidyalaya Doreen had been appalled to find that the boarders were charged fifty cents for contributions to Poppy Day. In Sri Lanka the annual ceremonies and jingoist displays held on this day caused some resentment. And in 1931 local ex-servicemen's organizations started a protest against Poppy Day by selling a rival yellow flower (suriya mal). The campaign was then taken over by the Colombo Youth League. Doreen Wickremasinghe was made president of the Suriya Mal campaign, which in the years 1933 to 1936, became one of the important political actions by the radicals of the period. It united the left-wing socialists who had returned from abroad with the local Youth Leagues, which were already agitating on nationalist issues.

The Wickremasinghe's residence became the nerve center of the Suriya Mal movement, with the school teachers and senior students joining enthusiastically to make suriya flowers for sale. Their intense campaign included publicity for the movement in schools, factories and offices, and the Youth League members wrote articles in journals and to the daily press to explain the political importance of the agitation.[10] Doreen also wrote an article entitled "Suriya or Poppy?" in which she answered criticisms of the campaign. "It is useless to sigh as you think of the glorious dead" she wrote "and ignore the duty you owe to the living whose inglorious conditions are in part the responsibility of every citizen" (*Ceylon Daily News,* 11 November 1932). She posed the question, "whose need is more dire, the ex-servicemen in England or the poor of this country?" adding that the country needed people who could think clearly and had the courage to stand up for their convictions.

Naturally the British authorities and residents resented not only the challenge to the sacrosanct celebrations of November 11th, but also the fact that a British woman was in the forefront of the movement. The pro-British local press also joined the criticism; one paper referring to the "lack of decent sensibility of the Suriya Mal organizers" who were conducting a campaign which was "a crude political move...utterly in bad taste" (*Ceylon Independent:* 12 November 1933). And the principal of the leading Christian girls' school (Ladies College) warned the students and teachers not to become associated with such a seditious campaign.

Doreen Wickremasinghe was also involved in challenging local social structures, including the caste system. The fight against caste was one of the significant struggles waged by the Socialists of the early 1930s. While working in the countryside during the malaria epidemic of 1934 to 1935, they came in touch with the social realities of caste oppression and discrimination. It was, therefore, not surprising that the proceeds of the Suriya Mal campaign were used for the education of a girl of the most depressed caste, (the Rodi caste) in order to prove that in both caste and gender terms, a person of such a community could be educated and do well if taken away from the oppressive environment and given a chance in life. The child lived at the Ananda Balika residence with the Wickremasinghes and attended that school. When the Wickremasinghes went to Britain in 1936, she stayed with other friends and attended the leading Buddhist girls' school in Colombo, Visakha Vidyalaya; she qualified as a nurse, worked at the T.B. Hospital and went to Britain for further training, doing very well in her studies.[11]

From 1931 to 1936, Dr. S.A. Wickremasinghe was an elected member of the legislature. He was the sole representative of the left and consistently challenged the colonial government on political, economic and social issues. Doreen played an important part in this work, helping to draft speeches and reports including, for example, the dissenting report by Dr. Wickremasinghe on the commission to inquire into child servants. But by 1936, major changes occurred in the Wickremasinghe household. There was increasing anxiety among conservative Buddhist educators that the Suriya Mal campaign was too political to be overtly linked to a Buddhist girls' school. In addition, the coming and going to the principal's residence of young men who were politically active, and who freely mixed with the teachers, was frowned upon. Doreen was replaced as principal by Hilda Kularatne but continued to work as a teacher until June 1936. But Dr. Wickremasinghe lost his seat in the general elections of 1936 and both the Wickremasinghes were suddenly unemployed.

Doreen returned to Britain and found a job doing housework in London at the home of Mrs. Haeglar, a theosophist who worked in the India League and was an ardent supporter of the Indian freedom movement. In 1937, Dr. Wickremasinghe came to London and the family had difficulty making ends meet. Doreen's parents then came to the rescue, lending their savings to enable Dr. Wickremasinghe to buy a medical practice in Camberwell in South London where the family lived until 1939. They participated in the Communist-led agitation of these years against British Prime Minister Chamberlain. The menace of Fascism and the drift to world war were to affect the lives of the Wickremasinghe family. Dr. Wickremasinghe returned to Sri Lanka and Doreen and her daughter followed at the end of 1939, only to find that Dr. Wickremasinghe had been arrested and jailed for sedition.

THE LINKING OF THE LIVES OF DOREEN AND HEDI

Doreen Wickremasinghe's arrival back in Sri Lanka coincided with the return of Hedi and Pieter Keuneman, who had married in Switzerland in 1939.[12] The return of the Wickremasinghes and the Keunemans to Sri Lanka took place at a critical period. The left, which began with the formation of a broad-based party—the Lanka Sama Samaja Party (LSSP) in 1935—split in two in 1940 over the issue of Trotskyism, and the nature of the USSR. The minority led by Dr. S.A. Wickremasinghe rejected Trotskyism and broke away to form the United Socialist Party and later the Ceylon Communist Party (CP) in 1943. The LSSP (which became an openly Trotskyist party) also had disagreements with the Communists over the Second World War, especially after 1941 when the Trotskyists continued to oppose the war. But the Communists supported the allied war effort after the invasion of the Soviet Union by Germany. The LSSP was banned in 1942 and the LSSP leaders went to India or went underground. But after 1943, the CP was allowed to function because of its stand on the war. Using this favorable opportunity, the Communists organized the Colombo working-class and formed the Ceylon Trade Union Federation. They also cashed in on the popularity of the USSR as an ally against Fascism and formed the "Friends of the Soviet Union," an organization that included many non-Communist professionals and politicians. It started a reading room and library, held exhibitions and meetings, and published journals and numerous pamphlets on the USSR, also organizing a "Medical Aid for Russia Fund" (Perera 1967:39).

While the Communists were making their mark politically, Doreen Wickremasinghe went back to her earlier vocation, this time to start a school of her own based on modern methods. In Britain in 1937 she had studied for a post-graduate Teachers' Diploma and worked in a kindergarten and primary school in Camberwell. The new school Doreen started in Colombo in 1940 was significantly called the Modern School, which lasted until 1942 when disruptions due to the Second World War and the evacuation of children led to its closure. This venture in modern education was an important landmark in Sri Lankan education.[13] The school also became an after hours meeting place for politicians of the United Socialist Party and the left intelligentsia and significantly, for discussions on the formation of the Communist Party. Doreen Wickremasinghe and Hedi Keuneman, who were linked to the Communist Party from its inception, worked together on many issues during the war years, Hedi regarding Doreen as "a wiser and more experienced sister" (Personal communication, December 1990). Hedi taught classes held in the Modern School for older students doing public examinations. Many of the political cadres of the Communist Party were teachers of these courses. During her first two years in Sri Lanka, Hedi Keuneman also lectured in Logic at the university in Colombo where she made many political contacts among students. With the closure of the Modern School, after the Japanese air raids, the Wickremasinghe family moved south to Sri Lanka, where Dr. Wickremasinghe had a medical practice. Their house became a center for political discussion and activities in support of the war effort against Fascism. From the nearby Koggala army camp and airfield, many British servicemen who were Labour Party supporters or leftists visited the Wickremasinghes and their two children. There was also a lot of socializing between British troops sympathetic to the Soviet Union and local Communists and supporters.

Hedi Keuneman was involved in many aspects of party work and strike activity in Colombo. She wore the sari, lived very simply, often walking barefoot, traveling by bus and identifying closely with the lives of the working people. Pieter Keuneman recollects how Hedi and a group of women trade unionists lay down in front of the trams to prevent them functioning during a tramway strike and also marched to the police station to rescue a strike leader who had been taken into custody (Personal communication from Pieter Keuneman, July 12, 1991). She was also active in helping to run the "Friends of the Soviet Union" and recalls that many interested in this work were English-educated middle-class persons, students, teachers and clerks.[14] Hedi was always very conscious of women's status. In Sri Lanka she actively helped several women to make inter-ethnic and inter-caste marriages and she also publicized the atrocities against women that were taking place in Germany. She wrote a pamphlet, *Under Nazi Rule,* one of the first of its kind published in Sri Lanka, exposing Nazi tyranny and especially highlighting the oppression of German women under Fascism.

During the war Hedi also trained in air-raid precaution work, worked in the food distribution program of the co-operative societies and was elected the president of a local co-operative society in Colombo.[15] At the end of the War, Hedi, aged thirty, returned to England to see her mother and then decided to stay on. This decision was taken after she met Peter Stadlen, a fellow Viennese, who was a musicologist and pianist exiled in London, whom she had known in Vienna. She decided not to return to Sri Lanka and divorced Keuneman to marry Stadlen. It was, she writes, "a hard decision" because she had "wholeheartedly identified" with the Sri Lankan people. "My relationship with Sri Lanka was intense…and I think that I identified more with the people there than I had with the people of Austria" (Personal communication, October 1991). Although Hedi had played such an important role in leftist politics, she did not continue to be politically active. She helped her husband in his music career and had two sons. Pieter Keuneman also married again but Hedi was not forgotten by those "old timers" who were active during the early 1940s. Hedi's influence continued even after her departure, and her popularity and activism in the working-class heartland of Colombo contributed to the success of Pieter Keuneman at the parliamentary election of 1947 when he won a seat in the Colombo Central electorate.[16]

THE AUTONOMOUS WOMEN'S MOVEMENT OF THE LEFT

At the end of the war in 1945 Doreen Wickremasinghe and her two children went back to Britain, staying in West Hampstead, where she was active in the local Communist group. She participated in many of the struggles led by Communists in post-war Britain and was involved with a women's organization composed of housewives who led many militant actions, giving Doreen an experience of the way women could effectively organise as a broad-based group unattached to a party. The family returned to Sri Lanka in 1946 and a year later, inspired by Doreen, women party members of the LSSP, Communist Party and other non-party leftist women came together to form the EKP—Eksath Kantha Peramuna (the United Women's Front)—the first autonomous Socialist women's group in Sri Lanka. It was formed during a period when the three leftist parties had agreed to work together on certain issues. The EKP activists included many party women, women trade unionists, party leaders' wives, and independent women Socialists. The Secretary was Helen Gunasekera, whose mother, Dr. Mary Rutnam, née Irwin, from Toronto, was a doctor and a pioneer fighter for women's rights in Sri Lanka. Another Socialist activist in the EKP was a Hungarian psychoanalyst of Jewish origin, Edith Gymroi Ludowyk, a refugee from Nazism.

The EKP had secretaries for the Sinhala, Tamil and English sections of the organization and had a publication in Sinhala. It was particularly involved in highlighting the situation of working women, conditions of life in the slums, women's health, maternal and infant mortality, conditions of women's wards of the hospitals and housing for the poor. It also campaigned for the right of women to join all branches of the public services. Apart from practical work, debates were also conducted on a more theoretical level, the EKP taking pains to assert its Socialism, and to distinguish its policies from those women's organization fighting merely for equal rights within a capitalist framework. The EKP in January 1948, a month before independence, made it clear that as a Socialist organization it was for changes in "the fundamental structure of society."[17]

The EKP managed to get considerable publicity for its work in the press. In March 1948, Doreen Wickremasinghe attacked the government for its "callous festivity and rejoicing" over independence, while calling on the poor to make increased sacrifices in conditions of mass poverty and high infant and maternal mortality rates (*Times of Ceylon,* March 5, 1948). She also wrote a critique of a locally held I.L.O. Conference showing the gap between the country's adher-

Doreen Wickremasinghe and trade unionist
Ponsinahamy after Doreen's electoral victory, 1952.
(Picture courtesy of Doreen Wickremasinghe.)

ence to International Labor Conventions and the realities of unemployment, child labor and unequal pay, making the point that "industrial legislation has come first, whilst we still await the industries." (*Times of Ceylon,* November 8, 1948). In spite of its successes the EKP had to face the problem of the deteriorating relationship between the leftist parties, their lack of interest in women's issues and the hostility to the idea of an autonomous women's organization separate from the parties. By the end of 1948 the dissolution of the EKP was decided upon by the CP and the LSSP and, to the great regret of the women of the EKP, its activities ceased. It is remembered, however, not only as an important historic moment in Sri Lankan feminism, but also as an attempt that brought the issues of Left politics and feminism to crisis.

With the demise of the EKP, Doreen turned again to educational activities, trying to revolutionize teaching methods and, along with a group of teachers, writing a series of First Readers for children based on the modern methods of teaching reading through sentences and interesting pictures. The text was in spoken Sinhala with plenty of colored pictures, in contrast to the unattractive books then in use. The books were criticized by the Government Publications Board for not having pictures of Buddhist temples. When this was rectified and the books published at Doreen Wickremasinghe's expense, there was still opposition to their use because of Doreen's politics; as a result the books were not recommended and an opportunity to modernize reading methods was lost.

DOREEN WICKREMASINGHE IN PARLIAMENT

In the post war years in Sri Lanka, the left made its first significant electoral gains. At the general elections held in 1947, leftists obtained over twenty percent of the vote and eighteen seats, with several independents associating in parliament with the left. At the next general elections in 1952 the left had high hopes of making more gains, but by then its popularity had declined. It was at this election that the Communist Party fielded many candidates, hoping to make gains—including Doreen Wickremasinghe in an electorate where the Wickremasinghe family had their ancestral home. Doreen was contested by Dr. Wickremasinghe's sister's husband, a leading businessman from the ruling party. The contest was a bitter one and many attacks were directed against Doreen for being a white woman and a foreigner. Apart from political and family loyalties, Doreen was a popular candidate, speaking Sinhala, moving among the people, canvassing in remote rural areas, and expressing her views on social change at public meetings. She polled 16,626 votes and won by 1,001 votes; her victory was historic, the first time in Sri Lanka that a foreign woman was elected to Parliament. Doreen Wickremasinghe was an M.P. from 1952 to 1956, during a period of right-wing ascendancy in the country. She worked regularly in her constituency, hearing complaints and making it a special point to visit schools and see that amenities were made available. In parliament she contributed to the debates, highlighting the lack of health and educational facilities for the poor, criticizing the government for its policies and speaking out on issues of foreign policy during a period when the government took a very pro-Western stand (See Jayawardena 1991).

Doreen was also involved in numerous activities connected with the political work of Dr. S.A. Wickremasinghe as party leader and member of parliament; she spent time helping to run the dispensary and small hospital that Dr. Wickremasinghe had in Matara. She was in numerous organizations concerned with non-alignment, Afro-Asian solidarity and peace, campaigning and appearing at public meetings on these issues and also supporting the women's organizations of each of the leftist parties. After Dr. Wickremasinghe's death in 1981 she continued to be active in many fields, always participating in International Women's Day meetings.

What was perhaps most remarkable about Doreen Wickremasinghe and Hedi Keuneman was the way they were accepted by locals, including Communist party members, trade union activists, women organisers, students and even by the electorate. For many middle-class radicals too, they were an example of how Western women with high educational and other class privileges could devote their energies to causes ranging from education to national freedom, women's liberation and Socialism. In terms of colonialism and gender they were the antithesis of the memsahib, the missionary and the Holy Mother. Their foreign origin increased rather than decreased their popularity, for in choosing to go against Western imperialism, they had made an important internationalist intervention. And in confronting the Sri Lankan establishment on issues of Socialism and social change, they were among the pioneers of alternative policies. In this way, Socialist women were able to tackle conflicting agendas of nationalism and feminism, make a serious effort to include local women in anti-imperialist movements and bring gender issues into the leftist and nationalist movements.

CONCLUSION

AN ASIAN FEMINIST GAZE

> An English magazine stated that Indian women considered English women fair-
> er and more divine than anything imagined before. That was "very nice to
> read," said Amy, but her own experience proved it preposterous. She was taken
> for a "great white man" because of her sun helmet. There was an argument over
> whether she was man or woman. All agreed that she was an "appalling specta-
> cle." Questions were fired: What is your caste? Married or widow? Why no jew-
> els? What relations have you? Why have you left them and come here? What
> does the government pay you for coming? Amy explained...they were there to
> bring Good News. And what did the people do when they heard the news? They
> simply stared. They sat on the floor and chewed betel leaf and stared.
>
> —Amy Carmichael, a missionary, in Elisabeth Elliot, *A Chance to Die* (1987:143)

THIS BOOK HAS TAKEN A FEMINIST PERSPECTIVE OF THE WORK OF FOREIGN
women in South Asia during British colonial rule who responded in many
different ways to colonialism and to the condition of colonized women of all
classes, thereby raising important issues of nationalism and feminism. While
some were supportive or ambivalent about British rule, others distanced
themselves from colonial policies, from white colonial society, from their own
ruling hierarchies at home, and especially from conformism and tradition in
education and culture. And on crucial issues like women's subordination,
caste, and other social evils, many of the Western women—Christians,
reformers and Socialists, opposed the prevailing system and attitudes and
intervened actively to change or challenge these structures and practices.

Many of the foreign women were of middle-class origin, but some were
nuns, missionaries and women revolutionaries who were from the working-

class. Their political commitment ranged from orthodox to revolutionary, and there were also differences in terms of race and religion, a special concern for the oppressed being seen in the number of Irish and Jewish women who supported the struggles of colonial peoples, as did clergymen's daughters (and wives) who had broken away from Christianity. Western women in South Asia were involved with a wide range of local women and girls cutting across class, caste, religion and ethnic group. These included child widows, orphans, abandoned girls, women who suffered from poverty, sickness and caste oppression, as well as women workers and peasants and middle- and upper-class women. All these different instances show how varied and multi-faceted were the roles of white women in a colonial context and how it is misleading to label them "goddesses" or "devils." For the context was a shifting one in terms of colonial and nationalist history. Those who were considered "goddesses" because of their sympathy with local societies and their anti-colonialism, emerge with tarnished halos on gender issues, while the "devils" who critiqued local society and women's status were more truthful and courageous than has been admitted by local nationalists.

One aspect of "underground" colonial history has been the important connection between Western women, involved in numerous religious, liberal, revolutionary, and feminist movements in Europe and the United States, and South Asians working for national revival, social reform, political independence and women's rights. Many were dissenters who challenged orthodox ideologies, political establishments and the social structures they lived under, and who sympathized with the other victims of oppression—the colonized peoples—and were attracted by their cultures, religions and their ways of seeing and doing. While records are available of the history of Empire and of the struggles of the ruled against the colonizers, this book has concentrated on some of the lesser-known linkages between Western women and South Asia. The links were many and varied, often unofficial and unknown to the colonial rulers, with much mutual inter-action at many levels. They brought together two worlds—the Western Socialists, dissenters and feminists with the Indian religious and social reformers, nationalists and revolutionaries. Moreover, foreign women influenced the local movement on women's rights by their own rebellion against patriarchal subordination in the West, their assertion of independence and their commitment to changes at home and in the colonial world.

If there is one issue that is common to the foreign women of this book it is education, which was the key factor in the emancipation of local women. Many foreign women in the colonies were the early products of womens' higher education in the West. Modern educational methods pioneered by Pestolozzi, Froebel and Montessori were brought to South Asia by foreign missionary teachers in girls' schools and also by socialist and theosophist women and "Holy Mothers" who started their own schools. All these efforts contributed to the creation of a freedom of spirit in local women not only through high school education but also through encouragement to pursue higher studies and new avenues of employment. Western women also introduced some cultural trends of Europe, such as modernism in art and literature to South Asia, in addition to the classics and Western music and art. They also encouraged the revival of indigenous arts and crafts and inspired local artists to break free from Victorian realism.

Among the most visible Western women and the earliest group of foreign activists in South Asia were the missionaries and the nuns. Their work in education and health made them conscious of the condition of women in these societies. They were brought face to face with various social and religious practices that affected women adversely; based on their notions of Christian universality, they attacked social evils, thus showing considerable awareness of women's issues. Their own roles helped them to develop this awareness; in their missions and convents, they had to assume a leadership that sometimes brought them into conflict with male church hierarchies. Their struggles for equal recognition and remuneration, the autonomy of their organizations and for the rights of single women, were continuous. But their lasting contribution was their creation of modern schools for girls, which imparted a good liberal education, including a concern about women's status. The negative aspects were the religious intolerance, racial arrogance, cultural conformism and eurocentrism of the missionary project. But narrow intentions of proselytizing had the unexpected effect of producing the "new woman" in the colonies.

The secular women social reformers and doctors also present clear aspects of feminist concern because (unlike nuns and missionaries), many of them had been involved in contemporary struggles against slavery and particularly in campaigns for women's education, franchise and other rights. They brought their feminist consciousness to South Asia and in many cases were able to battle colonial patriarchs (both British and local) because of their earlier experiences against entrenched male hierarchies. Their struggles, which had led to the acceptance of women in the professions in the West, had an immediate impact in the colonies in respect of higher education for women.

The role of women in alternative movements is somewhat ambivalent. Theosophists and Holy Mothers became immersed in South Asian religions and cultures and their own examples of female leadership, rebellion, independence as women and freedom from domestic ties, influenced local women. Even local men were able to relate to women from the West, who were in sympathy with the political aspirations of the colonized. But in their anxiety to promote local culture and traditions, some of these liberated foreign women rejected equal rights for local women and denied to South Asian women some of the benefits of the modernizing process that the missionaries and others had provided. In an era of colonial rule, although they sympathized with the colonized, they also romanticized the past, and harked back to the traditions of the majority community, often ignoring minority groups, thereby promoting dubious and sometimes reactionary agendas.

During the period discussed in this book, male Marxists both in the West and in South Asia did not show too much interest in raising the "woman question" in a colonial context, and argued that this was a problem that could be tackled after national liberation. Many women Marxists in the West, however, were sympathetic to the issue of women's equality and discussed questions of women's exploitation under colonialism. Most of the women of the left who worked for national liberation and Socialism in India and Sri Lanka, had a feminist consciousness and an internationalist outlook that came to the fore in their writings and work. Unlike the missionaries and reformers, they represented a more liberated and well-educated group of people who did not hesitate to raise basic feminist issues; these included questions of birth control, female sexuality, relationships with men, and mixed marriages as well as Socialist feminist issues of employment, wages and conditions of work of colonial women workers and the organization of these women in trade unions. Not surprisingly, some of the issues—such as birth control in India and autonomous feminist socialism in Sri Lanka—were opposed by local male leftists, who saw these as threatening to the leftist movement.

But none of the Western women discussed in this book could ignore the basic issue of national liberation. Many of them supported gradual reforms and visualized a benevolent British Empire where women would be free of their shackles; others hoped that social reform and radical changes in women's lives would be made easier after the independence of the region from imperialism. To local political leaders, nationalists, and leftists, foreign women (memsahibs) were generally merely the lesser half of the foreign rulers, supporting their men in the colonial project; those foreign women who did not fall into this category were judged by their commitment, not to local women, but to local independence. Hence the annoyance when foreign women criticized religious traditions and customs and reprimanded local men for their subordination of women. There were some possible arguments in reply: to deny any oppression and claim that local women were free, to declare certain practices to be cultural and religious and therefore sacred and unchanging; to blame the colonialist intruder for social evils, or to say that any such evils affecting women would be best tackled by South Asians themselves and that it was not the business of foreigners to interfere in local domestic arrangements.

But what of the Rights of Man that South Asians claimed to be universal and therefore applicable in a colonial situation? Were there then some universal rights of women, on which South Asian males were failing the test? This became an issue of contention; for missionary women were not only claiming one true religion, but also universal values and "global sisterhood." Whatever governments or local leaders said, Western women reformers insisted on their international duty to save their "sisters" from atrocities, and in many cases, defied all types of patriarchs in their crusade for women. But the "sisterhood" that was envisaged could not exist in a colonial situation of unequal relationships between rulers and ruled; such relationships between women were often "maternalistic," deciding that in terms of religion, culture, education and patterns of social behavior "mother knows best" (Ramusack 1981a). Local women, however, could also make their own decisions—rejecting what they did not need (someone else's religion) and only taking those products of Western society that were advantageous to women.

The theosophists and Holy Mothers had a different relationship with South Asians, and though the kinship they claimed as mother, daughter and sister was fictive, it was nevertheless nearer the concept of sisterhood than that of the Christians. For in embracing South Asian religions and celebrating their cultures and traditions, these women were making a sharp political statement in a colonial context and were therefore behaving like real sisters. It was satisfying for South Asian men to see that even the worst of their social practices could be justified, thus saving them from the shame that missionaries and reformers tried to impose on them. Even if some of the strange Western women spoke of Mahatmas in Tibet, New Messiahs in Madras and the Superman of the Future, they were to be honored for their identification with South Asia. The key test was the stand on colonialism and in this, the theosophists and Holy Mothers—with their earlier commitments to alternative political and social ideologies in the East and West, stood firm against the colonial policies of their own governments. Hence foreign women, who at the height of imperial domination, could challenge the might of Empire and even be imprisoned on this issue—as were Annie Besant, Margaret Cousins, Nellie Sen Gupta and Mira Behn—were to be honored and remembered.

One key question that remains to be discussed and researched further is how did local women react to foreign women claiming to be "sisters"? The responses were many and varied, changing with the rise to prominence of educated Indian and Sri Lankan women. Missionaries, for example, provoked sharp and intense reactions from local women, ranging from allegations of complicity with colonial rule, to angry rejection and ridicule of Christianity and Western social practice. As Amy Carmichael noted:

In one house an old lady leaned forward and gazed with a beautiful earnest gaze. Then she grabbed her hair and pointed to mine. "Are you a widow too," she asked, "that you have no oil on yours?" After a few such experiences that gaze loses its charm. "Oil! No Oil!...why not? Don't any white Ammals ever use oil?" (Elliot 1987:143)

But converts like Pandita Ramabai, for whom Hindu patriarchy could only be negated by adopting Christianity, were inspired and elated by the new faith. There was also a more pragmatic view by women who declined Christianity but appreciated the modern education and health benefits offered by the missionaries, as well as the projects for social reform and medical education sponsored by foreign women.

An important reaction to Western women who were idealizing South Asian societies and beliefs came from local women who were in movements to reform these very structures and ideologies. A group of women in the reformist Brahmo Samaj in Bengal, for example, protested against Sister Nivedita's romantic and unrealistic view of Hindu society and Kali worship, complaining that her sentimentality and goals of renunciation had produced "spinelessness and cowardice" (Reymond 1953:172). There were, however, important differences of opinion among local women about the foreign "sisters." To give a few instances, while Dr. Rukhmabai held foreign women doctors in high esteem and fought her personal battles against child marriage with their support, another early doctor, Dr. Anandabai, surprised her Christian benefactors in America by publicly defending child marriage. As Indian women came to the forefront of political struggles, many were bound to find Western women in leadership roles somewhat of an anachronism. But when foreign women defied British rulers and went to jail as Gandhi's supporters, they became heroic figures. Annie Besant's courage in promoting Home Rule inspired several generations of Indian women. The nationalist and Socialist leader Kamaladevi Chattopadyaya states that her mother held up Annie Besant to her as "a guiding star" and to Kamaladevi, Besant historically had few women equals, "her activities...working on my heart and mind powerfully" (Chattopadyaya 1986:32—33).

But even the most committed of the Western women could have problems. Margaret Cousins' pioneering work organizing Indian women met with dual responses; many like Kamaladevi claimed her as a true sister, applauding her courageous stand on women's rights and Indian national liberation, while others felt that foreigners had a diminishing role to play on these issues. Such problems were also faced by Gandhi's collaborator and disciple Mira Behn who became less indispensable as competent Indian women took over the running of his ashram by the mid-1930s. But feelings of solidarity also existed.

Kamaladevi Chattopadyaya and Mira Behn were in jail together and shared food, books and the spinning wheel. "We enjoyed each other's company, we had so much to say to each other, we read together, sang *bhajans*" (ibid 1986:171–72). Others like Sister Nivedita and the Mother of Pondicherry also inspired strong feelings of devotion and admiration among local women, which continue even to this day. However, the very controversial issue of child marriage continued to put Indian women in an awkward position. When Katherine Mayo made her fierce criticisms of Indian family life, in 1927, Indian men took on the bitter fight while Indian women were rather silent. But by 1934, when Eleanor Rathbone raised the same issue, some critical voices were heard among Indian women like Dhanwanthi Rama Rau who challenged "the right of British women to arrange a conference on Indian social evils in London" without Indian women's participation (Ramusack 1981a:115–16).

But unlike outside critics, it was the foreign women who devoted their lives to education of a radical type and to anti-imperialist and Socialist movements, who were most appreciated by local women, especially those who were politically active. In the girls' schools run by liberal and Socialist foreign women in Sri Lanka, a former pupil claimed

> we breathed an air of peace and freedom such as we had not known before. No fear of rigid rules and strict discipline haunted us. It was a process of mental and physical development at the hands of…eminent women of the West fired with a sense of dedication. (Gladys Abeysekera, *Ceylon Daily News,* 13 March 1987)

This was particularly true of Socialist women like Doreen Wickremasinghe who in her schools, introduced so many progressive reforms that "left their indelible mark on the pupils" (ibid), and in her political career, inspired many local women to confront feudal values, to repudiate caste and ethnic barriers and participate in movements for social and political change. Foreign women who did not live in India, but supported the Indian nationalist and Socialist causes, also inspired local politicized women. Writing of Agnes Smedley (whom she had sometimes criticized), Kamaladevi Chattopadyaya claims that Smedley "was one of the most remarkable women" she had known; "…she strode forward into some of the stormiest earth shaking events of international history…. She braved wars and shattering turmoil because of her single-minded devotion to the downtrodden, and the oppressed" (Chattopadyaya 1986:57).

This was perhaps the nearest to sisterhood that was possible in the colonial period. And this sisterhood could only be achieved through difficult and sometimes disparate tasks: first, confronting and opposing their own subordination under patriarchal structures of religion, state and family; second, taking a firm stand against imperialism by supporting local independence movements and associating with their leaders; and third, by speaking out against the exploitation and oppression of women and other social evils in South Asia.

NOTES

CHAPTER I

1 A committee of the House of Commons stated in 1781, "any interference with the religion of the native would eventually insure the total destruction of the British power"
   (Pathak 1967:16). However, in 1784, Charles Grant argued that only Christianity could
   morally and materially transform India: "I certainly am for helping these poor people...to become acquainted with *the truth and excellence of Revelation, with the improvements of the
   rights of man*" (ibid:12, emphasis added).

2 Harriet Winslow, a Methodist missionary described her visit to a Buddhist temple in 1820:
   "The moment I entered the building...horror seized me. I approached with trembling
   the hideous figure called Boodhu" (Winslow 1840:182). Her reaction to Hinduism was
   equally extreme; it was a religion "suited to their corrupt inclinations"; she referred to
   "their yells and horrid music...prostrating themselves before an idol" (ibid).

3 Millenarianism had its origin in the scriptural text of Revelations denoting the thousand
   years between the First and Second Coming of Christ, with the appearance of the
   "woman in the wilderness," who casts out the dragon and ushers in the Kingdom of
   God. Many dissident and heretical sects rejected the authority of the Church and State,
   advocated simplicity in life, dualism in theology, free will and non-violence and the
   expectation that the Second Coming would bring a female messiah (Desroches 1971).

4 George Fox, the founder of the Quakers, wrote in favor of women's right to prophesy,
   speak in church, be ministers, and have separate women's meetings. His wife, Margaret
   Fell, was at the forefront of Quaker feminism, writing a book (while in jail for her religious beliefs) called "Women's Speaking," using Bible sources to prove the prophetic roles
   given to women (Bacon 1986:16).

5 Born in 1736, Mother Ann experienced both the hardships of the early factory system
   and the violent resistance to exploitation. Many Shaker communities in the United States
   were run on the dual system of administration (half men and half women) in the belief
   that God embodied male and female elements. Friedrich Engels claimed that the Shakers
   were the first in the world "to found a society organized according to the principal of
   the common ownership of goods" (Desroches 1971:295).

6 The link between missionary activity by women abroad and fund raising for such activity by women church-goers at home dates back to the New England Great Awakening
   between 1798 and 1826. In 1800, the Boston Female Society for Missionary Purposes was
   formed to raise funds. Subsequently, the "Female Mite Society" and the "Female Cent
   Society" (1811) were started to collect small sums of money from women for church purposes. In 1819, there was a significant step forward when a women's auxiliary to the
   Missionary Society of the Methodist Episcopal Church was formed. (Butler 1904:24)

7 Educated women between the ages of twenty-five and thirty, desirous of spreading the
   gospel, were chosen and sent to India for an initial three years, with a salary of £ 120 a
   year at a time when male missionaries from Britain got £ 300 and Indian women missionaries had £ 60 a year (Forbes 1986: WS4).

8 In 1796, William Carey had spoken of the need for female missionaries "to communicate
   the gospel...in a situation where superstition secludes all women of respectability from
   hearing the word, unless from their own sex" (Potts 1967:38). In 1809, a pioneer in female

education in India, Hannah Marshman, started a Baptist day school for girls (Fuller 1899:255). By 1812, the Calcutta school run by the "Baptist trio," Carey, Marshman and Ward, had 310 male and 102 female students (Potts 1967:128–29).

9   As Anna Davidson of the "Ladies' China Missionary Society of Baltimore" (1848) stated, "an independent organization was considered an infringement of Church usage (and) the...rights of the Missionary Board; consequently *official brethren—Ministers and laymen— with a few honourable exceptions, gave the cold shoulder*" (Butler 1904:25–26, emphasis added).

10 Geraldine Forbes has observed that "espousing the cause of...universal sisterhood they expressed compassion for wrongs inflicted on all women...that Western women were beginning to make progress..was possible only because they were Christians. Eastern women were male-oppressed, but...male-oppression was sanctified by religion" (1986: w57).

11 The policy followed seems to have been an enlightened one, with the school not limiting itself to "any class or caste, and...breaking the walls that are so quick to form" between Europeans in India and other races (Baker 1898:186).

CHAPTER 2

1   The Maternal Society in Dorchester, Massachusetts in 1816, banded women together to discuss "how to fulfill their highly responsible situation as mothers and as professing Christians." The popularity of these autonomous women's groups made some of the clergy uneasy (Rendall 1985:79). Winslow linked the Jaffna maternal society to a similar group in Portland, Maine, informing it that the "female members of our mission" had come together "for mutual aid, in adopting the best methods for training up their children for usefulness in the church of God" (1840:249).

2   An American missionary in 1816 commented on the lack of female education in Jaffna: "I saw two native females, who could read and write, one in Alavetty, and one in Udupitty. I heard of another, but never saw her. I think there were no others" (Harrison 1925:4).

3   "The business of their marriage is superintended by the Christian Missionaries." The Mission gave each girl a dowry of £ 4.10 for the "purchase of dress and ornaments," (American Mission April 1839:8). On the question of dowry, there was criticism in America (ibid:6).

4   Betsey Pomeroy's conversion was not without problems from her family. Winslow records that "Betsey's father keeps a temple dedicated to a female devil, and is said to have devoted a sister of her's to its service. Probably he wants her for the same object; but I trust the Lord has better things in store for her" (Winslow 1840: 307).

5   In 1901, Eunice John passed the Calcutta entrance with a first class, also winning the prize given in the name of the Bengali reformer Keshab Chandra Sen for the best girl candidate from India, Burma and Ceylon (Harrison 1925:94–95).

6   Mrs. O'Flanagan of Limerick (the widow of an Irish soldier who had died in Sri Lanka) had earlier started a Catholic girls' school in Jaffna, assisted by her daughter Catherine. On the arrival of the Holy Family sisters, however, this school was handed over to them and the O'Flanagans went to Trincomalee on the East coast to take over St. Mary's English and Tamil schools (Peiris 1980:19–20).

7   As the principal of the Holy Family Convent in Colombo said in 1912: "The education of girls...is to fit them to occupy...their stations in the higher sphere of life they are expected to follow hereafter. Imbued as we are in Ceylon with Western ideas of civilization, men wish their wives to have had the same educational advantages as themselves" (Sessional Paper of 1911–1912:65, quoted in Jayaweera 1990:329).

8 The Institute was founded in 1625 by Mary Ward in Yorkshire, for teaching and keeping alive the Catholic ideal in Protestant England. The convent in York attracted many Irish, including Mother Mary Teresa Ball who pioneered and developed the Loreto Abbey as a first-rate girls' school for upper-class Irish girls (Colmcille 1968:8).

9 We read of the "good old Irish lay-sisters" who were "simple country girls (who) found it natural to offer themselves as cooks, laundresses or maids of all work in a convent." They had "endless recipes, and home-made remedies, and an equally unfailing supply of legends and fairy tales" (Colmcille 1968:94–95).

10 The Archbishop ordered that Loreto House premises be given to the St. Xavier boys' school. He also interfered in the convent administration; the nuns "could hardly venture to move a doormat without his approval!" (Colmcille 1968:38–39).

11 Mother Hogan was born in Limerick, educated at the Loreto Abbey, and had taught in two leading schools in Dublin. Arriving in India in 1844, she founded the convent in Chittagong in 1845 (Colmcille 1968:101–102).

12 Reluctantly, Mother Teresa Mons took on the task of running the hospital. The sisters' experience in the hospital was evidently very unpleasant and harrowing, so much so that the convent chronicles cut out many pages of "experiences narrated" (Colmcille 1968:4).

13 Beale also started "the three St. Hilda's" named after the famous Abbess of Whitby, patron of learning and founder of a monastery. They were St. Hilda's College in Cheltenham for advanced studies, which later got university status, St. Hilda's a women's college in Oxford, and St. Hilda's in the East End of London for social work among the poor (Clarke 1953).

14 Author's discussions with Doreen Wickremasinghe and Nita Muttucumaru.

CHAPTER 3

1 For a time they lived in a forest but her parents and sister died of starvation during the great famine of 1876–77. Ramabai, aged sixteen, and her brother then traveled on foot to North and East India searching for food and work (Dyer 1900).

2 Rachel Little Bodley had the chair of chemistry at the Women's Medical College, Philadelphia, becoming its Dean in 1874, a post she held for fourteen years. She was involved in supporting medical missionary work, keeping in touch with Dr. Clara Swain and Dr. Anna Kugler who worked in India (James et al., 1971).

3 The reformer, M.G. Ranade, first married at the age of 13. His second marriage, at 31, was to a girl of 11, in order to please his father; T.T.Telang, a critic of child marriage, had his daughter married off at a young age; and Deshmukh who publicly called for widow remarriage, refused to attend such a wedding due to family pressure (Kosambi 1988:w.s.45).

4 One of the Vice-Presidents was Rev. Phillips Brooks (1835–93), whose Trinity Church was a "social landmark in Boston" (Goonetileke 1976:180–81). He had traveled in India and Sri Lanka and in 1891, he became Bishop of Massachusetts. He was a liberal Christian, "ever open to the cry of the distressed and oppressed of whatever nation" (Ramabai Association 1893:24–25).

5 Pauline Agassiz Shaw (1841–1917) was a well-known educational philanthropist, active in social work, including day nurseries and training schools in the poorer parts of Boston; in the 1890s she became a suffragist and a supporter of peace movements (James et al., 1971, Vol. 13: 278).

6 "I was delighted to see the chivalrous spirit rising in the hearts of my young countrymen, who thus manifested their desire to honour woman.... I felt very proud to think

that the time was not far distant when my sisters would be honoured by our brothers, not because they were mothers or superior beings, but because they were women" (Ramabai Association 1890:15)

7 Kartini in 1902 wrote: "I read of her in the paper. I trembled with excitement; not alone for the white woman is it possible to attain an independent position, the brown Indian too can make herself free.... For days I thought of her.... See what one good example can do" (Geertz 1976:177–78).

8 "We are wanting, first and foremost, in UNITY. We are so many castes...clans...families and...individuals." Ramabai posed a rhetorical question to Hindus, "Why did you not go to England to trade...and establish Hindu rule? Why could we not be masters and mistresses of a glorious empire?" The answer was that British rule was not based on "lies and deceitfulness of a few unprincipled traders, but on right Christian principles" (American Ramabai Association, 1909).

9 The President of the American Ramabai Association referred to the slogan "India for the Indians," and predicted that "the great movements of the future" would be those with "great and powerful native leaders" while also sympathizing in "difficulties that confront the people there from a religious point of view" (American Ramabai Association 1909:39).

10 As the Rev. Lyman Abbot said, Christians "should be more wise than we have been in our missionary movements" and should concentrate on "spontaneous and indigenous movements like that of Ramabai"; Christianity, he said, had been confounded with "that particular form which it has taken on in our Anglo-Saxon race". (Ramabai Association 1892:36–37).

11 Hamlin had been bold enough to ask whether this was not in violation of the pledge of non-sectarianism given to the American funders (Ramabai Association 1890:28).

12 Allegations that pupils were being converted led to a crisis. Thirty pupils were withdrawn and the school "seemed in danger of annihilation." Ramabai was accused "of disloyalty to her own people, of obtaining money from American people under false pretences, of defiantly interfering with the religious customs of her pupils, and of dismissing the Managing Board that she might openly teach Christianity in her school" (Ramabai Association 1892: 14). Allowance was made for both the enthusiasm of the convert and Ramabai's "Indian" ways. Judith Andrews in the Executive Committee Report for 1900 wrote: "Her oriental nature leads her to more ardent utterances than some of her Occidental sisters are accustomed to hearing. Might it not be well to ask ourselves if some of our restrained and seasoned utterances may not seem as inadequate to her as hers seem extravagant to us?" (American Ramabai Association 1900:30).

13 While the Sharada Sadan remained overtly secular, the school at Kedgaon called Mukti (salvation) with 365 women and girls, was "Christian pure and simple" (American Ramabai Association 1899:13).

CHAPTER 4

1 In 1859, Bessie Rayner Parkes started the Ladies Sanitary Association to teach British women who were "living on a dung heap," the advantages of pure water, fresh air and soap; there were also "Training Work House Girls" schemes started by Louisa Twining to teach poor girls a "useful occupation," and Jessie Boucherett's "Society for Promoting the Employment of Women" (Hollis 1979).

2 Roy campaigned against sati (which was made a crime in 1829) and in 1828, along with other enlightened Bengalis, formed the Brahmo Samaj, which drew inspiration from all

religions, challenged obscurantism, orthodox beliefs, and championed women's rights.

3 The Prarthana Samaj (Prayer Society) formed in 1867 by Dr. Atmaram Pandurang (1823–1898) promoted social reform and the propagation of theistic worship as opposed to idolatry. Jotirao Phule (1827–1890), founded the Satyashodak Samaj in 1873 as a movement of the "low" castes against Brahmin domination; he also spoke out for women's education and widow remarriage and opposed polygamy and child marriage. Gopal Deshmukh (1823–1892) in the 1840s, had attacked the caste system, child marriage and the harsh treatment of widows. Numerous writers, poets and reformers from all over India campaigned against injustices against women (Jayawardena 1986:84–87).

4 In 1831, she became the superintendent of the church Sunday school at Lewin's Mead; many of the children came from poor homes, which she visited. The Bristol riots of 1831 and the cholera epidemic the next year made her aware of the "consequences of poverty and of ignorance" (Saywell 1964:4).

5 "Miss Carpenter and her allies stressed the need for reformation. Kindliness versus corporal punishment became a subject of debate in press and pamphlet" (Saywell 1964:6).

6 Over the next twenty years, 417 girls passed through the school, which taught non-sectarian religion, reading, writing, simple arithmetic, singing, general knowledge, needlework and knitting. The older girls were trained for work as domestics (Saywell 1964:9–10).

7 While in London, Roy's son stayed with Rev. D. Davidson; an infant born to the Davidsons, was named Rammohan Roy and Mrs Davidson recalled that the elder Roy used to come to the nursery "to visit his namesake" (Carpenter 1850:112–13).

8 These included Harriet Martineau, Miss Dale, Mrs Thomas Woodforde and Miss Acland who wrote,

> Sons of the Western main around thee hung
> While Indian lips unfolded Freedom's laws,
> And grateful woman heard the Brahmin's tongue
> Proclaim her worth, and plead her widowed cause.

(Carpenter 1850:176)

9 In 1884, the Ilbert Bill was passed with a compromise provision that Europeans would be tried by a jury, with at least half composed of Europeans (Sinha 1992:98). One local paper, commenting on the unprecedented agitation by white women in India, stated that they had refused "to submit to the jurisdiction of the Calibans lusting after the Mirandas of Anglo India" (ibid:99).

CHAPTER 5

1 "Many of the male students went to considerable lengths to harass and annoy them publicly and privately; sometimes even obscenely, with the covert approval of a few professors" (Lutzker 1964:63). The university refused to grant degrees to the women medical students, claiming that thier admission had been a mistake. They were expelled in 1874, sued the university and won, but the verdict was reversed on appeal; the payment of £2,000 costs was met by help from a newly-formed committee which appealed for public funds (ibid:63). Attempts to get legislation in parliament to allow medical degrees for women were defeated; in 1875, a bill was defeated by 196 to 153, and the Senate of the University of London also rejected the proposal.

2 These included three M.Ds from the university of Zurich: Louisa Aikins (1872) who became house surgeon in Birmingham hospital for women, Eliza Dunber (1872), Elizabeth Hoggan (1870), and Anna Kingsford, who in 1881 qualified in Paris (Lutzker 1964:58)

3 Pioneer American women doctors in India included Dr. Sara Norris, sent to India in 1873 by the Women's Board of Missions of the American Congregational Church, and Dr. Sara Seward of the Presbyterian Foreign Missionary Society who opened a dispensary in Allahabad in 1872. After her death in 1891, the Sara Seward Hospital was constructed as a memorial to her (Balfour & Young 1929).

4 In 1881, Dr. Elizabeth Bielby qualified in Ireland and Switzerland. Midwifery was a particular concern of hers, and in a talk to the National Indian Association in England in 1885, Bielby described Indian midwives as ignorant of medical knowledge "whose fables, charms and nostrums have been handed down from generation to generation"; surmising that 40 million Indian women were in need of help, she wrote that "the need for duly qualified medical women for the women of India cannot be exaggerated" (Lutzker 1973:93).

5 Other pioneers were Dr. Maria White of the American Methodist Mission, who started a hospital in Sialkot in 1875; Dr. Ida Faye of the American Baptist Missionary Union, an M.D. from Pennsylvania who came in 1881 to Vellore, opening a dispensary and a hospital in 1897 (Balfour & Young 1929:22–23); and Dr Rose Greenfield of Britain who came to Ludhiana in 1875, opened a dispensary in 1881, a hospital in 1889, and helped in the establishment of the Women's Medical School with a new hospital attached to it in 1893. She retired in 1924 after forty-nine years in India (ibid:18–19).

6 Dr. John Scudder (1795–1856), studied in New York, and was influenced by accounts of William Carey's mission work in India. He was the first medical missionary to join the American Board for Foreign Missions, arriving in Jaffna (Sri Lanka) in 1819. There he was ordained as a Methodist priest and served as a doctor until 1836 when he moved to South India to start a mission in Arcot. Scudder's perception of his own vocation included medical work, fights against local customs, and the spread of the Gospel (Jeffery 1938:29).

7 Ida Scudder recalled, "I thought very seriously about the condition of the Indian woman and I went to my father and mother...and told them that I must go home and study medicine, and come back to India to help such women" (Jeffery 1938:51)

8 Another generous donation by Gertrude Dodd (of the Women's Auxilary and the Foreign Mission Society Board), the daughter of a wealthy contractor, helped in starting a tuberculosis sanatorium; Dodd visited India twice and finally in 1917 settled in Vellore to help Dr. Scudder in her work (Jeffery 1938:66).

9 Scharlieb was involved in her husband's legal work, especially in helping to edit two monthly law journals; "My share of the work" she wrote, was in "the collection of materials, writing notes of law cases...and occasionally in the contribution of articles" (Scharlieb 1924:28).

10 As Scharlieb wrote, "I frequently heard through my husband's native clients...Brahmin clerks, and from our servants, of the...unncessary suffering of the women of the country, Hindu as well as Mohammedan, in sickness and in childbirth" (Scharlieb 1924:29).

11 Dr. Cockerill of the Madras Lying-in-Hospital disapproved of women studying medicine. "He told me that the work was not suitable for a English lady, that it involved much unpleasantness...that my husband could not possibly approve (Scharlieb 1924:32).

12 Scharlieb was helped by the matron Mrs. Secluna. "She was English by birth, a big fair woman, who had fifteen children herself, and was one of the most skillful midwives and most kindly people that I ever had the good luck to meet. She, at any rate, approved of my desire to learn practical midwifery (Scharlieb 1924:32).

13 Among the other women students who passed the LMS (Licentiate of Medicine, Surgery and Midwifery) were Dora White, who subsequently worked for the government of

Hyderabad, Miss Mitchell, who qualified but gave up work on marriage, and Miss D'Abreu, an Anglo-Indian who worked with medical missionaries (Scharlieb 1924:43).

14 Along with Sophia Jex-Blake, Pechey went to Berne, Switzeland for studies after the Edinburgh fiasco, receiving the M.D. degree in 1877. The same year they gained admission to the Royal College of Physicians in Ireland to sit for the final examination and thereby got a licence to practice in Britain. She was a founding member in 1878, of the Medical Women's Federation in England (Lutzker 1973:64).

15 In 1865, an Indian doctor referred to the ignorance of midwives who were unable to learn since "not even one in hundred can write her name" (Lutzker 1973:93). In 1884, the widow of an Indian doctor started a fund with an annual award to the best student of midwifery (ibid:81).

16 Pechey tactfully praised aspects of Indian family life but denounced child marriage as a "pernicious custom," stating that it was "a retrogression from the early civilization of your race; it is a stigma on your religion; a blot on your humanity which…would disgrace you in the eyes of the whole civilized world" (Lutzker 1973:195).

17 "Educate yourselves, educate yourselves" Pechey said—"Upon you depends the future of the country, whether it is to progress or stand still…. You must do it yourselves…. All the results of educational associations in England are due to the hard work of women themselves, and so it must be with you" (Lutzker 1973: 186).

18 Rukhmabai's lawyer had argued that she was married without her consent while the husband's lawyer claimed that "marriage among the Hindus is not a contract…but a religious duty, and want of personal consent through infancy is immaterial." Justice Pinhey concluded that "it would be a barbarous, a cruel, a revolting thing to compel a young lady…to go to a man whom she dislikes, in order that he may cohabit with her against her will" (Lutzker 1973:202–203).

19 A journal called *Native Opinion* argued that "Hindu girls married in childhood…seldom if ever feel it a grievance to go and join their husbands when they grow up…and on the average are as happy as the women of any other country in the world" (Luzker 1973:204). Tilak claimed that while Rukhmabai tried to sow discontent in Hindu family life, Anandibai had passed through many ordeals and was a noble example to Hindu society (Pradhan & Bhagwat 1959:50).

20 An English writer to the *Indian Magazine* stated: "We do our best to raise the women of India out of the condition of helplessness, social slavery and degradation in which we find them; and then… allow our laws to become an instrument for riveting their chains…. Does England govern India in order that we may send to prison a woman who will not live with a husband against whom her whole nature rises up in most justifiable abhorrence?" (Lutzker 1973:204)

21 "Why should English law…aid in the restitution of conjugal rights?" Müller inquired, adding that "What concerns Englishmen and Englishwomen, is that…English law should not be rendered infamous in aiding and abetting unnatural atrocities. When so many questions are asked in Parliament, will no one ask a question about Rukhmabai?" (Lutzker 1973:206)

CHAPTER 6

1 In London, *The Times* had an article on "The Hindoo Child-Widow" stating that the Viceroy, "on the advice of nine of the ten provincial governments," delayed reforms on this issue "until Indian public opinion declared itself more openly in favour" (*The Times*, 15 October 1886).

2   Tilak pioneered "the use of religious orthodoxy as a method of mass contact" through his emotive attacks on reformers as anti-Hindu and, therefore, unpatriotic. He acquired a mass base by resorting in the 1890s to Hindu religious symbolism and appeals to past glory. He launched a "patriotic-cum-historical cult" of the Hindu warrior-king Shivaji, who fought the British and was made into a "central symbol of nationalism" (Sarkar 1983:99).

3   Tilak replied "You are not told to find new discoveries in *Dharma Shastra* and you are not asked to bring "good tidings" out of them. (Wolpert 1962:55–56) Bhandarkar hit back alleging that "Mr. Tilak thinks that our present practice prevails in all part of the country, and has descended to us from very olden times. He thus belongs to the school of those who find the steam engine and the electric telegraph in the Vedas" (ibid:56). Tilak took the fight against the social reformers into the Indian National Congress, succeeding by 1895 in getting Congress to sever links with the National Social Conference of Ranade and the reformers.

4   A picture in her book of an obese holy man had the caption: "Talk of beasts in human shape!… But he is a temple saint—earthly, sensual, devilish. Now put beside him a little girl—your own little girl—and leave her there—you leave her there in his hand" (Carmichael 1903:188).

5   Rev. Downie, an American Baptist praised Carmichael: "That she has painted a dark picture of Hindu life cannot be denied…. I rejoice that she had the courage to do what was so much needed, and yet what so many of us shrank from doing lest it should injure the cause" (Carmichael 1906:vi–vii).

6   In 1917, Mayo campaigned for a State police force for New York State to "curb rowdy immigrants and labor disputes and also defend lonely women and children against drunken husbands, ruffians and rapists…. the causes which most occupied reform-minded women of her time did not involve her: slums…suffrage, the conditions of labor" (Handlin 1971:516)

7   Mayo traveled to the Philippines and wrote *The Isles of Fear* in 1925; she opposed self-government for the Philippines, praised the benefits of American rule as proof of "Anglo-Saxon performance" and denounced sexual crimes against local women by Filipino officials and school teachers (Handlin 1971:516).

8   "Bengal is the seat of the bitterest political unrest—the producers of India's main crop of anarchists, bomb-throwers and assassins. Bengal is also among the most sexually exaggerated regions of India: and medical and police authorities in any country observe the link between that quality and queer criminal minds—the exhaustion of normal avenues of excitement creating a thirst and a search in the abnormal for gratification" (Mayo 1927:122). In a rejoinder the editor of the *Indian Social Reformer*, K. Natarajan said: "Miss Katherine Mayo need not have come all the way to India to verify the observation of medical and police authorities about…a thirst and a search in the abnormal for gratification. *"Mother India,"* we fancy, had its origin in such a thirst leading to such a search. *The muck is in Miss Katherine Mayo's mind more than in Bengal or any other part of India*" (Natarajan 1928:50, emphasis added).

9   Tagore also cited others whose "views have been misinterpreted, their words mutilated, and facts tortured into a deformity which is worse than untruth" (Mukerji 1928:105–8). Tagore also denounced the review of *Mother India* in the *New Statesman*, which had accused him of supporting the consummation of marriage before puberty. In this he refers to "propaganda…against individuals, whose countrymen have obviously offended the writer by their political aspirations" (Natarajan 1928:99).

10 "If Miss Mayo had confessed that she had gone to India merely to…examine the drains…there would perhaps be little to complain" he said, but to Mayo "The drains are India." However, Gandhi urged Indians to read the book, "We may repudiate the charge as it has been framed by her, but we may not repudiate the substance underlying the many allegations she has made. It is a good thing to see ourselves as others see us. We need not even examine the motive with which the book is written. A cautious reformer may make some use of it" (Natarajan 1928:103–106).

11 Lajpat Rai claimed that there was "an unholy combination of all the white people of the earth against India's aspirations to political freedom," adding that, "India's freedom means the freedom of the whole coloured world"; the political awakening of the East he said had "frightened both Europe and America," Mayo being "only the mouthpiece of the oppressors of the East" (1928:xviii)

12 Ellen Wilkinson, a Labour M.P., accused the British government of helping Miss Mayo because it had "a very shrewd idea of the kind of book she was going to produce." At this meeting Lady Emily Lutyens, the theosophist, said that assuming Mayo's statements were partially true, it was an indictment on the British government; similarly, Lady Cynthia Moseley alleged that Mayo's book was not intended to promote social reform, but to "stand up for the British in India" (Natarajan 1928:120–23).

13 In Calcutta a newspaper had an article captioned "Indian Women Blasphemed" (*Amrita Bazaar Patrika*, 28 August 1927 quoted in Field 1929:9) and the *Forward* called Mayo's book "A Libel against Indian Womanhood" (ibid:9).

14 Another critic, Mahendra Pratap, who wrote *Long Live India* in reply to Mayo, argued that the modern woman was callous and cruel, sparing none, not even her mother and sisters, in keeping with "her modern enthusiasm for bobbed hair and nude fashion" (1932:4).

15 In a reply to Mayo entitled *Father India* (1927) C.S. Ranga Iyer called her a "forward American spinster" (1927:11, 13). Sir C P Ramaswami Aiyar referred to "persons like Miss Mayo with filthy minds who in all probability are suffering from inhibited instincts and who have no eyes, but for evil, dirt and degradation" (Natarajan 1928:109). Lajpat Rai wrote: "Her mind is obscured by our excessive sensuality, and on the Freudian hypotheses her frequent references to this topic, in season and out of season, suggest morbidity of an uncommon order" (1928:xiii).

16 These included the problems of Liverpool's dock-workers, widows, and dependents of soldiers. She pioneered the idea of family allowances in the form of payments to mothers directly, and her book on this question *The Dis-inherited Family* (1924) became wellknown. Rathbone, in 1909 became the first woman member of the Liverpool city council, and was also involved in issues of women's equality in Britain and other countries.

17 Apart from her concern for Indian women, Rathbone also took up the issue of female circumcision in Africa and forced marriage in the Arab countries (Banks 1985:167).

18 Another supporter of India's struggle for freedom and a champion of Indian women's rights was Agatha Harrison (1885–1954) the Secretary of the India Conciliation Group, formed to keep the political links open between India and Britain. Harrison mobilized prominent British personalities who were for Indian independence and helped to organize visits of Indian leaders to Britain. She was also a link between British feminists interested in India and Indian women leaders, and on her many visits to India, she attended several conferences of the All India Women's Conference where she was "warmly received" (Ramusack 1981a:130–37, 149).

CHAPTER 7

1   Henry Thomas Colebrooke became Professor of Sanskrit at the College of Fort William in Bengal in 1801 and published "Essays on the Religion and Philosophy of the Hindus." Charles Wilkins translated *The Bhagawad Gita*, *The Hitopadesha* and a Sanskrit grammar in 1801. H.H. Wilson, translated the epic poem *Meghadhuta* in 1813 and produced the first Sanskrit-English dictionary in 1819, becoming the first Professor of Sanskrit at Oxford in 1833; he also translated the first book of the Rig Veda in 1850 which "caused considerable stir" (Schwab 1984:39).

2   Thoreau in 1856 wrote his famous Vedantic poem "Brahma." Also inspired by Hinduism was Edgar Allan Poe (1809–1849) whose *Eureka* (1848) "showed thought closely akin to that of the Upanishads" (Rolland 1984:67).

3   Several British painters popularized the monuments of India. They included William Hodges, *Select Views of India* (1786); Thomas and William Daniels in *Oriental Scenery* (between 1795 and 1808) and *A Picturesque Voyage to India* (1810) described as "the very quintessence of romantic India" (Mitter 1977:126).

4   Emmanuel Swedenborg (1688–1772) had experienced "mystical states" and "supernatural flashes of light." Dr. Franz Anton Mesmer (c 1734–1815), wrote of planetary influences on the human body and popularized the practice of trances, where spirits speaking through mediums conveyed messages from the dead; he also used magnetic cures through "mesmeric sleep" (Webb 1988a:20–25). In the United States Katherine and Margaret Fox, who lived in a "haunted" house, claimed to talk to spirits through raps. The movement spread to Britain, attracting a distinguished clientele, while also capturing some working-class interest. Robert Owen the Utopian socialist was involved, as were the writers Conan Doyle and Bulwer-Lytton, and "even Queen Victoria and Gladstone were known to have dabbled" (Owen 1989 :19).

5   In Britain, a spiritualist, Emma Hardinge Britten, who had been in the women's rights and abolitionist struggles in America, argued forcefully for full political and social equality of women, but denounced "free love" (Owen 1989:37). In America, some spiritualists influenced by the Swedenborgians put forward controversial theories that masculine and feminine qualities were to be found in both sexes. (ibid:14).

6   "The generation of women empowered by Spiritualism did not lose their inspiration when the movement ceased to provide it. Instead they used skills gained within Spiritualism for campaigns for women's emancipation…. The ranks of the trance lecturers provided a corpus of experienced female speakers for the suffrage campaign" (Brande 1989:192–93).

7   On this question, Colonel Olcott, her close associate, wrote: "She is no more a *she* than you or I. I have pumped enough out of her to satisfy me that the theory…was correct—she is a man, a very old man, and a most learned and wonderful man, a Hindu man." (Nethercot 1961:322).

8   Blavatsky argued that since there was a similarity in all religions, there was a common origin. This was the famous "Lost Doctrine," only preserved in Tibet by an ancient brotherhood of "Masters" which Blavatsky believed would be revealed to her. Ellmann caustically comments, "Two masters in particular, Koot-Hoomi and Morya, had graciously indicated their willingness to transmit some of the secret doctrine to the world through the good offices of the Theosophical Society" (1988:59–60).

9   Despard also noted that "the Masters of Wisdom in their latest message to Humanity, have found some of their best interpreters in women, chiefly those two who are venerated…everywhere throughout the world—H.P.Blavatsky and Annie Besant (1913:9)

10 Blavatsky quotes a Parsi paper, which sarcastically commented on this wedding where "the bride who was carried in arms, greeted the guests, not with smiles, but with a dreadful howl" adding sarcastically that this showed "with the exactitude of a barometer the progress of our speedily developing nation" (1975:228).

CHAPTER 8

1 "The ideal humanity of the Christian is the humanity of the slave, poor, meek, submissive to authority, however…unjust; the ideal humanity of the Atheist is the humanity of the free man who knows no Lord, who brooks no tyranny…proud…brave (Besant 1984:137).

2 "I refused to reprint the *Law of Population* and to sell the copyright, giving pain to the brave and loyal friends who had so generously stood by me in that long and bitter struggle" (Besant quoted in Paxton 1990:342).

3 The petition against Besant alleged that she associated herself with an "infidel" Charles Bradlaugh, publishing pamphlets, whereby "the truth of the Christian religion is impeached and disbelief in all religions inculcated" (Besant 1984:189).

4 Besant's "spectacular performance as a laywoman lawyer" led to the formation of an "Association to Promote Women's Knowledge of the Law," which reported on women's disabilities in entering the Inns of Court and practising law (Nethercot 1961:153).

5 The famous scientist Thomas Huxley had been one of Besant's examiners in botany and he signed a petition calling upon the Council to reconsider its action in preventing her admission. But by the time the Council met, Huxley had been elected president of the Royal Society, and when it came to voting on her issue, he abstained (Nethercot 1961:192).

6 Besant was part of the protest against the ban on demonstrations the government had imposed on unions and socialist organizations; this culminated in "Bloody Sunday," the massive demonstration at Trafalgar Square in 1886, brutally dispersed by the police. Shaw referred to Besant as the "heroine of Trafalgar Square and its aftermath" (Nethercot 1961:258).

7 Besant was also the first woman elected to the London School Board. She then began a campaign exposing poverty, sweated labor, child labor and "the absurdity of trying to educate half-starving children," also pioneering many reforms in the schools system (Nethercot 1961:277–78, 283).

8 Kumari Jayawardena, *Sinhala Buddhism and the "Daughters of the Soil"* (in *Pravada*, vol 1, No 5, May 1992).

9 Arundale was a member of the French Order of Co-Masonry, which unlike freemasons, included both men and women among its members (Nethercot 1963:73–74). In 1902, Annie Besant joined the group and became active in founding many Co-Masonry lodges in Britain. When Arundale's nephew, George Arundale, a Cambridge graduate and theosophist, came to India to teach at the Central Boys College, Francesca Arundale came to India with him (ibid:71).

10 Besant published *How India Wrought for Freedom*, "a savage indictment of England's past treatment of the country"; this made the authorities suspicious of her activities as President of the Home Rule League, which by 1917 had 150 branches with over 10,000 members (Nethercot 1963:249, 257).

11 In 1903, another missionary, Amy Carmichael, referred to a Hindu whose home the missionaries had visited; "he knew all about Mrs. Besant…and was up in the bewildering tangle of thought known as Hindu Philosophy" (Carmichael 1903:11, 129).

12 In 1911, M.C. Nanjunda Rao, a doctor, questioned how the untutored Krishnamurti could have written the book and, ridiculing Besant on her claim to clairvoyant powers, sug-

gested that she should place them "at the service of the authorities for the discovery of bombs, …anarchists and murderers." The *Hindu* was gratified "that responsible members of the community" were realising the need for a "critical examination of the Theosophical movement" and said that "only fools or madmen could believe in this 20th century that the boy Krishnamurti is an incarnation of the Divinity" (Parthasarathy 1978:205–207).

13 As Nethercot notes "Brotherhood and youth were in the air. National Star Conferences and Theosophical youth meetings were held all over the world." In the twenties Krishnamurti, surrounded by loyal English women, traveled to several theosophical society conventions and claimed that his Order of the Star had sixty to seventy thousand members (1963:324–24). See also Mary Lutyens (1975), *Years of Awakening* (London: John Murray).

CHAPTER 9

1 Florence Farr's father William Farr (1807–1883) was a doctor, and renowned medical statistician. A close friend of Florence Nightingale, he discussed with her the need for trained nurses (Johnson 1975:13). Dr. Farr was also a pioneer social reformer committed to changing society and was interested in women's emancipation.

2 "The novelty of *Widowers' Houses* lay in the anti-romantic use to which Shaw put a theatrical cliché"; the father makes a bargain with the hero offering him "money for social position." Blanche is a strong woman with a fierce temper, "over whom the pact between aristocratic respectability and financial exploitation is made" (Holroyd 1988:281, 283).

3 Horniman, who like Farr belonged to the Golden Dawn occult group, was also a classic example of the independent woman of the period; she rode a bicycle, wore trousers, smoked, and sported a "huge jewelled dragon in oxidized silver round her neck" (Holroyd 1988:299).

4 The character Louka, which Farr played, was mistakenly referred to as Loica by Ezra Pound in Canto 28. *Arms and the Man* caused a sensation; it was a "deconstruction of heroism—professional soldiers who carry chocolates instead of cartridges and weep when scolded"; moreover, wars were waged "mostly by paperwork and won through ludicrously lucky errors." The cynical exposure of war, soldiers, mercenaries and patriotism shocked and excited audiences in Britain and the United States (Holroyd 1988:302–303).

5 As Holroyd writes of Shaw, "for all his knowledge, his vitality, his busy politics, there seemed…no mystery, no beating of a religious pulse," adding that for Farr, "It was a relief to turn from the hectic Shavian vocabulary to…Yeats…. He came bearing esoteric apparatus…. She began to replace Shaw's elocution with Yeats' cantillatory polemics, put down Fabian and picked up magical tracts. She meditated on colours, plucked interesting discords, muttered verse invocations and trance-like intonements" (1988:307–308)

6 Ramanathan's visit impressed the President of the American Ramabai Association, Rev. Charles Cuthbert, who had traveled and lectured in India. Cuthbert remarked on the increasing frequency of contact between "Westerners with the East,…(and) Orientals with the West" and referred to his meetings with P. Ramanathan who had given "lectures upon Philosophical Hinduism" (American Ramabai Association 1906:38–39).

7 As Ramanathan stated, "The boys in Jaffna had many high schools conducted on Saiva principles; but the girls had either to seek admission to Christian schools or be at home entirely neglecting their studies. I found the parents…complaining bitterly of the poison instilled into the minds of…their boys and girls (in) Christian schools" (Vythilingam 1971:546).

8 Ramanathan's biographer, exaggerating somewhat, spoke of her as "a name to conjure with in the literary and philosophical world of her time" (Vythilingam 1971:549). During the Silver Jubilee celebrations of Ramanathan College (in 1939) Florence Farr was claimed to have had "a great reputation as a scholar" and was described as "a deep thinker, a brilliant speaker...sought after by the universities to lecture to learned scholars in England" (Ramanathan College Souvenir 1939:16).

9 According to Ramanathan, the school aimed to give Hindu girls "such a training as would make them not only thoroughly efficient at home and in society without being denationalized, but also devoted to God, loyal to the King and desirous of the welfare of the people." It was based on the ancient Indian system of *guru kula vasam*, or residence with the teacher. Instruction was to be in Tamil and English and the school laid special emphasis on a knowledge of Tamil literature and Hinduism (Vythilingam 1971:550–51).

CHAPTER 10

1 In Britain the victory of the Liberal Party over the Conservatives in 1906 had ushered in a period of social welfare, reforms and legislation in favor of trade union rights. By 1910 the aggressive battles of the British suffragists had made female franchise a national issue. Around the same period, the struggles in Ireland were becoming more violent, culminating in the Proclamation in 1916 of the Irish Republic. The growth of militant trade unionism and the rise of the Labour Party in Britain and the 1917 Russian Revolution, gave a filip to Socialists all over the world, including the colonial world.

2 Margaret Cousins was "subjected to the cultural influence and romance which were the warp and woof of Ireland" (Cousins and Cousins 1950:23). She was inspired by the Irish Home Rule movement and sympathized with Parnell and the Irish "fighters for freedom" (ibid:25). She began to notice the inequality of opportunity for females and favoritism toward her brothers in the family; she claimed that she "rebelled from that early age against any differential treatment of the sexes" (ibid:22–23, 54).

3 Cousins was influenced by Walter Besant's *All Sorts and Conditions of Men*, which aroused in her "a desire to do slum social service," and W.T. Stead's journal *Review of Reviews* which, in one issue, contained a character sketch of Helena Blavatsky (Cousins & Cousins 1950:27).

4 "My memories of that month sum themselves up as a species of living death because of the solitariness of the confinement.... No writing materials were allowed. There was a short church service daily which each prisoner was expected to attend. I always went because I could see my companions then, though no conversation was possible" (Cousins & Cousins 1950:180–81).

5 James Cousins helped start the Arts League and was in touch with the Indian Society of Oriental Art in Calcutta. In 1916 he went to Calcutta and met the Tagores, later organizing an exhibition of Indian modern art in Madras (Cousins and Cousins 1950:260).

6 Cousins wrote: "In the midst of its charm and sweetness I was assaulted in my heart by the tragedy of premature motherhood....' I was revolted by the slavery and indignity put on womanhood by the inconsiderate domination of men, and there grew within me a determination to do all I could to forward all circumstances calculated to bring women into public and particularly legislative life" (Cousins & Cousins 1950:331).

7 They were Kamaladevi Chattopadyaya, a South Indian (married to the Bengali poet, Harindranath Chattopadyaya, brother of Sarojini Naidu) and Hannah Angelo, the Secretary of the Nurses Association in Madras. After both lost, Cousins lobbied for the nomination of Kamaladevi and three other women to the Legislative Council. Kamaladevi was considered to be "a possibly dangerous revolutionary" and was over-

looked in favor of Dr Muttulakshmi Reddy (Ramusack 1981a:128). Dr. Reddy, who was a close friend of Cousins, became a leading voice in the Madras legislature, agitating on many social reform issues, including child marriage and temple prostitution.

8 The Indian delegates included Sarojini Naidu, the best-known Indian woman political activist, and two pioneer women legislative councillors, Dr. Muttulakshmi Reddy of Madras State and Dr. Poonen Lukhose of Travancore State, who had also served as the Minister of Health for three years. The Ceylon (Sri Lankan) delegation was led by Lady Daisy Dias Bandaranaike of the Women's Franchise Union, grandmother of Chandrika Kumaratunga, who became the country's President in November 1994.

9 Other resolutions were passed on the need for free and compulsory primary education for both sexes; a comparative study of world religions in order to promote "harmony among communities," support of the League of Nations, better health facilities and the promotion of campaigns against drink and drugs (All-Asian Women's Conference; 1931, Lahore).

CHAPTER II

1 Several British women in India were well-known novelists, poets and writers; among them was Flora Annie Steel (1847–1929) who wrote short stories and novels, the most successful was one about the 1857 rebellion called *On the Face of the Waters* (1896), which shows "more than usual insight and sympathy into the lives of her Indian characters" (Paxton 1990:337).

2 As Bader wrote (on sati), "Ardent piety, spiritual and ascetic tenderness, complete negation of herself, unlimited devotion to family, a boundless need for love formed the character of such women" (Bader quoted in Chakravarti 1989: 46).

3 Rhys Davids devoted his life, after retiring from the Ceylon Civil Service, to Buddhist studies, and formed the Pali Text Society. He taught Pali and Buddhist literature at University College, London and in 1907 he and others formed the Buddhist Society of Great Britain and Ireland (Wickremeratne 1985:198).

4 Caroline Rhys Davids writes of "The bereaved mother, the childless widow...emancipated from grief and contumely...the wife of the raja...from the satiety and emptiness of an idle life, the poor man's wife from care and drudgery, the young girl from the humiliation of being handed over to the suitor who bids highest, the thoughtful woman from the ban imposed upon her intellectual development by convention and tradition (Rhys Davids 1909: xxiv).

5 Praising "the singular character of Tibetan women" and their "tranquil courage," David-Néel wrote: "Very few Western women would dare to live in the desert in groups of four or five or sometimes quite alone. Few would dare under such conditions to undertake journeys infested with wild beasts and brigands" (David-Néel 1978: 50–51).

6 In 1907 and 1908, Dharmapala received individual contributions of $1,000 which enabled him to buy a two-storeyed house for the Maha Bodhi Society in the heart of Calcutta for Rs.11,000; it was the Foster donation that gave the society its first permanent premises. Foster also gave Rs. 30,000 to the Vihara Fund for the building in the mid-1920s of a Vihara temple in Saranath, India, one of the places sacred to Buddhism (Guruge 1965: 740).

7 When the First World War broke out, Dharmapala invested Rs. 18,000 from the Foster Fund and Rs. 9,000 from the Vihara Fund in war bonds, also giving a donation of Rs. 1,000 to the Carmichael War Fund on behalf of the Maha Bodhi Society (Guruge 1965: 734). In 1928 the Foster Fund totalled Rs. 391,000 (Maha Bodhi Society Report, 1928).

8 Coomaraswamy's second wife was Alice Richardson, one of his pupils, who took on the

name Ratan Devi, and became known for her recitals of Indian music and song around 1912 to 1916, which were praised by Tagore and Yeats (Lipsey 1977:92). His third marriage to the American painter Stella Bloch also ended in divorce in 1930, and that year he married an Argentinean Dona Luisa Runstein, who worked in Boston as a photographer. Their marriage lasted until his death in 1947 (ibid: 92, 161–62).

CHAPTER 13

1 Noble studied at the Congregational College at Halifax; in 1866 she began to teach in Wrexham, a mining town, and to write for the local newspapers on poverty, especially among women (Foxe 1975:12–15).

2 Vivekananda admired the material development and technology of the West, while being appalled by its inhumanity, violence and arrogance. He met William James, Max Müller, and liberal theologians and dissident Socialists like Edward Carpenter, while lecturing and giving courses on Hinduism to Westerners who were interested in comparative religion.

3 "You have not the capacity to manufacture a needle, and you dare to criticise the English! Fools! Sit at their feet and learn their arts and industries." He believed that the country had to be cleansed of caste, irrational practices, blind orthodoxy in religion and stagnation in national life. Both Western and Eastern attitudes were needed, "for they were complementary, awaiting the word to unite them…, and it was he, who was to open the path to union" (Rolland 1984:106).

4 Vivekananda wrote, "If the Brahmin has more aptitude for learning on the ground of heredity than the Pariah, spend no more money on the Brahmin's education, but spend all on the Pariah. Give to the weak, for there the gift is needed" (Rolland 1984:112).

5 As Foxe notes, "She went on lecturing, writing letters to the papers, appealing for funds, rolling up her sleeves and supervising…striding into houses where she was asked for help" (1975:78).

6 The day began with Sanskrit prayers and the singing of *Bande Mataram* (I salute the Mother), later to become a prohibited political slogan and the anthem of the independence struggle in India. The children were taught a variety of handicrafts (drawing, clay modelling, mat weaving, paper cutting and sewing) as well as Bengali, English, arithmetic, geography, history and games (Foxe 1975:158–64).

7 As Vivekananda had advised: "Let your girls draw and model and paint their ideal of the gods; gather all sorts of animals; cows, dogs, cats, birds. Revive old arts, and sewing, embroidery, filigree…serve humanity, pay homage to beggars and sick babies and poor women every day as a practical training of heart and head together (Reymond 1953:166).

8 It was clear from letters to her friends that Nivedita's devotion to Vivekananda bordered on the obsessive. For example, describing a lecture given by Vivekananda in New York in 1900, she writes: "Then as we sat and waited for him to come in, a great trembling came over me, for I realised that this was…one of the test moments of my life…my own life…where was it? Lost, thrown away like a cast off garment that I might kneel at the feet of this man (Ananyananda 1983:285).

9 In 1908, Nivedita stated, "Rightly considered, the home was a cloister, the Hindu woman a nun, giving her wifely and maternal duties all the devotion which the nun bestowed…in her worship of the Madonna" (Ramusack 1987:5).

10 "Long ago, when a child's solemn betrothal often took place at seven or eight years of age, it was to gratify the old people's desire to have more children about them…it was she who comforted "the minute grand daughter-in-law in her hours of homesickness"

(Nivedita 1988, Vol.II:29–30).

11 "Few books offer such delight to their readers as that known as the 'Laws of Manu'....
The conception of domestic happiness which they reveal is very complete, and no one
who has seen the light on an Indian woman's face when she turns to her husband can
doubt that the conception is often realised in life" (Nivedita 1988, Vol.II:36–37).

12 Nivedita notes that "there is no other rite to be compared in depth to that which binds
together the mother and her child...with the coming of her first-born...the young wife
has advanced, as it were, out of the novitiate...." (Nivedita 1988, Vol.II:17).

13 "There is no excuse made for the sin of abandoning the husband, and deserting the burdens and responsibilities of wifehood. If one does this, the East never plays with the idea
that she may have fled from the intolerable, but holds her gravely responsible for all the
ensuing social confusion" (Nivedita 1982a, Vol.IV:251–52).

14 Nivedita wrote, "The inviolability of the marriage tie has nothing whatever to do with
attraction and mutual love. Once a wife, always a wife...her feet should be ready at all
times to go forth on any path, even that of death, as the companion of her husband.
These things constitute the purity of the wife in India" (Nivedita 1988, Vol.II:25).

15 Bharathi dedicated his collection of poems, *Janmabhumi* (1909), to Nivedita, saying, "she is
my guru, who enabled me to realise the nobility of the ascetic life and the dignity of
labouring for the Mother." His poem *Nivedita Devi* compares Nivedita to the image of a
sun dispelling darkness, and fire that destroys slavery (Mahadevan 1957).

16 Isherwood notes, "the unpleasant and the pleasant are equally real (or unreal)...Kali...is
Shakthi...the Power which both creates and destroys.... The Mother and the Destroyer,
giver of life and death, blessings and misfortunes, pleasures and pains"(1980:51). Another
aspect of Kali is that of "abnegation of the male"; she is depicted with decapitated heads of
men in her hands and trampling the male under her feet. "Here then is the reverse of
the Vedic rituals, the mother goddess is all powerful, the male is crushed" (Obeyesekere
1984:443–44).

17 Valentine Chirol, in a book on Indian unrest, mentions the invocation of Kali in the
Bengali press to arouse hostility to British rule (Payne 1933:104).

18 Nivedita wrote, "Yet again shall come the great re-establishment of Dharma when the
whole of this nation shall be united together, in a great...ever strong, consciousness of
the common nationality, the common heritage, the common struggle" (Foxe 1975:155).

19 In London, Nivedita's friends included Kropotkin, Gokhale, R.C. Dutt, Bipin Chandra
Pal, Ananda Coomaraswamy, Wilfrid Scawen Blunt, and British politicians such as Keir
Hardie and others who were interested in India. Foxe notes that "inevitably there were
rumours that dark political deeds were afoot. But in fact it was a time of discussion and
rallying" (1975:196).

20 G.S. Ray Choudhury alleges that Aurobindo's revolutionary group (Anusilan Samiti)
was actually Sister Nivedita's party, since "it was she and not Aurobindo who conducted the working and training of the secret revolutionary party because she knew the
techniques of it," adding that Nivedita, "before coming in contact with the Swami...was
a dangerous anarchist. We have heard that she was a nihilist of the worst type. What she
was, she again became, after the Swami's death" (Chatterjee 1968:222).

CHAPTER 14

1 An admirer of British liberalism, Gandhi was also influenced by dissident thinkers, among
them Thoreau, who advocated civil disobedience, Ruskin, who believed that the "good
life" was to be found in the practice of crafts and agriculture; and Tolstoy, who repudiat-

ed violence and lived like a peasant. Gandhi's first community project in South Africa was named Tolstoy Farm.

2 Schreiner wrote to Gandhi, "Surely you, who would not take up arms even in the cause of your own oppressed people cannot be willing to shed blood in this wicked cause" (First and Scott 1980:304).

3 Gandhi replied, "You are welcome…only please remember that the life at the Ashram is not all rosy…. Bodily labour is given by every inmate. The climate…is also not a small consideration. I mention these things not to frighten you, but merely to warn you" (Mira Behn 1960:63).

4 "My job was to see that Bapu's personal routine went on smoothly and in the midst of all this rush…to see that water was heated…and that the bathroom was clean, then one inquired for the goat's milk and vegetables" (Mira Behn 1960:104).

5 Romain Rolland called her "proud of figure, with the stately bearing of a Demeter" (Morton 1953:192–93).

6 As Mira Behn recalled, "The meetings and receptions continued without a break, also every sort of question was asked…while the political aspect, so much to the fore in England, was of secondary importance. Gandhi the man, the Apostle of Truth, was what they sought" (1960:187–88).

7 Outstanding Indian women around Gandhi included Prabhavati, wife of the Indian socialist leader Jaiprakash Narayan, and Rajkumari Amrit Kaur (who was active in the women's movement) and also helped in Gandhi's secretarial work.

8 "When the camp opened and training began I took on the job of guidance and inspection of sanitation, clothes washing, and a little instruction in horse riding and bicycling" (Mira Behn 1960:226).

9 Mira Behn argued that "If things go on as they are going, the peasants of Orissa will garland the Japanese when they land…. The people with whom you associate…are out of touch with the masses…. What do your Knights and Barons of the Viceroy's Council count for? Nothing!…You are faced with two alternatives; one to declare India's Independence, and the other to kill Gandhiji, and once you kill him you kill for ever all hope of friendship between India and England" (1960:236–37).

CHAPTER 15

1 *Bhawani Mandhir* was to be a religious and political training center with "spiritual exercises…given almost as much importance as bomb manufacture." It marked, as Sarkar says, the beginning of "the metamorphosis of Aurobindo from revolutionary leader into mystic guru," and as a secular revolutionary, Hemachandra Kanungo, observed, "the means to the end of political emancipation was turning into an end in itself" (Sarkar 1977:486). Writing of the use of religion by political extremists, Lord Ronaldshay claimed that Aurobindo "did more than anyone to breathe into the sinister spectre of anarchy the vitalising influence of religion" (Payne 1933:103–105).

2 In 1907, Aurobindo successfully lobbied at the Indian National Congress for a resolution calling for independence as the goal of Congress, leading to a split between its "moderates" and "extremists."

3 In 1914, Aurobindo spoke of Paul Richard as "one of the Nivedita type, a brother in Yoga, who was practically an Indian in belief, culture and aspirations." Richard, he said, works for "a general renovation of the world by which the present European civilisation shall be replaced by a spiritual civilisation," adding that "he and Madame Richard are rare examples of European Yogins who have not been led away by Theosophical and other

aberrations" (Srinivasa Iyengar 1978, Vol. I:49).

4 James Cousins (See Chapter 10) recalls a conversation with some Japanese at Mirra Richard's home in Tokyo. "Politics were then at the top of the conversational bill. On that occasion I heard more socialism talked than I had done since my early twenties" (Cousins & Cousins 1950:352). Cousins returned to Madras via Colombo where he again met up with the Richards, who were on their way to Pondicherry (Cousins & Cousins 1950:380).

5 Every morning the Mother would appear for darshan (appearance in public), whereby, in her words, "after establishing a conscious contact with each of those who are present, I identify myself with the Supreme Lord and merge myself completely in Him." There were also special darshan days such as the birthdays of the Mother and Sri Aurobindo, when visitors were given a few minutes "to spend in the presence of the two avatars" (Wilfried 1986:43).

6 Aurobindo deplored the physical training as contemptible, the moral training as non-existent and the mental training as "meagre in quantity and worthless in quality, giving the student a store of facts and second-hand ideas" (Dowsett and Jayaswal 1974:43).

7 The student was encouraged "to learn by himself, choose his subject of study, progress at his own pace and ultimately take charge of his own development. The teacher is more an adviser and source of information than an instructor" (Patel 1986:86).

8 A French architect designed it and by 1967, a pioneer colony had been formed. In 1971, a huge "Matrumandir" in the form of a globe visible for miles was begun which was to be the "soul of Auroville," with a meditation hall inside. It remains uncompleted (Wilfried 1986:90).

CHAPTER 16

1 Among the world-famed Russian women revolutionaries were Vera Zazulich, who shot a Tsarist official in 1876; Vera Figner, who was part of a plot that killed a Tsarist General in 1881; and Sofya Perovskaya, who was hanged in 1881 for being a member of a group responsible for killing the Tsar Alexander II (Maxwell 1990).

2 Emma Goldman went to jail many times and in 1917 was tried for opposing the war and deported to the Soviet Union. She was later highly critical of the Soviet system and lived in other parts of Europe until her death in 1940.

3 In 1921 Kollontai was in the "Workers' Opposition" tendency in the Communist party against Lenin, and she also, in theory and practice, raised the issue of women's liberation. Another Russian revolutionary, Angelica Balabanoff (1878–1965), went to universities in Belgium and Italy and stayed on in Italy to become an important figure of the Italian Socialist party and a critic of the Soviet system (Mullaney 1983:Chapter IV).

4 As Angela Davis has written, Zetkin was "a pioneering theorist of women's status in capitalist society…(who) sought to understand the special oppression of women…and became one of the outstanding Communist leaders in the decades surrounding the October Revolution" (Foner 1984:9).

5 Luxemburg, born in Poland, studied in Switzerland and Germany and became an active leader of the German Social Democratic Party. The left opposition led by Luxemburg and Karl Liebknecht formed the Spartacist group, which was involved in an attempted revolution in 1919. This failed, ending in their murder by state forces.

6 Mother Mary Jones moved with the wives of workers and organized a children's march to Washington in 1903 to highlight the plight of child labor. She continued to organize strikers, and was active in Socialist politics even after she was over eighty.

7   Several Irish women, all feminists in their own way, including Margaret Noble, Annie Besant and Margaret Cousins had made the important decision to devote their energies to the re-awakening and eventual liberation of India.

8   Philip Gunewardena's sister Caroline acknowledged Bilstad's existence and gave me the first clues. I also found a few details about her through the University of Wisconsin Archives and through conversations with Bilstad's relatives in Cambridge, Wisconsin. I also thank Philip's daughter, Lakmali Gunewardena for her help.

9   I thank Alys Faiz of Lahore for this information.

10 The de Silvas co-authored two books, one on Poland, *Peace on the Vistula*, and the other, *American Friends*, described as "biographies of leading American warmongers." In 1953 Rhoda produced a pamphlet on the execution of Julius and Ethel Rosenberg called *The Rosenbergs—what was their crime?*

11 Rhoda de Silva challenged its legality and won a case against Pan American Airlines on which she had been deported. On arrival in New York at the height of the Macarthy witch-hunts against Communists, she was interviewed by a *New York Times* journalist who asked if she was a Communist; she refused to confirm or deny it, calling herself "a kid-napee of the American Government" *(New York Times,* 20 March 1954). Deported at the same time was Claudine Leibowitz, a Belgian, who lived with an Estonian painter Karl Kassman in Sri Lanka. Both were involved in Communist politics, and although Claudine made a marriage of convenience with a local Communist party activist in order to obtain citizenship she was expelled from Sri Lanka. The suspicions of the local Communist Party that Rhoda was a spy were unfounded (personal communication with Communist Party veteran leader Pieter Keuneman, October 1994).

12 Born in Kent, England in 1924, Jeanne Hoban had joined the Communist party in her youth and was an organizer in the Transport and General Workers' Union.

13 The local Trotskyist party leader referred her case to the Prime Minister and warned him that there would be major political protests if she were deported (personal communication with Jeanne Moonesinghe).

14 Jeanne Moonesinghe was active in the LSSP (a Trostkyist Party) and was assistant secretary of the Ceylon Mercantile Union. She was dismissed for her trade union links and subsequently led a strike of machine shop workers in *Lake House*, the leading newspaper group in the island.

CHAPTER 17

1   Details are from Sibnarayan Ray (1987) and personal communication from the Registrar, Stanford University, 28 September 1989, and notes in the Evelyn Trent Jones Collection at the Hoover Institute, Stanford.

2   An American Socialist described Roy at that time as "tall, with long, slim, expressive hands...and black eyes that flashed frequent wrath out of a dark face" (Ray 1987, Vol.1:14–15).

3   Attempts were made to smuggle German arms to Bengal through a shipment from California via Java, and M.N. Roy left for Java in 1915. Roy returned to India with no arms, but some German money. On a second trip to Java, the arms did not arrive and Roy decided not to return to India, arriving in California in 1916 (Overstreet & Windmiller 1959:20–21).

4   M.N. Roy was less enthusiastic than Lenin about the potential of nationalism and claimed that "the real strength of the liberation movements in the colonies is no longer confined to the narrow circle of bourgeois democratic nationalists. In most of the colonies there

already exist organized revolutionary parties.... But if from the outset the leadership is in the hands of the Communist vanguard, the revolutionary masses will not be led astray" (Overstreet & Windmiller 1959:29–30).

5 Lajpat Rai was an early Indian nationalist who had come to the United States in 1914 and remained there for five years, popularizing the cause of India among the American public, and winning support among Irish Americans, liberals, Socialists, feminists, and journalists such as Oswald Garrison Villard who gave him access to *The Nation* (MacKinnon & MacKinnon 1988:37).

6 Chattopadyaya's father, a nationalist, was also a very Westernized person who was principal of a college in Hyderabad where Islamic influences were strong. His sister Sarojini Naidu was a leading figure in the Indian National Congress and its best-known woman; and his brother Harindranath, a writer and poet, was active in Communist organizations along with his wife Kamaladevi, one of the foremost women leftists of the pre-independence period (MacKinnon & MacKinnon 1988:70).

7 In Berlin, Chattopadyaya worked with the Germans to mobilize Indians abroad against British rule and to send money and arms to revolutionaries in India. He was the co-ordinator of the Berlin Indian Revolutionary Committee, which included Bhupendra Nath Dutta (brother of Swami Vivekananda), described by the British as "one of the most dangerous revolutionaries Bengal has produced" (Petrie 1972:309).

8 As a non-Indian and a woman, Smedley was highly vulnerable, and from the beginning she became a chief target for attack. Roy accused her not only of immorality but also of stirring up opposition to him and probably working as a spy for the British. This led Smedley to exclaim, "Think of it—not even an American spy—but a British one!!!" (MacKinnon & MacKinnon 1988:72–73)

9 The British police in the 1920s described Evelyn Roy as a "prolific writer of Communist pamphlets," noting that she "is said to be a cleverer and more capable Communist than Roy himself" (Petrie 1972:335). Abdul Qadir Khan, who worked in Tashkent with the Roys, later recalled that M.N. Roy derived his communism "mainly from his gifted Californian wife Evelyn Roy" (Overstreet & Windmiller 1959:35–36).

10 In 1921, Evelyn Roy unsuccessfully tried to get an Indian woman to participate in the International Women's Conference in Moscow; among Indian women known to Evelyn Roy was Prabhabati Das Gupta, who was associated with Indian revolutionaries in the United States. Police reports said, "she was on very friendly terms with Mrs. Roy to whom she gave a list of addresses in America to which copies of the *Vanguard* could be sent" (Petrie 1972:308).

11 In New York Smedley knew Margaret Sanger and other feminists and, in Germany she was helped and supported by many independent women friends, including actresses, political activists, psychoanalyists, artists (Kathe Kollowitz), and feminists such as Dr. Helena Lange, founder in Germany of the first girls high school (see MacKinnon & MacKinnon 1988:32, 129, 127).

12 Smedley even had to repay money owed by Indians to others, on the ground that the honor of India was at stake. "The honor of India be damned!" she wrote. "It came out of my body, and never did I have one second of rest and peace trying to do my housework and at the same time trying to make extra money writing" (MacKinnon & MacKinnon 1988:81).

13 As the MacKinnons noted, "Indian men dodged the problem of birth control in India by writing abstractly about the geopolitical concerns of the issues, much to Smedley's chagrin" (1988:114).

14 Smedley's articles may have had some impact, for when Margaret Sanger traveled to India in 1935, on the invitation of the All-India Women's Conference, the climate of opinion on the issue had changed; Sanger was greeted with great warmth by Indian political leaders and the medical profession, but Gandhi, whom she tried to convince, advocated abstinence instead of birth control (Lader:1975:289).

15 Smedley contrasted the Indian leaders (in India) "poisoned by their English education (and) an English interpretation of world events," with Indian revolutionaries abroad who could see "the world situation through Indian eyes." Lajpat Rai replied "Miss Smedley is mistaken if she thinks we are all babies and do not understand even elementary politics," while Chattopadyaya's sister-in-law Kamaladevi attacked Smedley for her dogmatism. The tension eased when Lajpat Rai apologized (MacKinnon & MacKinnon 1988:124–25). In later years Kamaladevi was close to Smedley and wrote warmly about her courage. (Chattopadyaya 1986:57)

16 Smedley said that Mayo "displayed a remarkable genius for meeting English men and women who could show her the darkest side of India…for picking out just those Indians who are bootlickers…for meeting Indian princes who are such noble chaps…or extracting passages from books…damning India and lauding British rule." She also noted that "long before Miss Mayo went to India," she and Indian progressives had condemned social evils, such as child marriage, womens' seclusion and enforced widowhood, adding that "England should get off India's back. Slavery produces…ignorance, bigotry, cruelty, superstition." She also denounced Mayo as a believer in "Nordic supremacy" with "nothing but contempt for the national movement" (Smedley 1927:26).

17 In his memoirs, written in the 1950s, Roy is harsh on Smedley, but generous to his old enemy Chattopadyaya, and one senses a feeling of Bengali male-bonding. "Chatto," he writes, was "a restless soul of indomitable energy" whose "unconcealed hostility" to Roy in Moscow was puzzling, and was due to Smedley poisoning his mind. "She seemed to believe that to fall in love with famous Indian Revolutionaries would be the expression of her loyalty to India" (Roy 1964:291, 487).

18 On Zetkin's sixty-fifth birthday, Roy was chosen by the President of the Comintern to move a resolution congratulating her (Ray 1988 Vol.II:307).

19 It was attended by many non-Communists such as Nehru, Bertrand Russell, Henri Barbusse, Romain Rolland and Mme. Sun Yat Sen; Chattopadyaya became the League's executive secretary (MacKinnon & MacKinnon 1988:117–18).

20 Ironically, this group had been the majority in the Communist Party in 1929 but having been accused of right-wing deviation had been expelled from the Communist International (Comintern) and replaced by a minority group led by William Foster, more submissive to the discipline of the Comintern in Moscow.

21 Evelyn Roy claimed that "his was the first voice raised along Marxist lines in India and he…is responsible for the tremendous awakening and change that has overswept the national revolutionary movement in the last ten years—a change towards internationalism and Marxism" (E. Roy 1931).

22 Jones was a journalist in Sacramento and had earlier run his own newspaper in Sierra Madre; he also held various jobs in California in the State Emergency Relief Administration and the State Department of Employment. During 1938–39, Evelyn also worked as a free-lance writer for these organizations. (Evelyn Trent Jones Collection, Hoover Institute, Stanford).

23 Indian Communists and American scholars frequently asked Evelyn to comment on M.N. Roy and write her memoirs, but she was sensitive and reticent about this phase of

her life, insisted on complete anonymity, and never wanted to be quoted. To a Stanford Professor she wrote, "As I read these scholarly tomes, I wonder which is more exhausting, to have lived through some of these experiences, or to have done research to write about them" (Letter of 7 March 1960 in Evelyn Trent Jones Collection Hoover Institute, Stanford).

24 Louise's sister Eva lived with A.C.N. Nambiar, a famous leftwing Indian residing in Berlin in the late 1920s. Louise Geissler came to India in 1931, but was forced by the British to leave (Ray 1979:27–29, and personal communication from Prof. S. Ray, 28 October 1990).

CHAPTER 18

Parts of this chapter have appeared in a pamphlet, *Doreen Wickremasinghe—A Western Radical in Sri Lanka,* Women's Research and Education Centre, Colombo, 1991. Much of this chapter is based on interviews with Doreen Wickremasinghe and Hedi Stadlen.

1 Weare left school at age nine; his childhood was "without joy and brightness, with little love, often without bread, or boots or fire to keep him warm." Being also a devout Christian at the time, Weare attended Sunday school, and using Cassells's "Self-educator," he taught himself geography, history, French, science and literature. As a young man he also became a Sunday School teacher and member of a Mutual Improvement Society run by the Church (Young 1922).

2 Young started working, at age eleven, delivering telegrams; he worked in many parts of Britain, and in South Africa (during the Boer war), retiring as post-master of York. He wrote a book about Robert Weare, and traveled extensively in India and Sri Lanka in 1932–33 with his wife. He was one of the pioneers of postal trade unionism and was the national representative of the Postal Clerks' Association, at the same time being active in the Labour Party.

3 Many future Labour leaders, including Ramsay McDonald (Labour Prime Minister in 1924 and 1931), Ben Tillet (the trade union leader) and several future Labour M.Ps had been part of the Bristol Socialist group, which had several remarkable feminists, Miriam David, Helena Born (a writer), Katherine Conway (a classics teacher) and Enid Stacey a popular lecturer on Socialism.

4 "It was a very lively place…among the people I personally remember were Bruce Glacier, Kate (Conway) Glacier, Bob Gilliard, Edward Carpenter, Robert Sharland, Dan Irwing, Will Petherick and Charlie Sixsmith…the Clarion Club and its publication 'The Clarion' was a force in our home" (personal communication from Doreen Wickremasinghe, January 17, 1988).

5 Wickremasinghe was influenced by its British principal, a theosophist and Pali scholar (F.L. Woodward) and by the Vice-Principal (F. Gordon Pearce) who had been a British Labour Party supporter.

6 Some of the Jewish women included a theosophist, Paula Kemperling, née Stein, a refugee from Vienna who came to Sri Lanka around 1940 and taught in a Buddhist girls school; Anne Ranasinghe, née Katz, a refugee from Germany, who married a Sri Lankan doctor and is today a well-known poet; Edith Gymroi Ludowyk, a psychoanalyst, known in left circles in Budapest in the 1930s, who arrived in Sri Lanka in 1938 and married a Sri Lankan Professor of English; Rhoda Miller de Silva (of the United States), a journalist, and Claudine Leibowitz (from Belgium), who were close to the Communists in Sri Lanka in the 1950s and were deported by the government; Ruth Prawer Jhabwala, a refugee from Germany to Britain, who married an Indian architect and is now famous internationally for her novels set in India, and her film scripts.

7 In 1918, after the collapse of the Austro-Hungarian Empire, the new Republic of Austria came into being. Soon after, there were unsuccessful Communist revolutions in 1919 in Germany and Hungary, and attempts in Austria by Communists to gain power. While there were non-Socialist governments in power between 1920 and 1927, Vienna remained a stronghold of the Socialists. They concentrated on ambitious working-class housing, health and adult education measures which were financed by heavy property taxes. "Red Vienna" became the showpiece of Europe, but the success was short-lived. Civil war, the defeat of the Socialists and Fascist ascendancy finally led to *anschluss*, incorporation with Germany in 1938.

8 A pupil of the school recalled in later years the influence of these teachers, and especially Doreen Wickremasinghe who "introduced so many progressive reforms that left their indelible mark on the pupils...senior pupils received a training which few other schools would dare give at a time when public opinion was very conservative." (Gladys Abeysekera in *Ceylon Daily News,* March 13, 1987).

9 For example, in 1934, when Rabindranath Tagore came to Colombo with his students (singers and dancers) from Santiniketan, they used to have their meals at the school and the teachers and girls of Ananda Balika looked after the Indians during their stay. The Wickremasinghes had even earlier been frequent visitors to India. In 1932, at the height of Indian agitation led by Gandhi, along with Doreen's parents, they visited India, met Gandhi in jail and also visited Tagore at Santiniketan and Annie Besant in Adyar.

10 Terrence de Zylva, writing on the Suriya Mal movement in 1932, called for the establishment of a "Socialist Democratic Ceylon" *(The Searchlight,* October 18, 1933), and Leslie Goonewardena, in 1933, stated that money should not be sent to help the British Empire "wage wars for the purpose of partitioning the world" (*Young Ceylon,* October 1935).

11 She returned to Sri Lanka and for a time worked at Dr. Wickremasinghe's hospital and dispensary in Matara, but finally decided to settle down in Britain.

12 The issue of whether Keuneman should marry Hedi Simon had been a political question. As Hedi recalls: "It was discussed within the colonial section of the party whether it was advisable for Pieter Keuneman to bring home a European wife, whether that might not harm his work in the party and among the wider sections of the people—but I believe that my commitment to the cause was taken to be so total that permission was granted" (personal communication, December 1990).

13 The Modern School had around fifty pupils ranging from ages four to nine, and evening classes for older students doing public examinations; many of the children at the school were from families of left and liberal professionals and political activists who appreciated the benefits of a school which was "progressive" in both its educational methods and political ambiance.

14 Hedi recalls, "I was, therefore, able to address meetings in English. I worked in the reading room and library helping with the publication of journals and leaflets and traveled outside Colombo to other centres in order to widen membership. I loved doing this since it gave me an opportunity to stay at the homes of supporters and make many friends" (personal communication, December 1990).

15 Hedi writes, "I remember this as perhaps the most satisfying work I did because it made a genuine contribution to help the local population to get a fair supply of foodstuffs with their coupons. The chief enemies were the black marketeers and I remember arriving at our co-op very early, long before opening time every morning, in order to prevent illegal black market dealings in food" (personal communication, December 1990).

16 I thank Eric Hobsbawm (who knew Hedi Simon in Cambridge in the 1930's) for telling

me that she was alive and well in London. I met Hedi and wrote an article about her in a Sri Lankan paper (the *Sunday Island*) on 6th January 1991, her seventy-fifth birthday. After this, the newspaper received many letters about her from enthusiastic readers who had fond memories of Hedi Keuneman. One Sri Lankan recalled Hedi and Pieter Keuneman surrounded by a crowd outside the main railway station of Colombo when they were promoting alternative cereals to rice as a part of the war effort: "It was not the usual pavement astrologer, musician or the snake-bite specialist, but a diminutive lady clad in a cheap cotton sari and...a tall young man in shirt and shorts. They were serving a steaming cereal to the people around them.... I was simply thrilled and spent a considerable length of time watching the humanitarian drama" (G. Nanayakkara, *Sunday Island*, 20 January 1991).

17 The EKP stated that a large rural women's organization—the Lanka Mahila Samiti, functioned "in the village economy of a slave colony" and while praising it for trying to uplift women (helping them to cultivate vegetables, sew, weave and make lace), it pointed out the limitations of such work. "We consider that even the most prosperous village where every plan and endeavour of the Mahila Samiti has flourished and borne maximum results will still leave our sisters living in conditions unacceptable to us in a world of scientific discovery and achievement in social organization" (*Times of Ceylon*, 30 January 1948).

BIBLIOGRAPHY

Ahmad, Muzaffar. 1962. *The Communist Party of India and Its Formation Abroad*. Calcutta: National Book Agency. (Pvt) Ltd.

All-Asian Women's Conference. 1931. "Proceedings of the Conference." Lahore.

American Ceylon Mission. 1839 April and 1843 July. *First and Second Reports of the Female Boarding Schools at Oodooville*. Jaffna, Press of the American Mission. (1843 Oct.), *First Report of the Female Boarding School at Varany*. Jaffna: Press of the American Mission.

American Ramabai Association—See Ramabai Assocation.

Ananyananda, Swami. 1983. *Reminiscences of Swami Vivekananda*. Calcutta: Advaita Ashrama.

Annan, Noel. 1990. *Our Age: Portrait of a Generation*. London: Weidenfeld & Nicholson.

Anthias, Floya and Nira Yuval-Davis. 1983. "Contextualizing Feminism—Gender, Ethnic and Class Divisions," in *Feminist Review*, No. 15. London: Feminist Review Collective.

Anzaldua, Gloria. 1990. *Making Face, Making Soul, Creative and Critical Perspectives by Feminists of Color*. San Francisco: Aunt Lute Books.

Aurobindo, Sri. *Collected Works* in 30 Volumes. Pondicherry: Sri Aurobindo Ashram.

———. 1986. *Sri Aurobindo and the Mother on Education*. Pondicherry: Sri Aurobindo Ashram.

Bacon, Margaret Hope. 1986. *Mothers of Feminism—The Story of Quaker Women in America*. San Francisco: Harper & Row.

Bader, Clarisse. 1964. *Women in Ancient India*. (1867), Varanasi: The Chowkhamba Sanskrit Series.

Baker, Frances J. 1898. *The Story of the Women's Foreign Missionary Society of the Methodist Episcopal Church 1869–1895*. Cincinnati: Curtis & Jennings.

Balfour, Margaret I. and Ruth Young. 1929. *The Work of Medical Women in India*. London: Oxford University Press.

Ballhatchet, Kenneth. 1980. *Race, Sex and Class under the Raj: Imperial Attitudes and Policies and Their Critics, 1793–1905*. London: Weidenfeld and Nicholson.

Banks, Olive. 1985. *The Biographical Dictionary of British Feminists 1830–1930*. New York: New York University Press.

———. 1986. *Faces of Feminism, 1986: A Study of Feminism as a Social Movement*. London: Basil Blackwell.

Barr, Pat. 1976. *The Memsahibs—The Women of Victorian India*. Bombay and London: Secker and Warburg.

Bartholomeusz, Tessa. 1994. *Women Under the Bo Tree—Buddhist Nuns in Sri Lanka*. Cambridge: Cambridge University Press.

Bax, Clifford, ed. 1946. *Florence Farr, Bernard Shaw, W.B. Yeats Letters*. London: Home & Van Thal Ltd.

Behn, Mira. 1960. *The Spirit's Pilgrimage*. London: Longmans, Green & Co.

Bernays, Robert. 1931. *Naked Fakir*. London: Victor Gollancz.

Besant, Annie. 1879. *Marriage As It Was, As It Is, And As It Will Be*. New York: A.K. Butts.

———. 1901. *Ancient Ideals in Modern Life*. London and Benares: The Theosophical Publishing Society.

———. 1904. "The Education of Indian Girls." Pamphlet reprinted in Besant (1913).

———. 1913. *Essays and Addresses Vol. IV, INDIA*. London and Madras: The Theosophical Publishing Society.

———. 1914. "Women and Politics." London: The Theosophical Society.

———. 1984. *An Autobiography*. (1893). Madras: The Theosophical Publishing Society.

Beveridge, William. 1947. *India Called Them*. London: George Allen and Unwin.

Blake, Susan L. 1990. "'A Woman's Trek': What Difference Does Gender Make?" in *Women's Studies International Forum*, Vol 13, No. 4.Tarrytown, NY: Pergamon Press.

Blavatsky, H.P. 1973. "The Women of Ceylon as compared to Christian Women" (1889). In *Collected Writings Vol. XI*. Illinois: The Theosophical Publishing House.

——. 1975. "On Child Marriage" (1879). In *Collected Writings From the Caves and Jungles of Hindustan*. Illinois: The Theosophical Publishing House.

Blaze, B.R. 1948. *The Life of Lorenz*. Colombo: Associated Newspapers of Ceylon.

Bose, Mihir. 1982. *The Lost Hero: a Biography of Subhas Chandra Bose*. London: Quartet Books.

Bracegirdle Commission. (1938). Report of Ceylon Sessional Paper No. 18.

Brande, Ann. 1989. *Radical Spirits—Spiritualism and Women's Rights in Nineteenth-Century America*. Boston: Beacon Press.

Burfield, Diana. 1983. "Theosophy and Feminism." In *Women's Religious Experience*,. ed. Pat Holden. London: Croom Helm.

Burke, Marie Louise. 1958. *Swami Vivekananda in America*. Calcutta: Adraita Ashram.

Burman, Debajyoti. 1968. "Sister Nivedita and Indian Revolution." In *Nivedita Commemoration Volume*, ed. A.K. Mazumdar. Calcutta: Vivekananda Janmotsava Samiti.

Burton, Antoinette M. 1991. "The Feminist Quest for Identity: British Imperial Suffragism and 'Global Sisterhood', 1990–1915." *Journal of Women's History*, Vol.3, No.2. (Fall).

——. 1992. "The White Woman's Burden—British Feminists and the Indian Woman, 1865—1915." In *Western Women and Imperialism, Complicity and Resistance*. Chaudhuri and Strobel, eds. Bloomington: Indiana University Press.

Butler, Clementine. 1922. *Pandita Ramabai Sarasvati*. New York: Revell and Co.

Butler, Mrs. F.A. 1904. *History of the Women's Foreign Missionary Society*. Nashville, Tennessee: Publishing House of the M.E. Church, South.

Capucin Mission Unit, Maryland. 1923. *India and Its Missions*. New York: MacMillan.

Carmichael, Amy Wilson. 1903 and 1906. *Things as They Are—Mission Work in Southern India*. New York: Fleming H. Revell.

Carpenter, Mary. 1850. *The Last Days in England of Raja Rammohun Roy*. London: Trubner.

——. 1867. *Addresses to the Hindoos delivered in India by Mary Carpenter*. London: Longman's, Green and Co.

——. 1868. *Six Months in India*. London: Longman's, Green and Co.

Chakravarti, Uma. 1989. "Whatever Happened to the Vedic Dasi?" In *Recasting Women, Essays in Colonial History*, eds. Kumkum Sangari and Sudesh Vaid. Delhi: Kali for Women.

Chalmers, Lord Robert. 1937. "W.T. Rhys Davids." In *The Dictionary of National Biography 1922–30*. ed. J.R.H. Weaver. London: Oxford University Press.

Chamberlain, W.I. 1925. *Fifty Years in Foreign Fields*. New York: Women's Board of Foreign Missions.

Chapman, Priscilla. 1839. *Hindoo Female Education*. London: R.B. Seeley.

Chatterjee, Partha. 1989. "The Nationalist Resolution of the Women's Question." In *Recasting Women, Essays in Colonial History*, eds. Kumkum Sangari and Sudesh Vaid. Delhi: Kali for Women.

——. 1993. *The Nation and Its Fragments—Colonial and Postcolonial Histories*. Princeton, NJ: Princeton University Press.

Chatterjee, Rakhahari. 1968. "Sister Nivedita in the Back-ground of Contemporary Indian Politics." In *Nivedita Commemoration Volume*, ed. A.K. Mazumdar. Calcutta: Vivekananda Janmotsava Samiti.

Chattopadhyaya, Kamaladevi. 1986. *Inner Recesses Outer Space*. New Delhi: Navrang.

Chaudhuri, Nupur and Margaret Strobel. 1992. *Western Women and Imperialism, Complicity and Resistance*. Bloomington: Indiana University Press.

Choudhuri, Keshab. 1979. *The Mother and Passionate Politics*. Calcutta: Vidyodaya Library Ltd.

Clarke, A.K. 1953. *A History of the Cheltenham Ladies' College*. London: Faber and Faber.

Cole, G.D.H. 1947. *A Short History of the British Working-Class Movement*. London: George, Allen & Unwin.

Colmcille, Mother Mary. 1968. *First the Blade, History of the I.B.V.M. (Loreto) in India (1841–1962)*. Calcutta: Firma K.L. Mukhopadhyay.

Comaroff, Jean and John L. 1989. "The Colonization of Consciousness in South Africa." In *Economy and Society*, Vol. 18 No. 3. New York: Routledge.

Coomaraswamy, Ananda K. 1905. *Borrowed Plumes*. Kandy: Printed for the author at the Industrial School.

———. 1910. *The Oriental View of Woman*. Broad Campden: Essex House Press.

———. 1957. "The Status of Indian Women." In *The Dance of Shiva* (1924). New York: Noonday Press.

Coomaraswamy, Ethel. 1906. "The Education of Girls in Ceylon," *Journal of the Ceylon University Association*. Colombo.

Cousins, J.H. and Margaret. 1950. *We Two Together*. Madras: Ganesh.

Cousins, L. et al. 1974. *Buddhist Studies in Honour of I.B. Horner*. Dordrecht: D. Reidel Publishing Co.

Crawford, Allen. 1985. *C.R. Ashbee, Architect, Designer and Romantic Socialist*. New Haven: Yale University Press.

David-Néel, Alexandra. 1978. *Buddhism: its Doctrine and its Method*. London: Unwin Paperbacks.

Daly, Mary. 1978. *Gyn/Ecology: The Metaethics of Radical Feminism*. Boston: Beacon Press.

Delaveney, Emile. 1971. *D.H.Lawrence & Edward Carpenter, a Study in Edwardian Transition*. London: Heinemann.

Denham, E.B. 1912. *Ceylon at the Census of 1911*. Colombo: Government Printer.

Despard, C. 1913. *Theosophy and the Women's Movement*. London and Madras: The Theosophical Publishing Society.

Desroches, Henri. 1971. *The American Shakers—From Neo-Christianity to Pre-Socialism*. Amherst: University of Massachussetts Press.

Dickens, Charles. 1980. *Bleak House* (1853). New American Library.

Dictionary of National Biography. London: Oxford University Press.

Douglas, Norman. 1930. *How About Europe? Some Footnotes on East and West*. London: Private printing.

Dowsett, N.C. and S.R. Jayaswal. 1974. *The New Approach to Education*. Pondicherry: Sri Aurobindo Society.

Durai Raja Singham, S. 1974. *Ananda Coomaraswamy: Remembering and Remembering Again and Again*. Kuala Lumpur: Published by author.

———. 1977. "The Two Gekkos—Ananda and Ethel." In *Ananda Coomaraswamy—the Bridge Builder, A Study of a Scholar Colossus*. Kuala Lumpur: Published by author.

———. 1980. *Who is this Coomaraswamy?* Kuala Lumpur: Published by author.

Dyer, Helen. S. 1900. *Pandita Ramabai: The Story of Her Life*. New York: Fleming H. Revell Company.

Du Cann, C.G.L. 1963. *The Loves of George Bernard Shaw*. London: Arthur Barker Ltd.

Elliot, Elisabeth. 1987. *A Chance to Die—the Life and Legacy of Amy Carmichael*. New Jersey: Fleming H. Revell Company.

Ellman, Richard. 1988. *Yeats—the Man and the Masks*. London: Penguin Books.

Engels, Friedrich. 1972. *Socialism: Utopian and Scientific* (1882). New York: International Publishers.

Evans, Ernestine. 1922. "Looking East from Moscow." In *Asia, The American Magazine of the Orient*. New York: Asia Publishing Company.

Farquhar, J.N. 1915. *Modern Religious Movements in India*. New York: Macmillan.

Farr, Florence. 1910. *Modern Woman: Her Intentions*. London: Frank Palmer.

Fast, Howard. 1991. *Being Red—A Memoir*. Boston: Houghton Mifflin.

Field, H.H. 1929. *After Mother India*. New York: Harcourt, Brace & Co.

First, Ruth and Ann Scott. 1980. *Olive Schreiner*. London: Andre Deutsch Ltd.

Fischer, Louis. 1982. *The Life of Mahatma Gandhi*. London: Grafton Books.

Foote, G.W. 1889. *Mrs. Besant's Theosophy*. London: Progressive Publishing Co.

————. 1889. *The New Cagliostro: An Open Letter to Madame Blavatsky*. London: Progressive Publishing Co.

Foner, Philip S. 1984. *Clara Zetkin: Selected Writings*. New York: International Publishers.

Forbes, Geraldine H. 26 April 1986. "In Search of the 'Pure Heathen': Missionary Women in 19th Century India." In *Economic and Political Weekly*. Bombay: EPW Research Foundation.

Foxe, Barbara. 1975. *Long Journey Home—A Biography of Margaret Noble* (Nivedita). London: Rider & Co.

French, Harold W. 1974. *The Swan's Wide Waters, Ramakrishna and Western Culture*. National University Publications. Port Washington, NY: Kennikat Press.

Fuller, Jenny. 1899. *The Wrongs of Indian Womanhood*. New York: F.H.Revell & Co.

Gandhi, M.K. 1985. *An Autobiography* (1927). London: Penguin Books.

Geertz, Hildred, ed. 1976. *Letters of a Javanese Princess*. Hong Kong: Heinemann.

Ghadiali, D.P. 1929. *American Sex Problems*. Malaga and New Jersey: Spectro-chro Institute.

Gidumal, Dayaram. 1891. *Behramji M. Malabari, A Biographical Sketch*. London: T. F. Unwin.

Goonetileke, H.A.I. 1976. *Images of Sri Lanka Through American Eyes*. Colombo: United States Information Service.

Gopal, Ram. 1967. *How India Struggled for Freedom*. Bombay: The Book Centre.

Gunawardena, R.A.L.H. 1984. "The People of the Lion." In *Ethnicity and Social Change in Sri Lanka*. Colombo: Social Scientists' Association.

Guruge, A., ed. 1965. *Return to Righteousness*. Colombo: Department of Cultural Affairs.

Hackler, Rhoda. 1986. *A History of Foster Park and Garden*. Honolulu, Hawaii: The Friends of Foster Garden.

Haggis, Jane. 1990. "Gendering Colonialism or Colonising Gender?" In *Women's Studies International Forum*, Vol. 13, Nos. 1–2. Tarrytown, NY: Pergamon Press.

Haithcox, John Patrick. 1971. *Communism and Nationalism in India: M.N. Roy and Comintern Policy, 1920–1939*. New Jersey: Princeton University Press.

Handlin, Mary F. 1971. "Katherine Mayo." In *Notable American Women, A Biographical Dictionary Vol. 2*, E.T. James, J.W. James and P. Boyer, eds. Cambridge: Harvard University Press.

Hardesty, Nancy A. 1980. *Great Women of Faith*. Michigan: Baker Book House.

Harrison, Minnie Hastings. 1925. *Uduvil 1824–1924, Being the History of One of the Oldest Girls Schools in Asia*. Tellippalai: American Ceylon Mission Press.

Hill, Patricia R. 1985. *The World Their Household, The American Women's Foreign Mission Movement and Cultural Transformation 1870–1920*. Ann Arbor: University of Michigan Press.

Hitchcock, Olive. 1957. *A History of CMS Ladies' College*. Colombo: Published by the Principal, Ladies' College.

Hobsbawm, Eric. 1987. *The Age of Empire 1875–1914*. New York: Pantheon Books.

Hollis, Patricia. 1979. *Women in Public, The Women's Movement 1850–1900*. London: Allen and Unwin:

Holmes, John Haynes. 1950. *Gandhi's Letters to a Disciple*. New York: Harper.

Holroyd, Michael. 1988. *Bernard Shaw*, Vol. 1, 1856–1898, *The Search for Love*. London: Chatto and Windus.

Hone, Joseph. 1942. *W.B. Yeats, 1865–1939*. London: Macmillan.

hooks, bell. 1981. *Ain't I a Woman?* Boston: South End Press.

Horner, I.B. 1930. *Women Under Primitive Buddhism—Laywomen and Almswomen*. London: George

Routledge Ltd.

————. 1940. *Alice M. Cooke—A Memoir*. Manchester: Manchester University Press.

Howe, Ellic. 1972. *The Magicians of the Golden Dawn*. London: Routledge and Kegan Paul.

Hunter, Jane. 1984. *The Gospel of Gentility; American Women Missionaries in Turn-of-the-Century China*. New Haven: Yale University Press.

Iggledon, R.E. and C.W. 1974. "Isaline Blew Horner: A Biographical Sketch." In *Buddhist Studies in Honour of I.B. Horner*, L. Cousins et al., eds. Dordrecht: D. Reidel Publishing Co.

Isherwood, Christopher. 1980. *Ramakrishna and his Disciples*. Calcutta: Advaita Ashram.

James, E.T., J.W. James and P. Boyer. 1971. *Notable American Women A Biographical Dictionary, 1607–1950*. Cambridge: Harvard University Press.

Jayawardena, Kumari. 1972. *The Rise of the Labor Movement in Ceylon*. North Carolina: Duke University Press.

————. 1986. *Feminism and Nationalism in the Third World*. London: Zed Books.

————. 1988. "So Comrade, What Happened to the Democratic Struggle?" in *Economic & Political Weekly*, 8 Oct. 1988. Bombay: EPW Research Foundation.

————. 1991. *Doreen Wickremasinghe, A Western Radical in Sri Lanka*. Colombo: Women's Education and Research Centre.

————. 1992. "Sinhala Buddhism and the "Daughters of the Soil." In *Pravada*, Vol.1, No. 5, May 1992. Colombo: Pravada Publications.

————. 1993. *Dr. Mary Rutnam: Pioneer of Women's Rights in Sri Lanka*. Colombo: Social Scientists' Association.

Jayaweera, Swarna. 1990. "European Women Educators under the British Colonial Administration in Sri Lanka." In *Women's Studies International Forum*, Vol 13, No. 4. Tarrytown, NY: Pergamon Press.

Jeffery, Mary Pauline. 1938. *Dr. Ida: India, The Life Story of Ida S. Scudder*. New York: Fleming H. Revell Co.

Jha, M. 1971. *Katherine Mayo in India*. New Delhi: Peoples Publishing House.

Jinarajadasa, C. 1925. *The Golden Book of the Theosophical Society*. Madras: The Theosophical Publishing House.

Johnson, Josephine. 1975. *Florence Farr—Bernard Shaw's "New Woman."* Gerards Cross: Colin Smythe.

Joshi, Kireet. 1989. *Sri Aurobindo and the Mother*. Delhi: The Mother's Institute of Research.

Kabbani, Rana. 1986. *Europe's Myths of Orient*. Bloomington: Indiana University Press.

Karaka D.F. 1945. *I Go West* (1938). Bombay: M. Joseph, Ltd.

Kaye, Cecil. 1971. *Communism in India*. (1925). Subodh Roy, ed. Calcutta: Editions India.

Keshavmurti. 1969. *Sri Aurobindo, The Hope of Man*. Sri Aurobindo Publications, Pondicherry.

Kosambi, Meera. 1988. "Women, Emancipation and Equality: Pandita Ramabai's Contribution to Women's Causes." In *Economic and Political Weekly*, 29 Oct. 1988. Bombay: EPW Research Foundation.

Kramnick, Miriam, ed. 1975. *Woolstonecraft's Vindication of the Rights of Women*. London: Pelican Books.

Lader, Lawrence. 1975. *The Margaret Sanger Story*. Connecticut: Greenwood Press.

Lajpat Rai, L. 1928. *Unhappy India*. Calcutta: Banna Publishing Co.

Lasreg, Marnia. 1988. "Feminism and Difference: The Perils of Writing as a Woman on Women in Algeria." In *Feminist Studies*, Vol.14, No. 1. University of Maryland: Feminist Studies, Inc.

Leitch, Mary and Margaret. 1890. *Seven Years in Ceylon*. New York: American Tract Society.

Lipsey, Roger. 1977. *Coomaraswamy, His Life and Work* Vol. 3. Princeton: Princeton University Press.

Lutzker, Edythe. 1964. "Edith Pechey-Phipson; Pioneer Doctor in India." In *Orient/West* Vol. 9, No. 5. Tokyo.

————. 1973. *Edith Pechey-Phipson, M.D.: The Story of England's Foremost Pioneering Woman Doctor*. New

York: Exposition Press.

MacKinnon, Janice R. and Stephen R. 1988. *Agnes Smedley—The Life and Times of an American Radical.* Berkeley: University of California Press.

Mac Millan, Margaret. 1988. *Women of the Raj.* New York: Thames and Hudson, Inc.

Mahadevan, P. 1957. *Subramania Bharati—Patriot and Poet.* Madras: Atri Publishers.

Mani, Lata. 1990. "Multiple Mediations, Feminist Scholarship in the Age of Multinational Reception." In *Feminist Review,* No.35, Summer 1990. London: Feminist Review Collective.

Maskiell, Michelle. 1984. *Women Between Cultures.* New York: Syracuse University Press.

Maxwell, Margaret. 1990. *Narodniki Women.* New York: Pergamon Press.

Mayo, Katherine. 1927. *Mother India.* New York: Harcourt, Brace & Co.

Mazumdar, A.K., ed. 1968. *Nivedita Commemoration Volume.* Calcutta: Vivekananda Janmotsava Samiti.

Mencken, H.L. 1919. "Among the Avatars." In *Prejudices.* New York: Knopf.

————. 1949. "Hooey from the Orient" (1931). In *A Mencken Chrestomathy.* New York: Knopf.

Middleton, Ruth. 1989. *Alexandra David-Néel, Portrait of an Adventurer.* Boston: Shambala Publications.

Mies, Maria and Kumari Jayawardena. 1981. *Feminism in Europe: Liberal and Socialist Strategies 1789–1919.* The Hague: Institute of Social Studies.

Mitra, Mukundabihari. 1968. "Nivedita as a Journalist." In *Nivedita Commemoration Volume,* ed. A.K. Mazumdar. Calcutta: Vivekananda Janmotsava Samiti.

Mitter, Partha. 1977. *Much Maligned Monsters, History of European Reactions to Indian Art.* Oxford: Clarendon Press.

Moghadam, Valentine. 1989. "Against Eurocentrism and Nativism." In *Socialism and Democracy,* Fall/Winter.

————, ed. 1994. *Identity Politics & Women: Cultural Reassertion and Feminisms in International Perspective.* Boulder, Colorado: Westview Press.

Mohanty, Chandra T. 1988. "Under Western Eyes: Feminist Scholarship and Colonial Discourses." In *Feminist Review,* No. 30. London: Feminist Review Collective.

Montgomery, Helen Barrett. 1910. *Western Women in Eastern Lands.* New York: Garland.

Morton, Eleanor. 1953. *The Women in Gandhi's Life.* New York: Dodd, Mead.

Mosse, George L. 1985. *Nationalism and Sexuality: Middle-Class Morality and Sexual Norms in Modern Europe.* Wisconsin: University of Wisconsin Press.

The Mother (Mirra Richard). 1978. "Words of Long Ago." In *Collected Works of The Mother, Vol 2.* Pondicherry: Sri Aurobindo Ashram Trust.

————. 1984. *On Women.* Compiled from the writings of Sri Aurobindo and The Mother. Pondicherry: Sri Aurobindo Society

Mukerjee, Dhan Gopal. 1928. *A Son of Mother India Answers.* New York: E.P. Dutton and Co.

Mullaney, Marie Marmo. 1983. *Revolutionary Women, Gender and the Socialist Revolutionary Role.* New York: Praeger Publishers.

Muller, Erin. 1957. "Colombo in 1900." In *A History of CMS Ladies' College.* Hitchcock, ed. (1957). Colombo: Published by the Principal of Ladies' College.

Muller, Henrietta. 1893. "Theosophy and Women." In *Theosophical Congress.* Chicago, New York: The Theosophical Society.

Mumtaz, Khawar and Farida Shaheed. 1987. *Women of Pakistan.* London: Zed Books.

Murray, Janet Horowitz. 1982. *Strong-Minded Women and Other Lost Voices From Nineteenth-Century England.* New York: Pantheon Books.

Nahar, Sujata. 1985. *Mother's Chronicles, Book One, Mirra.* Paris, Auroville and Tamilnadu: Mira Aditi Centre.

Natarajan, K. 1928. *Miss Mayo's Mother India, a Rejoinder.* Madras: G.A.Natesan & Co.

Nethercot, Arthur H. 1961. *The First Five Lives of Annie Besant*. London: Rupert Hart-Davis.

———. 1963. *The Last Four Lives of Annie Besant*. London: Rupert Hart-Davis.

Nivedita, Sister (Margaret Noble). 1973. "The Function of Art in Shaping Nationality." In the *Complete Works of Sister Nivedita*, Vol.III. (2nd ed). Calcutta: Ramakrishna Sonada Mission.

———. 1982a. "Civic Ideal and Indian Nationality." in *The Complete Works of Sister Nivedita*, Vol.IV. (2nd ed), Calcutta: Advaita Ashrama

———. 1982b. *Kali, the Mother*. In *The Complete Works of Sister Nivedita* Vol. I (3rd ed). Calcutta: Ramakrishna Sarada Mission.

———. 1988. *The Web of Indian Life*, (1904). In *The Complete Works of Sister Nivedita*, Vol.II. (3rd ed). Calcutta: Advaita Ashrama.

Obeyesekere, Gananath. 1984. *The Cult of the Goddess Pattini*. Chicago: University of Chicago Press.

Offen, Karen. 1988. "Defining Feminism: A Comparative Historical Approach." In *Signs*, Vol.14, No.II. Chicago: University of Chicago Press.

Olcott, Henry Steele. 1954. *Old Diary Leaves, 1878–1883*, 3rd edition. Madras: Theosophical Publishing House.

Overstreet, G. and M. Windmiller. 1959. *Communism in India*. Berkeley: University of California Press.

Owen, Alex. 1989. *The Darkened Room*. London: Virago Press.

Padmanabha, Jayanta. 1947a. "A Tribute to Florence Farr Emery—I and II." In *Ceylon Daily News*, 10, 11 Feb. 1947.

———. 1947b. "In Memoriam: Florence Farr Emery—I and II." In *Ceylon Daily News*, 29, 30 April 1947.

Pandit, M.P. 1983. *Integral Perfection—A Collection of Talks*. Colombo: Sri Aurobindo Society of Sri Lanka.

Parthasarathy, Rangaswami. 1978. *A Hundred Years of the Hindu; The Epic Story of Indian Nationalism*. Madras: Kasturi & Sons Ltd.

Patel, Chandrakant. 1986. *Study of the Psychological Foundations of the Free Progress System as Evolved in Sri Aurobindo*. Bokhira: International Centre of Education.

Pathak, S.M. 1967. *American Missionaries and Hinduism: A Study of their Contacts from 1813–1910*. Delhi: Munshi Ram Manoharlal.

Paxton, Nancy L. 1990. "Feminism Under the Raj: Complicity and Resistance in the Writings of Flora Annie Steel and Annie Besant." In *Women's Studies International Forum*, Vol. 13, No. 4. Tarrytown, NY: Pergamon Press.

Payne, Ernest A. 1933. *The Saktas, An Introductory and Comparative Study*. Calcutta: YMCA Publishing House.

Peiris, Rt. Rev. Edmund. 1980. *The Story of the Holy Family Sisters in Sri Lanka*. Colombo.

Pieris, Ralph. 1980. "The Enigma of Anagarika." In *Lanka Guardian*, 15 Oct. 1980. Colombo.

Perera, Basil. 1967. *Pieter Keuneman, A Profile*. Colombo: The Ceylon Communist Party.

Petrie, Sir David. 1972. *Communism in India*. Calcutta: Editions Indian.

Potts, E. Daniel. 1967. *British Baptist Missionaries in India, 1793–1837*. Cambridge: Cambridge University Press.

Pound Ezra. 1928. "Portrait d'une Femme." In *Selected Poems*. London: Faber & Faber.

———. 1933. "Canto XXVIII." In *Draft of XXX Cantos*. London: Faber & Faber.

Pradhan, G.P. and A.K. Bhagwat. 1959. *Lokmanya Tilak*. Bombay.

Prasad, Narayan. 1976. *Education for a New Life*. Pondicherry: Sri Aurobindo Ashram.

Pratap, Mahendra. 1932. *Long Live India*. Peking, China: The World Federation.

Purani, A.B. 1987. *Life of Aurobindo*. Pondicherry.: Sri Aurobindo Ashram.

Ramabai Association. *Reports of the Annual General Meetings, 1887–1898*. Boston: American Ramabai

Association. *Reports of the Annual General Meetings, 1899–1909.* Boston: American Ramabai Association.

Ramabai Circle. 1887. "Address of Ramabai to Cornell University."

Ramabai, Pandita. 1887. *The High-Caste Hindu Woman.* Philadelphia and London: George Bell.

———. 1903. *Pandita Ramabai, the Widow's Friend.* Australian edition of *The High-Caste Hindu Woman.* Melbourne: .

Ramanathan College Silver Jubilee Souvenir, 1939. Colombo.

Ramusack, Barbara N. 1981a. "Catalysts or Helpers? British Feminists, Indian Women's Rights, and Indian Independence." In *The Extended Family: Women and Political Participation in India and Pakistan.* Gail Minault, ed. Delhi: Chanakya Publications.

———.1981b. "Women's Organisations and Social Change—The Age-of-Marriage Issue in India." In *Women and World Change: Equity Issues in Development.* Naomi Black and Ann B. Cottrell, eds. Beverly Hills: Sage Publications.

———. 1987. "Sister India or Mother India? Margaret Noble and Katherine Mayo as Interpreters of the Gender Roles of Indian Women." Paper presented at the 7th Berkshire Conference on the History of Women, Wellesley College, 20 June 1987.

———. 1990. "Cultural Missionaries, Maternal Imperialists, Feminist Allies—British Women Activists in India, 1865-1945." In *Women's Studies International Forum,* Vol. 13, No. 4. Tarrytown, NY: Pergamon Press. Also in *Western Women and Imperialism—Complicity and Resistance.* 1990. Chaudhuri and Strobel, eds. Bloomington: Indiana University Press.

Ranga Iyer, C.S. 1927. *Father India.* London: Selwyn and Blount Ltd.

Rathbone, Eleanor. 1934. *Child Marriage: The Indian Minotaur.* London: George Allen & Unwin Ltd.

Ratnatunga, Sinha. 1991. *They Turned the Tide: The 100 Year History of the Maha Bodhi Society of Sri Lanka.* Colombo: Maha Bodhi Society.

Ray, Sibnarayan, ed. 1979. *The World Her Village, Selected Writings and Letters of Ellen Roy.* Calcutta: Ananda Publishers Private Ltd.

———.1987. *Selected Works of M.N. Roy, Vol. I 1917–1922.* Delhi: Oxford University Press.

———.1988. *Selected Works of M.N. Roy, Vol. II 1923–1927.* Delhi: Oxford University Press.

Rendall, Jane. 1985. *The Origins of Modern Feminism: Women in Britain, France and the United States 1780–1860.* London: MacMillan.

Reymond, Lizelle. 1953. *The Dedicated: A Biography of Nivedita.* New York: John Day.

Rhys Davids, Caroline. 1909. *Psalms of the Early Buddhists. I. Psalms of the Sisters.* London: Pali Text Society.

———. 1940. *Wayfarer's Words Vol. I.* London: Luzac & Co.

———. 1941. *Wayfarer's Words Vol. II.* London: Luzac & Co.

Richard, Paul. 1920. *The Dawn Over Asia.* Aurobindo Ghose, trans. Madras: Ganesh & Co.

Rolland, Romain. 1984. *The Life of Vivekananda and the Universal Gospel.* Calcutta: Advaita Ashrama.

Rosenthal, A.M. 1957. "Mother India, Thirty Years After." In *Foreign Affairs.* Vol. 35, July. New York.

Rowbotham, Sheila. 1992. *Women in Movement, Feminism and Social Action.* London & New York: Routledge.

——— and Jeffrey Weeks. 1977. *Socialism & the New Life—Edward Carpenter and Havelock Ellis.* London: Pluto Press.

Roy, Evelyn. 1923a. "The Metamorphosis of Mr. C.R. Das." In *Labour Monthly,* June 1923. London.

———. 1923b. "Mahatma Gandhi: Revolutionary or Counter Revolutionary?" In *Labour Monthly,* Sept. London.

———. 1924a. "Some Facts About the Bombay Strike." In *Labour Monthly,* May. London.

———. 1924b. "The Revolution in Central Asia." In *Labour Monthly,* Sept. London.

————. 1925. "Indian Political Exiles in France." In *Labour Monthly*, April. London.

————. 1931. "M.N. Roy and Indian Communism." In *Revolutionary Age*, Nov. New York: The Communist Party of the U.S.A.

Roy M.N. 1957. "The Ideal of Indian Womanhood." In *Fragments of a Prisoners Diary, Vol I, Crime and Karma*. Calcutta: Renaissance Publishers Private Ltd.

————. 1964. *Memoirs*. Bombay: Allied Publishers.

Said, Edward W. 1979. *Orientalism*. New York: Vintage Books.

————. 1994. *Culture and Imperialism*. New York: Alfred A. Knopf.

Sarkar, Sumit. 1977. *The Swadeshi Movement in Bengal, 1903–1908*. New Delhi: People's Publishing House.

————. 1983. *Modern India 1885–1947*. Madras: MacMillan India Ltd.

Satprem. 1979. *Mother or the Divine Materialism*. Paris: Institut de Recherches Evolutives.

Saywell, Ruby J. 1964. *Mary Carpenter of Bristol*. Bristol Historical Association.

Scharlieb, Mary. 1924. *Reminiscences*. London: Williams-Norgate.

Schneir, Miriam, ed. 1972. *Feminism, the Essential Historical Writings*. New York: Random House.

Schwab, Raymond. 1984. *The Oriental Renaissance: Europe's Discovery of India and the East 1680–1880*. New York: Columbia University Press.

Sen Gupta, Sukhendu Bikas. 1975. *Nellie Sen Gupta*. Calcutta: C. Das.

————. 1985. *Jatindra Mohan Sen Gupta*. Calcutta: C. Das.

Sethna, K.D. 1978. *Glimpses of Mother's Life*. Pondicherry: Sri Aurobindo Ashram.

Sethna, Khorshed Adi. 1987. *Madame Bhikhaiji Rustom Cama*. New Delhi: Publications Division, Ministry of Information and Broadcasting.

Shastri, K.R. 1931. *The Bombshell of Today*. Madras: Triplicane.

Shulman, Alix Kates. 1979. *Red Emma Speaks*. London: Wildwood House.

Simon, Mabel E. 1957. "This is the Victory—Our Faith," in *A History of CMS Ladies' College*. Hitchcock, ed. Colombo: Published by the principal of the Ladies' College.

Singh, Karan. 1963. *Prophet of Indian Nationalism, A Study of the Political Thought of Sri Aurobindo Ghosh 1893–1910*. London: George Allen and Unwin.

Sinha, Mrinalini. 1992. "Chathams, Pitts and Gladstones in Petticoats." In Chauduri & Strobel (1992).

Sitarammayya, B.P. 1946. *History of the Indian National Congress. Vol I*. Bombay: Padma Publications.

Smedley, Agnes. 1927. "'Bootlickers' Handbook of India." In *New Masses*, Nov. 1927.

Sorabji, Cornelia. 1908. *Between the Twilights*. London & New York: Harper and Brothers.

————. 1934. *India Calling*. London & New York: Nisbet & Co. Ltd.

Speir, Charlotte. 1973. *Life in Ancient India*, (1856). Reprinted as *Phases of Indian Civilization*. Delhi: Cosmo.

Sri Prakasa. 1962. *Annie Besant as Woman and as Leader*. Bombay: Bharatiya Vidya Bhavan.

Srinivasa Iyengar, K.R. 1978. *On the Mother, The Chronicle of a Manifestation and Ministry, Vols. I & II*. Pondicherry: Sri Aurobindo International Centre of Education.

————. 1988. *Swami Vivekananda*. Madras: Samata Books.

Strobel, Margaret. 1991. *European Women and the Second British Empire*. Bloomington: Indiana University Press.

Studdert-Kennedy, Gerald. 1990. "Gandhi and the Christian Imperialists." In *History Today*, Oct.

Symonds, J. 1960. *The Lady with the Magic Eyes: Madame Blavatsky, Medium and Magician*. New York: T. Yoseloff.

Taylor, Anne. 1992. *Annie Besant: A Biography*. Oxford & New York: Oxford University Press.

Thapar, Romila. 1989. "Imagined Religious Communities; Ancient History and the Modern Search for a Hindu Identity." In *Modern Asian Studies*, Cambridge 23(2).

Tiffany, Sharon, and Kathleen Adams. 1985. *The Wild Woman: An Inquiry into the Anthropology of an Idea*. Cambridge, Mass: Schenkman Books.

Urquhart, Margaret. 1926. *Women of Bengal. A Study of the Hindu Pardanasins of Calcutta*. Calcutta: Association Press, YMCA.

Vivekananda, Swami. 1986. *Women of India*. Madras: Sri Ramakrishna Math.

Vythilingam, M. 1971. *The Life of Sir Ponnambalam Ramanathan Vol. 1*. Colombo: Ramanathan Commemoration Society.

Webb, James. 1988a. *The Occult Underground*. La Salle, Illinois: Open Court

———. 1988b. *The Occult Establishment*. La Salle, Illinois: Open Court.

Wickremeratne, L. Ananda. 1985. *The Genesis of an Orientalist: Thomas William Rhys Davids and Buddhism in Sri Lanka*. New Delhi: South Asia Books.

Wilfried. 1986. *The Mother—A Short Biography*. Pondicherry: Sri Aurobindo Society.

Wilson, D. Kanagasabai. 1975. *The Christian Church in Sri Lanka*. Colombo: Study Centre for Religion and Society.

Winslow, Rev. Miron. 1840. *Memoir of Mrs. Harriet Winslow, Thirteen years a member of the American Mission in Ceylon*. New York: American Tract Society.

Wolpert, Stanley. 1962. *Tilak and Gokhale: Revolution and Reform in the Making of Modern India*. Berkeley: University of California Press.

Young, William. ca1922. *Robert Weare of Bristol, Liverpool and Wallasey—An Appreciation*. Published privately.

Yuval-Davis, Nira and Floya Anthias, eds. 1989. *Women-Nation-State*. London: MacMillan Press.

———. 1994. "Identity Politics and Women's Ethnicity." In *Identity Politics and Women, Cultural Reassertions and Feminisms in International Perspective*, Valentine Moghadam, ed. Colorado: Westview Press.

Zaidi, A.M. and Dr. S.G. 1980. *The Encyclopaedia of the Indian National Congress, Vol. 10 : 1930–5*. New Delhi: S. Chand & Co.

Zinn, Howard. 1980. *A People's History of the United States*. New York: Harper & Row.

INDEX

Abai, Saiyad Abdul Wahid, 226
Abhayananda, Swami (Marie Louise), 186
Ackroyd, Annette, 6, 14–15, 63, 67, 71–74, 209
age of consesnt, in Indian marriages, 84, 91–94, 128
Age of Consent Bill, 93
Aikin, Lucy, 6, 63, 69–70
Aiyar, Subramamia, 123, 133
Alexandra Native Girls English Institution (Bombay), 84
Alfassa, Maurice, 207
Alfassa, Mirra (Mother of Pondicherry), 206, 207–209 (photo), 210–17
    Sri Aurobindo and, 207–217
All-Asian Women's Conference, 152–53
All-India League for Maternity and Child Welfare, 89
All-India Sarada Sub-Committee, 102
All-India Society for the Abolition of Child Marriage, 102
All-India Trade Union Congress, 234
All-India Women's Conference, 101, 102, 152, 154, 277(n18), 289(n14)
American Methodist Mission to Ceylon, 34
American Ramabai Association, 60, 272(n9), 280(n6)
Ananda Balika, 251, 253, 291(n9)
Anandabei. See Joshi, Anandibei, M.D.
Anderson, Elizabeth Garrett, 76
Anglican Church, 24, 32, 33
Anglo-Indians, 43, 45–46
Anketell, Daisy, 40
Annan, Noel, 137–38
anti-feminism, of Ananda Coomaraswamy, 170
anti-imperialist movements, 225, 249, 259
    Western women in, 219–59
anti-Semitism, 247, 248
Anushilan Samiti, 231, 284(n20)
Arunachalam, Ponnambalam, 142
Arundale, George, 279(n9)
Arya Mahila Samaj, 54
"Aryan myth", 110
ashram
    of Aurobindo, 213–14, 216
    of Gandhi, 196, 199, 202, 226, 285(n3)
Asian Women's Conference, 148
Association of Medical Women in India, 88–89
atheism, 125, 279(n1)
Aurobindo, Sri, 6, 16, 72, 112, 177, 179, 180, 191, 192–93, 230, 231, 284(n20), 285(n1–n3), 286(n5, n6)

    Mirra Alfassa and, 207–17
Auroville, 216, 286(n8)

Baha, Abdul, 208
Bahai religion, 208
Ball, Teresa (Loreto nun), 45, 271(n8)
Baltimore Women's Missionary Society, 29
Bandaranaike, Daisy Dias, 282(n8)
Bandaranaike, Sirima, 42–43
Bande Mataram, 193, 210, 234, 283(n6)
Baptist Church, 22, 24, 27, 274(n5)
Bapu, Gandhi as, 180, 199, 201, 203, 205, 285(n4)
Bapu Raj Patrika, 205
Barbusse, Henri, 236, 242
Baroda College, 210, 214
Beale, Dorothea, 48, 136, 271(n13)
Bedford College (London), 71, 76
Bedi, B. P. and Freda, 226–27
Beecher, Catherine, 29–30
Behn, Mira. See Slade, Madeleine (Mira Behn)
Benares, Maharajah of, 129
Bengal, 192–93, 195, 210, 213, 276(n8), 287(n4), 288(n7)
Bengal Social Science association, 70
Benson, Annette, M.D., 89
Bernal, J. D., 249
Bernays, Robert, 201
Besant, Annie, 6, 16, 61–62, 97, 98, 109, 114, 117, 118, 122, 123–27(photo), 128–34, 138, 148, 153, 176, 178, 189, 196–97, 222, 246, 265, 266, 278(n9), 279(n1–n12), 291(n9)
    in India, 128-31, 150, 151, 153, 154, 164, 168, 287(n7)
Beveridge, Annette, 73, 74. See also Ackroyd, Annette
Beveridge, Henry, 73, 74
Beveridge, Laetitia, 73
Beveridge, William, 73
Bhaduri, Anadi and Inger, 226
The Bhagavad Gita, 208, 278(n1)
Bhandarkar, R. G., 93, 276(n3)
Bharathi, S., 190, 284(n15)
Bielby, Elizabeth, M.D., 78, 83(photo), 88, 274(n4)
Bilstad, Esther, 226, 287(n8)
Bird, Isabel, 162
Birkbeck Institute, 126
birth control, 125, 222, 232, 237, 239, 288(n13)
Blavatsky, Helena Petrovna, 16, 114, 115(photo)–120, 123, 127, 165, 196, 208, 278(n8), 279(n10), 281(n3)

in India, 120–122, 155, 176
Bode, Mabel, 158
Bodley, Rachel, M.D., 54, 55–56, 271(n2)
Bondfield, Margaret, 223
Bose, Jagdish, 112
Bose, Subhas Chandra, 6, 226
Bradlaugh, Charles, 109, 124–25, 279(n3)
Brahmins, 54, 60, 120–21, 283(n4)
Brahmo Samaj, 54, 177, 178, 192, 266, 272(n2)
Brande, Ann, 107, 113, 114
Bristol Socialist Society, 246
British Committee for Indian Women's Franchise, 101
British National Association of Spiritualists, 113
Brooklyn Ethical Society, 61
Brooklyn Ramabai Association, 61
Buddhism, 109, 159, 160, 164, 171
    women in, 161–62
Buddhist Theosophical Society, 117, 250

Calcutta Municipal Corporation, 155
Calcutta University, 39, 54
Cama Hospital, 61, 88
Cambridge Local Examinations, 42, 47, 48, 49, 168
Cambridge Union Socialist Club, 249
Cambridge University, 49, 76, 161, 196, 208–209, 214, 248, 249, 250, 279(n9)
Canavarro, Miranda de Souza, 166–67
Carew, ___. (Jesuit Archbishop of Calcutta), 44, 45
Carey, William, 22, 55, 91, 269(n8), 274(n6)
Carmichael, Amy W., 14, 94–95, 96, 261, 265–66, 276(n5), 279(n11)
Carpenter, Edward, 246, 283(n2), 290(n4)
Carpenter, Lant, 67–68, 69
Carpenter, Mary, 6, 14, 63, 66, 67–69(photo), 70–71, 72
castes, in India, 36, 39, 55
Catholic Church, 26, 32, 33, 40–47
celibacy, 239
Central Hindu College, 128, 129
Central Society for Women's Suffrage, 85
Ceylon Communist Party, 243, 254
Ceylon Daily News, 227
Ceylon Labour Party, 250
Ceylon National Congress, 251
Ceylon Social Reform Society, 167
Ceylon Trade Union Federation, 254
Ceylon University College, 50, 249, 255
Ceylon Women's Union, 88
Charter for Women's Freedom, 213
Chatterjee, Mohini Mohan, 112, 141
Chattopadyaya, Harindranth, 281(n7), 288(n6)
Chattopadyaya, Kamaladevi, 124, 153, 266, 267, 281(n7), 288(n6), 289(n15)
Chattopadyaya, Virendranath, 6, 17, 230, 232–34, 237, 238, 239–40, 288(n6, n7), 289(n15, n17, n19)

Cheltenham Ladies' College (England), 47, 48, 49–50, 54, 136, 143, 145
childbirth, in young Indian girls, 84, 96
child marriage, in India, 1, 14, 54, 61, 67, 77, 81, 84, 85, 87, 90, 91–103, 120, 121, 133, 151, 152, 189, 266, 273(n3), 275(n16), 283(n10)
Child Marriage Restraint Act, 101
child widows, in India, 55, 57–58, 60, 61, 93–94
Chinese revolution, 230, 240
Christianity, 63–64, 128, 262, 265, 266, 269(n1)
    in colonial South Asia, 8, 9, 11, 15, 19–62, 176
    feminization of, 25–26
    Ramabai's conversion to, 53–62, 272(n10, n12)
Christian Socialists, 109
Churchill, Winston, 149, 202
Church Missionary Society, 47, 48, 48–49
circumcision, of females, 277(n17)
Clements, Mrs. Major, 158
Colmcille, Mary (Loreto nun), 33, 44, 45
Colombo Youth League, 252
colonialism, in India, 2–3
Comintern, 239, 241, 289(n18), 289(n20)
Communism, 17, 208, 249, 256, 287(n11)
Communist International, 231, 232, 235, 241
Communist Party, 223, 226, 228, 229, 231, 238, 240, 245, 249, 254, 256, 258, 286(n3), 289(n20)
Communist Women's International, 223–24
Congress of Oppressed Nationalities, 236
Congress Working Committee (Allahabad), 203–204
Contagious Disease Act (1964), 66
convent education, in India, 40–47
Conway, Katharine, 222, 290(n3)
Conway, Moncure, 124, 167
Coomaraswamy, Ananda, 141, 142, 161, 167–70, 171, 188, 282(n8), 284(n19)
Coomaraswamy, Ethel, 16, 167–71
Coomaraswamy, Mutu, 141, 167
Cooper-Oakley, Isabel, 118
Cornell University, 39, 56, 78
Court of Wards Act (India), 93
Cousins, James, 148, 150, 154, 281(n5), 286(n4)
Cousins, Margaret, 16, 97–98, 118, 149(photo), 265, 266, 281(n2–n4, n6, n7)
    in India, 147–55, 287(n7)

Daly, Mary, 8, 99–100
Darjeeling Loreto convent, 455
Darwin, Charles, 108, 116
Darwinism, 15
David-Néel, Alexandra, 16, 157, 162, 163(photo), 164, 171, 208, 282(n5)
Delhi Women's Medical College, 89
Delphine, Mary (Loreto nun), 41(photo), 43, 44–45
Democratic Women's Association, 227
Deshmukh, Gopal, 67, 271(n3), 273(n3)

de Silva, Joseph, 227, 287(n10)
de Silva, Rhoda Miller, 227, 287(n10, n11), 290(n6)
Despard, Charlotte, 118, 119, 148, 278(n9)
Devi, Ratan (Alice Richardson Coomaraswamy), 282(n8)
Devi, Santa. *See* Trent, Evelyn
Dharma, 193, 211
Dharmapala, Anagārika, 112, 134, 164–67, 178
doctors
    female, in South Asia, 75–90
    women missionary school graduates as, 49, 50
Dolmetsch, Arnold, 138, 139
Doyle, Gabriel (Loreto nun), 44
Dufferin, Lady, 88, 158
Dufferin, Lord, 88
Dufferin Fund, 88, 89
Dutt, Bupendranath, 193, 288(n7)

Edinburgh School of Medicine for Women, 82
education
    of Indian women, 128–31, 141–45, 187–88, 281(n9)
    methods of Aurobindo and Mirra Richard, 214–17
    methods of Besant, 262–63
    methods of Farr, 141–46
    methods of Nivedita, 187–88
Eksath Kantha Peramuna, 256, 257
Ellmann, Richard, 115, 278(n8)
emancipation of women, in South Asia, 28–32
Emery, Florence. *See* Farr, Florence
Engels, Friedrich, 108, 269(n5)
English, as subject in Indian missionary schools, 39, 40, 42, 44
Evanston College for Ladies, 56

Fabian Society, 126, 128, 222
Faiz, Alys George, 227, 287(n9)
family life, in India, 1
Farquhar, J. N., 116, 117
Farr, Florence, 16, 118, 135–40(photo), 141–46, 155, 280(n1)
Fascism, 249, 254, 255
"female devils", Western women as, 2, 18, 21
"Female Mite Society", 269(n6)
feminism, 224, 288(n11)
    of Annie Besant, 125
    Christianity and, 25–26
    in First World, 12
    in India, 14
    of Margaret Noble, 185
    of Pandita Ramabai, 55
    Quakers and, 25, 269(n4)
    in South Asia, 8–9, 26, 261–68
    in Third World, 12–13
    women revolutionaries and, 236–37

feminists
    British liberal, 72
    early Indian women as, 51, 55, 62
Finch, Christine (Loreto nun), 46
Fitingof, Rosa, 226, 243
Foley, Caroline. *See* Rhys Davids, Caroline
Foote, G. W., 109, 128
Foster, Mary Elizabeth, 16, 164–67, 171, 282(n6, n7)
Foster Buddhist Seminary (Kandy), 165
Foster Robinson Hospital (Colombo), 165
Foxe, Barbara, 184, 185
France, early Oriental scholarship in, 110–11
Free Church of Scotland, 23
Froebel, Friedrich, 58, 119, 184, 262
fund-raising, for Indian women physicians, 88–90

Gandhi, Firoze, 250
Gandhi, Indira, 215
Gandhi, Kasturbai, 197
Gandhi, Mohandas K., 1, 6, 16–17, 79(photo), 97, 98, 99, 112, 117, 131, 148, 154, 177, 179–80, 186, 234–35, 235–36, 239, 277(n10), 284(n1), 285(n2–n4), 289(n14), 291(n9)
    Madeline Slade (Mira Behn and, 16–17, 195–206, 266, 285(n4–n9)
Geissler, Louise, 241, 290(n24)
George, Alys. *See* Faiz, Alys George
Geraghty, Alphonsus (Loreto nun), 44
Germany, 110, 288(n7)
Ghadiali, Dinshah, 97, 98
Ghadr Party, 226, 233
Ghose, Aravinda Ackroyd. *See* Aurobindo, Sri
Ghose, Aurobindo. *See* Aurobindo, Sri
Ghose, Krishnadham, M.D., 209
Ghose, Manmohan, 72, 209
Gillespie, Margaret, 147, 148. *See also* Cousins, Margaret
Gladstone, William E., 93, 278(n4)
global sisterhood, 10, 11, 53
Golden Dawn. *See* Order of the Golden Dawn
Goldman, Emma, 223, 232, 286(n2)
Good Shepherd Order (Catholic nuns), Indian convent schools of, 41
Gopal Ashram, 205, 206
Grant Medical College, 85
Grenstidel, Christine, 184(photo), 186
Grey, Nellie. *See* Sen Gupta, Nellie
Guild of Handicraft, 169
Gunawardena, Philip, 225–26, 287, 287(n8)
gurus
    foreign women disciples of, 16–17
    Western Holy Mothers and, 175–81

Hamlin, Sarah, 59, 272(n110)
Harijan Colony (Delhi), 202
Henry Street House Settlement, 202

Herald Tribune, 240

Hewavitana, Don David. *See* Dharmapala, Anagarika

Hindu Conspiracy Case, 231

Hinduism, 94, 97, 109, 120–21, 189–90, 278(n2), 279(n11)

Hindu Mahila Vidyalaya, 72

Hindu patriarchy, 53–62, 176, 265

Hoare, Samuel, 101, 202

Hoban, Jeanne. *See* Moonesinge, Jeanne

Hobsbawm, Eric, 118, 222, 291(n16)

Hogan, Joseph (Loreto nun), 45, 271(n11)

Holmes, John Haynes, 195, 202

Holy Family Convent (Colombo), 42, 270(n7)

Holy Family Order (Catholic nuns), Indian convent schools of, 41, 42

Holy Mothers, 2, 4, 8, 11, 16, 18, 206, 225, 259, 263, 265
Indian gurus and, 175–81

Home Rule Bill, 149, 150

Home Rule for India, 16, 91, 124, 128, 131, 266

Home Rule League, 131, 151, 279(n10)

Honolulu Star Bulletin, 165

Horner, Isaline Blew, 16, 161–62, 171

Horniman, Annie, 137, 138, 280(n3)

Hospital for Indians (Calcutta), 45

human rights, early religious educators' promotion of, 42, 51

Huxley, Thomas, 184, 279(n5)

Ibsen, Henrik, 137, 232

Ilbert Bill (1883), 73, 273(n9)

imperialism, Western women against, 219–59

Independent India, 242

India
Annie Besant in, 128–31
Florence Farr in, 141–46
Helena Blavatsky in, 120–22
Madeline Slade in, 195–206
Margaret Cousins in, 147–55
Margaret Noble (Nivedita) in, 179, 183–94
social reformers in, 63–103, 155
women in, 120–22

India Conciliation Group, 277(n18)

India League (London), 246, 250

Indian Communist Party, 232, 235

Indian Majlis, 210

Indian National Congress, 92, 131, 132, 154, 155, 192, 196, 199, 200, 201, 202, 203–04, 210, 214, 226, 235, 285(n2), 288(n6)

Indian National party, 234

Indian Society of Oriental Art (Calcutta), 281(n5)

The Indian Spectator, 92

Institute of Ethnography (Leningrad), 239–40

intermarriages. *See* mixed marriages

International Brigade, 249

International Conference of the Women's Suffrage Alliance (1906), 85

International Congress on Defense of Culture, 242

International Labor Organization, 256–57

International Trade Union Conference, 127

International Women's Day, 223, 258

The Irish Citizen, 149

Irish Home Rule movement, 6, 147, 149, 150, 154, 184, 224, 281(n2)

Islam, 109

Ismaloun, Mathilde, 207–208

Jaffna Female Seminary, 42

Jagnathan, Annie, M.D., 82, 83(photo)

Japan, 211, 212

Jayawardena, Kumari, 279(n8)

Jesuits, in India, 41, 43, 44

Jesus and Mary Convent (Lahore), 42, 43

Jesus and Mary Order (Catholic nuns), Indian convent schools of, 41, 42, 43

Jews, 16, 17, 207, 214, 247, 248, 256, 290(n6)

Jex-Blake, Sophia, 76, 275(n14)

Jinarajadasa, Dorothy, 150–51

Jonas, Charlotte, 246, 247, 250

Jones, Dewitt, 240, 289(n22)

Joshi, Anandibai, M.D., 54, 81–82, 99, 266, 275(n19)

Joynt, Mary Gonzaga (Loreto nun), 44

Kali worship, 2, 5, 16, 99, 179, 180, 183, 190–91, 266, 284(n16)

Kandy Arts and Crafts Society, 167

Kandy School of Art, 167

Kartini, 58, 272(n7)

Kaur, Rajkumari Amrit, 101, 285(n7)

Keuneman, Hedi, 254–56, 258, 291(n14–16). *See also* Simon, Hedi; Stadlen, Hedi

Keuneman, Pieter, 6, 17, 248(photo)–249, 254, 255, 256, 291(n12)

Khan, Abdul Qadir, 288(n9)

Khankhoje, Pandurang, 226

Khetri, Rani of, 77

Kinnaird College (Lahore), 31

Kipling, Rudyard, 24, 75–76

Kisan Ashram, 204, 205, 206

Kisogotami, 160

Kollontai, Alexandra, 223, 286(n3)

Kotah, Maharajah of, 89

Kotahena Girl's Free School, 168

Krishna Menon, V. K., 6, 227, 246, 250

Krishnamurti, Jeddu, 6, 16, 17, 18, 124, 133–34, 279(n12), 280(n13)

Krishnamurti, Nityananda, 133

Kropotkin, Peter, 184, 185, 284(n19)

Kularatne, Hilda, 250, 251, 253

Kularatne, Patrick, 159, 250, 251

Kumaratunga, Chandrika Bandaranaike, 43, 282(n8)

Labour Monthly, 235, 236
Labour Party, 223, 242, 246, 255, 281(n1), 290(n2)
Ladies Association for the Promotion of Female Education among the Heathen, 27
Ladies' College (Colombo), 34, 47–51, 252
Ladies Sanitary Association, 272(n1)
Lady Aitchison Hospital (Lahore), 78
Lady Hardinge Medical College for Women (Delhi), 89
Lady Reading Hospital, 89
Lajpat Rai, Lala, 97, 98, 112, 233, 234, 277(n11), 288(n5), 289(n15)
Lake House newspapers, 227, 287(n14)
Lanka Estate Workers Union, 227
Lanka Mahila Samiti, 88, 292(n17)
Lanka Sama Samaja Party (LSSP), 251–52, 254, 256, 257, 287(n14)
Lathrop, Harriet Wadsworth. *See* Winslow, Harriet
Law College (Colombo), 251
Lee, Ann (Mother), 25, 269(n5)
Leeds Suffrage Association, 85
"Left Quartet", 239–40
Leibowitz, Claudine, 287(n11), 290(n6)
Lenin, Vladmir, 223, 226, 235, 236, 286(n3), 287(n4)
liaisons, of European men and Indian women, 3–4
Liebknecht, Karl, 241, 286(n5)
Life, 96
London Economist, 227
London School of Economics, 246
London School of Medicine for Women, 76, 81, 87
London University, 125–26
Loreto Abbey (Dublin), 43, 271(n8)
Loreto House (Calcutta), 44, 45, 271(n10)
Loreto Order (Catholic nuns), Indian convent schools of, 33, 41, 43–47, 209
Loreto Teachers College, 46
Louise, Marie. *See* Abhayananda, Swami (Marie Louise)
Ludowyk, Edith Gymroi, 256, 290(n6)
Luxemburg, Rosa, 224, 241, 286(n4)

M. N. Roy Archives, 242
Madanapalle College, 150
Madras Legislative Council, 151
Madras Medical College, 80
Madras Standard, 131
Maha Bodhi societies, 165, 166, 282(n6–n7)
Mahinda College, 246
Mairet, Ethel (Ethel Coomaraswamy), 169
Majlis, 249
Malabari, Behramji Merwanji, 92
Manning, Elizabeth, 74, 196
Marchand, Marie Xavier (Holy Family nun), 42
marriage
  among mission school girls, 37
  Hindu view, 129–30

of Indian children. *See* child marraige
  between Indian men and European women, 167–69, 225–27, 264
Martineau, Harriet, 6, 27, 66, 69, 273(n8)Marxism, 217, 222, 224, 235, 249, 264, 289(n21)
Maternal Society (Jaffa), 35, 270(n1)
Mayo, Katherine, 1–2, 8, 14, 15, 67, 91, 95–100, 101, 102, 238, 267, 276(n6–n8), 277(n10–n15), 289(n16)
McDonnel, Xaviera (Loreto nun), 45
medical education, for South Asian women, 79–81
medical missionaries, in India, 75–90
"Medical Women for India Fund", 82
mediums, women as, 113, 114
memsahibs, 4
Mencken, H. L., 16, 118
Mesmer, Franz Anton, 113, 278(n4)
messiahs, 132–34
Methodist Church, 23, 24, 26, 32, 33, 34–36, 274(n5, n6)
Methodist Women's Foreign Missionary Society, 77
midwives, 78, 79, 274(n4, n12), 275(n15)
missionaries
  in South Asia, 8, 9, 13–14, 263, 265–66
  women as, 21, 26–28
missionary schools, feminist and reformist content of, 33–51
mixed marriages, 4, 167–69, 225–27, 264
Modern School, 254, 255, 291(n13)
Mons, Teresa (Loreto nun), 43, 271(n12)
Montessori, Maria, 119, 215, 262
Montessori system, 143, 144, 215
Moonesinghe, Jeanne, 227, 287(n12–n14)
Morris, William, 136, 169
Morton, Eleanor, 196–97
Moseley, Cynthia, 277(n12)
The Mother. *See* Richard, Mirra (Mother of Pondicherry)
"Mother Jones", 224, 286(n6)
Mother of Pondicherry. *See* Richard, Mirra (Mother of Pondicherry)
Mount Holyoke College, 31, 39, 49
Muller, Henrietta, 119, 186
Müller, Max, 86–87, 93, 110, 275(n21), 283(n2)
Museaus College (Colombo), 250
"Music in Ceylon" (Coomaraswamy), 168
Muslim League, 204
Mussolini, Benito, 201, 249

Naidu, Sarojini, 99, 112, 151, 281(n7), 288(n6)
Narodnik movements, 223
Natal Indian Congress, 196
Natarajan, K., 98, 276(n8)
National Association to Supply Female Medical Aid to the Women of India (Dufferin Fund), 88, 89

National Conference of Women, 148
National Indian Association (England), 71, 74, 196, 274(n4)
National Secular Society, 109, 124, 125
National Social Conference (India), 92, 276(n3)
National Union of Societies for Equal Citizenship (England), 100
Nazism, 249, 256
Nehru, Indira, 250
Nehru, Jawarhalal, 6, 112, 117, 131, 204, 205–206, 215, 240, 242, 289(n19)
Nethercot, Arthur H., 116, 124, 280(n13)
New India, 131, 150
New York Evening Post, 96
New York Herald, 179
New York Times, 287(n11)
Nietzsche, Friedrich, 177, 232
Nightingale, Florence, 66, 93, 280(n1)
Nivedita, Sister. *See* Noble, Margaret (Sister Nivedita)
Nixon, Lilian, 48, 49–50
Noble, Margaret (Sister Nivedita), 2,6, 16, 61, 99, 151, 169, 175, 176, 177, 179–80, 181, 183, 184 (photo)–194, 195, 202, 211, 213, 216, 230, 266, 267, 283(n1), 284(n11–15), 287(n7)
non-violence movement. *See* passive resistance movement
Northfield Seminary for Girls, 78
nuns, Indian missionary schools of, 40–47

Olcott, Henry, 114, 116, 120, 165, 278(n7)
Opie, Gwen, 50, 51
Order of Nuns (Buddhist), 159–60
Order of Ramakrishna, 187
Order of the Golden Dawn, 16, 137–39, 280(n3)
Order of the Star, 280(n13)
Orientalists, 2, 4, 8, 12, 105–171
   women as, 157–71
Oriental Renaissance, 110–12
Owen, Robert, 68, 278(n4)
Oxford University, 50, 159

Pali Text Society, 158, 159, 162, 282(n3)
Pandurang, Atmaram, 67, 273(n3)
Pankhurst, Christabel, 148, 149
Parkes, Bessie Raynor, 71, 272(n1)
Parliament, Doreen Wickremasinghe in, 258–59
Parliament of Religions (Chicago), 164, 178, 185
Parliament of Women (London), 149
Parnell, Charles Stewart, 210, 281(n2)
Parsi religion, 178
Partridge, Ethel. *See* Coomaraswamy, Ethel
Pashulok, 204, 205, 206
passive resistance movement, of Gandhi, 180, 196, 197, 198, 236
Patiala, Maharajah of, 4

Pechey, Edith, M.D., 14, 76, 82–83(photo), 84–85, 87, 275(n14)
Pechey-Phipson Sanatorium, 83
Pestalozzi, Johann H., 119, 262
Philippines, 96, 276(n7)
Phule, Jotirao, 63, 272(n3)
physicians. *See* doctors
Placer Country Welfare Department, 240
polygamy, in India, 84
Pomeroy, Betsey C. (Chinnachi Vyravi), 38, 270(n4)
Pondicherry, Mother of. *See* Richard, Mirra (Mother of Pondicherry)
Portugal, as source of Indian Catholicism, 40, 41
Pound, Ezra, 16, 135, 139, 145, 146, 280(n4)
Prarthana Samaj, 54, 273(n3)
professional women, missionary school graduates as, 49, 50
Protestant ethic
   in early Indian women's schools, 47–51
   of Nivedita, 193

Quakers, 10, 25, 102, 201, 269(n4)
Queens College (London), 48, 136, 145
"Quit India" movement, 204, 214

Radda-bai. *See* Blavatsky, Helena Petrovna
Ramabai, Pandita, 14, 15, 32, 48, 57(photo), 81, 86, 95, 96, 123, 128, 176, 266, 271(n1)
   American fund-raising for, 53–62
Ramabai Association, 55–57, 188
Ramakrishna Paramahamsa, 176, 177, 185, 191
Ramanathan, Ponnambalam, 16, 141, 142, 143, 146, 280(n6), 281(n8)
Ramanathan College (Jaffna), 141, 144–45
Ramusack, Barbara, 10, 14, 101, 189
Ranade, M. G., 67, 92, 93, 271(n3), 276(n3)
Rathbone, Eleanor, 14, 15, 67, 91, 100–103, 267, 277(n17–18)
Rau, Dhanwanthi Rama, 100, 154
Ray, Sibnarayan, 240–41, 242, 287(n1)
Ray Choudhury, G.S., 284(n20)
Reddy, Muttulakshmi, 147, 153, 281(n7), 282(n8)
religion, East-West exchanges of, 178–81
revolutionaries, women as, 221–28
Revolutionary Age, 240
Rhys Davids, Caroline, 16, 159–61, 171, 282(n4)
Rhys Davids, Thomas William, 118, 159, 161, 282(n2)
Richard, Mirra (Mother of Pondicherry), 162, 267, 286(n4)
   Sri Aurobindo and, 16, 177, 179, 180, 285(n3), 286(n5)
Richard, Paul, 208, 211, 213, 285(n3)
Ripon Hospital (Simla), 89
Rodi caste, 253

Rolland, Romain, 186, 198, 201, 236, 242, 283(n3), 285(n5–n6)

Rosenthal, A. M., 95, 99

Roy, Evelyn. *See* Trent, Evelyn

Roy, Manabendra Nath, 6, 17, 226, 227–32, 233, 234, 235, 238–42, 287(n2–n4), 288(n8), 289(n17)

Roy, Rammohan, 6, 63, 66, 68–69, 91, 100, 177, 272(n2), 273(n7)

Royal University of Ireland (Dublin), 48, 148

Roy Defense Committee, 242

Royists, 242

Rukhmabai, ____, M.D., 82, 83(photo), 266, 275(n18, n19, n21)

Rukhmabai Defense Committee, 85

Ruskin, John, 169, 284(n1)

Russell, Bertrand, 249, 289(n19)

Russian Revolution, 223, 224, 225, 281(n1)

Rutgers University, 78

Rutnam, Mary, M.D., 87–88, 256

St. Bridget's Convent (Colombo), 43

St. Christopher's (Letchworth), 246

St. Mary's English and Tamil schools, 270(n6)

St. Xavier's (Calcutta), 41

San Francisco Chronicle, 240

Sanger, Margaret, 232, 233, 288(n11), 289(n14)

Sanghamitta School, 250

Sarada Act, 101

Sara Seward Hospital (Allahabad), 274(n3)

sati, in India, 14, 84, 121, 170, 190, 272(n2)

satyagraha. *See* passive resistance

Satyashodak Samaj, 272(n3)

Scharlieb, Mary, M.D., 14, 75, 79–80(photo), 81, 88, 89, 274(n9–n12)

School of Oriental Studies (London), 159

Schreiner, Olive, 6, 197, 222, 285(n2)

Scudder, Ida, M.D., 78–79(photo), 274(n7, n8)

Scudder, John, Jr., M.D., 78

Scudder, John. M.D., 78, 274(n6)

Scudder, Sophia, 78

secular missionaries, 14

Sen, Keshab Chandra, 6, 67, 71–72, 177, 178, 179, 270(n5)

Sen Gupta, Jatindra Mohan, 154, 155

Sen Gupta, Nellie, 154–55, 265

Sesame Club, 184

Sewagram (ashram), 203

Shakers, 10, 25, 269(n5)

Sharada Sadan, 57, 58, 60, 272(n13)

Shastri, 2

Shaw, George Bernard, 16, 123–24, 126, 135, 136–37, 141, 143, 184, 222, 280(n2, n5)

Shaw, Pauline Agassiz, 56, 271(n5)

Sikkim, 163, 164

Simon, Hedi, 17–18, 227, 248(photo)–250, 291(n12). *See also* Keunemen, Hedi; Stadlen, Hedi

sisterhood, of women, 11, 21–32, 265, 266–67

Slade, Madeleine (Mira Behn), 177, 179, 180, 181, 265, 267

Gandhi and, 16–17, 195–206, 266, 285(n3–n9)

Smedley, Agnes, 17, 98, 224, 227, 229, 230, 232, 233(photo)–236, 237–40, 243, 267, 288(n8, n11, n13), 289(n14–n17)

Social Democratic Party (SDP), 223, 286(n5)

Socialism, 2, 246, 248, 256, 267, 281(n1)

Socialist Party, 224, 232

Socialist women, 219–59

social reformers, 25

in India, 63–103

Society of Friends. *See* Quakers

Somerville College (Oxford), 93, 100

Sorabji, Cornelia, 93–94, 96

South Asia, Western women in, 6–7, 16

Soviet Union, 249, 286(n2)

spiritualism, 112–14, 116, 119, 278(n4–n6)

Springield Republican, 118

Sri Aurobindo International Centre of Education, 215

Sri Lanka

arts and crafts studies of, 167, 171

foreign women in, 17, 141–46, 227

leftist politics in, 245–59, 287(n11)

missionary schools of, 33

women missionaries of, 27

Stacey, Enid, 222, 290(n3)

Stadlen, Hedi, 245, 247–49, 255. *See also* Keuneman, Hedi; Simon, Hedi

suffrage movement, 9, 148, 149, 159

Sujatha Vidyalaya (Matara), 250, 251, 252

Suriya Mal movement, 252, 253, 291(n10)

Swain, Clara, M.D., 77, 78, 83(photo), 271(n2)

Swedenborg, Emmanuel, 113, 278(n4)

Syndicalism, 223

Tagore, Rabindranath, 97, 112, 139, 141, 150, 169, 211, 276(n9), 281(n5), 291(n9)

Tamil girls, mission schools for, 33, 34–40

Tamil Women's Union, 88

Tashkent, 232, 243

Theosophical Society, 114, 115, 116–17, 119, 123, 134, 138, 148, 149, 150, 154, 178, 246, 278(n8)

theosophists, 2, 4, 8, 11, 16, 105–171, 189, 196, 221–22, 225, 246, 247, 250, 253, 263, 264, 279(n12), 280(n13)

theosophy, 114–20

Thoreau, Henry David, 111, 278(n2), 284(n1)

Tibet, 163, 164, 171, 208, 265, 282(n5)

Tilak, Bal Gangadhar, 58, 60, 85–86, 92, 93, 176, 275(n19), 276(n2)

Time, 227

The Times (London), 275(n1)

trade unions, 222–23, 224, 246, 255, 258

women in, 127

Trent, Evelyn (Evelyn Roy), 17, 227, 229, 230, 231(photo)–232, 233, 236, 237, 2239–41, 242–43, 288(n9, n10), 289(n21, n23)

Uduvil School (Sri Lanka), 33, 36–40, 142
Unitarian Church, 23, 56, 67–74, 102, 124
untouchables, in India, 186, 202

Varany Girls' Boarding School, 36, 37
Vedanta, 16
Victoria, Queen of England, 66, 70, 81, 86, 88, 93, 278(n4)
Village Industries Association, 202
Villard, Oswald Garrison, 96, 288(n5)
Visakha Vidyalaya (Colombo), 250, 251, 253
Vivekananda, Swami, 2, 6, 16, 61, 111, 112, 150, 165, 166, 169, 175, 176, 177, 178–79, 180, 183, 185–90, 191, 193, 194, 195, 210, 230, 231, 283(n2, n4, n7, n8), 288(n7)
    Margaret Noble (Sister Nivedita) and, 185–91, 283(n8)
von Racowitz, Princess, 116

Weare, Robert, 246, 252, 290(n1, n2)
Webb, Beatrice, 118, 124, 222
Webb, James, 112, 118
Webb, Sidney, 124, 126, 222
Westbrook, Jessise Duncan, 158–59, 250
Western women
    as Indian guru disciples, 16
    in South Asia, 16, 105–171
"white feminism", 11
"white goddesses", Western women as, 1–18, 175–81
white women, as goddesses and devils, 1–18
Wickremasinghe, Doreen, 245, 246–47(photo), 250–57(photo), 258, 267, 271(n14), 290(n5), 291(n8, n9)
Wickremasinghe, S.A., M.D., 6, 17, 246, 250, 253, 258, 291(n9, n11)
widow remarriage, in India, 188, 189, 273(n3)
widows, inIndia, 120
Willard, Frances E., 56, 224
Winslow, Harriet, 34–36, 37, 40(photo), 269(n2), 270(n4)
Winslow, Miron, 23, 34, 36, 110
Winter, Helen (Holy Family nun), 42
"woman question", 238
women
    education in early India, 33–52, 128–31, 187, 190
    emancipation in South Asia, 28–32

Indian, 120–22, 281(n6), 282(n4)
    as missionaries, 26–28
    as revolutionaries, 221–28
    sisterhood of, 21–32
    spiritualism and, 112–14
    Westernized Asian, 33–51
    white. See white women
Women in the Pulpit, 56
Women's Board of Missions, 30, 274(n3)
Women's Education Society, 250
Women's Foreign Missionary Society (Boston), 26, 31
Women's Franchise Union, 88, 282(n8)
Women's Indian Association, 131, 150, 151, 152, 154
Women's Medical College of Philadelphia, 54, 78, 81, 271(n2)
Women's Medical College (Vellore), 78
Women's Medical School (Ludbiana), 274(n5)
Women's Medical Service (India), 89
Women's Missionary Advocate, 27
Women's Missionary Union (U.S.), 28
women's rights, 2, 5, 25, 139–41, 159, 238–39, 269(n4), 277(n16), 280(n1)
    Florence Farr and, 139–41
    in India, 42, 47, 51, 60, 66, 77, 150–55, 262, 277(n18)
    in South Asia, 6
    in Sri Lanka, 256, 257
Women's Social and Political Union, 148–49
Women's Suffrage Society (Liverpool), 100
Women's Training College (Cambridge), 48
"women's work for women", in India and Sri Lanka, 32
Woodhull, Victoria, 114
Woodard, F. I., 290(n5)
Working Women's College (London), 71
World War I, 230, 231, 241

Yeats, W. B., 16, 21, 135, 137, 138–39, 141, 142, 145, 148, 150, 184, 280(n5)
Yongden, 163
Young, Doreen, 17, 227, 250–51. See also Wickremasinghe, Doreen
Young, William, 246, 290(n2)
Youthful Offenders Act (1854), 68
Yuval-Davis, Nira, 10

zenana education, 27–28
Zenana Missionary Society of the Church of England, 78
Zetkin, Clara, 223–24, 239, 286(n4), 289(n18)